'Strategy is a word of comparatively recent origin but Beatrice Heuser shows us that "strategic thinking" about the role of military force in the achievement of state policies long preceded the great nineteenth-century masters of military thought. Her writing is accessible, even entertaining, her scholarship impeccable. To properly understand Mahan, Corbett and the rest of them we need to know who and what came before them to supply the foundations on which they built. Thanks to Beatrice Heuser, we now do.'

—Geoffrey Till, King's College London, UK

'Beatrice Heuser's excellent new book shows that – historically – there was strategy before "strategy" both in theory and practice, across the boundaries of time, space and even gender. Heuser illustrates the richness and wisdom of thinking about war before strategy became tragically dominated by the pursuit of military victory at all cost. This book should be read by all who wish to understand how the world we live in today came into being and, in particular, by those who want to make sure that we have a world to live in tomorrow.'

—Brendan Simms, University of Cambridge, UK

'In this boldly innovative collection of essays, Beatrice Heuser challenges us to reconsider the notion that military strategy was of little consequence before the modern era. She shows how there was considerable evidence of strategic awareness in earlier periods, whether in the use made of dynastic marriages, the prioritising of diplomatic goals, or the allocation of financial and technological resources in the pursuit of war. And she insists that Europe boasted a long tradition of strategic thinking long before Clausewitz, citing authors from Christine de Pizan to Guibert. It was, the book argues, a tradition to which Clausewitz himself belonged: as the final essay shows, he had read many of these works and fully understood their import.'

—Alan Forrest, University of York, UK

STRATEGY BEFORE CLAUSEWITZ

This collection of essays combines historical research with cutting-edge strategic analysis and makes a significant contribution to the study of the early history of strategic thinking.

There is a debate as to whether strategy in its modern definition existed before Napoleon and Clausewitz. The case studies featured in this book show that strategic thinking did indeed exist before the last century, and that there was strategy making, even if there was no commonly agreed word for it. The volume uses a variety of approaches. First, it explores the strategy making of three monarchs whose biographers have claimed to have identified strategic reasoning in their warfare: Edward III of England, Philip II of Spain and Louis XIV of France. The book then analyses a number of famous strategic thinkers and practitioners, including Christine de Pizan, Lazarus Schwendi, Matthew Sutcliffe, Raimondo Montecuccoli and Count Guibert, concluding with the ideas that Clausewitz derived from other authors. Several chapters deal with reflections on naval strategy long thought not to have existed before the nineteenth century. Combining in-depth historical documentary research with strategic analysis, the book illustrates that despite social, economic, political, cultural and linguistic differences, our forebears connected warfare and the aims and considerations of statecraft just as we do today.

This book will be of great interest to students of strategic history and theory, military history and IR in general.

Beatrice Heuser is Professor of International Relations at the University of Glasgow, Scotland, and currently a visiting professor at the Sorbonne and at Sciences Po in Paris. She is the author of many books, including *The Evolution of Strategy* (2010) and *Reading Clausewitz* (2002).

Cass Military Studies

For a full list of titles in this series, please visit www.routledge.com

Researching the Military
Edited by Helena Carreiras, Celso Castro and Sabina Fréderic

Drones and the Future of Air Warfare
The Evolution of Remotely Piloted Aircraft
Michael P. Kreuzer

Transforming Warriors
The Ritual Organization of Military Force
Edited by Peter Haldén and Peter Jackson

Space Warfare in the 21st Century
Arming the Heavens
Joan Johnson-Freese

Strategy Before Clausewitz
Linking Warfare and Statecraft, 1400–1830
Beatrice Heuser

Special Operations Forces in the 21st Century
Perspectives from the Social Sciences
Edited by Jessica Glicken Turnley, Kobi Michael and Eyal Ben-Ari

Civilians and Warfare in World History
Edited by Nicola Foote and Nadya Williams

STRATEGY BEFORE CLAUSEWITZ

Linking Warfare and Statecraft, 1400–1830

Beatrice Heuser

 Routledge
Taylor & Francis Group

LONDON AND NEW YORK

First published 2018
by Routledge
2 Park Square, Milton Park, Abingdon, Oxon OX14 4RN

and by Routledge
711 Third Avenue, New York, NY 10017

Routledge is an imprint of the Taylor & Francis Group, an informa business

British Library Cataloguing-in-Publication Data
A catalogue record for this book is available from the British Library

Library of Congress Cataloging-in-Publication Data
Names: Heuser, Beatrice, 1961– author.
Title: Strategy before Clausewitz : linking warfare and statecraft, 1400–1830 /
    Beatrice Heuser.
Other titles: Linking warfare and statecraft, 1400–1830
Description: Abingdon, Oxon ; New York, NY : Routledge, [2018] | Series:
    Cass military studies | Includes bibliographical references and index.
Identifiers: LCCN 2017011137 | ISBN 9781138290907 (hardback) |
    ISBN 9781138290914 (pbk.) | ISBN 9781315265834 (ebook)
Subjects: LCSH: Strategy—History. | Military history, Modern—Europe—Case
    studies. | Military art and science—Europe—History. | Europe—Relations.
Classification: LCC U162 .H483 2018 | DDC 355.409/03—dc23
LC record available at https://lccn.loc.gov/2017011137]

ISBN: 978-1-138-29090-7 (hbk)
ISBN: 978-1-138-29091-4 (pbk)
ISBN: 978-1-315-26583-4 (ebk)

Typeset in ApexBembo
by Apex CoVantage, LLC

For my mother, Dr Emma Brigitte Heuser,
née Paulus.

Se qualche d'uno s'abbate à caso à leggere questi fogli, sappia di prima vista ch'io non gli ho scritti à lui, ma a me stesso, e che non havendo havuto altro fine, che di piacer, che di giovar all'animo mio, ho à questo scopo solo diritta tutta la forma di quest'opra. [sic]

(If somebody should deign to read these pages, let him know from the beginning that I have not written them for him, but for myself, and that I had no other aim than to please, to entertain my spirit, and have to that sole aim shaped the entire form of this work.)

—Raimondo Montecuccoli, writing as a prisoner of war in Stettin (Szczecin), c. 1640.[1]

CONTENTS

List of figures   xi
List of maps   xii
Preface and acknowledgements   xiii

1   Was strategy practised before the word was used?   1

2   Christine de Pizan, the first modern strategist:
    good governance and conflict mediation   32

3   Denial of change: the military revolution as seen
    by contemporaries   48

4   The invention of modern maritime strategies:
    the Anglo–Spanish War of 1585–1604   69

5   A national security strategy for England:
    Matthew Sutcliffe, the Earl of Essex and the
    Cádiz Expedition of 1596   91

6   Command of the sea: the origins of a
    strategic concept   117

7   Lazarus Schwendi, Raimondo Montecuccoli and
    the Turkish wars: peaceful coexistence or rollback?   136

8   Guibert: prophet of total war?   167

9   What Clausewitz read: on the origins of some
      of his key ideas   185

Bibliography   *208*
Index of personal names   *227*
Index of place names and states   *233*
Index of wars and strategic concepts   *237*

FIGURES

1.1	Medal of Philip II of Spain: 'non sufficit orbis'	15
1.2	Titian: *Religion Saved by Spain* (or *Spain Succouring Faith*), 1572–1575	16
6.1	Edward III's noble	119
6.2	Queen Elizabeth I's armada portrait	125
7.1	Peter Aubry: Raimondo Montecuccoli, c. 1650	150

MAPS

1.1   English possessions on the Continent   7
4.1   Atlantic and European routes of the Spanish navy and armies   77
7.1   The Habsburg Empire and the Ottoman Empire   139

PREFACE AND ACKNOWLEDGEMENTS

This book deals mainly with strategic theory, but also with strategic practice, in the centuries before the 1770s, when the word 'strategy' was introduced to Western European languages, or at any rate (when we come to Clausewitz), before the term was defined as it is now in military doctrine. The chapters in this book broach the subject from a number of different angles.

The first chapter sets the scene for the following chapters. Giving a very roughly sketched overview of the causes and aims of warfare in Europe, it will home in on three case studies of strategic practitioners – men who had a grand strategy and applied it. By 'grand strategy' we mean, following the British strategist Basil Liddell Hart, the coordination and direction of 'all the resources of a nation, or band of nations, towards the attainment of the political object of the war – the goal defined by fundamental policy'.[2]

Several of the following chapters will deal exclusively with one or two theoreticians – the thinkers who wrote works on strategy – in the context of their times. We have two civilians – Christine de Pizan, and the clergyman Matthew Sutcliffe. We have several writers with extensive military experience: Lazarus Schwendi, Count Guibert and Clausewitz, even though they did not necessarily have much influence on strategy making. And we have two writers who as senior military commanders did at least at times have a considerable impact on the practice of strategy, albeit usually in a collegiate decision-making context: the Earl of Essex, and Raimondo Montecuccoli.

One chapter analyses how a phenomenon that is claimed to have characterised early modern warfare – namely profound change in military technology leading to change in many other areas, especially the formation of the modern fiscal-military state – was perceived by contemporaries. Another contains a diachronic study of the evolution of a key concept of naval strategy. The final chapter also takes a diachronic approach, aiming to break down the wall in strategic studies which cuts off just

about all twentieth- and twenty-first-century theoretical work from the thinking
and the literature that originated before the French Revolution. In that chapter, I
shall try to track some of Clausewitz's key ideas to their antecedents.

This book does not aspire to be a comprehensive study of all aspects of strategy
before the word was introduced to our vocabulary. But the chapters serve as illus-
trations of the *constat* that it is language and at times conceptualisation more than
social, economic, political (let alone mental or educational) limitations that differentiate us from our forebears.

★

This book would not have seen the light without the generous support of a large
number of very kind colleagues. Among those who have commented critically on
earlier drafts of chapters are above all Dr Michele Margetts and Dr Rosemary Gill. Dr
Frank Tallett and Professor Andrew Lambert gave sterling advice on several chapters.
Further invaluable advice on Chapters 1 and 2 was given by Professors Françoise
Le Saux, Elizabeth A. R. Brown, Anne Curry, John Gillingham, Clifford Rogers, Natalie Fryde, Caroline Barron, Geoffrey Parker, Joël Félix and Guy Rowlands;
on Chapter 3 by Dr Sylvie Kleiman-Lafon; on Chapters 4, 5 and 6 by Professors
Enrique García Hernán, Andrew Lambert, John Hattendorf, Geoffrey Parker, Alan
Cromartie, N.A.M. Rodger and Drs Neil Younger and Benjamin Redding; Chap-
ter 7 by Dr David Parrott; Chapter 8 by Dr Thierry Wiedemann, Professors Stig
Förster, Roger Chickering and Patrice Gueniffey; Chapter 9 by Dr Sibylle Scheipers
and Professor Andreas Herberg-Rothe. All remaining mistakes are my own entirely.

While I have not had any major research grant for any of its chapters, several of
them are the result of invitations to conferences or to give papers which prompted
me to research and study the respective subjects, and often enabled me to visit
libraries which I would otherwise not have been able to reach. My thanks in this
context are due particularly to Hofrat Dr Erwin Schmidl, whose support for a
research visit to Vienna included invaluable battlefield and geostrategic tours, Professor Enrique García Hernán, Dr Mauro Mantovani, Professors Roger Chickering
and Stig Förster; and Professor Guy Rowlands. The maps were made by Alex Bund,
whom I thank for his patience. The index was compiled by Adam Gavin.

As far as the libraries are concerned, other than the library of the University
of Reading, where staff have supported me patiently with inter-library loans, my
thanks go, in order of *ancienneté*, close to home, to the staff of the Bodleian Library
in Oxford, and further afield, the Bibliothèque Mazarine in Paris, the Biblioteca
Estense in Módena, the Bibliothèque de l'École militaire and the Bibliothèque
nationale in Paris, the British Library, the Österreichische Staatsbibliothek and the
Kriegsarchiv with its library in Vienna, and finally the Jefferson Library at West
Point Military Academy.

I also need to thank the following publishing houses and editors of volumes in
which four chapters included in this book have previously been published:

Chapter 3 was previously published as "Denial of Change: The Military
Revolution as seen by Contemporaries", in Mauro Mantovani (ed.): *International*

Bibliography for Military History, No. 32 (Leyden: Brill, 2012), pp. 3–27, reprinted here with permission of Koninklijke Brill NV and editor.

Chapters 4, 5 and 6 draw on two previous publications: "A National Security Strategy for England: Matthew Sutcliffe, the Earl of Essex, and the Cadiz Expedition of 1596" was published in Óscar Recio Morales (ed.): *Redes y espacios de poder de la comunidad irlandesa en España y la América española, 1600–1825* (Valencia: Albatros Ediciones, 2012), pp. 117–135, reprinted here with permission of the publishers and editor; and "Regina Maris and the Command of the Sea: The Sixteenth Century Origins of Modern Maritime Strategy", in *Journal of Strategic Studies*, published online (Dec. 2015), pp. 1–41.

Chapter 7 was previously published as "Guibert (1744–1790): Prophet of Total War", from Roger Chickering, Stig Förster (eds), *War in an Age of Revolution, 1775–1815*, Series: Publications of the German Historical Institute (Cambridge: Cambridge University Press, 2010), pp. 49–68, reprinted here with permission of the Press.

Finally, I have to thank my family for listening, not always patiently, to my ramblings about the various strategists who are the protagonists of this book, and having allowed family holidays and other logistics to be configured around visits to libraries, battlefields and other sites connected with their lives and their works. In this line of business, clear distinction can be made between my private life or holidays and research. This has good sides and bad.

Notes

1 Raimondo Montecuccoli: *Trattato della guerra* (Biblioteka Estense, Módena, MS italiano 21 α.P. 9.15), trans. into German in Hauptmann Alois Veltzé (ed.): *Ausgewählte Schriften des Raimond Fürsten Montecuccoli*, Vol. 1 (Vienna: Wilhelm Braumüller, 1899), p. 1.

2 B.H. Liddell Hart: *The Decisive Wars of History: A Study in Strategy* (London: G. Bell & Sons, 1929), p. 150f.

1

WAS STRATEGY PRACTISED BEFORE THE WORD WAS USED?

Above all, the supreme military commander and the supreme decision-maker in the war should consult, so that they may ascertain on what [aim] they want to stake most of their assets and hopes, and by which ways and means they hope to achieve victory in war, or to bring or force the enemy to agree to an acceptably good treaty and peace. Once such a resolution and decision is made, one should abide by it in all cases.
—*Lazarus von Schwendi, 1522–1583*[1]

This book presents a challenge, as it purports to deal with strategic thinkers in Europe, most of whom lived and wrote before the word 'strategy' was introduced to European languages.[2] Even then, European definitions of 'strategy' at the time of the French Revolution and Napoleon would still be far from what we understand by 'strategy' today. For example Clausewitz's definition is very narrow: he defined 'strategy' merely as 'the use of engagements for the object of the war'.[3] Admittedly today, more than ever, the word is a catch-all for a vast array of meanings, ranging from a simple synonym for 'planning' to 'foreign policy making in a hostile environment' and to more complex definitions. These are many and varied, and might be summed up as 'Strategy is a comprehensive way to try to pursue political ends, including the threat or actual use of force, in a dialectic of wills.'[4]

So how can we find a definition that is a useful starting point for the question of whether people thought (and argued) 'strategically' before the word was generally used? A different approach suggests itself. Rather than seeking one recent definition which could be projected into the past, we might begin with certain commonly recognised features of strategy. Strategy is about linking the use of force with political ends, or, when a more sophisticated polity has been created with its division of labour and its political and military leadership, about the relationship between warfare and statecraft. In this relationship, warfare is the tool of statecraft, next to others (e.g. the many tools of diplomacy, including forming coalitions, or alliances through marriage, or enticing an enemy's allies away from him; or economic tools, such as trading concessions or tariffs; or 'chequebook diplomacy', the buying off of an adversary). As we shall see, warfare and statecraft went hand in hand throughout the centuries covered in this volume, and were not thought of as separate as they would be in the nineteenth and early twentieth centuries.

Strategy is also about identifying aims, as Lazarus Schwendi put it earlier. Moreover, it is about planning, and about making choices: the choice of ends, means and ways to apply the means. Strategy is about prioritising some tasks over others (this becomes especially salient when wars are prosecuted against more than one adversary, on more than one front, with potential naval and land dimensions). One may have to prioritise fighting one adversary over another, one front over another, one service over another, because one simply cannot afford to employ all possible means. Hence, strategy is about prioritising defence spending in some areas rather than others. And finally, to the extent possible, it is about choosing between different ways to prosecute a war. This may be entirely or in part because some forms of warfare would produce effects that would preclude the overall political ends pursued in the war (e.g. one would not want to destroy the prosperous town that one wishes to conquer). As the classicist Kimberly Kagan has put it, strategy is 'the setting of a state's objectives and of priorities among those objectives' in order to allocate resources and choose the best means to prosecute a war.[5] In other words, we can discern strategy – or reflections on strategy or strategic prescriptions – in the sources we are looking at once we can see that such choices or prioritisations were made.

This could apply even at the simplest level. If a group of humans is attacked, they may have three choices: fight back, surrender or try to buy off the attackers. Such a choice depends in part on the adversary: Genghis Khan's hordes might have wiped out a village before its elders could attempt to negotiate. In classical antiquity, surrender might not have been a serious option: it might have brought no hope of survival as the adversary might still have massacred all adult males and abducted all women and children into slavery. With other adversaries, other considerations might influence choices. Fighting meant death, destruction and suffering, but a significant part of the population might survive to live in freedom. Surrender would inevitably mean a curtailment of freedom and sacrifice of prosperity, but lives might be saved. Buying off an attacker would avoid deaths and loss of freedom, but it could transform the relationship into one commonly associated with Mafia practices, where the criminals, well pleased with this bargain, would come back regularly to collect more 'protection money'. (A historic example of this was the Viking raids on the British Isles, which were later turned into the 'Danegeld' taxation of the local populations.)

Besides being about planning, choosing and prioritising, strategy is also about consulting and explaining. Unless the prince is also the supreme military commander, to use Schwendi's terms again, the prince will have to explain to his general what he or she intends to do, and consult him on how to do it. Such explanations would also be contained in communications with ambassadors or leading ministers, when they were not in the same place as the prince where communication could take place orally, and without a record kept. Unless one was dealing with an absolute monarchy, princes also would have to explain themselves to those who would help them finance their war – those providing money or men through taxation or feudal levies, or both. These, then, are the contexts in which we shall look for examples of the articulation of strategic reasoning in surviving sources.

This chapter endeavours to identify instances where strategy was indeed applied – or strategic decisions were made – in the context of war in the centuries and the writings covered in this book. And to repeat, most of these date from before the introduction of the word 'strategy' into Western languages shortly before the French Revolution. Thus before claiming, in the following chapters, that theoreticians of warfare conceived of strategy, we shall apply here the test of whether strategy was *practised*, using three case studies dating from before the time when the term 'strategy' made its first appearance. I have chosen three monarchs, because their biographers have claimed that they thought and acted strategically: the kings Edward III of England, Philip II of Spain and Louis XIV of France. In other words, I shall lazily dig where others have already prospected and found precious metal. Nevertheless, this exercise is worth doing, as I shall be applying the same criteria to define 'strategy' – the definition of objectives, the prioritisation of conflicting needs – that is the allocation of resources when these were not sufficient to address all needs at once – to all three. Only then can we tell if the precious metal found is gold in all three cases. In each case, one or two documents examined in greater detail will serve to conduct this test.

Polities, dynasties and wars of succession

To set the stage, we should briefly summarise the main patterns of relations between European polities in the Late Middle Ages. Throughout Central and Western Europe, systems of governance had emerged by which populations were ruled at several different levels and in a variety of ways. Many people were subjects of a local lord, who in turn came under a prince, or a more highly ranking aristocrat who in turn owed loyalty to a prince. Others lived in towns or cities which might have been directly under a prince's authority and below that, to some extent, governed by their own elites. Some cities – especially in Italy, from which Christine de Pizan hailed – were themselves sovereign polities.

The king of France or the Holy Roman emperor did not have direct ownership of all the lands of their respective kingdom or empire, even if they expected an oath of fealty from the other land owners within their realm. England was something of an exception to this rule, as nominally, William the Conqueror claimed to have inherited all of England in 1066, and had merely loaned parts of it to his loyal vassals. But the fundamental principle of property that pertained throughout Europe – namely that parents would pass on the lands they occupied to their children – conflicted with the notion that the king of England was the ultimate proprietor of all lands. When the king asserted this right and denied his vassals an automatic succession right, or re-appropriated their territory, he asked for trouble. Three such waves of re-appropriations of land by Edward II, his wife and his son Edward III occurred in the fourteenth century, the earlier two each followed by a minor civil war.[6] When in

1399, King Richard II tried to prevent his exiled first cousin, Henry Bolingbroke, from taking full possession of his late father's Lancastrian lands, many peers of the realm rose up in support of Bolingbroke: Richard's transformation of the ritual of automatic confirmation of succession – still marked as taking place by the king's grace by being coupled with the payment of a fee or inheritance tax – into something the king could veto jeopardised their own children's guaranteed succession rights.[7]

The problems of dynastic succession also lay at the roots of other wars, civil or domestic and foreign: the dividing line was quite blurred throughout this period. In principle, by the High Middle Ages, many polities accepted primogeniture. But in practice, this pattern of succession continued to compete with elective rulership, which applied to the supreme power in the Holy Roman Empire, or the doge of Venice, or the king of Poland even in the early modern period. Elected rulers quite liked to turn the principle of election into heredity for their children, and the process into something on a sliding scale between, on one hand, a mere going through the motions, and acrimoniously negotiated consensus on the other. This would always be a potential cause of war.

Prior to the general acceptance of primogeniture, there had been two patterns that were at odds with it, but which actually survived the *general* convergence towards a pattern of primogeniture. One was that of the succession, within a dynasty, by the worthiest or most able male in the family (in France it was later asserted that Salic law excluded all females, but whether this also excluded inheritance by males through their mothers or grandmothers was at the centre of the Hundred Years' War). Given mortality patterns at the time, primogeniture brought a number of young children (or occasionally, somebody with a mental illness) to the throne, and inevitably the question arose whether the succession of an uncle or elder cousin would not be better for the security and good governance of the realm. Often such an uncle was appointed regent, like the York prince famous for his deformed back, the future Richard III, who would acquire a taste for the power this brought that he would not want to forego later. Or else several uncles or cousins would dispute the regency among them, the pattern underlying the Armagnacs vs Bourguignon Civil War, which Christine de Pizan lived through in France, and subsequently the Wars of the Roses in England.

The other was the division of lands, at the father's death, among his sons. This pattern, which had moved even Charlemagne to divide his possessions among his sons, would be recognisable almost until the end of the period covered here. Thus William the Conqueror's lands were disputed among his sons, so that initially, his two eldest sons, Robert Curthose and William II Rufus, laid claim to England and Normandy respectively; his third son, Henry I, ultimately reunited the territories after going to war with his surviving elder brother, Robert. After all the empire-building of his ancestors, Habsburg Charles V divided his global possessions between his brother, Ferdinand (I as Holy Roman Emperor), and his son Philip (II of Spain). Even Louis XIV of France, coming from a tradition which had upheld primogeniture and exclusively male succession rigorously for centuries, merrily departed from this principle when it suited his dynasty. He thus claimed a part of his father-in-law's heritage for his wife in the form of the 'devolution' of the Spanish Netherlands. Later he was prepared to settle for an outcome of the War of the Spanish Succession that would secure the Spanish crown for one of his wife's and his younger descendants (*not* the dauphin), in return for the latter's renunciation of all claims to the French crown. This pattern and further quarrels over whether heredity through the female line was acceptable, and whether lands inherited through the female line by definition had to stay separate from the father's lands and thus go to a younger offspring, were a recurrent cause of wars throughout our period, from Edward III's claims to the crown of France to Louis XIV's to the crown of Spain for his grandson.

Dynastic marriages, a tool of diplomacy widely practised by the late West Roman emperors and by the Byzantines, and warfare were two sides of the coin of Medieval and early modern statecraft: alliances through marriage were at least as valuable as whole armies. But both came at a price: allies expected reciprocity in commitment, and armies were hugely expensive. Add to this multiple alliances with interested relatives and their respective families, or partisan (arch)bishops or abbots with their lands and riches (and sometimes, private armies), and a pattern emerged which could be managed only by deft statecraft: allied interests would always have to be taken into consideration in decisions over what to prioritise, and where to concentrate one's forces.

If land was acquired through dynastic marriages, it was not necessarily the coveted strip of land adjacent to one's own hereditary territories (although the kings of France managed to absorb several such areas through marriage, and the Habsburgs did pretty well within the Iberian Peninsula). Ruling families and nobles throughout Europe thus ended up as owners of widely scattered territories, and the same was true for abbeys or other churches that were bequeathed lands by rich, childless benefactors. Inevitably, this meant quarrels over border regions, as many boundaries were vague if they ran through particularly inhospitable and sparsely settled regions, such as mountain ranges that were less coveted by rulers on either side. As rulers delegated the control of such areas – usually remote from their centres of power – to 'lords of the marches' or marquesses, the latter enjoyed relative freedom from control. Clashes with the central authority easily ensued. Thus the English king's northern vassals would be reluctant to send him forces for campaigns in France when they feared (or desired, for their own aggrandisement) border clashes with the Scots.

The need to rely on vassals for the levying of troops for any campaign created the need to persuade them that this was necessary – even for the English kings who claimed sovereignty over all of England. The paradox was thus that the English king theoretically owned all of England, but was dependent on his vassals for most of his income. The vassals potentially got more out of such a bargain than mere security: the booty, plunder and ransom money for hostages taken in war were all important incentives to support war, but such investments were risky, even though the risks were limited as long as the wars were confined to the Continent. Since Anglo-Saxon times, the English monarch was expected to consult his nobles in what was called the *magnum concilium* or large council. Monarchs who acted without such consultation – especially Henry II and his youngest son, King John – incurred the ire of their peers, leading to the latter's humiliation by his barons and his forced signing of *Magna Carta* in 1215.[8] From Edward I's reign onwards, English monarchs met with their subjects through 'parliaments' in order to persuade them to pay more taxes. These were assemblies of nobles and bishops, but also knights and burgesses from the towns which provided a substantial part of the royal revenue to extend the basis of consent. Monarchs were thus forced to articulate their motivations and plans for war, and in return had to satisfy at least some of their subjects' demands, as such parliamentary assemblies gave their subjects the chance to voice grievances. The exchanges between monarch and Parliament are thus an occasion where we might look for articulations of strategic reasoning.

Edward III and strategies in the Hundred Years' War

As our first theorist writing on the link between statecraft and the art of war is Christine de Pizan, it is appropriate to start here with an example of strategy making that she witnessed in her own lifetime: the warfare between the Plantagenet king Edward III (1312–1377) and his heirs, and Christine's patron Charles V (1338–1380) and his heirs. Like his father and grandfather before him, Edward tried to acquire overlordship over Scotland, and also made a bid for the crown of France after the successive deaths of his mother's three elder brothers, all of whom had been kings of France. Instead, claiming that Salic law applied which purportedly excluded women from the succession, the descendants of their uncle, Charles of Valois, claimed the throne. This pitted Edward III first against Philip VI (Charles of Valois's son), and then John II the Good (Philip's son). This phase ended with the nine-year Peace of Brétigny (1360–1369; see Map 1.1).

War resumed still under Edward III, but on the French side under Charles V the Wise (John's son). Another peace treaty was concluded at Bruges in 1375, which initially held when Charles VI the Mad succeeded his father, Charles V. The new king even gave his daughter (aged seven) in marriage to Edward's heir, Richard II. Unsurprisingly, this marriage remained without issue, for as we recall, only three years later, Richard was deposed by his Lancastrian cousin Henry Bolingbroke (crowned as Henry IV) and subsequently murdered in what would turn into a civil war which kept the Valois-Plantagenet conflict from boiling up again. Yet Henry IV's son Henry V and Charles VI's youngest son, Charles (the future Charles VII), would be at each other's throats again for the last phase of the Hundred Years' War (referred to as the Lancastrian war). Another spell of peace followed after the battle of Agincourt in 1415, when in the Treaty of Troyes 1420, Charles VI was forced to resort again to the statecraft-tool of peace-by-marriage, offering another daughter in marriage, this time to Henry V. This union did produce a son – Henry VI. Like Edward III he would claim his mother's heritage and would even be crowned king of France, but at the same time he was cursed with his maternal grandfather's hereditary mental illness, thus replicating the conditions for civil war in England that had engendered the Armagnac-Bourguignon War in France. This gave Charles VI's surviving son Charles all the more reason to contest the Treaty of Troyes agreed by his father and to reclaim the French crown, with the help of Joan of Arc. The Hundred Years' War would thus continue and end well after the deaths of Henry V and Christine de Pizan, when Charles VII – this time truly decisively – defeated the Lancastrian forces at the Battle of Castillion in 1453.

Let us focus here on the conflict in the fourteenth century. To repeat, Edward III's ambitions lay both in France and in Scotland. His grandfather had already brought Wales firmly under Plantagenet control, and like France, Scotland had a series of succession

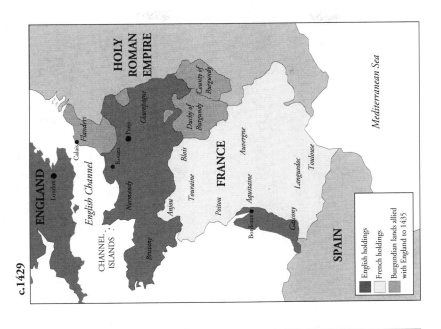

c.1360

ENGLAND
London

English Channel

CHANNEL ISLANDS

Calais
Flanders

Rouen
Paris

HOLY ROMAN EMPIRE

Champagne

Normandy

Anjou

Brittany

Touraine

Blois

Burgundy

Auvergne

Poitou

Aquitaine

Bordeaux

Gascony

Languedoc

Toulouse

FRANCE

SPAIN

Mediterranean Sea

English holdings
French holdings

c.1429

ENGLAND
London

English Channel

CHANNEL ISLANDS

Calais
Flanders

Rouen
Paris

HOLY ROMAN EMPIRE

Champagne

Duchy of Burgundy

County of Burgundy

Normandy

Anjou

Brittany

Touraine

Blois

FRANCE

Auvergne

Poitou

Aquitaine

Bordeaux

Gascony

Languedoc

Toulouse

SPAIN

Mediterranean Sea

English holdings
French holdings
Burgundian lands allied with England to 1435

MAP 1.1 English possessions on the Continent

crises of which Edward III sought to take advantage. Eventually Edward and his heirs had to make a strategic choice: they would concentrate their efforts on France and leave Scotland alone, as they could not in the long run sustain a war on two fronts. (Even their marriage politics concentrated on France throughout. The English royal house did not make a Scottish match from the early twelfth until the early sixteenth centuries.)

With Edward seeking to extend his rule both to the North and to the South-East, the respective kings of Scotland and France realised that they had a common adversary, and an interest in making common front against him. Already their forebears of the late thirteenth century had concluded an alliance against the expansionist Plantagenets, and the treaty would be renewed several times in the subsequent centuries. In the Peace of Brétigny, Edward III managed to prise the 'auld alliance' of France and Scotland apart, at least temporarily, but in turn had to give up his own alliance with the Flemings and stop pursuing his claim to the French throne.[9] Thus balance-of-power politics – albeit not always fully translated into grand strategies of co-ordinated alliance warfare – can be identified at this point not only in the relations between the rivalling Italian city states but also among the kingdoms of Western Europe.[10]

It has been argued by some historians that medieval strategies differed substantially from later strategies, as different mindsets and culture prevailed. Philippe Contamine has characterised medieval strategy making as dominated by two principles: the avoidance of pitched battles and the 'obsidional reflex', the tendency to seek refuge in fortifications.[11] Battles were indeed rare in the High and Late Middle Ages, for which Jan Willem Honig has put forward a cultural explanation – namely that they were seen as divine ordeals, and thus shunned by any prince aware of his own sins and shortcomings in the eyes of God.[12] By contrast, John Gillingham favours practical, non-cultural explanations: the high risk involved in battles that they would not lead to the desired end, the scarcity of resources, the weak economic bases of the small overall populations and thus the small size of armies that were raised ad hoc for every campaign and poorly trained, containing few experienced soldiers, and in which losses would be difficult to replace.[13] Yet princes whose claim to the throne was contested in some way needed victories to show that the Divine Judge was on their side; only, argues Clifford Rogers, both sides' wish to give battle coincided less frequently than in later times.[14] Nevertheless, the few pitched battles that did take place in the Hundred Years' War tended to be important turning points.

What were alternative strategic options to giving battle? One was the construction of castles or fortifications around key towns to defend inherited or conquered territories, and the other side of that same medal was, of course, siege warfare to take such 'places', as both were called during our entire period. Both fortifying 'places' – a strategic measure adopted in the mid-fourteenth century and sometimes referred to as the 'Barbicans Strategy' – and sieges took a long time and were costly although on different scales. It took years and huge amounts of money and manpower to build fortifications; it would generally take months to get a 'place' to surrender, and in the meantime, one's own forces might well demand to be released as they generally owed their lords only 40 days of military service per year, and would also run out of supplies. So even sieges tended not to occur as frequently before as after 1500.

Much more common were border raids and the *chevauchée*, a form of warfare that is difficult to comprehend let alone justify even with the medieval mentality in mind. It consisted of inflicting great suffering on the civilian population by ransacking and burning villages and harvests – and this despite the concern of the princes on both sides of this conflict to be seen as the legitimate ruler who – according to all standards of European kingship – had a duty to protect just that civilian population. Moreover, to our minds, the *chevauchée* clashed with the self-denying ordinances which both sides adopted for war more generally, and which tended to include the proscription of pillaging and stealing food.[15] It must be remembered, however, that Edward III was not much more compassionate in his dealings with his own subjects in England: similarly cruel measures of extortion were used to seize provisions for his armies, and the officials he sent out to collect this revenue in money and kind, the *escheators*, were the most detested among the royal officials, even more so than his sheriffs.[16] Edward also seems to have been inspired to adopt the *chevauchée* by his experience of the Scottish border raids into English territory, and applied it to France. Much of the Hundred Years' War consisted of such raids, usually conducted by the Plantagenet and later Lancastrian forces, within France. According to Rogers, Edward III's main strategy in the Hundred Years' War was to take repeated recourse to the *chevauchée*, in order to force the French monarch to give battle.[17]

Another strategic option was to take the war to sea. Yet outside the Mediterranean, notwithstanding the Vikings' extraordinary naval exploits, naval warfare beyond the mere transport of soldiers, horses and supplies was in its infancy. On the south coast of England, at the end of the Anglo-Saxon era which was at once the end of the era of Viking invasions, King Edward the Confessor had granted the 'Cinque Ports' special privileges in return for their provision of ships with its purely defensive aim; in 1066 these ships were cooped up in port by the same winds that allowed William the Conqueror to set sail for England. This arrangement with the Cinque Ports was continued by the Norman kings, and by around 1300 had been increased to include three more towns.[18] Even the kings involved in the Hundred Years' War did not have their own navies but merely the right to requisition ships. Proper naval battles away from ports and estuaries had not taken place outside the Mediterranean. Even naval battles over the access to estuaries like the Battle of Damme on the Zwyn River (today a silted-up arm of the Scheldt estuary) in 1213, which pitted ships requisitioned by Plantagenet king John against ships requisitioned by King Philip II of France and involved ramming and burning rather than any form of manoeuvre, were most rare. In 1340, English merchantmen were blocked from access to their crucial trading partners in Antwerp by a fleet anchoring, again in the estuary of the Scheldt, near the river Zwyn and the town of Sluis. The fleet was under French command, assembled from various Genoese and Flemish ships. Edward III in turn pulled together a fleet to break through this inbound blockade, carrying off one of the few celebrated naval victories of the Middle Ages. The outcome of this battle secured England's politically unchallenged domination of the Channel for the next two centuries (admittedly, piracy continued to be rife), but did not put an end to French raids on southern English coastal towns, nor did it decide the outcome of the Hundred Years' War.

Let us thus look at how this naval battle fitted into Edward's strategy, by turning to one exemplar of a document that might serve us here as evidence that Edward reasoned strategically. On 9 July 1340, Edward wrote to his parliament – his 'dukes, archbishops, bishops, earls, barons and others' – from Bruges. He recounted how he was on the point of crossing the Channel to Flanders on 24 June, 'with a certain number of men-at-arms':

> News came to us that our enemy of Valois had arrayed a great armada of ships, which was before us in the river Zwyn. Having heard this news, and considered the perils which might come if they left there in order to damage our realm of England or our people elsewhere, and what a comfort which it would have been to our enemies, and especially the Scots, if such a force came to them, we immediately decided to seek them out wherever we could find them.

As noted, Edward's navy proceeded to win this naval battle (see also Chapter 6). But immediately thereafter,

> the country of Flanders, and also other lords, our allies, came to us, and informed us how our enemy was on the border, ready to enter Flanders or elsewhere against our allies, wherever he could most harm them and most effectively drive them to withdraw from our alliance.
>
> Considering the pursuit of our right, and most importantly the keeping of our faith and the resisting of his malice, and by the assent of our said allies and of the lords of our realm and of the land of Flanders who were then around us, we decided to land and to split our host; one part going with us towards Tournai, where there would be 100,000 armed Flemings, and [the other with] lord Robert d'Artois towards St. Omer with 50,000. That is aside from all our allies and their forces.

Both armies moved south in a pincer movement to engage the French, if the latter were prepared to give battle. 'To govern and lead such a host requires a very great sum of money,' Edward continued, 'on top of the debts that we must necessarily pay before our departure.' Therefore

> We pray you dearly, each one of you, that you first of all weigh the right that we have; next the great peril which will come, unless we are quickly succoured with money and goods, in order to satisfy the said land [of Flanders] and our allies and the soldiers who have already been retained by us and who will withdraw if they are not paid. And also if our allies are not paid, they may even perhaps go over to our enemy; and considering his malice and their power rejoined to his, bear in mind that our land, ourself, our children and all the lords and others would be on the point of perdition. . . . [By contrast] if we are quickly aided, we hope to take him at a disadvantage, and to triumph over him forever after – if only you will arrange that we should be hastily succoured by money or by goods in such a way as to give satisfaction for our debts and to retain our forces.[19]

This, according to our definition is a clear example of strategic reasoning. Having secured the Channel, Edward III took the war to the Continent, continuing to prioritise the campaigns against and in France to those against Scotland. Given these different options, Clifford Rogers rightly argues that Edward III did indeed make strategic choices, and used warfare strategically, along with other tools of statecraft, within the social, economic and fiscal limitations of this age.

★

Eighty years later, Edward's great-grandson Henry V made an attempt to create a standing fleet under royal ownership, but it did not survive him.[20] Even though Charles V of France had already developed a system of coastal patrols in 1369/1370, when war with the Plantagenets had resumed, France moved to create a permanent navy only after the end of the long wars with England, in 1455. In short, while we see nascent attempts to develop the naval component of warfare, the infrastructure in the form of ships and the economic base that could have supported a standing fleet were simply too feeble to allow the growth of these limited moves into full-fledged naval strategy. It is illustrative that despite the problems of movements on land, no English invasion of Scotland was attempted by sea. At best, some ships were sent to resupply land forces that had marched north through the borders.[21]

To sum up, given the constraints posed by economic and social factors, it is plausible to argue with Francisco García Fitz that medieval monarchs, just like their modern successors, did seek to impose their will on their adversaries (to use Clausewitz's definition of the aims of any war). Like the great leaders of classical antiquity or modern rulers, they did draw on a selection of tools, military as well as diplomatic and economic, and they were quite capable of articulating choices and weighing different options.[22] Different preferences in their selection of tools notwithstanding, medieval princes thought and acted no less 'strategically' than Thucydides's protagonists in the Peloponnesian War, Rome's emperors or, later, Philip II of Spain or Louis XIV of France.

Religious wars

Recommended by Christine de Pizan, and implemented by Charles VII of France as he emerged triumphant from the Hundred Years' War with England, the reinvention of a standing army (as the Romans had of course had standing armies) on the basis of important changes in fiscal-military relations ushered in a new age of warfare in Europe. While many of their ambitions were far-reaching, princes in the intervening millennium may not have lacked the strategic imagination, but certainly the means to realise them. Such limitations would equally apply to the Tudor and early Stuart monarchs of England for a long time yet. It would in due course strengthen their dependence on their aristocracy and nobility, which in turn would result in the progressive reduction of the powers of the monarch, until Britain was turned into a constitutional monarchy. By contrast, French monarchs would be set on the path towards absolutism. The path would be long as the process would be slowed down by the religious wars that tore the polity apart and led to the assassination of two successive monarchs and several attempts on the lives of others.[23]

Although they diverged in this critical area of state structure, both countries were affected similarly by other, more general trends, revolving around the centralisation of government and the gradual growth of a bureaucracy to administer states. Royal courts were still peripatetic throughout the sixteenth century; Spain did not even have a *permanent* capital city until around 1600. Philip II (1527–1598) ruled his empire from the Escorial Palace 50 kilometres outside Madrid, which would gradually evolve into this capital city only around the turn from the sixteenth to the seventeenth centuries.[24] France was ahead of other states in forming central institutions, but by the reign of Henry VIII and Elizabeth, English monarchs also relied greatly on a very small number of trusted ministers. This pattern can also be seen in other European polities. Philip II still prided himself on holding all the threads of the government of his vast realm in his own hands. Sitting in his small study in the Escorial, a special window overlooking the high altar of the huge adjacent chapel, he insisted on being his own first minister. Only in the following century would his heirs entrust the government of their extensive possessions to ministers, such as the Count-Duke Olivares or Don Baltasar de Zúñiga.

Like Edward III of England (and the English monarchs throughout), Philip needed the support of the representatives of his estates, especially the *Cortes* of Castile, the largest and richest entity among his European possessions, to finance his military enterprises; his other revenues, though considerable, did not suffice. The transformation of state finances, along with an equally steady growth of European populations, and an increase in trade and revenues brought in from the taxation of such trade would gradually allow several countries, including Burgundy, Hungary and Spain, to follow the French example of establishing a standing army.[25] Meanwhile warfare changed slowly but comprehensively under the effects of the introduction of firepower, first in the form of cannon, and gradually in the form of handheld weapons (see Chapter 3). The same growth of fiscal-military states allowed for the creation of navies owned directly by the crown. Key innovations in the maritime sphere had led to the discovery of the New World. By the late sixteenth century the globe had been circumnavigated. Philip II of Spain, scion of the Habsburg dynasty, wearing in personal union the crowns of Spain and Portugal, could look on an empire extending not only to the Americas in the West but also to the islands named after him in the Far East.

In the immediate context of the discovery by Columbus in 1492 of the western passage to what was originally thought to be Asia, the respective monarchs of Spain and Portugal had asked the Spanish-born Borgia pope Alexander VI for adjudication, and his bull *Inter caetera* of 1493, modified slightly by the Treaties of Tordesillas (1494) and Saragossa (1496), divided the extra-European world with two longitudinal lines. America west of the western line was to go to Spain, territories between both lines (from modern Brazil to Macao, but generally taken to exclude the Mediterranean and its littoral) to Portugal, and anything east of the eastern line (above all, the Philippines) again to Spain (see Map 4.1). And no other state was to meddle and claim land in the New World. Any boat 'crossing the line' by sailing from Europe to the New World (or indeed to any other part of the globe), as Queen

Elizabeth's voyagers so often would, for purposes other than mere exploration, thus could be interpreted by Philip to have committed an act of war. This needled the English in particular, and they came to see Philip as aspiring to world domination.

Yet the Habsburgs – both the Austrian branch that was hogging the Holy Roman emperorship and the Iberian branch – encountered a huge challenge to their pre-eminence arising from a new feature in European politics: war based on confessional differences. From 1520 until 1648, almost all wars in Europe had a religious dimension.[26] This made warfare more difficult to contain and to steer by the rulers who engaged in it, as it inflamed public passions which were not easy to calm down again. Once the opponent had been stigmatised as the Antichrist, it was difficult to explain why one would want to sit down and negotiate peace with him. Religious wars then and now have a tendency to develop a momentum of their own and to drag on.

In the 1570s, 1580s and 1590s, several at least partly religiously motivated civil wars or insurgencies took place across Western Europe. From 1562, France was rent apart by a series of such wars. In 1568 the Protestant Dutch began an 80 years' insurgency (or war of independence) against their Habsburg overlord, who was king of Spain as Philip II. Despite the shocking implications of such a rebellion against the God-given authority of a prince, Protestant opinion throughout Europe rapidly took the side of the Dutch in view of the brutal and infamous repression of the rebels and local populations. External Protestant powers – especially England and, later, Sweden – would intervene on the side of the Protestants in their fight in what Nicholas Rodger has aptly called the worldwide 'Catholic International', with the Roman papacy formulating its doctrines and, through its churches everywhere, taking care of propaganda.

In reality, this 'Catholic International' was no more a 'monolith' than the Communist world after the Second World War. Already from the early sixteenth century, the Catholic Valois monarchs would break ranks and ally with anybody from the Ottoman sultan to the Protestants to spite the Habsburgs in their own dynastic balance-of-power game in which they sought pre-eminence in Europe for themselves, a pre-eminence which they traced back to seeing France as the 'oldest daughter of the Church' and to their own descent from Charlemagne. Yet like world Communism in the Cold War, the 'Catholic International' (or at least the House of Habsburg with all its branches) was *perceived* as a monolith by its adversaries.[27] Moreover, regardless of whether they intended to (see ahead), the Habsburgs were *seen* as wanting to re-establish a universal monarchy, and thus rule the planet, something the medieval Holy Roman emperors had never quite managed to do.[28] Therefore, European strategy began to acquire a global dimension even in the sixteenth century.

In the French Religious Wars, Protestant queen Elizabeth's England and Catholic king Philip's Spain took opposite sides, each favouring the French monarchs or pretenders closest to their own religious inclinations. Thus Elizabeth sided with the Protestant Prince of Condé, and Protestant Henri Bourbon, king of Navarre; Philip II sided with the Catholic Guises (to whom Mary, Queen of Scots, had belonged on her mother's side). When Henri of Navarre, as the legal heir, claimed the French crown after the death of the last Valois king in 1589, Philip made a rival bid for the French crown on behalf of his daughter, the Infanta Isabella Clara Eugenia. His several invasions of French territory did not, however, allow him to gain a permanent foothold in France, as the forces of Henri of Navarre expelled him each time, usually with English support, either financial or in the form of actual soldiers.

Moreover, the Protestant princes supported Prince William of Orange, leader of the Dutch rebels, who would be assassinated, a fate wished also upon Elizabeth by Catholics. As we shall see, the Dutch even had the sympathy of loyal servants of the Habsburgs, such as Lazarus von Schwendi (see Chapter 7). The religious strife of this period was thus a crucial cause of war, and a crucial factor in strategy making.

Philip II's ambitions and strategies

As we have noted, the sixteenth and early seventeenth centuries were marked by the House of Habsburg's flirtation with world rule, a *monarchia universalis* surpassing that of any former empire in its geographic span. True, Charles V in the mid-1550s divided his heritage between his brother, Ferdinand I (to whom he left the Eastern Habsburg lands and who got himself elected emperor in Charles's place), and his son Philip II (to whom he left Spain, the Netherlands, the Mediterranean possessions and the colonies), but he had hoped that upon Ferdinand's death (which came in 1564), Philip might succeed to the empire and not Ferdinand's son Maximilian. In fact within a decade after the religious peace between Catholics and Protestants within the empire had been agreed with the edict of Augsburg (1555), Philip with his support for the Inquisition, the burnings of Protestants on Spanish soil from 1559 (as acts of faith, Port. *autos da fé*) and his fierce suppression of the Dutch insurgency had made himself so unpopular among more liberal-minded Catholics, not to mention the Protestants, that there was no chance of his being elected emperor.[29]

Even without the Holy Roman Empire, however, the heritage received by Philip was colossal. Moreover, through his marriage with Mary Tudor, Philip hoped to gain England for his heirs, a hope frustrated when she died childless in 1558. But as king of Naples and Sicily, Duke of Milan from 1554, ruler of Netherlands from 1555, king of Spain from 1556 and, through another quirk of fate in the game of royal (in)fertility, heir and successor to a childless king of Portugal from 1581, Philip was the most powerful monarch in Europe. His dangerous ambitions for global, indeed universal, hegemony seemed confirmed with the medal he had coined in 1580, depicting a horse poised to leap off the globe and into space, with the modest little caption 'non sufficit orbis': the world is not enough (Figure 1.1).

(It is known that Sir Francis Drake got his hands on a copy of the medal; what he made of it, we can imagine.[30]) It was only Philip II's eponymous grandson, Philip IV, who in the following century would be called the *Rey Planeta*, king of the entire planet (captured in an equestrian portrait by Rubens in which Philip carries the world upon his shoulders, a personification of Faith marking Spain with a cross, while the personification of Divine Justice destroys heresy with Jupiter-like arrows of lightning).[31] But the symbolism linking dominion over the entire planet with the Spanish monarch was already well established in the iconography of Philip II's reign, and was promoted by writers, such as Jaime Vadés, who called him *Emperador del Nuevo Mundo y de Europa* – emperor of the New World and of Europe.[32]

FIGURE 1.1 Medal of Philip II of Spain: 'non sufficit orbis'[33]

Turning back to Philip II, according to historian Geoffrey Parker, his overall strategy was, first, to preserve his inheritance, threatened especially by the insurgence of the Protestant Dutch in quest of independence. Secondly, he tried to keep what he had acquired in his own lifetime: the English crown through his marriage with Mary Tudor, lost again once she predeceased him without issue, and that of Portugal. Thirdly, he was encouraged to follow in the Spanish tradition of defending Christianity against the infidel, the long-standing leitmotif of the Reconquista, but now also to be the *defensor fidei*, champion of – by now worldwide – Catholicism against the Protestant heresies, with the ultimate aspiration of re-establishing a universal monarchy.[34] This is illustrated by the Titian painting dating from the early 1570s (the Dutch Revolt was well underway) where *ecclesia* is threatened by the Turks from the sea, and by the snakes of heresy behind her (see Figure 1.2).

There was even an initiative dating from 1596 to create a religious order (in the tradition of the crusading orders) to operate at sea, with a navy of 21 galleons, against the infidel and against heretics.[35] The choice of galleons – ships relying entirely on wind power – is of course an indicator that this fleet was to be used mainly in the open waters of the Atlantic rather than in the Mediterranean, where in 1571 the Christian forces under Spanish leadership had triumphed against the Ottoman navy using galleys and galleasses – that is ships propelled mainly by power of oar.

FIGURE 1.2 Titian: *Religion Saved by Spain* (or *Spain Succouring Faith*), 1572–1575 (Madrid: Prado)[36]

Parker doubts that Philip himself espoused the goal of a 'universal monarchy', but to repeat, contemporaries were convinced that he embraced it fully, and felt threatened by it much as the liberal democracies of the twentieth century would feel existentially threatened by the expansionist, universalist ambitions of 'world Communism'. Either way, as it was Philip's unquestionable aim to assert his authority over the Netherlands, against the Dutch uprising, he needed to continue with his counter-insurgency campaign there. The Dutch fielded an increasingly regular force, with the open support of Elizabeth's England and, periodically, Henri IV's France. Spain's lines of communication lay either overland on the '*camino español*' (the preferred route during 1568–1638), through Habsburg possessions from Milan through the Franche Comté to the low countries, or by sea, along the coast of France through the Channel to the Dutch ports. Two of these – Brill (Brielle) and Flushing (Vlissingen) – were controlled by England, on the basis of the 1585 Treaty of Nonsuch concluded with the Dutch rebels.[37] Following this treaty, Anglo-Spanish hostilities, never formally taking the form of a declared war, turned into direct military clashes.

With hindsight we can see that the Anglo-Spanish War of 1585–1604 (see Chapter 4) was a sideshow to the main rivalry between the Habsburgs and the French kings that was to dominate European politics until 1756. Even after that, the French Revolutionary and Napoleonic Wars were mainly directed against the (Austrian) Habsburgs. (The rivalry really only ended when Napoleon claimed the imperial heritage from Rome via Charlemagne for himself and for France in 1804, and two years later caused the dissolution of the Holy Roman Empire, to be replaced by a Franco-Prussian and then Franco-German rivalry.) The Habsburgs in general and the Spanish Habsburgs in particular with their ever growing empires were rising to become the French kings' rivals for pre-eminence in Europe, and later, in large parts of the world. France's religious wars were closely linked with the Dutch insurgency in what was to some extent a Europe-wide civil war that would later grow into the Thirty Years' War. The Franco-Habsburg conflict was muted when Bourbon king Henri IV became a Catholic and above all tried to assert his authority within France, which hinged on interdenominational reconciliation; despite the troubles which followed his assassination, this put an end to foreign meddling in French domestic affairs.[38] Even so, until the Spanish War of Succession, Spain's wars were dominated mainly by the confrontation with France, a bloody sparring that was concluded only when Henri IV's descendant, King Louis XIV, managed to put one of his grandsons on the Spanish throne. At least between 1570 and 1625, France had no navy that could threaten any other country, so the conflict took place almost entirely on land, and mainly within France's possessions.

Another major and mortally dangerous adversary of Philip, the House of Habsburg and indeed all of Christendom was the Ottoman Empire. The immediate threat to Spain and its North African possessions was naval, and this was largely but by no means entirely rebutted in the Battle of Lepanto in 1571, which only retrospectively can be seen as a turning point in favour of Christendom. During Philip's lifetime it was uncertain whether the many campaigns of the Ottoman fleet that took place even in the Western Mediterranean, and that would secure most of North Africa for the sultan's rule, could not again pose a threat to South-Western Europe. For the naval operations which led to the Battle of Lepanto, Philip joined a coalition of Christian powers and navies whose interest in fending off the Turks converged: this was the short-lived Holy League that had been brought together by Pope Pius V, counting also among its members Venice, Genoa, Savoy and some other Italian states and the Knights of Malta. Its navies were commanded by Philip's handsome half-brother, Don John of Austria; thus Philip ensured that he could dominate this successful venture and could claim leadership among the Christian powers in the defence against the Turks, an enduring concern. Meanwhile South-Eastern Europe was of course firmly under the sultan's control. Local piracy along the Barbary Coast added to Philip's worries about the security of his southern flank and naval lines of communication in and around the Mediterranean. Nevertheless, in the following decades of Philip's reign, the Ottoman threat receded behind the Dutch rebellion which began in 1568, and Spain's wars with France and England.

Spain's strategic options and choices

If further evidence of strategic thinking is needed for Philip II, but also of the statecraft in presenting it and garnering support for it, we might look for it in the arguments presented on behalf of Philip to the Castilian *Cortes*, the representatives of the estates of Castile from which Philip drew his main revenue. One such example of a letter from Philip read out to the *Cortes* by his secretary, Francisco de Eraso, can be found in 1570, when the Ottoman threat was at its greatest, and the Dutch Revolt had only just started. Here Philip asked the *Cortes* for more funds. He explained not only that it behoved him to ensure the security of his kingdom's frontiers, its fortified places and the good provisioning of his armies and navy, but also that he needed the means to 'castigate . . . the rebels' in Flanders – that is the rebellion in the Netherlands, 'with a great example and authority'. To do so he needed to help the last Valois French king, Charles IX, against the 'heretics' in his own country, but also to support a campaign to quell an uprising of the Moriscos in Granada, which assumed a further dimension as possible preparation to help a landing in Spain by a Turkish fleet. Philip added that he needed ships to fend off the Turks and also pirates operating in the Mediterranean. In this letter, Philip stressed that the priority for him and all the faithful – '*prima y principalmente*' – must be the defence of the Catholic faith, in fact the justification for *all* these campaigns and expenses. In his negotiations with the *Cortes*, he thus made it quite impossible for the Castilian emissaries to take issue with this long list of obligations or to unpick it by arguing that some might be less pressing than others. Admittedly, strategy making in this case was a denial of choice, and an insistence that all these points must be met. (Things would look different once the Dutch War of Independence had been underway for some years.) The *Cortes* on this occasion promised to support the king's plans.[39]

While at this stage, Philip could aspire to have it all, as the Dutch wars dragged on he had to choose between different priorities and focus on other enemies as well. Spain proved unable to defeat France in a head-on campaign (which would have required a massive confrontation of land armies either in France's north or along the Pyrenees or both); nor did Philip II have hopes of doing so. Instead, as we have seen, he meddled in the French Wars of Religion by supporting the Catholic side. He repeatedly seized (but subsequently lost again) French ports along the English Channel in order to secure his naval lines of communication to the Netherlands, but henceforth, France was not his priority. From 1876 until his death in 1598, the dithering king as one might also call him weighed the options of concentrating his strategic options on the defeat of the Dutch rebellion, or on a direct or indirect assault on their principal supporter, Queen Elizabeth of England.[40]

After Philip's courtship of Elizabeth was rejected, he began to see Elizabeth as a danger to Spain's great Catholic programme. Already in 1563, Spain's ambassador to England, Alvaro de Quadra, wrote to King Philip about Queen Elizabeth:

> This woman desires to make use of religion in order to excite rebellion in the whole world . . . If she had the power today she would sow heresy broadcast in all your Majesty's dominions, and set them ablaze without compunction.[41]

Swayed by evidence of Elizabeth's support for the Protestant rebels against his rule in the Netherlands, Philip proceeded to back Catholic Mary Stuart, Queen of Scots, as pretender to the English crown, through conspiracies and plots, a strategy of 'all mischief short of war' (one definition of the Cold War of the twentieth century). Don John was keen to replace Elizabeth on the English throne himself, and from 1576 until his own death in 1578 tried hard to manipulate his half-brother, Philip II, into prioritising an invasion of England.[42]

The Turkish threat was always lurking in the background and we know only with the benefit of hindsight that the sultan would cause Philip no further grief. Philip managed to bribe him to accept an armistice, which in turn did not please Pope Gregory XIII, who would have preferred Philip to win back the Christian lands that had been conquered by the Ottoman Empire. If Philip was not willing to go on an all-out *Reconquista*, the pope could threaten him with the revocation of the 'Three Graces', special taxes paid by the Spanish churches to their monarch that had originally been granted to fend off the Turks. From 1582, Pope Gregory XIII also expressly urged Philip to invade England. At the very least, thus the pope's demand, Philip should invade Ireland to force out the English and restore Ireland fully to the Catholic fold. This option was attractive not least as Philip could do unto the English as they were doing unto him: as they were supporting the Dutch against him, he might support a rebellion against Tudor rule in Ireland. Until 1574, Spanish ships could freely approach the coasts of Ireland, for in 1553, the first year of his spouse's Mary I's reign, Philip had bought the right for Spanish fishermen to fish in that region for a period of 21 years.[43] Thereafter, Spanish relations with the Irish were maintained, and indeed, elites of both nations were united in their antipathy towards English Protestantism. The archbishop of Dublin, for example, was a Spaniard, and Spaniards were among the soldiers who were to invade England in Philip's campaigns. Indeed, in September 1581, Philip footed the bill for a small fleet to take 800 Spanish and Italian volunteers to the coast of Ireland to help the Irish expel the English. But news of this had travelled, and they were met by an English contingent and soundly beaten.[44]

Further challenges deflected Philip from the 'Enterprise of England'. While his realm and colonial empire doubled in size with his succession to the Portuguese throne in 1581, his rule was challenged by Dom Antonio, an illegitimate grandson of the late King Manuel I of Portugal. Dom Antonio managed to establish himself in the Azores. Philip sent a fleet to evict him from there, upon which Dom Antonio fled to France and then to England. In 1585 Queen Elizabeth imposed an embargo on English trade with the Spanish in the Netherlands, to which Philip retaliated by arresting the crews of foreign ships in Spanish harbours; it transpired that his reason was one of deterrence: 'hearing that the Hollanders seake ayde in England and fearing they shalbe ayded' Philip 'meaneth by this arreste to fear [=deter] the Englishe from ayding them'. It was only after Sir Francis Drake's surprise attack on Cádiz in the same year that Philip moved from deterrence to aggression and opted for an invasion of England, even though the preparations – including building the necessary navy – and final decision would be another three years in the making.[45]

As England could threaten Philip II's maritime line of communication with his Dutch possessions, especially in the Channel, one strategic option for Philip was to try in turn to dominate the Channel by gaining a foothold in Brittany and seizing Calais in Normandy. This is indeed an option he pursued, but as we have noted, the forces of Henri IV, with English help, ousted his each time.

While Philip's resources – local taxation in his united kingdoms covering the Iberian Peninsula but also revenue from his overseas' empire – were much larger than those of Elizabethan England, there were still limits, not merely financial but also physical, to what he could do to harm England.[46] Yet this became clear only during the Anglo-Spanish War. Both Philip and Elizabeth tried throughout to avoid direct confrontations. Indeed, both Philip II and Elizabeth I are counted among the hesitators or 'Fabians' among strategic decision-makers.[47] Even after 1585, Philip postponed the invasion of England several times. For reasons of economy alone, both the Tudor and the Habsburg monarchs needed a lasting peace.

Philip's and Elizabeth's hesitations and last-minute cancellations of campaigns are not in themselves evidence of an absence of strategy, but of the dilemma monarchs faced repeatedly: the cost for their economies of raising armies was considerable, in terms of not only losses of manpower to the economy as a whole but also the money lost for their provisioning. Unless one had a standing army like France, an army that had been assembled and that waited for a long time to be deployed usually cost nearly as much as an army actually sent into action, and the same applied to armies that were disbanded again without seeing action.[48] Navies, whose operations were frequently cancelled or delayed due to unfavourable winds, often consumed large parts of their dearly acquired victuals while waiting in port or trying to brave the storms. To decide to call off action meant an even greater waste of money.

Eventually, Philip and Elizabeth were so committed to the Europe-wide war confessional and dynastic strife that their credibility was at stake; they could not easily pull back, and their own subjects would not have allowed this to happen. While Philip II along with his dynasty was imbued with Catholic missionary zeal, Elizabeth's claim to the English throne was strongly supported by the English Protestants. Their conflict was thus ideologically inescapable. Even now, Philip hesitated, trying to bring Elizabeth's rival Mary Stuart to the throne of England through conspiracy rather than invasion. After her execution in 1587, he sought a match between Mary's son, James, and his daughter Isabella Clara Eugenia, and wanted James to claim the English crown (he wanted Isabella on the throne of either England or France; unsuccessful, he later gave her the Netherlands to administer).[49] Only an invasion would put her on the throne, however. In 1588, a year after Mary Stuart's execution, Philip finally ordered his *gran armada*, configured around this set of crown-owned vessels built for this specific operation, to sail. The strategic flaw in his 'masterplan' was that he tried to do three things simultaneously – launch a surprise attack on England's southern shores, but also pick up a Spanish army in the Netherlands and ferry them across the Channel (preparations for which could not go undetected by English spies), and also meet an English fleet, now assembled and prepared, in open battle.[50] Famously, Philip's armada was repulsed by an English fleet that was assembled defensively ad hoc, and then scattered by the winds.

When the news of this calamity reached Spain, Philip on 1 October 1588 had a letter read out to the *Cortes*, in which he explained that he had launched this campaign 'in the service of God and the Holy Catholic Faith, and for the benefit of [his] kingdoms'. Anything could happen now, he argued, and the security of the seas and of the Indies was at risk, and even that of 'our own homes'. He implored them as his good vassals to support him in what he needed to do, given his 'great and inexcusable obligations'. The war with England now topped the Spanish list of strategic concerns, and Philip asked for support above all for a defence of Spain and its shipping against England.[51] After six days' deliberations, the *Cortes* grudgingly agreed to give the crown 16,000 ducats.[52] Nevertheless, Philip's prioritisation of the 'Enterprise of England' forced him to make economies elsewhere, and he chose to make cuts in his fortification scheme for his African and Asian possessions.[53]

Delayed by more pressing demands on his attention – revolts in Castile, Sicily and Aragon – Philip attempted to carry out another naval invasion of England only in 1595 with a little success (the Spanish fleet succeeded in burning Penzance, Moushole and Newlyn in Cornwall), and two more, one unsuccessfully in 1596 and one again unsuccessfully in 1597, when adverse winds persuaded the armada to turn back. In 1595, Don Bernardino de Mendoza, who had been Quadra's successor as Spanish ambassador to the Court of St James (London) and was then expelled for plotting with Mary Stuart, argued implicitly against the creation of a standing Spanish royal navy, and explicitly for configuring a navy each time it was needed, according to the purpose it was to serve in any particular campaign.[54] His view either reflected the king's views or persuaded him: the armadas of 1596 and 1597 were thus again assembled and in part built specifically for the operation against England. This joint venture character of the armadas was perhaps an additional reason for their failure besides the adverse winds that met them on their operations: the decision to turn back was taken more easily by captains of privately owned vessels, as the prospect of booty slipped from their grasp.

Philip also returned to the Irish option. After Spain's unsuccessful attempt in 1581 to help the Irish in an uprising against English rule, Philip decided to support Tyrone's Rebellion (or the Nine Years' War, 1594–1603), which was being prepared through contacts with Spain. From 1591, Tyrone received first Spain's indirect and later direct support, initially only with Spanish advisers helping the Irish to develop increasingly successful guerrilla tactics, and then with the actual deployment of Spanish troops. Eventually, England had to deploy larger forces to Ireland than it had been able to finance in support of the Dutch Rebellion. The Spanish strategy of supporting the Irish against England of course relied heavily on naval communications with Ireland, and thus on vessels as vehicles for transport, rather than equipped for naval battle. The Nine Years' War was brought to an end only well after Philip's death and indeed years after the Battle of Kinsale (1601), where Irish rebel and Spanish regular forces clashed with and were defeated by an English army.[55] (Irish resistance against English rule would break into flames again in the War of the Three Kingdoms, when the Irish even offered Spanish king Philip IV the Irish crown. He declined.)[56]

Both monarchs under whom the Anglo-Spanish War had started were dead and buried before peace would be concluded under their respective successors, Philip III and James I and VI. (The Dutch Rebellion, however, was not over, and would drag on for 80 years, eventually ending with the independence of the United Provinces at the end of the Thirty Years' War, into which the rebellion merged.)

Geoffrey Parker, who first argued that Philip had a grand strategy, shows that he had to make decisions about the prioritisation of investments in his military (creating a royal navy, raising and deploying troops in his various theatres of war, ensuring the openness of his own lines of communication, etc.), as well as using (or attempting to use) diplomatic tools, such as dynastic marriages and the kinship with the Austrian Habsburgs. Despite the great revenues which the Spanish crown drew upon, not least from its American possessions, Philip's budget was overstretched by his multiple ambitions. While Philip was convinced that in all of this, he was doing God's bidding, this did not translate itself into good fortune in all his campaigns. He managed to keep most of his realm, but could not reconquer England or contain the Dutch independence movement. Nor could he put the genie of Protestantism back in the bottle.[57]

Parker has seen a link with a deficiency in statecraft on the part of Philip: his very style of personal government drove him into a rut in which he ended up so preoccupied with all details of administration that bagatelles in all shapes and forms prevented him from a more coherent application of strategy on higher levels. Philip was too reactive to have been a very successful grand strategist, and too preoccupied by daily events to be able to keep on top of greater developments.[58] But even if weaknesses in Philip II's statecraft and strategy making can be identified, he managed to leave to his successors a global empire that lasted until the death of the last Habsburg monarch triggered the war of succession that would be won by Louis XIV of France.[59]

War in the grand siècle of Louis XIV

Louis, who acceded to kingship at the tender age of four, as a youth was very keen to shake off the joint tutelage of his mother and of Cardinal Mazarin. In later life, however, he would make excellent use of his ministers, generals and other advisers, including Jean-Baptiste Colbert; his son, the Marquis of Seignelay; father and son Telliers, who would both be Marquis de Louvois; Sébastien Le Prestre de Vauban; Jules-Louis Bolé de Chamlay; and Godefroi, Count d'Estrades.[60] Louis would delegate tasks to them to an extent that his maternal great-grandfather Philip II would not have dreamt of.

Between the two monarchs lay a period of wars which engulfed all of Europe, from Ireland and Britain (in the Wars of the Three Kingdoms) to Poland, and from Sweden to Spain and the Balkans (the Thirty Years' War). On the periphery even the Russian and Ottoman Empires got involved. A number of factors lay at the origins of this: attempts by the Austrian Habsburgs, at the helm of the Holy Roman Empire, to roll back Protestantism and support the Counter-Reformation, and on the other side attempts to counter the 'Catholic International'; centrifugal forces of regional self-assertion; blank opportunism on the part of several princes. These wars were civil wars and interstate wars at once, and the strategic aims of all parties were exceedingly complex and shifted often.[61] It is perhaps because of this complexity that only two serious strategic theorists wrote at the time of this war or soon thereafter: Raimondo Montecuccoli (see Chapter 7) and the considerably less brilliant Paul Hay du Chastelet Jr.[62] (A few other works appeared at the time that are at best of tactical interest.)

Louis XIV was himself only ten when the Thirty Years' War was ended with the 1648 Peace Treaties of Münster and Osnabrück. The former turned Alsace into a part of France but oddly gave the French king a seat of the Imperial Diet of the Holy Roman Empire (although Cardinal Mazarin managed to avoid making the French king a subordinate prince of the empire: that would have been reminiscent of the status which the Plantagenet kings had had as vassals of the French king, for their possessions in France).

Henceforth, religion was theoretically and generally speaking no longer a major factor in European warfare. While religious strife was off the agenda, the Bourbon-vs-Habsburg rivalry that had succeeded the rivalry between the French and imperial heirs of Charlemagne was fully unleashed. And this despite or because of the intermarriage between the House of Bourbon and the House of Habsburg: not only was Louis's mother the granddaughter and daughter of Spanish Habsburg kings Philip II and Philip III respectively. Louis himself married his first cousin, daughter of his mother's brother, Philip IV, king of Spain. Indeed, while war drew to a close in 1648 elsewhere in Europe, war between France and Spain dragged on until 1659. In that year's Peace of the Pyrenees, France obtained a swathe of territory to its north that had previously been parts of the Spanish Netherlands, including Artois and Hainault, and to the south, the Roussillon and a chunk of Catalonia called Cerdanya (Cerdagne). This territorial enlargement of France was the achievement of the two faithful servants of the Bourbon dynasty, Cardinals Richelieu and Mazarin. The most striking illustration of this is the splendid building facing the Louvre on the Left Bank of the Seine, which today houses the Institut de France. Cardinal Mazarin left his fortune to its construction, to house a *Collège des Quatre Nations*, meaning the new 'nations' or populations that had been integrated into the Bourbon realm with the Treaties of Münster and the Pyrenees. The College was designed to educate future loyal civil servants of France who hailed from these areas. Louis XIV's own strategic aims of enlarging his kingdom even further were thus in principle a mere continuation of the aims of his father's reign, and of the two cardinals. Their respective strategies, however, differed considerably. Louis XIV in his relentless pursuit of his expansionist aims could use the far greater means left to him by the two cardinals. The means with which he pursued his objectives distinguished him in particular.

Louis XIV had considerable advantages over all his predecessors. Religious strife was on the whole reduced in prominence in interstate relations if not in the domestic politics of France (Louis still had to face the Camisard uprising in the Cevennes and was ultimately obliged to negotiate with a baker's son and had to concede

religious freedom to the rebels). But on the whole, the monarchs' absolutist powers increased significantly, and with it, a fiscal-military state on a scale that Europe
had not seen since the end of the Roman Empire in the West. The French state
apparatus that was fostered by the two cardinals, and later by Louis's finance minister Jean-Baptiste Colbert, allowed Louis XIV to embrace expansionist strategic
aims. Richelieu had begun to build up a navy which provided Louis with a strategic tool that his predecessors had lacked, even though in 1695, due to financial
constraints, the king had to choose between navy and army, strategically choosing to concentrate his remaining funds on the latter. Louis had a whole series of
extremely talented servants and ministers dealing with the many dimensions of
warfare, of whom Sébastien Le Prestre de Vauban, famous for his system of fortifications along France's land frontiers, was but one.[63] Despite the demographic
dip due to the famine of 1695, France's population was significantly larger than it
had been in previous reigns. That, together with the previous and ongoing fiscal
reforms, allowed Louis to double and then more than triple the size of his standing
army: where his father's army had had a paper strength of 125,000 when France
entered the Thirty Years' War in 1635, the Sun King had 279,000 soldiers during his Dutch War of 1672–1678, and up to 420,000 during his Nine Years' War
against the League of Augsburg (the Holy Roman Empire, Spain, Great Britain and
Savoy) during 1688–1697.[64]

Louis XIV of France as strategist

There is no doubt that Louis himself formulated the strategic priorities of his reign,
albeit with the help of his counsellors.[65] In ascertaining these, the 358 notes produced for Louis by Chamlay between 1690 and 1709 are revealing: 145 concerned
the Netherlands, 140 the Habsburg Holy Roman Empire, 122 Italy and only 49
concerned Spain (and that mainly from 1700, as the Spanish succession crisis came
to the fore). Only six concerned Britain, and a further eight the defence of the
French coast.[66]

Louis's own hand could be seen when, upon Philip IV of Spain's death in 1665,
much like Edward III of England before him, the French monarch would invoke an
obscure principle of inheritance to increase his territories. Thus began the first of
Louis's wars, the 'War of Devolution' of 1667–1668, aimed to enlarge France to the
north. From the beginning, Louis's grand strategic objectives were to increase his
dynasty's possessions wherever he could. A letter he sent to the Count d'Estrades on
19 December 1664 may serve as an example for strategic thinking that integrated
warfare, the forging and undoing of alliances, reflections on short- and long-term
consequences of actions, the application of the laws of war (*ius ad bellum*) and other
aspects of statecraft. Louis had concluded a treaty of mutual assistance with Johan
de Witt, the grand pensionary (or republican head of government) of Holland,
internally opposed by the faction of William III of Orange, son and husband to Stuart princesses (family bonds he would eventually use to seize the crowns of England
and Scotland in 1688). In late 1664, de Witt called upon Louis to support him in a

war against England. In the letter to Estrades – our next piece of evidence for the presence of strategic reasoning before the word was coined – Louis explained his hesitations to fulfil his treaty obligations.

Louis wrote that he wanted to secure the Spanish Netherlands, interposed between de Witt's state and his own, for his wife and their heirs. But at this point Louis hoped for a peaceful succession, as the heir of Spain and half-brother of Louis's wife, the future Carlos II, might be prevailed upon to cede the Spanish Netherlands peacefully. Louis noted that London was on the point of concluding a similar treaty of mutual assistance with Madrid, and going to war against England was likely to obviate his wife's peaceful succession to the Spanish Netherlands. Nor was Louis confident that de Witt would pass up the occasion of such a war – which might escalate to bring Spain into it – to seize the Spanish Netherlands for his country. King Charles II of England and Scotland was obviously aware of de Witt's attempts to bring in France as an ally, and had cleverly suggested to Louis XIV a way of reneging on his treaty commitments to de Witt, by suggesting that an *unjust* war was not covered by such a treaty of mutual assistance. Charles defined de Witt as the aggressor, thus claiming the moral high ground. The Dutch-British quarrel concerned possession of the Dutch West India Company, so another excuse for Louis not to honour his treaty commitments was to claim that the treaty did not pertain to extra-European conflicts. In short, on this occasion, Louis XIV did not want to go to war.[67] In his memoirs, Louis explained the choice that he was facing: to try to keep his own pursuit of the succession of the Spanish Netherlands separate from de Witt's war, or to join forces with him at the risk of seeing him play false at the end, or otherwise losing the Spanish Netherlands while deeply alienating Spain and what was from 1707 the United Kingdom of Great Britain.

Then there was the choice of means, were he to go to war: would he use his navy or his army? He opted for the latter. As 'the wellbeing of my kingdom did not permit that I expose myself to the caprices of the sea,' and as naval warfare would force him to delegate all his authority 'to his lieutenants, without the ability to intervene personally', he was reluctant, he said, to espouse a mainly naval strategy. Moreover, he had a large standing army which he was maintaining at the expense of his subjects, so he would prefer to make use of that and to 'throw it into the Spanish king's estates' to fight. Given that he was faced with a war on two fronts, he preferred to concentrate on his fight with Spain, and to leave the naval dimension of this war to the Dutch.[68]

Louis's calculations changed when in the following year, the likelihood increased that a Dutch defeat in this (Second) Anglo-Dutch War was likely to lead to the overthrow of de Witt, and to the rule of William III of Orange with his family links with the crown of England and Scotland. Louis eventually joined the fray in 1666 on the side of de Witt. In the following year, however, Louis would clash with de Witt over his attempts to secure the Spanish Netherlands under Louis's wife's claim to succession, a war that would become known as the War of Devolution (1667–1668).

The following phase of Louis's reign, lasting from roughly 1675 up to 1697, he intended to be one of consolidation. But in fact the Nine Years' War of

1688–1697 that pitted Louis against a Grand Alliance of all Habsburgs and some other princes of the Holy Roman Empire, the Dutch and Victor Amadeus II of Savoy brought huge reversals for France, including the temporary loss of Lorraine.[69] Louis had no inhibitions about employing scorched earth tactics to break resistance to French occupation in contested areas, or to make them unattractive to his adversaries;[70] his tactics closely resembled those of the *chevauchées* of Edward III and other English monarchs in France in the Hundred Years' War. Louis's earlier wars with Spain had paradoxically been conducted mainly along France's northern frontier with the Habsburg lands in Flanders. Briefly, in 1694, at Chamlay's advice, Louis attempted an offensive move against Catalonia and the Basque country. In 1697, this led to the French seizure of Barcelona, which proved decisive in persuading Madrid to sue for peace, leading to the Peace of Rijswick of the same year.[71]

Even during the last phase of Louis's wars (1701–1714), centring on the War of the Spanish Succession waged over his wife's claims to the crown of Spain itself, the main theatres of the wars between Louis's forces and those of the Spanish Habsburgs were the Low Countries and Northern France, and Italy, with Spain being a theatre of tertiary importance. It curiously became a war in which the Bourbons mainly fielded land forces but were faced with a coalition of the Austrian Habsburgs, the Dutch and the British with a strong naval element which Louis could not match, either in terms of numbers of ships or of reach: France's ports were shallow and always on the verge of silting up, and only Toulon on France's Mediterranean coast and Brest in Brittany could support larger vessels. Moreover, Britain's conquest of Gibraltar in 1704 would be a serious blow not only for Spain but also for France, as Britain henceforth controlled the waters along France's western and southern coasts, along with the passage between the Mediterranean and the Atlantic, through which France might want to move her ships if ever she wanted to concentrate her navies in one area.[72]

Louis's secondary strategic aim in the War of the Spanish Succession was to seize also the Spanish Habsburg possessions in Italy (especially Milan and its dependencies). The Austrian Habsburgs under Prince Eugene of Savoy were also trying to secure these lands, and Austrian and French armies would thus clash in northern Italy. Access to Italy presupposed the passage through the Alps in the areas controlled by Victor Amadeus II of Savoy, who would thus continue to hold the key to Louis's successes and failures.[73]

Despite the impressive fiscal-military state and the exceptionally talented ministers Louis could draw upon, even he did not have enough revenue to develop fully all strategic options. He was able to extend France's frontiers to the north, east and south, and to fortify the frontier regions with Vauban's constructions permitting a defence-in-depth. But he could not also finance a big enough standing navy to deal Britain or the Netherlands a decisive blow; historian Jean-Philippe Cénat has argued that the *Royale* (French Navy) was in part sacrificed to the other parts of the military budget. Neither did France have the means to assure the long-term defence of France's colonies in North America. But Louis's personal lack of interest in territories outside of Europe was another strong factor in this lack of a colonial strategy: French emigration to North America was not particularly encouraged, so that during his reign, the number of British settlers in North America grew to be almost 20 times as large as that of French settlers. The peace of Utrecht of 1813 formalised this imbalance by transferring the Hudson Bay, Terre-Neuve (Newfoundland) and Acadia (renamed Nova Scotia) to Britain.[74] Even if France clung onto the Antilles and stole other Caribbean islands away from the Dutch, on the whole conquests beyond Europe were not part of Louis's grand strategy.

Even during the defensive middle phase of Louis's wars, his expansionism antagonised all neighbouring states; intimidation was key to his overall strategy.[75] Louis was always on the look-out for new allies, courting the Ottomans and even the king of Siam, but he was less keen to follow through on alliance commitments. Louis followed a few strong stragetic principles: the 'sanctuarisation' (i.e. the protection and defence) of French territory; the preference of sieges over battles with their uncertain outcome and their tendency rapidly to bring a campaign to a potentially adverse conclusion; and overall risk minimisation, unless a preventive war promised success. And finally, he had a tendency to concentrate the bulk of his forces on one of the several fronts on which his wars took place, while employing diversions and peripheral moves, forming temporary alliances or promising aid where none would eventually be forthcoming.[76]

At the end of Louis's reign, France had acquired almost its present shape, except for parts of its northern frontier, the parts of the Duchy of Savoy in the south-east which France obtained later, and the repeated changes in the status of Lorraine until the twentieth century. Louis's France had Europe's largest population, defended in depth guaranteed by Europe's largest army and an awe-inspiring system of fortified 'places', mainly towns and cities, that at the time set the gold standard for the entire Western world. But it had come at a considerable price in blood and treasure, and also of resentment which all of France's neighbours bore this country.[77] As the motto that Louis XIV chose for himself put it,[78] France was superior to many, and many were those who begrudged her this. On his deathbed, Louis told his heir, Louis XV,

> Darling, you will be a great king, but your entire happiness will depend on your obedience to God and the care you will ease the burdens of your people. For this purpose you must avoid war as much as possible: it is the ruin of the peoples. Do not follow the bad example that I have given you in this matter; I have often undertaken war too easily and I have carried on out of vanity. Do not imitate me, but be a pacific prince, and let it be your principal undertaking to ease the burdens of your subjects.[79]

Even though he had presented all his wars as a *defence* of his dynastic interests and obligations, Louis had united all of Europe against France in a fashion that only Napoleon would manage to do again.[80]

Conclusions

The three examples we have sketched admittedly show that the war machines, the administrative and military apparatus upon which the three monarchs could draw, expanded and changed spectacularly over 300-odd years. Armies grew in size, especially under Louis XIV; but even then it would be said not of his country but of Frederick William I's Prussia that it was an army with a state, not a state with an army. At the beginning of the period considered here, the western hemisphere was as yet out of reach, while naval exploits of the subsequent two centuries would come to transform warfare. By then, and thenceforth, European wars, particularly those prosecuted by the littoral powers of the Atlantic, could assume a global dimension.

Despite all this change, we do see some patterns in common across all three case studies, and these confirm that strategies can be found in all of them. To use the criteria for this that we have defined at the outset, in all three cases, we find careful planning of campaigns. This involved choosing between several fronts on which to concentrate the forces and choosing between various forms of war. Thus all three monarchs considered here used navies to force battle, to attempt invasions, to capture or hold and supply territory, but less so than they might have done (or in the case of Philip II, were ill favoured by wind and weather to a degree well beyond his control). All three effectively prioritised their armies. Edward III and Louis XIV used the *chevauchée* or its more modern form of scorched earth tactics to badger the local populations into submission and sow terror; Philip's generals, especially the dreaded Duke of Alba, used massacres and mass executions to similar effect. Only Louis invested heavily in defensive fortifications, very much a strategic choice.

It is also striking how all three monarchs used diplomatic and economic tools of statecraft to complement and offset military measures, most visibly perhaps their dynastic politics, their marriages and their claims to land as their inheritance. While Louis was not good at forging alliances or making friends, Edward had some Continental allies and Philip could count on the allegiance of most Catholic princes in Europe and, of course, the pope. And within their realms, while all three had to contend with insurgencies by their own peers and populations on whom they otherwise had to rely to finance their wars, famously, after the Fronde Louis managed to re-establish law and order by rendering his central government structures more effective, and taking absolutism to unprecedented heights in France.

With greater or lesser success, with more or less enduring outcomes, all three monarchs can thus safely be said to have been strategists, and to have made strategy. To draw on the description of strategy making that we find in Lazarus Schwendi's work, they identified outcomes, they discussed them with their leading generals (or admirals) and ministers and, in the cases of Edward III and Philip II, articulated their aims and priorities to their parliaments (representatives of the estates). They prepared means and defined ways to use them, and they can be said to have pursued their aims by carefully choosing and applying their strategies and a variety of tools of statecraft (ranging from warfare to dynastic marriages).

Notes

1 Lazarus von Schwendi, Freyherr zu Hohen Landsperg etc: *Kriegsdiscurs, von Bestellung deß ganzen Kriegswesens unnd von den Kriegsämptern* (Frankfurt/Main: Andree Weichels Erben Claudi de Marne & Johan Aubri, 1593), p. 45.

2 Beatrice Heuser: *The Evolution of Strategy* (Cambridge: Cambridge University Press, 2010), Chapter 1.

3 Carl von Clausewitz: *Vom Kriege*, Book II (Berlin: Dümmler, 1832) trans. by Peter Paret and Michael Howard (eds): *On War* (Princeton, NJ: Princeton University Press, 1976), pp. 128, 177.

4 Heuser: *Evolution of Strategy*, p. 27f.

5 Kimberly Kagan: 'Redefining Roman Grand Strategy', *The Journal of Military History*, Vol. 70 No. 2 (2006), p. 348.

6 Natalie Fryde: *The Tyranny and Fall of Edward II, 1321–1326* (Cambridge: Cambridge University Press, 1979), *passim*.

7 Caroline Barron: 'The Tyranny of Richard II', *Bulletin of the Institute of Historical Research* Vol. 41 No. 103 (1968), pp. 1–18.

8 Natalie Fryde: *Why Magna Carta? Angevin England Revisited* (Münster: LIT Verlag, 2001).

9 Clifford Rogers: 'The Anglo-French Peace Negotiations of 1354–1360 Reconsidered', in J.S. Bothwell (ed.): *The Age of Edward III* (York: York Medieval Press, 2001), pp. 193–212.

10 This is not to claim that it had not existed previously – for example it had been practised deftly by Pope Innocent III in the early thirteenth century, see Natalie Fryde: 'Innocent III, England and the Modernization of European International Politics', *Innocenzo III, Urbs et Orbis*, Vol. 2 (1998), pp. 971–984.

11 Philippe Contamine: *La Guerre au Moyen Age* (Paris: Presses Universitaires de France, 1986²), p. 365.

12 Jan-Willem Honig: 'Reappraising Late Medieval Strategy: The Example of the 1415 Agincourt', *War in History*, Vol. 19 No. 2 (2012), pp. 123–151.

13 John Gillingham: 'War and Chivalry in the History of William the Marshal', reprinted in Matthew Strickland (ed.): *Anglo-Saxon Warfare: Studies in Late Anglo-Saxon and Anglo-Norman Military Organisation and Warfare* (Woodbridge: Boydell Press, 1992), pp. 251–263.

14 Clifford J. Rogers: *War Cruel and Sharp: English Strategy under Edward III, 1327–1360* (Woodbridge: Boydell Press, 2000); id.: 'The Vegetian "Science of Warfare" in the Middle Ages', *Journal of Medieval Military History*, Vol. 1 (2002), pp. 1–19.

15 For examples, see Sir Travers Twiss (ed.): *The Black Book of the Admiralty, vol. 55 of the Rerum britannicarum medii aevi scriptores or Chronicles and Memorials of Great Britain and Ireland during the Middle Ages*, Vol. 1 (London: Longman, 1871).

16 Nigel Saul: *A Companion to Medieval England, 1066–1485* (Stroud: Tempus, 2000), pp. 281–283.

17 Rogers: *War Cruel and Sharp*.

18 Which were by now: Sandwich, Dover, Hythe, New Romney, Hastings, Rye, Seaford and Winchelsea.

19 Clifford J. Rogers (ed. & trans.): *Edward III's Wars* (Rochester, NY: Boydell Press, 1999), Document No. 55.

20 Susan Rose: *Medieval Naval Warfare 1000–1500* (London: Routledge, 2002), pp. 123–131.

21 Frédérique Laget: 'Guerre sur Mer et Usage stratégique de la Mer, Manche, XIVe-XVe siècle', *Revue du Nord*, Vol. 95 No. 402 (Oct.–Dec. 2013), pp. 947–966.

22 Francisco Garcia Fitz: '¿Hube estrategia en la edad media? A propósito de las relaciones castellano-musulmanas durante la segunda mitad del siglo XIII', *Revista da Faculdade de Lettras*, Series II Vol. 15 No. 2 (1998), pp. 837–854.

23 David Grummit & Jean-François Lassalmonie: 'Royal Public Finance, 1290–1523', in Christopher Fletcher, Jean-Philippe Genet & John Watts (eds): *Government and Political Life in England and France, c. 1300-c. 1500* (Cambridge: Cambridge University Press, 2015), pp. 116–149.

24 For example the last time the representatives of Castile, the *Cortes de Castilla*, met in Valladolid before settling permanently in Madrid was in 1604.

25 Frank Tallett & David Trim (eds): *European Warfare, 1350–1750* (Cambridge: Cambridge University Press, 2010), p. 22f.

26 David El Kenz & Claire Gantet: *Guerres et paix de religion en Europe, XVIe-XVIIe siècles* (2nd edn, Paris: Armand Colin, 2008), p. 1.

27 N.A.M. Rodger: *The Safeguard of the Sea: A Naval History of Britain, 660–1649* (London: Penguin, 2004), p. 356; id.: 'Queen Elizabeth and the Myth of Sea-Power in English History', *Transactions of the Royal Historical Society*, 6th series, Vol. 14 (2004), pp. 153–174.

28 This fear would remain alive until after the Thirty Years' War, see for example Anon.: *Dessein perpétuel des Espagnols à la monarchie universelle avec les preuves d'iceluy* (s.l.: 1624), trans. into English by Robert Gordone (?): *The Spaniards perpetvall Designes to an Vniversall Monarchie* (s.l., 1624).

29 Friedrich Edelmayer: *Philip II: Biographie eines Weltherrschers* (Stuttgart: Kohlhammer, 2009), pp. 67–73, 97–107.

30 Carlos José Hernando Sánchez: 'Non sufficit orbis? Las estrategias de la Monarquía de España', in Luis Robot (volume ed.): *Historia Militar de España* III *Edad Moderna* Part II *Escenario europeo* (Madrid: Ministerio de Defensa, 2013), p. 30.

31 Equestrian Portrait of Philip IV after Rubens (the original has been destroyed), Florence, Galleria degli Uffizi, inv. 1890 no. 792. See also Sir Anthony Sherley's MS treatise, 'Peso político de todo el mundo', which the Bibliotéca nacional de España dates to 1601, see http://bdh-rd.bne.es/viewer.vm?id=0000174347&page=1, but it should probably read 1622. The frontispiece of J. van de Solorzano: *Political Indiana* (Madrid: Diego Diaz de Carrera, 1647) shows Philip IV enthroned with the globe as his footstool. See Peer Schmidt: *Spanische Universalmonarchie oder 'teutsche Libertet'* (Stuttgart: Franz Steiner Verlag, 2001), p. 435.

32 Schmidt: *Spanische Universalmonarchie*, p. 127.

33 ©The Trustees of the British Museum. All rights reserved.

34 Geoffrey Parker: *The Grand Strategy of Philip II* (New Haven: Yale University Press, 1998); see also Hernando Sánchez: 'Non sufficit orbis?', pp. 29–77.

35 Augustín Jiménez Moreno: 'Las Órdenes Militares y la defensa de la Monarquía hispánica. Un proyecto de organización naval atlántica: el memorial de Ramón Ezquerra (1596)', in Enrique García Hernán & Davide Maffi (eds): *Guerra y Sociedad en la Monarquía Hispánica: Política, Estrategia y Cultura en la Europa Moderna (1500–1700), vol. II: Ejército, economía, sociedad y cultura* (Madrid: Laberinto, 2006), pp. 700–705.

36 © Madrid, Museo Nacional del Prado. On the interpretation of the painting, see Hernando Sánchez: 'Non sufficit orbis?', pp. 32–34.

37 Geoffrey Parker: *The Army of Flanders and the Spanish Road, 1567–1659: The Logistics of Spanish Victory and Defeat in the Low Countries' Wars* (London: Cambridge University Press, 1972).

38 N.M. Sutherland: 'The Origins of the Thirty Years' War and the Structure of European Politics', *The English Historical Review*, Vol. 107 No. 424 (July 1992), pp. 587–625.

39 *Actas de las Cortes de Castila*, Vol. 3 (Madrid: Imprenta Nacional, 1863), pp. 16–24.

40 Geoffrey Parker: *Imprudent King: A New Life of Philip II* (New Haven: Yale University Press, 2014), pp. 237–350.

41 Quoted in David Loades: *England's Maritime Empire: Seapower, Commerce and Policy, 1490–1690* (Harlow: Longman 2000), p. 86.

42 Parker: *Imprudent King*, p. 237–246.

43 Sir John Boroughs: *The Soveraignty of the British Seas, Proved by Records, History, and the Municipall Lawes of this Kingdome, Written in the Yeare 1633* (London: Humphrey Moseley, 1651), p. 80.

44 Parker: *Imprudent King*, pp. 271–273.

45 Ibid., pp. 273, 280.

46 Parker: *Grand Strategy of Philip II*, pp. 179–268.

47 In the tradition of the Roman general Fabius Maximus, nicknamed *Cunctator*.

48 Robert Lacey: *Robert Earl of Essex: An Elizabethan Icarus* (London: Weidenfeld & Nicolson, 1971), p. 148.
49 Parker: *Grand Strategy of Philip II*, pp. 86, 161, 172.
50 Parker: *Imprudent King*, p. 307.
51 *Actas de las Cortes de Castilla*, Vol. 10 (Madrid: Los Hijos de J.A. García, 1886), p. 244f.
52 Ibid., p. 253.
53 Parker: *Imprudent King*, p. 311.
54 Don Bernardino de Mendoza: *Teórica y práctica de la guerra* (Madrid: Pedro Madrigal, 1595, repr. Madrid: Ministerio de Defensa, 1998), p. 128; trans. by Sir Edwarde Hoby, *Theorique and Practise of Warre* (Middelburg: Richard Schilders, 1597), p. 148.
55 Enrique García Hernan: *Ireland and Spain in the Reign of Philip II* (Dublin: Four Courts Press, 2009). These relations did not prevent the notorious massacres by the Irish of survivors of the 1588 Armada when those were shipwrecked on Irish beaches on their way back to Spain.
56 Hernando Sánchez: 'Non sufficit orbis?', p. 64.
57 Parker: *Grand Strategy of Philip II*, pp. 111–114.
58 Ibid., pp. 281–296.
59 Davide Maffi: 'El reducto desdeñado. el ejército de Flandes y la monarquía de Carlos II (1665–1700)', in Enrique García Hernán & Davide Maffi (eds): *War and Society in the Spanish Monarchy: Politics, Strategy and Culture in Early Modern Europe, 1500–1700*, Vol. 2 (Valencia: Albaros, 2016), pp. 277–300.
60 Significantly, all three of them would be given military as well as diplomatic missions.
61 For a discussion of these war aims, albeit not of strategy, see Peter Wilson: 'Habsburg Imperial Strategy during the Thirty Years War', in García Hernán & Maffi (eds): *War and Society in the Spanish Monarchy*, Vol. 1, pp. 245–267.
62 Excerpts from his works in English translation can be found in Beatrice Heuser (trans. & ed.): *The Strategy Makers: Thoughts on War and Society from Machiavelli to Clausewitz* (Santa Monica, CA: ABC Clio for Praeger, 2010), Chapter 6.
63 Hervé Drévillon: 'Vauban stratège', in Jean Baechler & Jean-Vincent Holeindre (eds): *Penseurs de la Stratégie* (Paris: Hermann, 2014), pp. 99–110.
64 John Lynn: *The Wars of Louis XIV, 1667–1714* (Harlow: Pearson Education, 1999), p. 50. See also David Parrott: *The Business of War: Military Enterprise and Military Revolution in Early Modern Europe* (Cambridge: Cambridge University Press, 2012).
65 Lynn: *Wars of Louis XIV*, p. 19f.
66 Jean-Philippe Cénat: *Le roi stratège: Louis XIV et la direction de la guerre, 1661–1715* (Rennes: Presses Universitaires, 2010), pp. 274, 293.
67 M. Mignet (ed.): *Négociations relatives à la succession d'Espagne sous Louis XIV*, Vol. 1 (Paris: Imprimerie Royale, 1835), pp. 414–416.
68 *Mémoires de Louis XIV*, quoted in Mignet (ed.): *Négociations relatives à la succession d'Espagne*, Vol. 1, pp. 425–427.
69 Guy Rowlands: 'Louis XIV, Vittorio Amedeo II and French Military Failure in Italy, 1689–96', *The English Historical Review*, Vol. 115 No. 462 (June 2000), pp. 534–569.
70 Bertrand Fonck & George Satterfield: 'The Essence of War: French Armies and Small War in the Low Countries (1672–97)', *Small Wars and Insurgencies*, Vol. 25 No. 4 (Aug. 2014), pp. 767–783.
71 Cénat: *Le roi stratège*, pp. 285–287.
72 Ibid., pp. 287–293.
73 Rowlands: 'Louis XIV, Vittorio Amedeo II.'
74 Cénat: *Le roi stratège*, pp. 257–264, 297.
75 Lynn: *The Wars of Louis XIV*, pp. 17–46.
76 Cénat: *Le roi stratège*, pp. 299–377.
77 Hervé Drévillon: *L'impot du Sang* (Paris: Eds Tallandier, 2006).
78 "Nec pluribus impar."
79 François Bluche: *Louis XIV* (Paris: Fayard, 1986), p. 890 (my translation).
80 Lynn: *The Wars of Louis XIV*, p. 350.

2

CHRISTINE DE PIZAN, THE FIRST MODERN STRATEGIST

Good governance and conflict mediation

An Italian at the French court

The rough details of Cristine or Christine de Pizan's[1] life are sufficiently well known for a short sketch to suffice here. Christine's mother was a Venetian, and it is in Venice that her parents were living at the time of her own birth in 1364. Christine's father, T(h)omasso da Pizzano, was himself born not in the town of Pizzano, to which the family owed its name, but in Bologna, for which reason he is sometimes referred to as T(h)omasso da Bologna. He studied medicine and astrology at the university there, and to these skills he owed the invitation from the French king Charles V to become a physician at his court in Paris. So the family moved to France when Christine was four years old. Despite her manifest devotion to the French royal family, the French people, their great virtues, and the French cause, she would continue to describe herself as an Italian.[2]

When Christine was 15, an age where this was normal for girls at the time, she was married to a young Picard gentleman, Etienne de Castel, probably the son of a court employee. The young husband became one of the secretaries to the court. The young couple had three children. When Charles V died in 1380, Tomasso's family initially continued to be employed by the royal family, but a long illness led to Tomasso's death in poverty some time before 1389. Disaster struck again in 1389 when Etienne de Castel died of a contagious disease while accompanying King Charles VI on a voyage. At the age of 25, Christine was left a widow without any income but with three children, her mother and an orphaned niece to feed.

Fortunately for her, she had soaked up all the knowledge she could at the court, and was able to read French, Italian and probably also Latin. Given her father's employment in the services of King Charles V, Christine seems to have had the privilege of access to the king's library. For about ten years, she put her talents to use by writing poems and other works on the subject of love and marriage, often tinged with sadness at her own loss, and her elegant writing became known even at courts abroad. She has been hailed as an early feminist in view of her famous *Book of the City of Ladies*, which celebrated the achievement of famous women. She also gained the patronage of several key members of the royal family, most importantly the new king himself, Charles VI; his queen, Isabeau of France (known as Isabeau of Bavaria, who herself had an Italian mother), and the two brothers of Charles V, John I (the Magnificent) Duke of Berry, and Philip II (the Bold), Duke of Burgundy, and their respective families. Her patrons commissioned her to write works with more political-philosophical content, including a biography of King Charles V – who had been a model of kingship and was thus known as 'the Wise' – and, crucially for our purposes, *The Book of Deeds of Arms and of Chivalry*, which must have been completed in 1410. It was written, in the tradition of other such works, for the education of the then crown prince, Louis de Guyenne, who like his two older brothers would eventually predecease his father. The need for such an early education of the young prince (who was only 13) was acute, as King Charles VI was afflicted with the same hereditary spells of dementia that would later plague his grandson Henry VI of England – and like England later, France was during the lifetime of Christine de Pizan beset by dynastic civil war stemming from this absence of a constant and capable ruler.

An erudite builder

In her biography of Charles V, Christine spelled out the relationship between the author who builds on the works of previous writers, and the sources. She explained that she worked like a builder who has not made the stones of the 'castle or house' he constructs, but took them ready-made.[3] With this methodology she was of course entirely mainstream in the tradition of Judaeo-Christian scholarship. To turn to her building blocks, then, most of the sources used by Christine have been identi-fied. They would have been found mainly in Charles V's library, which included Latin texts and recent translations into French commissioned by this great patron of the arts of Aristotle, Seneca, Ovid, Cicero ('Tulles'), Frontinus, Valerius Maximus, Boethius and, above all, Vegetius.[4] As we shall see, she was also familiar at least with some passages from Plato's *Republic*. She gleaned central arguments from other texts – such as John of Salisbury's twelfth-century *Policraticus* or the thirteenth-century writings of Giles of Rome – indirectly, through the translation of Gilles de Gauchi's late thirteenth-century *Gouvernement des Princes* and the writings of the sages of the French court, such as Charles V's most notable political philosopher, Nicolas d'Oresme. She also drew extensively on Honoré Bouvet's or Bovet's/Bonet's *Arbre des batailles* (*Tree of Battles*, c. 1387). She was thus by any standards among the most erudite people of her generation, but did not lay it on thick: she mentioned none of these sources by name, only alluding to a 'master' who had helped her (Bouvet, even though she seems never to have met him in the flesh), and citing the goddess Minerva as her chief source of inspiration. As Françoise Le Saux has demonstrated, however, Christine showed no awareness that the classical authors she cited had written in societies and with a system of references different from that of her own times and world; she made no distinction between the *equester* or cavalry-man of the late Roman Principate and the knight of her own times.[5]

Thus building on her talents, her education, which at the time made her exceptional not only among women, and her court contacts, Christine managed to support herself and her dependents. Indeed there is evidence that at various points she was invited to come to England and to Milan to continue her work there, offers which she declined; this was probably wise, as in the long run she could not have made do with sponsorship from only one source. Despite the generosity of various members of the French royal family, she often struggled to get by, and it was a great relief to her when she managed to find secure positions for her children. She attracted patrons for her only surviving son, Jean Castel, and her only daughter's livelihood was assured when she was sent off to a nunnery as a companion to one of the daughters of Charles VI. She kept herself afloat through patronage and commissioned works until about 1429, when she would have been 65; after that, we lose track of her; she may have retired to a convent.

War, society and the deficiencies of statecraft

Christine's life spanned an important part of the Hundred Years' War but also of internecine warfare in France. Generalising broadly, there were two main causes of war in France: one was essentially strife over family succession and influence, involving the descendants of King Philip III of France on the Capetian/Plantagenet/Lancaster and Valois sides respectively. The French crown was claimed by contenders on both sides of the Channel, one of whom (Edward III and his respective successors) as Duke of Aquitaine was not only a peer of the realm of France but also the king of England. Who had influence over the demented French king Charles VI Valois was fiercely disputed among his wife, his uncles and his brother. This family quarrel over inheritance and power took the form of a civil war inflicting suffering and death on both peasants and townsfolk. The other major cause of war – again civil war – was the long-term consequence of tectonic shifts in European society due to the dramatic fall in the population figures caused by famine and pestilence (especially the Black Death of 1348), and the consequent rise of the cost of living coupled with rising salary demands by the labouring classes. Peasants and townsfolk felt unjustly and excessively taxed, and exploited and underpaid, which led to a string of uprisings in the fourteenth and early fifteenth centuries. Kate Forhan lists seven major uprisings from the Jacquerie of 1353 to the Cabocherie in 1413, the last of which affected Christine de Pizan herself and explains her fear of popular insurrections and the suffering that their repression wrought upon civilians.[6]

'The common people', wrote Jean de Bueil 30-odd years after the death of Christine de Pizan, 'are the most hurt by the adversity of war'.[7] This was clearly also the case in France during her lifetime. There was one exception to the rule that it was the people who suffered most: the battle of Agincourt, where so many members of France's highest nobility were slain by the English side. But this battle was still in the future when Christine wrote her history of Charles V (1404) and her books *The Body Politic* (1404–1407), *The Book of Deeds of Arms and of Chivalry* (1410) and

Peace (1412/13). They illustrate that she was greatly moved by the ravages of civil war which tore France apart in the lulls between the campaigns waged by the Plantagenets and Valois in their struggle for the French crown. Already in 1402 or 1403, we find her lamenting that 'All the world is encumbered by wars.'[8] Christine de Pizan's experience was thus more of the effects of war on the population in general, not merely the nobility, and of the effects of constant and repeated devastation on society as a whole. This is thus a distinctive theme we find in Christine de Pizan's writings on war and society, and her prescriptions concern not only warfare but also, more importantly, good statecraft.

Consequently, Christine saw war and peace above all as a function of statecraft – that is of poor or good governance, and the virtues and vices of princes. Moreover, she saw the enforcement or lack of military discipline as a crucial variable in war and peace. She is the first and for a long time the only author I have found who articulated the view that insurgencies stem from poor governance and excessive demands made on the populations by princes (in the form of taxation, etc.), as we shall see presently. As a last resort, in her *Book on Peace*, she even advocated tyrannicide – in the medieval sense of killing an unjust ruler – to bring down a prince or magnate who ravages a land, just as Judith had slain Holofernes.[9] (This was a subject of particular poignancy, as this had been put forward as the excuse for the assassination of Louis Duke of Orleans, King Charles VI's brother, at the behest of the younger Duke of Burgundy, John the Fearless, in 1407; both of them had at some point financed Christine's writings, but Christine seems to have sided with Burgundy.)

Beyond poor governance and excessive taxation being causes for *internal* rebellion, Christine identified five causes of *external* wars proper, of which she deemed three just, and two unjust. The just causes included first, the defence of law and justice; second, the countering of 'evildoers who befoul, injure, and oppress the land and the people', and third, the recovery of anything stolen or usurped, whether it be land, movable possessions or titles belonging to a prince, a realm or its subjects. The two unjust causes, which she recognised as existing in reality, she saw as rooted in the 'will' of a prince or nobleman, with the motive of vengeance, or the motive of conquest. These causes she described as unjust, as vengeance should be God's alone, and the conquest of foreign lands without title to them was not justified by any divine law, and indeed created a just cause for war in self-defence for the opposite side.[10] Already in the *Livre du Chemin de long Estude* of 1403, Christine lamented that 'for lust of tribute and conquest of foreign lands, men destroy each other in mortal war.'[11]

How very different Christine's take is on this to that of the author whom she herself describes as her tutor,[12] Honoré Bouvet, who asked rhetorically, 'Whether this world can by nature be without conflict, and at peace?' He replied 'that it can by no means be so'. He argued this because men are governed by the stars, which themselves are in perpetual motion, and that the world contains more fools than wise men.[13] And he continued further on:

[T]he truth is that war is not an evil thing, but is good and virtuous; for war, by its very nature, seeks nothing other than to set wrong right, and to turn dissension to peace, in accordance with Scripture. And if in war many evil things are done, they never come from the nature of war, but from false usage . . . for all good things, and all virtue, come from God. . . . [W]ar comes from God, and not merely that He permits war, but that He has ordained it.[14]

Christine, by contrast, far from seeing war as 'good and virtuous' in principle, insisted strongly that war is a burden, a result of men's many vices, causing 'great harm', and acceptable only if it fulfils very restrictive criteria, the famous just war criteria.[15] In the *L'Avision Cristine*, written by her in 1405, we find a definition of this *ius ad bellum*:

> [the] nobles following the profession of arms . . . misunderstand chivalric deeds because they do not know or want to know the proper limits which are such that it is not permissible for anyone to fight or arm himself for war except for good reason. That is, in defence of God's law against miscreants or heretics who oppose the faith; and for the defence of the Church, his prince, his country, his land, the public good, the rights of the innocent, and his own possessions. There is no other law that permits it, nor is the fight just and approved otherwise.[16]

Given the particular situation in which she found herself, Christine relaxed the second condition for the justice of a war – namely that it must be declared by a person with the God-given authority to do so. Following the argument that a war could be just only if ordered by God, or His representative on earth, theologians normally admitted only the authority of the pope, the emperor or sovereign princes.[17] Christine by contrast listed also 'dukes and other landed lords and princes', but not 'barons' and other minor nobility or dignitaries.[18] After all, her *Book of the Deeds of Arms* was commissioned and paid for by John the Fearless, Duke of Burgundy, cousin of King Charles VI, for the benefit of the young dauphin Louis, Duke of Guyenne, whose guardian he was in view of the king's dementia.[19]

Yet she could not bring herself to approve of the Armagnac-Bourguignon Civil War waged between the two cadet branches of the royal family, the House of Orleans (or Armagnacs) and the Dukes of Burgundy (which in England would be replicated a generation later in the Wars of the Roses) as just wars.[20] In several works she pleaded with the nobles to put an end to this civil war. In her *Lamentation* about the state of France of 1410, she called upon women to storm the battlefield, babes in arms, to force men to make peace.[21] Overall, she saw war as an illness of society. Inspired by the legal and theological texts with which she was familiar, she called for good governance and statecraft, respect for laws and rules (including on the part of the rulers), discipline (especially among the military) and reason; these to her were the proper means to contain wars or even avoid them.[22]

Mediation as alternative to war

It took her some time, reading and reflection to come to this attitude to war. In one of her earliest works, in a poem on chivalry, Christine had naively exhorted knights, in order to 'acquire prowess, . . . [to] fight in many lands, . . . Do not flee from battle, nor retreat.'[23] The theme is still found in her *Livre des Trois Vertus* of 1405, where she wrote, 'The knight should be greatly ashamed who leaves the battle before the victorious end.'[24] But already in 1401, when she wrote her admonition of Hector by the goddess of wisdom, Othéa, she urged him 'Do not take up arms foolishly.'[25] Clearly, as she reflected further on what constituted good kingship, in the context of her biography of Charles V (written in 1404), she recoiled from the notion that war was worth fighting simply to acquire prowess, and no longer thought that avoiding battle was dishonourable. Charles V, she argued, had been a wise king because he had made peace with the English, even though he was victorious and had a big fleet he might have sent against them. His motivation was to spare his own country further warfare. Being a generous *chevalier*, he had even allowed the English king, Edward III, to keep most of his possessions in France.[26]

From analysis she turned to prescription in her *Book of the Deeds of Arms*, where she made her greatest and most original contribution to issues of war and peace: she suggested that the prince caught in such a dispute should gather

> A great council of wise men in his parliament, or in that of his sovereign if he is a subject, and not only will he assemble those of his own realm, but in order that there be no suspicion of favour, he will also call upon some from foreign countries that are known not to take sides, elder statesmen as well as legal advisors and others; he will set out or have [somebody else] set out the whole matter in full without holding anything back, . . . In short, in this way the affair will be put in order, clearly seen and discussed, and if through such a process it appears that his cause is just, he will summon his adversary to demand of him restitution and amends for his injuries and the wrong done to him. Now if . . . the adversary in question puts up a defence and tries to contradict what has been said, let him be heard fully without special favour, but also without wilfulness or spite. If these things are duly carried out, as the law requires, then the just prince may surely undertake war, which on no account should be called vengeance but rather the complete carrying out of due justice.[27]

Christine seems to have been inspired by the precedent of a 'parliament' assembled in Paris by Charles V, including 'wise jurists from Bologna' and elsewhere, in which he put his case for war against the English to the four estates represented here, and sought their support — and presumably, tax levy — for war. The English monarch could have been summoned to this parliament in his capacity of a prince of the realm and vassal of the French king, so that the step to the internationalisation of such a procedure is contained de facto if not de jure in this event.[28] Individual princes – for example Henry II of England in 1176 with regard to the quarrels over border towns between Alfonso VIII, king of Castile, and Sancho VI, king of Navarre,[29] and on other occasions, King (Saint) Louis IX – had been brought in as mediators in past interstate quarrels. Popes had mediated between princes, and church councils were an international forum for the settlement of disputes touching on religious issues or questions of ecclesiastical vs worldly powers. But to my knowledge there was no precedent for the international council of lay experts, princes and nobles as proposed by Christine.

Scholars seem to be in agreement, therefore, that this idea of convoking a council to settle a dispute between princes is an impressive and in this configuration original contribution to thinking about war and peace, as it does not involve the pope or the Church in any other personification as arbitrator or even mediator. It is at the same time her most lasting legacy, not only one which could have applied to her own times but also one which transcended her times and circumstances, unlike many of the other things she wrote. It could be seen to presage institutions such as the League of Nations, the United Nations or the Organisation for Security and Co-operation in Europe. There is no evidence, however, that later authors specifically picked up this idea of Christine's, despite Kate Forhan's assertion that the *Livre des Fais d'Armes* was so popular in the century or so after its first publication in manuscript form because of this ingenious approach to non-violent conflict resolution.[30]

The body politic

This, then, was Christine's main proposal for the resolution of conflicts between rulers. Her fear of popular uprisings, while leading her to pronounce firmly against any democracy or rule of the entire citizenry of a polity in her *Book of the Body Politic*, did not blind her to the need to address just grievances, and indeed to avoid strife by governing fairly and justly.[31] Indeed, the interconnectedness and interdependence of all classes were stressed by her as she subscribed to a vision of society as an organic whole, metaphorically a body in which all limbs and organs depended on each other, as the title of her book implies. This metaphor, which can be traced back to a story in Livy where the telling of a related fable is attributed to the consul Menenius Agrippa in 494 BC, was made famous particularly by John of Salisbury in his *Policraticus*.[32] Here is how Christine renders it:

> Once upon a time there was great disagreement between the belly of a human body and its limbs. The belly complained loudly about the limbs and said that they thought badly of it and that they did not take care of it and feed it as well as they should. On the other hand, the limbs complained loudly about the belly and said they were all exhausted from work, and yet despite all their labour, coming and going and working, the belly wanted to have everything and was never satisfied. The limbs then decided that they would no longer suffer such pain and labour, since nothing they did satisfied the belly. So they would stop their work and let the belly get along as best it might. The limbs

stopped their work and the belly was no longer nourished. So it began to get thinner, and the limbs began to fail and weaken, and so, to spite one another, the whole body died.

Likewise, when the prince requires more than the people can bear, then the people complain against their prince and rebel by disobedience. In such discord, they all perish together. And thus I conclude that agreement preserves the whole body.[33]

Thus depicting France as a body politic and emphasising the interdependence of its limbs made it necessary to delimit it against external enemies. Christine cast the king of England in this role of the other, the enemy against which France's body politic had to stand up to defend itself. Here our Venetian-born immigrant developed a staunch French proto-nationalism that would culminate in her epic work on the life and achievement of Joan of Arc, *Le Ditié de Jehanne d'Arc*, her last work, dating from 1429.

Throughout in her works, we find a consciousness of the need for all the parts of the body to work together, reflected also in her ruminations on when it is right for a prince to raise taxes to wage war (her answer: only with a just cause), to ransom a member of the royal family (John II the Good had been taken captive at the battle of Crécy and died in London as he was never ransomed) or as dowries of the prince's daughters.[34] Christine underscored the importance of spreading taxation equitably: 'And thus the rich in these cases should support the poor, and [it should] not [be] that these rich are exempt, as is the case today, and that the poor should bear all the heavier a burden.'[35]

The problems of financing war are a recurrent theme in Christine's writings. She was right to recognise that the prince had to think 'first of all . . . how many men are available and how much money', noting that it would be 'folly to wage war' if he is not 'well supplied with both these elements'. (Admittedly, she ignored the question of what to do if an overwhelmingly important just cause – for example a foreign invasion – forced a polity into collective self-defence.) Given her background, she also showed continuing awareness of developments in Italy, where she noted that 'especially Florence and Venice' fought wars 'more with their money than with their citizens' – that is by employing mercenaries.[36]

She gave much attention to the pay of soldiers, who were a central part of her reflection on the ills and woes of society.[37] If only soldiers were well paid, and taxes levied for this purpose were justified, there would be no reason for soldiers to pillage and steal. This emphasis on regular pay for professional soldiers makes Christine the main prophet and advocate in modern times of the creation of a standing army, a (re-)invention (given that the Romans of course had it) which France would spearhead and which would set the pattern for Europe after the end of the Hundred Years' War. Arguably, this was the most direct lasting impact of Christine's work on war.

In this context, Christine invoked another metaphor – the king was likened (much like Jesus) to a good shepherd, and the soldier should be his faithful sheepdog, but a dog that must not bite the sheep or harm them.

> The soldiers ought to have yet another duty. Just as the good dog brings back the strayed sheep, so they ought to bring back the common people or others who from fear or dread or evil want to rebel and take the wrong side. They ought to bring them back to the right path either by threats or by taking good care of them.[38]

This passage is strongly suggestive of Plato's analogous simile in his *Republic*.[39] Arguably, the last few words could be given a less benign meaning – 'emprendre bien garde' could be rendered 'guarded well'. But there is reason to think Christine took a humane stance even with regard to rebels, as elsewhere in her *Book of War*, she urges the prince not to use repression and excessive cruelty in his fight against them:

> Seneca says that just as trees that are cut back will regrow again, by means of many branches and shoots dividing themselves into diverse kinds of limbs, and spring back up, so does a king's cruelty increase and multiply the number of his enemies by making many people die, for their children or kin succeed them in hate. That is to say, for one enemy [slain], several others spring up.[40]

Interestingly, we find the same idea, explained with a different metaphor – that of a fight against the Hydra if excessive repression is used – in Machiavelli.[41]

Christine's concern about society as a whole was accompanied by a noteworthy and almost Protestant underscoring of the individual's responsibility to enquire about the justice of the cause of any war. 'In this matter', she wrote,

> the warrior should be well informed before he engages in it. You should know that if the quarrel is unjust, he that exposes himself in it condemns his soul; and if he dies in such a state, he will go the way of perdition without great repentance through divine grace at the last.

All depends, of course, on whom she meant by 'warrior': the question treated in this section was whether 'all subjects are bound to go to war with their lord if they are called upon to do so,' or whether they might refuse, given the injustice of the cause. Christine – or rather Bouvet, whom she seems to quote here as authority – did not expect the individual to judge this by himself, but to find out what 'competent jurists or lawyers' thought of the matter.[42]

Prudentia vs Fortuna

We have already mentioned one commonality between Christine's writings and those of Machiavelli. Another concerns the vicissitudes of fortune and ways to hedge against them, in peace and war. The dangers posed to all and sundry – from prince to pauper – by goddess Fortuna was a widely treated theme in medieval secular literature. It is a major theme also in the writing of Christine de Pizan. For example she wrote in her *Book of the Deeds of Arms*, 'the prince must not underestimate the power of any enemy, however slight it may appear to him, for he cannot know what *fortune* [my emphasis] another will have in his favour.'[43] And in the *Book of Peace* we read,

> [T]he wise counsellor advises the prince that he should not trust too much in his own power and strength; given that the strength of Fortune is so much greater, one must look with disfavour on all such approaches, as violence cannot continue for long, if evil is not to come of it. For as Tully [=Cicero] says: "The wise man watches out for good and evil before it happen, and so he does not find himself taken by surprise."[44]

For Christine, Providence and Prudence, very much seen by her as female figures, were crucial protectors against unforeseeable misfortune. Moreover, in her *Book on the Three Virtues* of 1405, the main virtues are Reason, Justice and Rectitude. Christine thus musters a whole team of virtues to support her against adversaries. She inscribed the second chapter of the first part of the *Book of Peace* with the motto 'fiat pax in virtute tua,' let there be peace in your virtue.[45]

This theme would be found again, a century later, in the work of Niccolò Machiavelli. Both saw the need to counsel their respective princes to field a major ally against the fickle goddess and 'the divers and wondrous cycles and stumbling of Fortune', as Christine put it.[46] In the case of Machiavelli, it is, famously, *virtù*, but also *prudentia*; in the case of Christine writing about war, it is mainly the feminine figure of *prudentia*, or in the vernacular, la *prud'homie d'homme*, governed by *justitia*. Justice in government and in dealings with friend and foe alike would deprive even adversaries of reasons for excessive harshness in their dealings with the prince, should the wheel of fortune turn against him.[47] For Christine, the imperative of dealing fairly even with an enemy ruled out outright deception – for example the seizing of an emissary who had come for a parley, or wiles and tricks that broke sacred rules (e.g. she disapproved of a feigned truce). Such emphasis on playing by the rules is explained by her view that conflicts unresolvable by human mediation could be settled only by divine ordeal, 'according to God and Holy Scripture'. (By contrast, ambushes and similar stratagems she thought entirely acceptable.)[48]

A considerable part of her *Book on Peace* thus discusses the immunity of emissaries, neutral travellers, students of the Sorbonne University, but also the immunity of the life of captured enemy commanders, unless they – as prisoners – conspired to harm their captors.[49] The recurrent theme running through this is the need for both sides to uphold conventions and to respect restraints on war. 'For this reason I say to you that the one who first breaks and oversteps the custom deserves to be treated likewise.' Thus she would argue about the need for the knight who was a prisoner of war to keep his word not to run away, but the tenor of this argument reflects her thinking more generally.[50] (Her general approach is much akin to the reasoning of what in the twentieth century would be called the 'English School' of international relations, which stressed the mutual interest of warring parties in establishing restraints in the conduct of war.)

A further parallel between the Venetian Christine at the French court and the Florentine Machiavelli is the genres into which they divided their writings. Both produced histories which gave them occasion to reflect on links between good statecraft and the mastery of fortune and fate: in the case of Christine, her biography – or should one say, secular hagiography – of Charles V; in the case of Machiavelli, the *History of Florence*. Both produced works of the genre of the 'mirror of princes', Christine most notably in the form of her *Book of the Body Politic* and her *Book of Peace*, Machiavelli in his *Prince*. Both produced manuals on the art of war, drawing heavily on Vegetius (of which Machiavelli's is the one lacking almost entirely in any political-strategic dimension, as he no longer thought it necessary to discuss the need for a just cause or reflect on the disadvantages of lacking one). Both used classical sources in similar ways, even Christine preferring secular sources over any biblical quotations. As Kate Forhan notes, while there is no hard evidence that Machiavelli read any of Christine's works, let alone these in particular, in the light of these parallels, her authorship over a century earlier makes Machiavelli's look less original, less of a departure.[51] If Machiavelli was truly not acquainted with Christine's political works, then one comes away with the impression that we are dealing with two students sitting down to similar essay-writing tasks – a mirror of princes, a book on the art of war – on the basis of much the same reading list, writing in what was, still, roughly the same political context of their own times.

Omissions

To turn back to Christine's work, the rest of the *Book of the Deeds of Arms* concerns what today we would call tactics, and technical preparations for war, from 'the manner in which a commander is expected to lodge his army' to the construction of castles and siege warfare or contemporary 'equipment for firing'.

There are notable omissions in Christine's ruminations on war, some of them clearly due to the circumstances of her writing, to which she was content to restrict herself (except with her brilliant vision of the mediating council). Most disappointingly, perhaps, from the point of view of a scholar of international relations, Christine did not dwell on the relationships between sovereign princes. Her comments on interstate relations were confined to casting England as the enemy which it behoved the body politic France to oppose. She did not explore or explain relations between France and the empire. She noted that Charles V had done well to receive 'Saracen' emissaries with courtesy and to reciprocate in the exchange of valuable gifts, but she did not expressly condemn or praise crusades.

Her scant mentioning of the pope – largely confined to decreeing that emperor and pope do not have the right to wage war against each other[52] – and her omission of any mention of the pope as potential source of arbitration in disputes must be connected with the decreased status of the papacy in view of the schism of 1378–1417. It does, however, coincide with an overall tendency in her writing to deny the clergy any particularly prominent part. Her *Book of the Body Politic* casts the clergy as a respected part of the third estate, not as the soul of the body politic, as the cleric John of Salisbury had done 250 years earlier.

Author of the first official war manual

Where should one locate Christine de Pizan as writer on war and peace? Her writings on this subject fall into conventional genres – mirrors of princes, a handbook on the art of war in the style of Vegetius's famous manuscript, and historiography. But all this she wrote a good century earlier than the great wave of such works that began to lap across Europe in the sixteenth century. Also, no author before Christine or between Christine and Machiavelli wrote works in *all* these genres. Moreover, her work is a world away from Honoré Bouvet's eulogy on war and its great virtues, and his *Tree of Battles* is the only original medieval work I know of which is entirely dedicated to the subject (the others were copies of Vegetius). As Françoise Le Saux has rightly noted, one suspects that authors glorifying war and turning a blind eye to the suffering of all classes below those of the knights would not have approved of Christine's concern for the people.[53]

Christine was firmly rooted in the pre-Christian Roman and subsequent Catholic traditions of the just war; she was conventional in defining war as the last resort where peaceful settlements would be preferable, calling for a just cause, legitimate authority and right intention as hard and fast preconditions. Without perhaps fully realising what she was doing or even putting the two side by side, she came shockingly close to making the case that there is a set of conditions not just for just war but also for just insurgency. At any rate she recognised poor governance and legitimate grievances as the roots of insurgencies, a view of causes of such insurgencies that would be found again fully articulated only in the eighteenth century (with a few early heralds in the sixteenth century). It would then be largely absent in the nineteenth century and would painstakingly be rediscovered only after the Second World War.

She was revolutionary and indeed visionary in proposing a mediatory council as an alternative to war (which she still accepted as the very last resort). She was probably the first writer in modern times to propose the creation of a standing, permanently paid army. She was precociously modern in emphasising the responsibility of the individual officer (and even soldier) in judging the rightfulness of the cause for he was fighting, and engaging his conscience in the matter. Admittedly, she was less original overall than Guibert or Clausewitz, but she was more scholarly, and curiously in some of her fundamental views – including her faith in mediation – closer to the views of our own time than they. She could have had interesting discussions with Machiavelli, and in disagreeing on some basic approaches, would also have found that they had much in common. She shared fundamental approaches and concerns with thinkers like Bernard Brodie or Michael Howard in the twentieth century, above all their concerns with the fate of civilians in wars. In short, she should be seen as the first Western, modern *stratégiste*, a thinker on strategy as a translation of political aims in conflicts – peace, justice, good governance and good statecraft – into the use of force, if mediation of disputes had failed.

Christine's work, like Clausewitz's, would gain fame particularly posthumously, and it is difficult to overstate her impact there. Not only has the influence of her *Book of the Deeds of Arms* been seen in the military reforms begun in the French armed forces in 1445, which would lead to the creation of the first modern stand-ing army.[54] Jean de Bueil, author of the *Jouvencel*, clearly built his instruction of the young knight on the material contained in her work.[55]

But also the book enjoyed international popularity. Two decades after her death, the *Book of the Deeds of Arms* was translated into German, probably in Berne.[56] On the other side of the Channel, John Talbot presented a copy of the *Book of the Deeds of Arms* to Margaret of Anjou, later one of the main protagonists in the Wars of the Roses, at her wedding to King Henry VI.[57] Translations into English soon circulated, one by Stephen Scrope, one by William Worcester and one by William Caxton.[58] And this last one is another impressive case of impact: King Henry VII Tudor himself commissioned the translation, and asked Caxton to print multiple copies for the education of his barons whom he thought to be in need of a better education in matters relating to warfare.[59] Christine's *Book of the Deeds of Arms* is thus the Western world's first officially commis-sioned, printed and distributed field manual on the art of war. Not bad for that 'simple little woman' (*simple femmelette*), as which she modestly described herself.[60]

Notes

1 She spelled her name Cristine in French, but presumably she would have been christened Cristina back in Venice. She is often referred to as Christine de Pizan, which leads to the confusion of the father's place of origin – Pizzano – with Pisa.
2 Thus in the preface to her *Le Livre de Fais d'Armes et Chevalerie*, I.iv, trans. by Sumner Wil-lard, ed. by Charity Cannon Willard: *The Book of Deeds of Arms and of Chivalry* (University Park, PA: Pennsylvania State University Press, 1999), p. 13.
3 Christine de Pizan: *Le Livre des Fais et Bonnes Mœurs du Sage Roi Charles V* (1404), ed. by S. Solente (Paris: Librairie ancienne Honoré Champion, 1936), II.xxi, p. 190.
4 Berenice A. Carroll: 'On the Causes of War and the Quest for Peace: Christine de Pizan and Early Peace Theory', in Eric Hicks (ed.): *Au Champs des Escritures: IIIe Colloque international sur Christine de Pizan* (Paris: Honoré Champion, 2000), pp. 337–348; Kate Langdon Forhan: *The Political Theory of Christine de Pizan* (Aldershot: Ashgate, 2002); Constant J. Mews: 'The Literary Sources of *Le Livre de la Paix*', in Karen Green, Constant J. Mews, Janice Pinder & Tania van Hemelryck (trans. & eds): *The Book of Peace by Chris-tine de Pizan* (University Park, PA: Pennsylvania University Press, 2008), pp. 33–40.
5 Françoise Le Saux: 'War and Knighthood in Christine de Pizan's *Livre des faits d'armes et de chevallerie*', in Corrine Saunders, Françoise Le Saux & Neil Thomas (eds): *Writing War: Medieval Literary Responses to Warfare* (Woodbridge: D.S. Brewer, 2004), pp. 93–105.
6 Forhan: *The Political Theory*, p. 6.
7 'Le peuple communiment est le plus grevé par les adversitez de la guerre.' Jean de Bueil: *Le Jouvencel* (1466, first printed Paris: Antoine Verard, 1493), Léon Lecestre (ed.): *Le Jouvencel par Jean de Bueil* (Paris: Renouard, 1887), p. 13f.
8 Christine de Pizan: *Le chemin de longue étude* (1403/1404), ed. by Andrea Tarnowski (Paris: Le Livre de Poche, 2000), ll. pp. 340–345.
9 Christine de Pizan: *Livre de la Paix* (1413), trans. by Karen Green, Constant J. Mews, Janice Pinder & Tania Van Hemelryck: *The Book of Peace by Christine de Pizan* (University Park, PA: Pennsylvania State University Press, c2008), III.4–5.
10 Christine de Pizan: *Le Livre de Fais d'Armes et Chevalerie*, I.iv, Sumner Willard (trans.), Charity Cannon Willard (ed.): *The Book of Deeds of Arms and of Chivalry* (University Park, PA: Pennsylvania State University Press, 1999), p. 16f.
11 Quoted in Carroll: 'On the Causes of War', p. 342.
12 In the Pizan: *Livre de Fais d'Armes*.

13 Honoré Bonet: *The Tree of Battles*, trans. & ed. by G.W. Coopland (Liverpool: Liverpool University Press, 1949), p. 118f.
14 Ibid., p. 125.
15 Quoted in Carroll: 'On the Causes of War', p. 342.
16 Trans. McLeod, p. 84, quoted in Forhan: *The Political Theory*, p. 147f.
17 Jonathan Barnes: 'The Just War', in Norman Kretzmann, Anthony Kenny & Jan Pinborg (eds): *The Cambridge History of Later Medieval Philosophy* (Cambridge: Cambridge University Press, 1982), pp. 775–777.
18 Pizan: *Le Livre de Fais d'Armes*, I.iii, Willard trans. p. 15.
19 Forhan: *The Political Theory*, p. 15.
20 Bertrand Schnerb: *Armagnacs et Bourguignons: la maudite guerre, 1407–1435* (Paris: Perrin, 2009).
21 Quoted in Carroll: 'On the Causes of War', p. 356.
22 Loïc Cazaux: 'Pour un droit de la guerre? La discipline militaire et les rapports entre combattants et non-combattants dans le *Livre des Faits d'Armes et de Chevalerie* de Christine de Pizan', in Dominique Demartini, Claire Le Ninan, Anne Paupert & Michelle Szkilnik (eds): *Une femme et la guerre à la fin du Moyen Âge: Le livre des faits d'armes et de chevalerie de Christine de Pizan* (Paris: Honoré Champion, 2016), pp. 89–102.
23 Gentil homme, qui veulx proesce aquerre,
    Ecoutes ci, entens qu'il te faut faire:
    Armes suivir t'estuet en maintes terres
    Estre loyal contre ton adversaire.
    De bataille ne fuir, n'en sus traire,
    Et doubter Dieu . . .
    From Balad No. L, in Forhan: *The Political Theory*, p. 69.
24 'Male honte ait le chevalier qui se depart de la bataille ains la fin de victoire', quoted in Christine Moneera Laennec: 'Unladylike Polemics: Christine de Pizan's Strategic Attack and Defense', *Tulsa Studies in Women's Literature*, Vol. 12 No. 1 (Spring 1993), pp. 47–59, here p. 50.
25 'Ne entreprens mie folles armes . . .', quoted by Forhan: *The Political Theory*, p. 142.
26 Pizan: *Le Livre des Fais et Bonnes Meurs*, II.xxix, p. 214.
27 Pizan: *Le Livre de Fais d'Armes*, I.iv, Willard trans. p. 17f.
28 Pizan: *Le Livre de Fais d'Armes*, I.v.
29 Fernando Luis Corral: 'Alfonso VIII of Castile's Judicial Process at the Court of Henry II of England: An Effective and Valid Arbitration?', *Nottingham Medieval Studies*, Vol. 50 (2006), pp. 22–42.
30 Forhan: *The Political Theory*, p. 159.
31 *Livre du Corps de Policie*, III.2; Pizan: *Livre de la Paix*, II.5.
32 Livy: *ab urbe condita*, II.32.
33 *Livre du Corps de Policie*, III.1, Forham trans. p. 91.
    The original in Kennedy (ed.), p. 92:

> Une fois sourdit moult grant murmuracion entre le ventre de corps humain et les membres. Le ventre se plaignoit fort des membres et disoit que ilz pensoient mal de lui, et que ilz ne le tenoient mie assez aise ne si bien nourri comme ilz deussent. Les membres d'autre part se plaignoient fort du ventre et disoient que ilz estoient tous lassez d'ouvrer, et que tout quanque il povoient lanbourer, aller et venir et traveillier, le ventre vouloit tout avoir, et encore ne le povoient asouvir, pour laquelle cause plus ne vouloient souffrir tel paine ne tel labour, lequel ne souffisoit encore au ventre rassadier, si cesseroient tous de œuvre, set se gouvernast le ventre si qu'il vouldroit. Si cesserent les membres de œuvre, et le ventre plus ne fu nourri, si commença a amagrir et les membres a deffaillir et affoiblier. Et ainsi en despit l'un de l'autre tout peri ensemble. Semblablement avient quant prince demande plus a peuple qu'il ne peut fournir, et que peuple murmure contre prince et se rebelle par desobeissance: tel descort perist tout ensemble. Et pour ce conclus que union d'accord est la conservacion de tout le dit corps de la policie.

34 Christine de Pizan: *Le Livre du Corps de Police*, ed. by Angus J. Kennedy (Paris: Honoré Champion, 1998), I.11.

35 "Et doivent les riches en tel cas supporter les povres, et non mie que yceulx riches en soient excens, si comme on le fait aujourd'hui, et que les povres en soient de tant plus chargiez." Pizan, *Livre du Corps de Police*, p. 17.

36 *Livre des Fais d'Armes*, I.v., Willard trans., p. 19.

37 *Livre des Fais d'Armes*, III.viii.

38 Pizan, *Livre du Corps de Police*, I.9, Forhan trans., p. 17. In Kennedy (ed.) p. 15:

> Ancore autre office doivent avoir les gens d'armes, c'est que ainsi que le bon chien ramaie la brebis que se forvoye, douivent-ilz, s'ilz voient gent de commune qui par crainte ou paour ou par aucune mauvaise voulenté se veulent rebeller t rendre a l'averse partie ou eulx y donner, les ramener a droit chemin, soit par menaces ou par eulx emprendre bien garde.

39 Plato: *The Republic:* in Book I he likens rulers to good shepherds, and in Book III he dwells on the danger of sheepdogs turning on their sheep, and soldiers are likened to watchdogs and guardians of the sheep.

40 In Karen Green, Constant J. Mews, Janice Pinder & Tania van Hemelryck (trans. & eds): *The Book of Peace by Christine de Pizan* (University Park, PA: Pennsylvania University Press, 2008), II.4, p. 235 (translation p. 99f.):

> Dit Senecque que tout ainsi et en la maniere que les arbres qui sont trenchiéz recroissent de rechief, par plusieurs branches et gictons en moult de diverses manieres de souches se fourchent et ressourdent, ainsi et par tel manière la cruaulté royalle acroist et multiplie nombre d'ennemis en faisant plusieurs gens mourir, car les enfans ou prochains d'iceulx succedent en hayne du singulier, c'est a entendre pour un ennemy sont ressours plusiers.

41 Niccolò Machivelli: *Discorsi* (1531), II.24.

42 Pizan: *Livre de Fais d'Armes*, III.vii, Willard trans., p. 152f.

43 Pizan: *Livre de Fais d'Armes*, Willard trans., p. 19.

44 In Green, Mews, Pinder & Hemelryck (trans. & eds): *The Book of Peace by Christine de Pizan*, II.5., p. 235 (translation p. 99f.):

> Le sage conseiller ammonest le prince qu'il ne se fie trop en sa puissance et force: veu que trop plus est grande celle de Fortune, pour rant doit ester deslouee toute tel voye comme chose violente ne puist avoir duree, afin que mal n'en conviengne. Car si que dist Tulles: "Le sage est pourveu du bien et du mal ains qu'il lui aviengne", et pour ce ne se treuve il deceu.

45 Psalm of David, Pizan: *Livre de la Paix*, I.ii.

46 'les tours et tresbuchemens de Fortune divers et tres merveilleux', in Green, Mews, Pinder & Hemelryck (trans. & eds): *The Book of Peace by Christine de Pizan*, II.5, p. 237f (translation p. 101f).

47 Pizan: *Livre de la Paix*, II.5. Christine had already admonished knights in her early poem to be 'loyal to your adversary'; see Balad No. L, in Forhan: *The Political Theory*, p. 69.

48 Pizan: *Livre de la Paix*, III.xiii, trans. Willard, p. 163.

49 Pizan: *Livre de la Paix*, III.xvii, see also III.xxiii.

50 Pizan: *Livre de la Paix*, III.xxiii, trans. Willard, p. 181.

51 Forhan: *The Political Thought*, p. 166.

52 *Livre des Fais d'Armes*, III.ii, iii.

53 Le Saux: 'War and Knighthood in Christine de Pizan', p. 104.

54 Charity Cannon Willard: 'Christine de Pizan on the Art of Warfare', in M. Desmond (ed.): *Christine de Pizan and the Categories of Difference* (Minneapolis: University of Minnesota Press, 1998), pp. 3–15; Demartini, Le Ninan, Paupert & Szkilnik (eds): *Une femme et la guerre*, p. 22.

55 Jean de Bueil: *Le Jouvencel*. MS 1466; first printed as *Le Jouvencel* (1466, Paris: Antoine Verard, 1493), Léon Lecestre (ed.): *Le Jouvencel par Jean de Bueil* (Paris: Renouard, 1887), and see Michelle Szkilnik: 'Le Jouvencel oule Roman des Faits d'Armes et de la Chevalerie', in Dominique Demartini, Claire Le Le Ninan, Anne Paupert & Michelle Szkilnik (eds): *Une femme et la guerre à la fin du Moyen Âge: Le livre des faits d'armes et de chevalerie de Christine de Pizan* (Paris: Honoré Champion, 2016), pp. 165–178.

56 Demartini, Le Ninan, Paupert & Szkilnik: *Une femme et la guerre*, p. 26.

57 Frances Teague: 'Christine de Pizan's *Book of War*', in Glenda McLeod (ed.): *The Reception of Christine de Pizan from the Fifteenth through the Nineteenth Centuries* (Lewiston: Edwin Mellen Press, 1991), p. 25f.

58 Andrew Taylor: '"Dame Christine" et la Chevalerie savante en Angleterre', in Dominique Demartini, Claire Le Le Ninan, Anne Paupert & Michelle Szkilnik (eds): *Une femme et la guerre à la fin du Moyen Âge: Le livre des faits d'armes et de chevalerie de Christine de Pizan* (Paris: Honoré Champion, 2016), pp. 179–190.

59 William Caxton (trans.): *Boke of the fayt of armes and of chyualrye* (Westminster: William Caxton, 1489). Christine's name, but not gender, was omitted from this translation, even if her authorship was acknowledged by name in the other English translations. The first French impression was published a year earlier, suppressing her authorship: *L'art de cheualerie selon Vegece* (Paris: Antoine Verard, 1488); Berenice A. Carroll: 'Christine de Pizan and the Origins of Peace Theory', in Hilda L. Smith (ed.): *Women Writers and the Early British Political Tradition* (Cambridge: Cambridge University Press, 1998), p. 27.

60 Preface to her *Livre de Fais d'Armes*.

3

DENIAL OF CHANGE

The military revolution as seen by contemporaries

Technological innovations in late medieval warfare

Medievalists have noted that from the late thirteenth century onwards, a whole series of critical technological inventions were made in or introduced to Europe, including the compass, the clockwork mechanism, spectacles (*ocularia*), gunpowder and printing.

Indeed, the Late Middle Ages are categorised as a distinctive period not least because of this steady increase in technological innovations, which of course would continue into modern times. Prior to this time, medieval men did not take a great interest in innovations, it seems. The terms *novitas* (invention) and *inventor* usually had negative connotations, linked to heresy, magic and new deviant doctrines. If *novus,-a,-um* was used with a positive connotation it was mostly linked with the restoration of a better world – the 'nova militia' (new soldiery) of the crusades replaced the Israelite hosts of God, and the underlying theme was that of *renovatio*, renewal of something that had existed before, in a better form. It was only from the mid-thirteenth century that there was a growing interest in '*novitates*', now with a positive connotation. The concept of the inventor and the invention was an innovation itself.[1] And yet the perception of innovation often lagged behind the impact of the inventions themselves, or the inventions were long regarded as curiosities, not necessarily as triggers of important changes. Even early Renaissance men were still convinced that their own times were inferior to those of classical antiquity, that they themselves were dwarves standing on the shoulders of giants (as Bernard of Chartres had put it); innovations were thus often seen not as big steps forward (in German *Fortschritt*) but as steps back towards a better albeit distant past.[2]

When speaking about the most crucial technological innovations in warfare, the introduction of gunpowder and its consequences usually come to mind. Other such innovations include the industrialisation of the production of military equipment and the transport and telecommunications revolutions which in the second nineteenth century allowed the creation of mass armies, quickly moved from theatre to theatre. The twentieth century saw the nuclear revolution, and then that involving precision-guided munitions and the space intelligence revolution, which merged into the much-celebrated revolution in military affairs of the tail end of that century.[3]

The introduction of gunpowder is commonly hailed as the first and most important of these. And yet it represented only one of a number of changes in warfare which began during the High Middle Ages. Europeans learned from other cultures in clashes with them, especially during the crusades.[4] Other changes were introduced by the rediscovery or reinvention of older technologies or the appropriation of simple technologies from other cultures. Thus the crossbow, which had been used in Ancient China and Greece, was reinvented in the eleventh century. The longbow was a Welsh invention of uncertain date, also in use in the twelfth century. Both caused great ravages on the battlefields of the Late Middle Ages. The Plantagenet kings appropriated the Welsh longbow and put it to decisive use against the French cavalry and infantry at Crécy (1346) and Agincourt (1415). They forced armourers to make their coats of arms ever thicker, more heavily padded under their metal coating, thus making the knight ever more unwieldy (to this day, body armour makes the fighter less mobile, and there is a trade-off between security and mobility).

The alternative (and complement) to body armour was the construction of fortifications. Settlements fortified by stone walls or at least by mud walls, wooden fences and/or ditches had of course existed since the Neolithic. It seems that Western Europeans for centuries forgot how to build stone castles and other stone fortifications, notwithstanding the fact that most of them must have lived within a few day's marches at most from surviving examples of Roman fortifications or at least stone walls.[5] Roman fortifications still remained standing more or less intact throughout those centuries in all parts of the Roman Empire, from Britain to Judaea, from the Danube to the North African littoral of the Mediterranean. The stone castle made its comeback in the late tenth century, after which it held up remarkably well even against cannon fire until early modern times. The relatively fast spread of castles around Europe, starting particularly in the West around 1000, is thus perhaps less a technological innovation than a return to older customs, a rediscovery or early renaissance of Roman castle architecture (as the name *castellum* itself suggests), after a decline in technology in the interval of AD 400–1000.

In the wars against the nomadic peoples of the great migrations, well-organised and co-ordinated infantry receded in importance and the fighter on horseback dominated the battlefield, seeing his cultural apogee in the medieval knight; Donald Neill has called this the 'cavalry interregnum'.[6] Yet from 1300 the writing was on the wall for medieval chivalric warfare, with its enormous focus on knights and its disdain for his retainers who fought on foot. Around 1300, the Scots, and the peoples of the Rhine, from Flanders to Switzerland, rediscovered what one could do with a tightly grouped infantry formation armed with shields and weapons that kept the attacking knights' weapons out of reach: pikes. These tightly packed formations of pikemen (the Swiss and German *Haufen*, the Scottish *schiltron*) can be considered as a rediscovery and further development of the Greek *phalanx*. At Courtrai in 1302 Flemish peasants, using such clusters of foot soldiers with pikes, won a victory over French knights, the famous battle of the Golden Spurs; in 1314 Scots led by Robert the Bruce prevailed over the mounted English forces at Bannockburn; in 1315 Swiss pikemen won a victory over Habsburg cavalry (and preserved the independence of the old Swiss Confederacy) at Morgarten. The Swiss perfected the technique of forming such gigantic porcupines, and further victories corroborated their independence from all expansionist surrounding powers: Sempach (1386) once again fended off the Habsburgs, and the battles of Grandson and Murten (1476) and Nancy (1477) not only thwarted Burgundian attempts to appropriate the Swiss states but also led to the death of Charles the Bold in battle.

Neither the pikemen nor the crossbow nor the longbow constituted a technological quantum leap in the way gunpowder did *in the long run* − spears, bows and arrows had all been among the oldest weapons known to man. Yet all of these came together to transform medieval warfare very profoundly, making lowly infantrists more important because more dangerous even to a well-protected knight, amounting to what has been called an infantry revolution in the fourteenth century. Infantrists were much cheaper to equip than the mounted 'man-at-arms'.

Battles probably also became more deadly in general, as historian Clifford Rogers has argued. From the eleventh century until the Hundred Years' War, European armies had been dominated by knights ('feudal warrior-aristocrats') on horseback, fighting to capture and exchange other knights for ransom rather than to kill. By contrast the armies after the Hundred Years' War

> differed from this description on every single count. They were drawn from the common population (albeit often led by aristocrats); they served for pay; they fought primarily on foot, in close-order linear formations which relied more on missile fire than shock action; and they fought to kill.[7]

Even after the piketeers or pikemen decreased in number, the infantry provided the large bulk of all armies, larger than the cavalry. In 1683, the Briton Sir James Turner wrote in *Pallas Armata*,

> the ancient distinction between the Cavalry and Infantry, as to their birth and breeding, is wholly taken away, men's qualities and extractions being little or rather just nothing either regarded or enquired after; the most of the Horsemen, as well as of the Foot, being composed of the Scum of the Commons.[8]

Siege engines also underwent great changes in the Late Middle Ages, even though some of them were rediscoveries or reinventions of classical models. The medieval trebuchet, despite its similarity to Roman siege engines, may have reached Europe from China through the Arabs. Its performance was improved at the hands of specialised European craftsmen, and in its most developed forms in the fourteenth and fifteenth centuries competed with cannon for popularity for use in sieges.[9] Rainer Leng draws attention to the multitude of manuscripts produced from about 1400 and, from the late fifteenth century, printed works devoted to the description of scorpions, catapults and other siege engines (most not using gunpowder in any form), but also on fortifications, which well into the seventeenth century constituted the main contribution Germanophone writers made to the literature on warfare.[10] This shows that the quest for innovation was widespread, and preceded or coincided with the introduction of gunpowder and cannon. It was not *caused* by the discovery of the effects of gunpowder when put to military use.

Gunpowder and guns

The first painting of a gun in the Chinese world is thought to be one dating from 1128, while probably the earliest cannon to be depicted and mentioned dates from 1326.[11] Only with the technique of 'corning' gunpowder from 1420, heavy gunpowder ordnance on land began to spread from France, Flanders and England to the rest of Europe. By this sort of siege warfare involving cannon England was driven out of most of its French possessions by the mid-fifteenth century; the Ottoman Turks captured Constantinople in 1453 by finally breaching the walls with cannon that exceeded anything seen earlier in size. The French used cannon against old-style castles in Normandy, thereby hastening the English withdrawal from its royal family's homeland. Thus for example Château Gaillard, the 'bold castle' of Richard I, was finally lost to the English, after many changes of hands, in 1449. The Catholic kings, Isabella and Ferdinand, turned the tables on Islam in their conquest of Granada, 1482–1492, in which they battered down the walls of fortresses that had previously withstood sieges of months. Then in 1494/95, King Charles VIII of France achieved rapid victories in his Italian campaign by using siege trains with more but lighter guns. The otherwise so advanced Arabs in Spain initially did not adopt gunpowder, the use of which they were shown only later by the Ottoman Turks; nor did the North African Muslims.[12] In 1486, one Muslim witness of the advance towards Granada of the Christian kings wrote that 'the Christian disposed of cannon with which he launched fire-bombs . . . These projectiles were one of the causes of the abandonment of the places on which they fell.'[13] By contrast, the Ottoman Turks in the fourteenth and fifteenth centuries rode on the crest of the gunpowder revolution. It was only in the seventeenth century that they were overtaken in this skill by the European powers. For several centuries, cannon were laboriously cast in small numbers by a specialist master and his assistants; industrial-scale production of big and small guns got under way only towards the end of the sixteenth century.

As cannon were used against castle walls from the fourteenth century, this led to changes in the construction of walled defences from the early sixteenth century. This was urged already by Leon Battista Alberti (1404–1472) in his *De Re Aedificatoria*, written before 1450, and printed in 1485;[14] the new architecture of fortifications that historians have called the *trace italienne* but which, as Geoffrey Parker now thinks, might better be called star-shaped or fortifications 'alla moderna' spread across Europe and to European colonies from Canada to India. The ramparts of defences of these new fortifications differed from previous ones in trading height for depth, with slowly rising sides, protected and backed by ditches. These early modern fortifications needed vast amounts of space, and were used to protect fortresses as well as towns and cities. John Hale dated this development of the early modern fortifications to 1450–1520; Geoffrey Parker saw the full development of the artillery-proof fortress only by 1530.[15] The first bastion design came into being in 1470, and by the seventeenth century most fortifications worth defending had taken this form.[16] They were particularly concentrated in northern and northeastern France, the Netherlands and western Germany. While entire cities had been protected by walls even in prehistoric times (Jericho) and in antiquity, the complex and deep fortifications that were developed from the sixteenth century knew no parallel in earlier times. From the later Middle Ages the pre-eminent form of warfare for some time became siege warfare. For this, horsemen are barely necessary; by contrast, the larger the area to be besieged, the larger the number of infantrymen needed, again increasing the overall emphasis on infantry, as Parker argued.

While the Romans had used artillery in battle, gunpowder-fired field artillery was used in battle for the first time in 1421, during a battle of the Hussites under Jan Zizka against King Sigismund of Bohemia's forces at Kutná Hora.[17] The spread and improved products of saltpetre factories in the fifteenth century were essential prerequisites for making the use of gunpowder (a compound of saltpetre, sulphur and carbon) more effective and therefore more frequent and widespread, and eventually truly useful also for small firearms.[18] Handheld guns spread only long after the longbow and the crossbow. Gunpowder used in muskets came to rival bow and arrow as portable arms only in the early sixteenth century. Gunpowder also revolutionised sea power. By the mid-fifteenth century, Mediterranean galleys had been developed with centre-line guns that could do serious damage to other ships. The first ship which could fire a 'broadside' with its cannon situated along the sides of its deck was the Scottish *Great Michael* in 1511.

The period of 1300–1600, as far as weapons technology and tactics in warfare are concerned, thus may well be said to have brought major technological changes in warfare. And yet it is not for this period but for the subsequent centuries that Michael Roberts and Geoffrey Parker have claimed to see a military revolution.

Historians' arguments about Roberts's 'military revolution'

The role of technology in warfare is at the centre of the debate about the dates of the military revolution, the great transformation of European and Ottoman warfare under the influence of the gunpowder revolution. The first historian to write about a 'military revolution' was Michael Roberts in 1955, who defined the period of 1560 to 1660, from the reforms of Maurice of Nassau, Prince of Orange, to those of Gustavus Adolphus of Sweden and innovations introduced just after the end of the Thirty Years' War, as revolutionary with regard to the conduct of war. At the centre of their reforms was the adaptation of infantry to the possibilities offered by artillery, and the synchronised use of cavalry for well-coordinated charges. Thus infantry came to be as important as or at times more important than cavalry. Drill and training were crucial to these reforms, which necessitated standing armies trained outside periods of campaigning. At the same time, the overall size of their forces increased. While none of these changes drew on technological innovations, they were expensive, and particularly standing armies required the support of a centralised state that raised taxes to pay for them. They had to be widely recruited, supplied, clothed, armed, housed and administered in every way.[19] The military revolution is characterised by the application of the new technologies surrounding the introduction of gunpowder: more intensive training of soldiers to give them the discipline needed for shooting in volleys, the move from militias of peasants with little training towards increasing proportions of professional soldiers, larger armies, the rise of military enterprisers and the rise of the modern state. This gave rise to the dialectic development of ever greater numbers of soldiers on the one hand and ever increasing firepower on the other, leading to a steady extension of the battle in space and time.[20] At the same time, in keeping with the development of ever greater firepower derived from stationary cannon, military architecture became significantly more expensive. Only the modern state with its bureaucracy, comprehensive administration and systematic taxation could afford all this; historians of early modern Europe have thus seen a mutually driving force in warfare and state building.[21]

John Hale, writing in 1961, accepted Roberts's dating for this revolution (late sixteenth to mid-seventeenth centuries), even though, contradictorily, he went on to say,

> Infantry became the chief arm, and the heavy armed horsemen who had dominated the battlefields of the Middle Ages virtually disappeared, their efficiency challenged first by the longbows of the English, then by the dense pike squares of the Swiss, and finally by cannon and handgun.[22]

All these developments, however, with the exception of that of the handheld gun, had taken place from the twelfth to the fifteenth centuries, not in the time of the 'military revolution'.

About two decades after Michael Roberts, his disciple Geoffrey Parker suggested a different time frame for this revolution. He emphasised not only the growth of armies but also the spread of siege warfare, including the sieges of sizeable cities, and thus he gave as the perimeters of the military revolution 1500 (the introduction of star-shaped fortifications) to the French Revolutionary Wars, when siege warfare was almost entirely abandoned.[23] In actual fact, army sizes fluctuated considerably from antiquity to the late eighteenth century. Even with total standing forces going up to 400,000, in the case of Europe's most powerful state, France,[24] armies rarely exceeded battle strengths of around 100,000 on one side before the wars of the French Revolution.[25]

Moreover, Parker's publications lent themselves to the interpretation that the development of the European state was driven by army sizes and that this was driven by the development of the new fortifications – said star-shaped fortifications – and the large armies these necessitated.[26] And star-shaped fortifications in turn had of course been the response to the invention of gunpowder. John Lynn has taken Parker to task over this simplification, and has emphasised that while there is consensus that army growth was possible only if the state became ever more effective in raising taxes and administration, the monocausality implied in Parker's words cannot be upheld.[27]

Jeremy Black, another leading specialist on early modern warfare, argued that, on the one hand, the main changes in European armies took place after 1660, and described the period of 1660–1792 as that in which truly effective armies and navies were formed, and in which warfare catapulted European powers to world power status. On the other hand, he thought the periods of 1470–1530 and 1792–1815 revolutionary in other ways, the first with respect to siege warfare, the latter with respect to battles.[28] Importantly, he situated the subject in a wider debate about what constitutes the arrival of 'modernity', challenging the narrative of one (exclusively European) path to modernity, and pointing out the many different criteria which, when applied, can lead to extreme divergences over the dating of the advent of modernity, even in Europe.[29] Even a supporter of the concept of a military revolution, Robert Frost, expert on East European and Baltic Wars of the early modern period, identifies a series of military revolutions in Europe, not just one.[30] Black himself urges a greater focus not on technological changes but on the motives that underlay them.[31]

For medievalist Clifford Rogers, a crucial starting point for transformation was the infantry revolution of the fourteenth century, and the artillery revolution of the fifteenth century. Clifford Rogers talks about a process of 'punctuated equilibrium revolution' – 'that is, a series of intense revolutionary episodes, each built on a more extended base of slow evolutionary change'.[32]

There is thus much debate about the time frame of the military revolution, and even its precise contents. The historian Martin van Creveld accepts 1500 as a very rough turning point from the age of tools – where the main power operating anything was muscle power – to the age of machines – where wind, water and gunpowder were applied to a by now significant extent.[33] But was it a revolution or a reformation, as John Hale suggested? The chief argument for the former is its scope, and for the latter, its extensive length.[34]

Unlike most of those arguing over time frames, historian Frank Tallett stressed the continuity between the main characteristics of medieval warfare and that of the two centuries after 1500, notwithstanding some changes made necessary by the introduction of gunpowder. As in the second half of the Middle Ages, sieges occurred more frequently in early modern Europe than battles, even though the frequency of battles increased spectacularly. For Tallett, there was an evolution, but not a revolution.[35]

Another attack on the paradigm of a military revolution came from a specialist on the Thirty Years' War, David Parrott, who argued that it was in fact irrelevant to the way war was fought between 1618 and 1648:

Battles were won and lost largely incidentally of the tactical changes of the period. Moreover, battles themselves were rendered almost irrelevant by the failure of a broader concept of strategy to come to terms with the real determinants of warfare in this period.[36]

Parrott held that while seventeenth-century states were good at raising armies, they were much worse at supporting them logistically over long periods, and at paying them regularly – a central feature was thus mass desertion.[37] In the Thirty Years' War, the commanders' freedom to act

in accordance with any overall strategy was almost completely curtailed. The growing size of armies initially reflected political considerations and ambitions; subsequently it became a necessary response to the commitment of other powers. Forced to increase beyond the resources available to the state, the insoluble powers of pay and supply became progressively all-embracing as the war moved into its final crisis. Tactics and strategy in the Thirty Years' War are perhaps best characterised as being undermined by two persistent failures: in the one case, to break the dominance of the defensive; in the other, to cope with logistical inadequacy.[38]

Like Parrott, Simon Adams argues that it is not technological/tactical causes that led to growth of armies, but political factors. Moreover he argues that the growth of army sizes has been exaggerated – they grew mainly on paper, not in real numbers.[39] The debate thus overlaps with that on the growth of the state and the relationship between this phenomenon and the extension of warfare in early modern Europe.

The bottom line of this debate is that historians on the whole do not deny that warfare underwent great changes, albeit gradually, and that gunpowder played a central role. But were these perceptions shared by those who witnessed these events?

The heritage of the Ancients: the denial of change

[W]ars have changed much since gunpowder weapons were first introduced: the cannon, the musket, the caliver[40] and pistol. Although some have attempted stiffly to maintain the sufficiency of bows, daily experience does and will show us the contrary.

Thus the Englishman Robert Barret wrote in 1598.[41] Indeed, many of his contemporaries distrusted the new invention and showed little appetite for its adoption. Many eyewitnesses were slow to perceive any major, let alone revolutionary, change since the introduction of gunpowder, or even to accept that warfare could become significantly transformed by new technology. Others even denied the importance of these changes. Curiously from our standpoint, they introduced many innovations, claiming that they were actually a return to ancient – pre-medieval – practices.

In perceptions of warfare, there was much continuity stretching all the way from antiquity to the French Revolution, reflected not least in the tremendous respect in which the writings of 'the Ancients' continued to be held. The early modern authors writing until the time of the French Revolution were all greatly influenced by the works of antiquity. For many of them, this was not a bygone era, but a codex of references setting standards for the present, much as the Bible, a perpetual model and exhortation for emulation. Just as paintings of biblical scenes from the Middle Ages well into the eighteenth century tended to show peasants and bystanders in contemporary attire (reserving classical dress only for Jesus, Mary and the Apostles, and casting other notables, including saints, in ageless fantasy garments), the references of authors on war were a merry mix between classical and biblical ones, with more recent experiences added sporadically.

Above all, this is reflected in the continued reading of the *Epitoma Rei Militaris*, written by the Roman Publius Flavius Vegetius Renatus towards the end of the fourth century.[42] To this day, this remains the archetype of all field manuals. There is only a short part of Vegetius's work, the 'General Rules of War' in Book 3, Chapter 26, which aspires to anything beyond technical prescriptions. Vegetius opined that anything that benefits the enemy necessarily harms us and vice versa. Vegetius preferred bloodless victories through ruses, or through starving or surprising the enemy, over bloody battles, and emphasised the need to keep one's own plans secret from the enemy for as long as possible.[43] He consequently emphasised the need for good logistics (otherwise one's own side might starve, providing the enemy with a bloodless victory),[44] for high spirits and good morale among the forces,[45] and the importance of chance (or good fortune), along with the luck required to exploit an unexpected opportunity.[46] Apart from echoes of these (fairly obvious) points, Vegetius's enduring influence over the centuries lay mainly in the remit, structure and style of his manual.

Surviving manuscripts of Vegetius's work date back at least to the ninth century, and it was the standard work on the art of war until Machiavelli and beyond. A particularly striking fact for readers of our age is that the students of Vegetius thought so very little of the changes brought about by technical innovations. Over 130 medieval manuscripts of the *Epitoma Rei Militaris* survive, an unusually large number for an ancient text, plus another 70-odd compilations of extracts or translations of the book into the vernacular. The translations more than the Latin original suggest that it was actually read by military commanders, as the strong Germanic strand in the European medieval aristocratic culture tended to value practical experience over all bookish learning, and deprecated the latter compared with all things physical. Accordingly, there are precious few references in sources to any practical application of Vegetius's ideas about warfare, and even with these, it can be argued that they were little more than the application of common sense, as much in Vegetius is the statement of the obvious.[47] This also sheds some doubts on the claims of modern scholars that medieval monarchs consciously applied Vegetius's teachings in their military campaigns; they might simply have done what was obvious.[48]

The Middle Ages offer us astonishingly little by way of original thoughts on the art or conduct of war, let alone on strategy (in the sense of a comprehensive way to try to pursue political ends, including the threat or actual use of force, in a dialectic of wills[49]), and even on its purposes. The very existence of tactics in medieval warfare has been denied by some historians, who retrospectively saw it as nothing but the sum of duels.[50] The Dutch historian Jan Frans Verbruggen, however, rightly noted that medieval battles were fought by composite armies made up of infantry, archers and cavalry, and the way these were deployed, used ditches and makeshift defences, and interacted on the battlefield merits being referred to as 'tactics'[51] in the Byzantine sense of the term (the 'science [*epistéme*] which enables one to organise and manoeuvre a body of armed men in an orderly manner'[52]). Changes in tactics that can be interpreted as a learning process after military defeats can be identified, but in the absence of written theoretical reflections on warfare, handed down to subsequent generations, these changes, where identified, were also ephemeral.[53]

Historian Bert Hall deliberately used the term 'Renaissance of warfare' both in view of the rediscovery of the crossbow and the pike formation, which had both existed in antiquity, and the increasing reading of Vegetius.[54] Students, commentators, translators and paraphrasers of Vegetius well into the sixteenth century saw no reason to think his work outdated and overtaken by new technology. Christine de Pizan followed Vegetius closely, adding text on new weapons;[55] her book was marketed in France as *The Art of the Knight according to Vegetius*.[56] While the medieval translations of Vegetius introduced ideas of chivalry into classical ways of waging war in which the *equester* had been culturally very different from his medieval counterpart, the knight, Christine de Pizan, William Caxton and the other followers of Vegetius were not conscious of any such basic cultural difference.[57] Even Machiavelli, the embodiment of the Renaissance, drew no attention to arms that had not existed in the late Roman Empire, and instead believed strongly in the immutability of all factors to do with warfare bar one. And this variable, which Machiavelli identified, was the nature of the state that waged it, and as part of this variable, whether its soldiers were mercenaries or citizens of the state they were to defend. Otherwise, his *Art of War* draws mostly on examples from Roman and Greek history as the database from which he constructed his recommendations about how to make war. He did introduce examples from the more recent past, and was impressed by the Swiss (whom he still counted as Germans). The military feats of the Swiss pikemen in defeating Burgundians, French and forces of the Holy Roman Empire to him seemed very comparable to the feats of the Roman Republican Army, which he most admired. His alter ego in the *Arte della Guerra*, Fabrizio, even wanted to equip his ideal army half with Roman, half with 'German' arms and armour. By the Roman arms he meant 'swords and shields'; by 'German' arms he meant pikes and harquebuses. While he fashioned his drill and order of battle on both the Swiss and the Romans, if asked to choose, he professed a preference for the Ancients.[58]

Machiavelli's approach to writing on war was followed by most other authors on war in the following centuries. Particularly prominent among them were the sons of the Nassau family in the Netherlands (later Nassau-Orange), who produced both active generals and writers on the art of war. Count John of Nassau-Siegen (1561–1623) in his *Book of War* quoted extensively from Vegetius, and the usual classical historians. As many of these works had recently become available in print,

John also drew on the *Strategikon* of the Byzantine emperor Maurice (539–602) and on the *Taktika* by one of his successors, Leo VI the Wise (865–912), that had recently been printed and for this first time translated into Latin.[59] Count John was guided by the ideas of his teacher Justus Lipsius, himself a great humanist steeped in these classical writings. More still than Machiavelli, John was obsessed with the ways of the Romans, and did not let more recent military events influence his quest for the perfect reconstitution of a Roman army. His *War Book*, a collection of essays and other papers in German and French on different aspects of war, is a particularly good example of early modern attempts to carry on regardless of technical innovations in the tradition of the Ancients. John added chapters of his own about the use of guns and muskets, but to him, technical innovations did not invalidate the classics he used.[60] John's cousin Maurice of Nassau (1567–1625) saw his own momentous reforms as a return to the Ancients, and this is how contemporaries conceived of them: in England, they were described in a publication that joined them with Aelian's *Tactica*, which had inspired Maurice to his reforms.[61] Another member of the family, Count William Louis of Nassau (d. 1620), in his youth prepared an elaborate study of the campaigns of Hannibal and Scipio Africanus, with a commentary; but he concentrated primarily on the ancient battles as examples for all times.[62]

The 'Beginning of a New Art', as Georg Heinrich von Berenhorst called the military innovations of Gustavus Adolphus of Sweden (1594–1632),[63] was thus regarded by its creators – Gustavus Adolphus himself, but also the Dutch Nassau princes of the late sixteenth century – not as an innovation but as a return to the customs of the Ancients, above all Vegetius. It went hand in hand with a renewed yearning for Roman (Republican) virtues, discipline and civic spirit. (Curiously, this had already been Vegetius's intention in writing his own treatise – he, too, deplored the loss of older skills and practices, and called for a return to these as well as to Roman *mores* and *virtus*.[64]) Their attitude was typical of the times. The fluctuations in the conduct of war from classical antiquity to early modern times, which culminated in the technological changes of 1300–1600, finally crowned by the realisation of the new possibilities created by the gunpowder revolution, were rarely perceived as a watershed by contemporaries.

One exception was Francesco Guicciardini, author of a history of Florence, who writing in 1520 described the French king Charles VIII's campaign to claim the crown of Naples in 1494/1495 as a watershed. From this relatively short and yet very successful campaign onwards, he reckoned,

> Wars became sudden and violent, conquering and capturing a state in less time than it used to take to occupy a village; cities were reduced with great speed, in a matter of days and hours rather than months; battles became savage and bloody in the extreme.[65]

The perception of a great transformation which can be read into this quotation from Guicciardini according to Geoffrey Parker was due to the superior cannon which Charles brought with him, which allowed him to invest cities and fortresses along his way in a flash, compared with earlier campaigns.

Some modern historians disagree that this campaign was *the* crucial turning point. For one, Simon Pepper has argued that Charles used the guns on only a few occasions. After he destroyed the walls of Monte San Giovanni in a mere eight hours, most places just surrendered to the French king at the news of his approach. At the celebrated bombardment of Castelnuovo in the first siege of Naples in 1494 the French even ran out of iron cannonballs and the place surrendered for other reasons.[66] Also, outside Italy this particular campaign was not seen as such a hugely important turning point in military affairs. It did not shake up the old world anywhere near as much as the conquest of Constantinople by Sultan Mehmet the Conqueror or the reintegration of Granada into Catholic Spain, both events, as we have seen, in which guns played a crucial part.

Moreover, the link between an intensification of warfare and an increase in the number of battles on the one hand and the changes in technology on the other hand was not necessarily made by contemporaries. A hundred years on, there was still a debate about whether these innovations had influenced war and its conduct in any fundamental way. Thomas Digges (1546–1595), an English scientist, one-time member of Parliament, and from 1586–94 muster-master general to the English forces fighting in the Netherlands, aptly summarised the debate. He himself claimed 'That neither the furie of Ordinance, nor any other like inuentions of this our age, hath or can worke' any great change in military affairs, 'But that the auncient discipline of the *Romane* and Martiall *Graecian* States, (euen for our time) are rare and singuler *Praecedents'* to be followed scrupulously in his day and age. He conceded, however, that many 'Captaines and Commaunders of the newe *Moderne Martiall Discipline'* claimed that since the invention of ordnance, 'all ancient *Romane or Graecian* Militarie Lawes and Orders of the Field' were outdated, as much as Roman and Greek prescriptions for government. He implied that they held this view as they were 'corrupt, base minded persons (as seeke the warres for gaine)', and intended 'excessiuely [to] enrich themselues, euen with the ruine of their countrey' by urging the adoption of these new inventions.[67]

Digges must have written this at much the same time as his compatriot Sir John Smythe (1531–1607) published his *Discourses*, which he began by saying that wise and humble men of later ages had acknowledged their own inferiority, compared with 'the excellency of men in all arts and sciences of former ages and of greater antiquity than to themselves'. By contrast, vain and self-important young men of his own time, especially in England,

> have not been ashamed to attribute unto themselves greater wisdom and sufficiency in all arts and sciences, and especially in the art military, than to the . . . great captains of former ages and of greater antiquity. . . . They say . . . that their wars are now grown to greater perfection and greatly altered from the wars of times past, under pretence whereof they have of late sought,. . . to reduce all our ancient proceedings in matters military . . . to their own errors and disorders,. . . by their vain and frivolous objections against our archery, to suppress . . . the exercise and . . . use of longbows.[68]

(Sir John Smythe could still argue at the time that more arrows could be shot per minute from a longbow than bullets fired from the handheld firearms of his time, which, imported from the Continent, were clearly the preferred weapon of the 'vain young men'.)[69]

The obsession with a return to ancient practices was not unique to weathered warhorses like Digges and Smythe, nor was it by any means unique to the Netherlands and England, but could be found throughout Europe. In 1568 the Spaniard Sancho de Londoño wrote a treatise dedicated to the Duke of Alba for application in his fight against the rebellious Dutch, which was passed through censure only a quarter of a century later. In it, Londoño pleaded for the *return of the military discipline to the best and antique state*. The Trojan War and Roman history were used by him to advocate a militia, not a mercenary army, and to formulate rules of conduct, tactics of employment and a code of honour.[70] His countryman Diego de Alava y Viamont, writing in 1589, still called the 'Science of Artillery' 'new'. His *Perfecto Capitan* was based entirely on the views expressed by classical authors, and examples drawn from classical history.[71] In 1638 the Frenchman Henri Duc de Rohan first published his *Parfait Capitaine*, a popular title in literature on war, which addressed military commanders in general and not just the commander-in-chief. This went through several reprints and for a century or more would be seen as a model handbook on the art of war. It was, in fact, an abridged and commented account in French of Caesar's wars.[72] Even in 1757, Count de Tressan in Diderot's and d'Alembert's French *Encyclopedia* commented that

> The invention or the discovery of gunpowder, which has resulted in the changes of the former sort of fortification, has not introduced many novelties in the offensive arms of the soldier. The gun corresponds quite exactly to the propulsive weapons of the Ancients.[73]

And as late as 1775, the French strategic theorist Guibert wrote about the army of Frederick II of Prussia, which he so admired,

> If the Prussians had made their tactics converge with that of the Greeks and Romans, who are our masters, and if they had adapted their discipline to the precision of their . . . movements, which army could have held out against them in a battle.[74]

The culmination: the *Querelle*

The culmination in this debate, which had clearly been under way since the sixteenth century, can be pinned to one event, although it was more symptom, less cause of the change, and its repercussions spread slowly. In 1687 a famous debate took place in the Académie Française, in which Charles Perrault – most popularly famous for his collection of fairy tales – led one group of intellectuals in arguing that the times of Louis XIV (the Great) of France were every bit as heroic and great

as those of the Ancients. The other faction continued to take the previously univer-
sally accepted line that the present never offered more than unsuccessful attempts
to live up the greatness of the Ancients. The 'Querelle' spread to the rest of Europe,
and only thenceforth did it become legitimate for the 'modernists' to draw increasingly on examples from the world around them as evidence for their writings about
society, economics, power – or war.[75] After the Querelle, majority opinion gradually
shifted towards recognition of the importance of the technical innovations engendered by gunpowder, but even then, old thinking was slow to go.

A typical statement of the way in which the art of war was thought about and
commented upon was that of Jacques François de Chastenet, Marquis de Puységur (1655–1743), marshal of France (i.e. one of the highest military commanders)
under Louis XIV. Himself son of a lieutenant general who had served under both
Louis XIV and his father, Louis XIII, he explained the usefulness of reflections on
war to complement actual practical experiences. It would be pointless, he argued, to
let every commander proceed entirely by trial and error; instead, one should learn
from other reflections on war. 'Wise persons' counselled him to turn 'to the Romans
and Greeks, going back to Homer', which Puységur duly undertook. He read (and
commented upon) Herodotus, Xenophon, Thucydides's Peloponnesian War, Arian's
feats of Alexander, Polybius, Plutarch's life of Philomenes, Caesar and Vegetius.
After Vegetius, he claimed, he had not until his own times found any author who
wrote on the subject of war in principle.[76] He added that he wanted

> to destroy the popular view that since the use of fire weapons war is waged
> in a very different way from how it was practiced before, and that all that one
> can read about war in the ancients is no longer of use. I say to that subject
> that the science and the art of war have always been and will always be the
> same, that they do not vary as a function of a few weapons we use, that the
> captains who have led armies and who have known war through principles
> have at all times been forced to formulate their orders of battle as a function
> of the different dispositions of the terrain where they had to fight, and as a
> function of the use they could make of their weapons. Our orders of battle
> to fight today have to be formulated along the same principles [as those of
> the Ancients].[77]

This he proceeded to demonstrate in the rest of his book, which was essentially
a commentary on select passages from the ancient authors listed earlier, plus the
memoirs of Montecuccoli and Turenne (1611–1675).

Interestingly, only four years after the original publication of this book in 1748,
extracts were edited by the Baron de Traverse, who prefaced it with the explanation
that he had left omitted references to 'the heroes of Greece and Rome in order to
instruct us':

> What use is it that we should be instructed which arms were used in ancient
> wars, and what were the machines that served to overthrow the towers and

walls of towns? It suffices that we should rest assured that the arms and artillery that are used currently are infinitely better. The same applies to engineering.[78]

The Habsburg general Raymundo de Montecuccoli (1609–1680), who had lived half a century earlier, in this point was much more modern than Puységur. Montecuccoli, who himself gained much military experience in the Thirty Years' War and in the Turkish wars, was exceptional in his times in that he cautioned against a 1:1 transfer of advice given by the Ancients and of examples from antiquity to the present, advocating instead an application modified in the light of different circumstances, and the differing spirit of the age. Nevertheless, in his *Trattato della Guerra* and *Delle Battaglie* he adopted classical Vegetian structures.[79]

Authors increasingly mixed more recent examples with those from Ancient Greece, Rome and the feats of the Israelites as recorded in the Bible. The third Marques of Santa Cruz de Marcenado (1684–1732) mixed stories from Livy, Josephus's Jewish Wars, Tacitus and the Hebrew Bible with military feats recorded in his own times, such as campaigns conducted under Louis XIV of France or Charles I of England and Scotland.[80] His contemporary Maurice de Saxe (1696–1750), marshal of France under Louis XIV, consciously tried in his *Rêveries* to stick as closely as possible to Vegetius as a model.[81] The same applies to the writings of Charles Tronson du Coudray (1738–1777), who like his contemporary Count Guibert was fascinated by the column and possible deployments in battle resulting from it. Yet again, in his manual he still followed Vegetius's structure.[82] Feuquières drew on Xenophon and Caesar, as well as on Santa Cruz, only without giving individual historical examples to support his maxims.[83] While the Welshman Henry Lloyd (c. 1718–1783) developed his principles on the conduct of war in the context of a history of the Seven Years' War, in which he had taken part, he devoted an entire section to the Greek phalanx and its merits, based on the descriptions of Thucydides.[84]

Half a century later Antoine Baron de Jomini (1779–1869), like his rival Clausewitz, wrote extensively not only on the wars of Napoleon but also, in his multi-volume work on tactics, on Frederick the Great's campaigns. In his works classical examples were scarce, as were reflections on recent technological changes; this is surprising as Jomini lived through the beginnings of the industrialisation of war and its logistic revolution by the railway.[85] Carl von Clausewitz (1780–1831) also stands accused of paying no attention to technological innovation, although he excluded all wars prior to the Thirty Years' War from his studies. Writing his famous *On War* in the 1810s and 1820s, he deliberately decided to leave classical wars out of his database of case studies on which he based his reflections. Clausewitz's argument was not based on technology, however: he argued that war changed with the culture of the age in which it was waged, and that the wars of the Ancients were the least relevant to his musings because they belonged to a different age, and that wars increased in relevance for his findings, the closer to his times they were.[86]

It was only when writing about the spirit of military institutions in 1845 that the French marshal Auguste de Marmont (1774–1852) gave a different explanation as to why he did not draw more on the Ancients: he thought that the discovery of gunpowder had so profoundly changed the 'science of war' that 'Polybius and Vegetius can still satisfy our curiosity, but let us no longer seek in their writing useful and applicable instructions. The ancient and the modern wars have no point of resemblance' other than issues of morale and the behaviour of men.[87] For multiple reasons, a new majority view was becoming established by the mid-nineteenth century that a narrow reading of the histories of the wars of the Ancients or the slavish copying of their tactics, drill or force structures was no longer the recipe for success. The impact of technological change was widely recognised as at least one reason; the paradigm shift was complete. Even so, this did not stop Count Schlieffen from looking to the Ancients for inspiration for his plans for the invasion of France worked out on the eve of the First World War!

Conclusions

Why did it take so long for technological change to be recognised as having had an enormous impact? There are several reasons. One consists of the parallel developments which first competed very successfully with gunpowder for influence on warfare, but ultimately became dead ends (the longbow and the crossbow, but also the pike formations). Another is the slow spread of gunpowder, and the slow development and calibration of guns fit for different purposes, from cannon cast especially to besiege towns or fortification to transportable field artillery to handheld fire arms with some precision in targeting. Gunpowder needed guns to fire it, and thus its application depended on the state of the art of founding. This in turn was still done in small numbers on a pre-industrial rate of production. The gunpowder innovation only slowly had a quantitative impact, illustrated by the flat star-shape applied increasingly to fortifications, and culminating in the seventeenth-, eighteenth- and nineteenth-century Vauban-type defences in depth that ultimately replaced the classical medieval curtain-wall defences. Given the rates of fire by handheld weapons, it *was* still reasonable for Sir John Smythe to note at the end of the sixteenth century that bows and arrows, handled by well-trained men, could be fired faster than the handheld guns available in England at the time.

Perhaps, however, we should listen to our 'ancestral voices' (Donald Neill) more carefully, and rethink the entire concept of the military revolution. Perhaps the technological element, especially gunpowder on its own, as *cause* of that revolution has been overemphasised. This is not to deny the sophistication and subtlety of the interpretations of Michael Roberts and Geoffrey Parker, but we should reject the simplification of the concept of the military revolution as it eventually percolates down the teaching chain and makes its way into student essays, not to mention political science writing. Perhaps we should take it more seriously if contemporaries rarely saw the great changes as caused directly or even predominantly by technology. The search for and adaptation of more effective military technology, as we have seen not only gunpowder but also the longbow, crossbow, pikemen and other more effective infantry formations, using little or no *new* technology, and the hundreds of siege engines and non-explosive catapults designed at the time, could be seen as much as the consequence of a gradual change of mentality as its cause. As we have seen, contemporaries talked about an increase in savagery (a change in the attitude in fighting), or emphasised the changes introduced by the re-emergence[88] of the religious element with its ideological fanaticism, changes in war aims and changes in social and political structures. Moreover, their perception of statehood changed from one which had no difficulties relating to states with territorial possessions scattered throughout different parts of a geographic region or even the European continent and the Americas to one that thought of the state as ideally comprising a solid landmass within one set of common borders, without any 'alien' territories within it.

To repeat: none of this is to deny that technology changed, and that this can be shown to have had consequences for the ideal way one had to train and structure armies, and to use them. But perhaps the most important changes are those in the minds of men, who seize new inventions in different ways, apply them with their own imagination conditioned, formed and limited by their mentality and culture.

Notes

1   Gerhard Dohrn-van Rossum: 'Novitates-Inventores: Die "Erfindung der Erfinder" im Spätmittelalter', in Hans-Joachim Schmidt (ed.): *Tradition, Innovation, Invention: Fortschritts-verweigerung und Fortschrittsbewusstsein im Mittelalter* (Berlin: Walter de Gruyter, 2005), pp. 27–49.

2   Volker Reinhardt: 'Goldenes Zeitalter, Zyklus, Aufbruch ins Unbekannte: Geschichts-konzeptionen der italienischen Renaissance', in Hans-Joachim Schmidt (ed.): *Tradition, Innovation, Invention: Fortschrittsverweigerung und Fortschrittsbewusstsein im Mittelalter* (Berlin: Walter de Gruyter, 2005), pp. 51–67.

3   For a listing of what can be seen as such revolutions in warfare, see Alvin Toefler & Heidi Toefler: *War and Anti-War* (Boston: Little, Brown, 1993).

4   Peter Thorau: 'Panzerreiter im Pfeilhagel?' and Daniel A. Rupp: 'Vom Gegner lernen? Zur Taktik französischer Heere in den Schlachten von Kortrijk, Arques und am Pevelenberg', both in *Militärgeschichtliche Zeitschrift*, Vol. 65 No. 1 (2006), pp. 63–78 and 89–112 resp.

5   Erich Sander: 'Der Verfall der römischen Belagerungskunst', *Historische Zeitschrift*, Vol. 149 (1934), pp. 457–476.

6   Donald A. Neill: 'Ancestral Voices: The Influence of the Ancients on the Military Thought of the Seventeenth and Eighteenth Centuries', *Journal of Military History*, Vol. 62 (July 1998), pp. 487–520, here p. 496.

7   Clifford Rogers: 'The Military Revolutions of the Hundred Years' War', in Clifford Rogers (ed.): *The Military Revolution Debate* (Boulder, CO: Westview Press, 1995), p. 56.

8   Quoted in Michael Roberts, 'The Military Revolution, 1560–1660', in Clifford Rogers (ed.): *The Military Revolution Debate* (Boulder, CO: Westview Press, 1995), p. 23.

9   Bert S. Hall: *Weapons and Warfare in Renaissance Europe: Gunpowder, Technology and Tactics* (Baltimore: The Johns Hopkins University Press, 1997), pp. 20–23.

10 Rainer Leng: *Ars belli: deutsche Taktische und kriegstechnische Bilderhandschriften und Traktate im 15. und 16. Jahrhundert*, 2 vols. (Wiesbaden: Reichert, 2002).

11 Peter Purton: *A History of the Late Medieval Siege, 1200–1500* (Woodbridge: Boydell Press, 2010), pp. 109, 116, and plate 7.

12 John F. Guilmartin Jr: 'The Origins and First Tests of the Military Revolution Abroad', in Clifford Rogers (ed.): *The Military Revolution Debate* (Boulder, CO: Westview Press, 1995), p. 323.

13 Quoted in J.N. Hillgarth: *The Spanish Kingdoms 1250–1516, vol. II: 1410–1516, Castilian Hegemony* (Oxford: Clarendon Press, 1987), p. 376. I am grateful to Dr Frank Tallett for having drawn my attention to this quotation.

14 Leo Baptista Alberti: *Leonis Baptista Alberti De Re Aedificatoria Libri X* (Florence: Laurentius Alamannus, 1485).

15 John R. Hale: 'The Early Development of the Bastion: An Italian Chronology, c. 1450-c. 1534', in J.R. Hale, J.R.L. Highfield & B. Smalley (eds): *Europe in the Late Middle Ages* (London: Faber & Faber, 1965), pp. 466–94; Geoffrey Parker: 'The "Military Revolution", 1560–1660: A Myth?', *The Journal of Modern History*, Vol. 48 (June 1976), p. 204.

16 John Lynn (ed.): *Tools of War: Instruments, Ideas, and Institutions of Warfare 1445–1871* (Urbana, IL: University of Illinois Press, 1990). In France, they are commonly associated with the extensive building scheme of Louis XIV's adviser Vauban, but long predated him.

17 Helen Nicholson: *Medieval Warfare* (Basingstoke: Palgrave Macmillan, 2004), p. 89.

18 Hall: *Weapons and Warfare*, pp. 67–104, 134–156.

19 Michael Roberts: *The Military Revolution, 1560–1660* (Belfast: Marjory Boyd, 1956), reprinted in Michael Roberts: *Essays in Swedish History* (London: Weidenfeld & Nicolson, 1967), pp. 195–225.

20 Martin van Creveld: *Technology and War from 2000 BC to the Present* (New York: Free Press, 1991), pp. 137ff.

21 Charles Tilly (ed.): *The Formation of National States in Western Europe* (Princeton, NJ: Princeton University Press, 1975); Johannes Burkhardt: *Der Dreissigjährige Krieg* (Frankfurt: Suhrkamp, 1992).

22 John R. Hale: *The Art of War and Renaissance England* (Washington, DC: Folger Shakespeare Library, 1961), p. 1.

23 Geoffrey Parker: *The Military Revolution: Military Innovation and the Rise of the West 1500–1800* (Cambridge: Cambridge University Press, 1988).

24 John Lynn: 'The Trace Italienne and the Growth of Armies: The French Case', *Journal of Military History*, Vol. 55 No. 3 (July 1999), p. 299.

25 Hall: *Weapons and Warfare*, pp. 202–235.

26 Geoffrey Parker: 'The Military Revolution 1560–1660: A Myth?', *Journal of Modern History*, Vol. 46 No. 2 (June 1976), p. 208.

27 Lynn: 'Trace Italienne', p. 299f; see also Bert Hall & Kelly DeVries: 'Essay Review: The Military Revolution Revisited', *Technology and Culture*, Vol. 31 No. 3 (July 1990), pp. 500–507.

28 Jeremy Black: *A Military Revolution? Military Change and European Society, 1550–1800* (Basingstoke: Macmillan, 1991); Jeremy Black: 'A Military Revolution? A 1660–1792 Perspective', in Clifford Rogers (ed.): *The Military Revolution Debate* (Boulder, CO: Westview Press, 1995), pp. 95–114.

29 Jeremy Black: *European Warfare 1494–1660* (London: Routledge, 2002), pp. 32–54.

30 Robert Frost: *The Northern Wars: War, State and Society in Northeastern Europe, 1558–1721* (London: Routledge, 2000); Robert Frost: *After the Deluge: Poland-Lithuania and the Second Northern War, 1655–1660* (Cambridge: Cambridge University Press, 2010).

31 Black: *European Warfare 1494–1660*, pp. 32–54.

32 Clifford Rogers: 'The Military Revolutions of the Hundred Years' War', p. 57.

33 Creveld: *Technology and War*, p. 2.

34 John R. Hale: *War and Society in Renaissance Europe, 1450–1620* (1985, this edn Baltimore, MD: Johns Hopkins University Press, 1986), pp. 46–74.

35 Frank Tallett: *War and Society in Early-Modern Europe, 1495–1715* (London: Routledge, 1992), p. 65.

36 David Parrott: 'Strategy and Tactics in the Thirty Years' War: The "Military Revolution"', in Clifford Rogers (ed.): *The Military Revolution Debate* (Boulder, CO: Westview Press, 1995), p. 228.

37 Geoffrey Parker: 'Mutiny and Discontent in the Spanish Army of Flanders, 1572–1607', *Past & Present*, No. 58 (Feb. 1973), pp. 38–52.

38 Parrott: 'Strategy and Tactics', p. 245f.
39 Simon Adams: 'Tactics or Politics? The "Military Revolution" and the Habsburg Hegemony, 1525–1648', in John A. Lynn (ed.): *Tools of War: Instruments, Ideas, and Institutions of Warfare 1445–1871* (Urbana, IL: University of Illinois Press, 1990), pp. 28-52.
40 A type of harquebus.
41 Robert Barret: *The Theorike and Practike of Moderne Warres, Discoursed in Dialogue Wise* (London: William Ponsonby, 1598), p. 2.
42 Philippe Richardot: 'La datation du *De Re Militari* de Végèce', *Latomus*, Vol. 57 No. 1 (Jan.–Mar. 1998), pp. 136–47.
43 Vegetius: *De Re Militari*, pp. 116–119.
44 Ibid., Book III.4, III,12 and III.26.
45 Ibid., pp. 69f, 92, 116–119.
46 Ibid., pp. 116–119.
47 One example is William Plantagenet, Count of Poitou, who while he was besieging the castle of Montreuil-Bellay in the mid-twelfth century, read Vegetius on siege warfare, and followed his advice – abandoning the siege; see Georges Duby: *France in the Middle Ages, 987–1460: From Hugh Capet to Joan of Arc*, trans. by Juliet Vale (Oxford: Blackwell, 1993), p. 178.
48 I owe this thought to Professor Michael Prestwick, of the University of Durham.
49 For the evolution of this term, see Beatrice Heuser: *The Evolution of Strategy* (Cambridge: Cambridge University Press, 2010), Chapter 1.
50 Hermann Meynert: *Geschichte des Kriegswesens und der Heeresverfassung in Europa*, Vol. 1 (Graz: Akademische Druck- u. Verlagsanstalt, 1973), p. 291.
51 Jan Frans Verbruggen: *The Art of Warfare in Western Europe during the Middle Ages; from the Eighth Century to 1340* (2nd edn, Woodbridge: Boydell Press, 1997), p. 75; see also Hans Delbrück: *Geschichte der Kriegskunst im Rahmen der politischen Geschichte*, vol. 3 (originally Berlin: Walter de Gruyter, 1901, repr. Hamburg: Nikol, 2003), pp. 316–324.
52 Heuser: *Evolution of Strategy*, p. 4.
53 For examples see the 'learning' from Arab and Turkic forces in the Middle East during the crusades and from French encounters with the superior Flemish infantry at the Battle of Courtrai in 1304; see Peter Thorau: 'Panzerreiter im Pfeilhagel?'; Rupp: 'Vom Gegner lernen?'.
54 Hall: *Weapons and Warfare*.
55 Christine de Pizan: *Livre. des fais d'armes et de Chevalerie* (1410) – see Chapter 2 of this book.
56 Anon [Christine de Pizan]: *L'Art de la Chevalerie selon Végèce* (Paris: Antoine Verard, 1488), later republished as *L'Arbre des batailles et fleur de chevalerie selon Végèce* (Paris: Phelippe le Noir, 1527); both printed versions deliberately hid Christine's translatorship and authorship of the additional chapters.
57 Philippe Richardot: *Végèce et la Culture militaire au Moyen Âge (Ve-XVe siècles)* (Paris: Economica, 1998).
58 Niccolo Machiavelli: *The Art of War*, trans. by Ellis Farneworth (originally 1521, Indianapolis: Bobbs-Merrill, 1965, repr. New York: Da Capo, 1990), pp. 47, 51.
59 Emperor Leo: *De bellico apparatu liber*, trans. by John Checo of Cambridge (Basle: s.e., 1554).
60 Johann von Nassau: *Das Kriegsbuch*, in Werner Hahlweg (ed.): *Die Heeresreform der Oranier* (Wiesbaden: Selbstverlag der Historischen Kommission, 1973), J.W. Wijn: 'Johann der Mittlere von Nassau-Siegen', in Werner Hahlweg (ed.): *Klassiker der Kriegskunst* (Darmstadt: Wehr- und Wissen-Verlag, 1960), pp. 119–133.
61 John Bingham (trans.): *The Tactiks of Aelian . . .; the Exercise Military of the English by the Order of That Great Generall Maurice of Nassau Prince of Orange . . .* (London: Laurence Lisle, 1616).
62 William (Guilhelmus) Count of Nassau & Alain Claude de Mestre: *Annibal et Scipion, ou les grands Capitaines, avec les ordres et plans de batailles* (Hague, 1675).
63 Georg Heinrich von Berenhorst: *Betrachtungen über die Kriegskunst, über ihre Fortschritte, ihre Widersprüche und ihre Zuverlässigkeit* (1733–1814, Leipzig: Gerhard Fleischer, 1827, facsimile repr. Osnabrück: Biblio, 1978), pp. 18–27.

64 Vegetius: *De Re Militari*, Book I.1.
65 Quoted in Parker: *The Military Revolution*, p. 10. Max Booth also sees this campaign as the crucial turning point: *War Made New: Technology, Warfare, and the Course of History, 1500 to Today* (New York: Gotham Books, 2006), pp. 1–6.
66 Simon Pepper: 'Castles and Cannon in the Naples Campaign of 1494–95', in David Abulafia (ed.): *The French Descent into Renaissance Italy, 1494–95: Antecedents and Effects* (Aldershot: Variorum, 1995), pp. 263–294.
67 Thomas Digges, in Thomas Digges and Dudly Digges: *Four Paradoxes, or Politique Discourses Concerning Militarie Discipline* (London: H. Lownes for Clement Knight, 1604), p. 40f.
68 Sir John Smythe: *Certain Discourses Military*, ed. by J.R.Hale (rev. edn, 1590, Ithaca, NY: Cornell University Press, 1964), pp. 3–5.
69 J.R. Hale: 'Introduction', in Sir John Smythe: *Certain Discourses Military* ed. by J.R. Hale (rev. edn, 1590, Ithaca, NY: Cornell University Press, 1964), pp. xxxvii–lxi.
70 Sancho de Londoño: *Discurso sobre la forma de reducir la Disciplina Militar a mejor y antiguo estado* (originally 1594?, Madrid: Ministry of Defence, 1992).
71 Diego de Alava y Viamont: *El Perfecto Capitán instruido en la Disciplina Militar y nueva ciencia de la Artillería* (orig. Madrid: Pedro Madrigal, 1590, repr. Madrid: Ministerio de Defensa, 1994).
72 Henri Duc de Rohan: *Le parfait capitaine, autrement l'abrégé des Guerres de Gaulle* (Paris: A. Courbé, 1638).
73 Comte de Tressan: 'Guerre', in Diderot & d'Alembert: *Encyclopédie ou Dictionnaire raisonné des Sciences, des Arts et des Métiers*, Vol. 7 (Paris: Briasson, David, Le Breton & Durand, 1757), p. 986.
74 Comte de Guibert: 'Observations sur la constitution militaire et politique des armées de S. M. prussienne, avec quelques anecdotes de la vie privée de ce monarque' (probably 1775), Bibliothèque Mazarine, MS 1888, p. 135.
75 For the most important texts on this quarrel, see Anne-Marie Lecoq (ed.): *La Querelle des Anciens et des Modernes, XVIIe–XVIIIe siècles* (Paris: Gallimard, 2001).
76 He was thus ignorant of a whole range of important authors, such as Fourquevaux, Matthew Sutcliffe, Bernardino de Mendoza, Paul Hay du Chastelet and his own contemporary Santa Cruz de Marcenado; see Beatrice Heuser (ed. & trans.): *The Strategy Makers: Thoughts on War and Society from Machiavelli to Clausewitz* (Santa Barbara, CA: Praeger/ABC Clio, 2010).
77 Brigadier Marquis de Puységur (ed.): *Art de la Guerre, par principes et par règles, ouvrage de M. Le Maréchal [Jacques Francois] de Puységur* (Paris: Charles-Antoine Jombert, 1748), p. 3.
78 Baron de Traverse: 'Preface', in id. (ed.): *Extrait de la première partie de l'Art de Guerre de M. le Maréchal de Puysegur* (Paris: chez Charles-Ant. Jombert et Hochereau l'Aîné, 1752), pp. viif., 1f.
79 For Raimundo Montecuccoli and his works, see Chapter 6 in this book.
80 Marquis de Santa Cruz de Marzenado: *Réeflexions militaires et politiques*, trans. from Spanish (Paris: Jacques Guerin, 1735).
81 Maurice de Saxe: *Rêveries sur l'Art de la Guerre* (written 1732, published posthumously in The Hague: 1756), trans. by US Army in Brig. Gen. T.R. Phillips (ed.): *Roots of Strategy*, Vol. 5 (Mechanicsburg, PA: Stackpole Books, 1985).
82 Charles Tronson du Coudray: *L'ordre profond et l'ordre mince considérés par rapport aux effets de l'artillerie* (Metz: Ruault et Esprit, 1776); Jacques Antoine Hippolyte Comte de Guibert: *Essai général de Tactique* (1770), in Guibert: *Stratégiques* (Paris: L'Herne, 1977).
83 Antoine de Pas, Marquis de Feuquières: *Mémoires sur la Guerre* (Amsterdam: François Champetier, 1731).
84 General Henry Humphry Evans Lloyd: *Continuation of the History of the Late War in Germany, between the King of Prussia, and the Empress of Germany and Her Allies*, Part II (1781), in Patrick J. Speelman (ed.): *War, Society and Enlightenment: The Works of General Lloyd* (Leiden: Brill, 2005), pp. 389–391.
85 Antoine Henri Jomini: *Traité des grandes Opérations militaires*, 4 vols. (2nd edn, Paris: Magimel, 1811), trans. by Col. S.B. Holabird: *Treatise on Grand Military Operations, or a Critical*

and Military History of the Wars of Frederick the Great, 2 vols (New York: D. Van Nostrad, 1865).

86 Carl von Clausewitz: *Vom Kriege* (1832), Book 2 Ch. 6 trans. by Michael Howard & Peter Paret: *On War* (Princeton, NJ: Princeton University Press, 1984), p. 173.

87 Maréchal Marmont, Duc de Raguse: *De l'Esprit des Institutions militaires* (Paris: Librairie militaire J Dumaine, 1845), Part IV p. 1f.

88 Which had been present in early medieval warfare during the original expansion of Islam and the bloody wars between early Christian denomination – Arian vs Orthodox vs Paulician/Manichaean . . . – and the wars of forced conversion to Christianity.

4

THE INVENTION OF MODERN MARITIME STRATEGIES

The Anglo-Spanish War of 1585–1604

On the eve of the French Revolution, Jacques Raymond Viscount de Grenier in a treatise on naval warfare accused his predecessors of having paid attention to little besides orders of battle, not 'tactics' (let alone 'strategy', but the term had not yet been introduced into the French language, and 'tactics' at the time covered both).[1] Writing in the 1930s, French admiral Raoul Castex claimed that there was an 'almost complete void in the writing on naval Strategy before the French Revolution, which stands in utter contrast to the work of authors writing about the army in the same period'.[2] While previously, I was inclined to agree with him,[3] further digging reveals that there was in fact an impressive body of writing on naval strategy in the sixteenth century. This was not always printed as we shall see, nor is it usually found in formal state archival collections, which barely existed then. Literature about naval warfare can be traced back even to classical times, but primarily in one of two forms: either as an historical record of wars, or in manuals of a prescriptive nature, in the tradition of Vegetius.[4] Christine de Pizan (c. 1364–1430) and the French admiral Jean V de Bueil (c. 1404–1477, the 'Scourge of the English'), in their treatment of naval matters (mainly concerning the construction of ships), did little but refer to Vegetius.[5] Tenth- and eleventh-century Byzantine writings on naval warfare – purportedly stemming from the pens of Emperor Leo VI the Wise, the Syrian Master and Nikephoros Ouranos – were equally technically-tactically oriented, and were known in Western Europe.[6]

From the sixteenth century onwards, however, we find books that emancipate themselves from a mere paraphrasing of Vegetius. In the sixteenth century, the Italians Lilio Gregorio Giraldi, Cristoforo Da Canal, Bartolommeo Crecentio (Bartolomeo Crescenzio) and Pantero Pantera, the Spaniards Martin Cortés, Alonso de Chaves, García de Toledo and Don Bernardino de Mendoza; the Frenchmen Antoine de Conflans, Lazare de Baïf and an anonymous Marseillais; and in Portugal, Father Fernando Oliveira tackled the subject, albeit with a heavy emphasis on practical issues, such as navigational mathematics, or preferred construction methods and shapes of galleys.[7]

It can generally be said that most of this literature dwelt more on practical and concrete choices rather than general principles of naval strategy. There are some notable exceptions, however, where we can find clear examples of generalised strategic thinking. The Venetian admiral Cristoforo Da Canal (1510–1562) with his plea for the setting up of a *Milizia Marittima* came the closest to treating parallels and differences between land warfare and naval war.[8] Fernando Oliveira (1507–after 1581) devoted an entire book to the subject of naval warfare which also included such strategic reflections, but was never translated into other languages.[9] Don Bernardino de Mendoza (1541-c. 1604), ambassador to the Court of St James (1578–1584), included quite extensive treatment of naval tactics in his *Theory and Practice of War*, as well a handful of strategic reflections, which we will deal with ahead.[10] England, too, produced some outstanding contributions. Indeed, as we shall see, most of the main options which navies present to the strategic decision maker were recognised and indeed applied by English practitioners-*cum*-thinkers even in the late sixteenth century.

This chapter focuses on the hitherto widely ignored yet very sophisticated articulations of naval strategy of the especially the late sixteenth century which belie the claims of Grenier and Castex. The Anglo-Spanish War of the late sixteenth century was the laboratory for experiments with the application of a series of naval strategies, several of them quite new, and for complex strategic reasoning, at any rate on the English side. These, in turn, were studied in detail by the key author who formed our thinking about naval and maritime strategy until this day, Sir Julian Corbett. A thumbnail sketch of Corbett's concepts will conclude the present chapter.

The Anglo-Spanish War

The Anglo-Spanish War of 1585–1604 was long in the making, as it was part of the larger religious strife that tore apart Christendom in the early modern period. In the mid-sixteenth century, the Catholic cause was symbolised by the alliance between Catholic Mary I Tudor of England and Philip II of Spain (both descendants from the formidable Catholic monarchs Isabel of Castile and Ferdinand of Aragon), until Mary's death in 1558. And yet these new *Reyes Catolicos* were at odds with Catholic France, which had temporarily turned its expansionist ambitions away from Italy and towards the Habsburg-owned Low Countries to its north, in a manifestation of feisty dynastic power-politics, adding another dimension to that of the religious-ideological conflict. Invading France from the Low Countries, Mary's then Catholic England and Philip's Spain jointly defeated France in the Battle of St Quentin in August 1557. Philip thought this victory so important that, in thanksgiving, he founded the gigantic, cold marble monastery of the Escorial near Madrid, which he would later use as his own residence. As an act of revenge, French forces under the command of the Catholic Francis Duke of Guise (uncle of Mary, Queen of Scots, herself a descendant of Henry VII Tudor and thus a future claimant of the English crown) seized Calais from England at the beginning of 1558, putting an end to the English monarchy's 500-year Continental empire.

As Enrique García Hernán has so ably demonstrated, the intermittent war between England and Spain in the following decades can be properly understood only if one takes into account England's interference in the anti-Spanish rebellion in the Low Countries, and Spanish involvement in the anti-English rebellion in Ireland. Each thus sponsored uprisings in the other's satellite state. Ever since Henry VIII had proclaimed himself 'king of Ireland' in 1541, the Tudors had aspired to control the entire island, even if effectively they controlled only a third, the area around Dublin known as 'the Pale'. Beyond the Pale, the local princes defending their standing and the Catholic elite were unhappy about Protestant Elizabeth Tudor's succession to her sister Mary's throne of England in 1558 and Elizabeth's claim to Ireland. They staged intermittent attacks on the English, which in turn were met with brutal repression, and scorched earth politics. Sir Humphrey Gilbert, who in the 1560s headed an army sent by Queen Elizabeth to subdue Ireland, was renowned for his cruelty: whenever he set foot in 'the enemies countrie, he killed manne, woman and child, and spoiled, wasted and burned, by the grounde, all that he might, leavying nothing of the enemies in saffetie, which he could possiblie waste or consume'. He lined the path to his headquarters with severed heads.[11]

Encouraged several times by Irish leaders to take control of Ireland, even to choose a new monarch for it, Philip II of Spain, foremost among the Catholic princes of Europe and nearer to Ireland than the Austrian Habsburgs, who had inherited the imperial crown, and above all commanded a strong fleet, first made plans for an invasion of both England and Ireland in 1571–1572. Many Irish would have welcomed the Spanish with open arms, and might have joined forces with them to attack England itself. The king's illegitimate half-brother, Don Juan of Austria, had led the Christian fleet that defeated the Turks at Lepanto on 7 October 1571, and a similar defeat now seemed to be in store for the English, as it became clear soon that Elizabeth sympathised with, and made money and then soldiers available to, the Dutch rebels. Pope Pius V went as far as making Elizabeth fair game for any regicides with his bull *Regnans in excelsis* of 1570 (a bull upheld by his successors), in which he excommunicated her, declaring her a heretic. This made it legitimate, from the Catholic Church's point of view, for any of her subjects to withdraw their obedience from her, and for any foreign monarch to go to war with her. To sever the link between Protestant Elizabeth and the Calvinist rebels in the Low Countries, Philip sought to harm England, either by direct invasion, or by stabbing it in the back through strengthening the anti-English forces in Ireland.[12]

Should they succeed in overthrowing Elizabeth, the Irish leaders wanted a marriage between Catholic Mary Stuart, Queen of Scots, and Don Juan, whom they might well have accepted as their king. Philip was not quite so keen to see his half-brother, who outshone him in looks, charm and charisma, become quite that powerful, but he, too, intermittently backed the plots of his scheming and active ambassador to the Court of St James, Don Bernardino de Mendoza, to replace Elizabeth with Mary Stuart. '*El rey prudente*', the prudent king, at least outwardly opted for a stand-off, calling off plans for an invasion, in 1573 concluding a commercial treaty with England instead. Yet by 1577, again encouraged by Irish Catholic leaders, Philip was back to planning an invasion of England, which he then put off again, in favour of another phase of secret plotting to overthrow or kill Elizabeth.

The death of the Portuguese sovereign in 1580 temporarily diverted Philip's attention from England, giving him the opportunity to seize this neighbouring kingdom, of which he had himself crowned king in 1581, and thus to control all of the Iberian Peninsula, including of course its entire Atlantic coast. Nevertheless, Philip continued to give indirect support to the Irish Catholics. From 1582, Pope Gregory XIII expressly urged Philip to invade England. Elizabeth's countermove was to conclude an alliance in late 1584 with several Protestant princes: King Henry of Navarre, Prince William of Orange (who would be assassinated later that year, a fate that was being wished by several sides also upon Elizabeth); the Count of the Palatinate; the French Huguenot leader, the Prince of Condé; and the Swiss Calvinist cantons. In this context of extreme Catholic-Protestant international tension, Elizabeth finally and reluctantly in early 1587 ordered the beheading of Mary, Queen of Scots – her own cousin, an anointed monarch – for her ceaseless and ill-concealed conspiracies to usurp her throne, backed by Spain. Elizabeth was all too aware that such action against another monarch (Mary was still the queen of a separate realm) could be seen as a precedent for such action against herself at a later time.

After this point, the gloves came off on both sides, as Philip's indirect approach, trying to overthrow Elizabeth, was definitively thwarted, and the queen in turn became more permissive of military enterprises against Spain. Regardless of whether this was a misperception, Philip's grand strategy was perceived by Queen Elizabeth's government as being 'by the means only of his Indies; not purposely to burn a town in France or England, but to conquer all France, all England, and Ireland', as even the prudent, war-weary Lord High Treasurer of Her Majesty, William Cecil, Lord Burghley, told Parliament in 1592. His opponent and head of the war faction, Robert Devereux, the second Earl of Essex, used starker images: war between Spain and England was not an ordinary quarrel to restore possessions unrightfully seized by an opponent, or to avenge particular injuries, which a mediator might settle. Instead, he wrote to the queen in 1596,

> you two are like 2 mightie Champions entred into the lists to fight for the two great general quarrels of Christendome, Religion and Libertie, hee forcing all to worship the beast, your Majesty standing for God and his truth, Hee affirming to an vniuersall Monarchy, your Majesty releeuing all the oppressed, and shewing that you are powerfull enough to make him feede within his tether.[13]

And in 1598 he told her Council that Philip's ambition was to 'establish . . . a *Spanish* universal monarchy'.[14] Thus the view from London was that this was a war for survival, at least for the queen and her supporters, and for Protestantism in Europe more generally.

England's strategic options

In Chapter 1 we have passed review on Spain's main strategic options, while merely touching on England's. What were the strategic options for Elizabeth in her confrontation with Philip II, apart from peace? The most defensive option can be traced to Henry VIII's strategy of studding the coasts of his lands with fortifications, such as Southsea Castle near Portsmouth, a forerunner of the nineteenth-century advocates of bricks-and-mortar defence. His daughter, Elizabeth, did not invest further in this option.

An arguably cheaper alternative was to shield England with a standing *fleet* closely hugging her coasts, as proposed by John Mountgomerie in 1570, but this second option – involving 40 ships – was apparently also dismissed as too costly by Queen Elizabeth.[15]

The Spanish sought to protect their own sea lines of communications through the Channel by seizing ports or other bases – the Spanish made several incursions on the coasts of Brittany, and repeatedly besieged and even seized Calais, which England had lost to France in 1558. England could help France drive out the Spanish from these bases.

Like the Spanish, the English had the option of the indirect approach of harming their adversary by supporting the rebellion against him – in the English case, supporting the Dutch against the Spanish. This they could do by deploying soldiers alongside the Dutch, or by paying or supplying them.

Another strategic option with a large land component was advocated two years after the Lisbon voyage by Antonio Pérez, a Spanish exile from Zaragoza in the kingdom of Aragon, which like Castile was now part of Philip II's patrimony. Unlike Portugal, Aragon boasted a movement to cast off Philip's rule. Pérez had antagonised the king, and had taken refuge in Zaragoza, where he found the protection of the high judge. Philip's forces marched into Zaragoza and executed the judge, while Pérez escaped, first to France, and thence to England. He advocated a military campaign from Southern France to free Aragon from Habsburg rule, an idea which was followed up by Henri IV of France, but the small French invasion aborted. Pérez then sought support for this project in England, without success: after all, Aragon, in the north-east of Spain, had no Atlantic sea frontier, and Zaragoza in any case was not a port. England could have given no direct support to such an endeavour with a navy, and an army would have had to cross all of France to get to the Pyrenees, and thence to Aragon, not a realistic option. In April 1596, Pérez may have resumed his lobbying for such an invasion.[16] This seems unlikely, however, as Pérez's interests mainly concerned the fate of Aragon.[17] Nothing in Pérez's correspondence with Essex, Burghley or indeed Henri IV of France around 1592–96 can be described as a strategic concept. Instead, there was much general waffle (in Spanish and Latin) about punishing Philip, serving the cause of justice, and about his admiration for England and France.[18]

Threatened by Spain with direct invasion, naval battle would have been difficult to avoid; the only alternative was to try to fend off an invading army on land, without being able to predict precisely where it would come ashore (and by sea, given favourable winds, a Spanish army could move faster than the land forces to counter it). Naval battle was also a strategy that England could – in principle – impose on the enemy, in his home waters. In that case England would have had the burden of keeping up long lines of communication, vulnerable to adverse winds. But how to draw Spanish ships out of their ports? Then, given a choice, did England really want a naval battle with Spain, or could Spain be weakened in ways more profitable and less destructive for England?

Imposing a 'blockade' – a term coined only in the following century – might be an answer, although it was logistically equally difficult. A blockade could also be used not to destroy Spanish ships but to intercept Spain's supplies of silver and gold from America. As Elizabeth's pirates had shown, Spain was constantly reinforced financially (and enabled to pay its soldiers, both Spanish and foreign mercenaries) through the periodic arrivals of treasure fleets from the West Indies and Americas. Many a naval captain in Plymouth was dreaming of intercepting such ships, with a letter of marque issued by the queen, in return for the commitment to share any booty with the crown. Many English naval exploits in these years thus aimed to waylay the treasure fleet on the dangerous high-seas voyage to America, leading to the not altogether misleading accusation on the part of the Spanish that the English were all pirates.[19] Intercepting the Spanish treasure fleet was most easily done around the Azores or Canaries, where it was bound to call for new provisions.

As ships could no more be found in the open seas than a needle in a haystack, this could be attempted only in three areas: at the source – that is where the Spanish convoys assembled the treasure and set out on their voyages from America (the 'Indies') to Spain; along the way, where the 'treasure fleet' had to stop at the Azores or Canaries to re-provision itself with water and victuals; or close to the destination harbours, mainly Cádiz, Lisbon and what the English called 'the Groyne' (A Coruña).

Any navy engaged in a blockade, however, would soon run out of provisions. Even the Spanish, when holding bases (temporarily in Brittany and Normandy and) in the Netherlands, did not opt for a blockade of the English coast to prevent the English from shipping troops and supplies to Brill and Flushing. How, then, could this be an option for England?

The answer suggested by the English monarchs' long history of Continental lordship was to establish bases on the adversary's shores (that would be supplied from the hinterland or surrounding region). The improvement of navigation made Englishmen bold – why not establish bases even on the Iberian Peninsula? Having lost Calais in 1555, England needed secure access to one or more new ports on the opposite coast to facilitate troop transport for this purpose, and supplies – hence the temporary dominion of Flushing and Brill conceded by the Dutch. Another option was to support rival claimants to the throne, or at least one of Philip's thrones – namely that of Portugal – relying on local support to rise up against him and end his rule.

An easier and less costly albeit indecisive option was that of harassing Iberian shipping and staging short attacks on Philip II's territorial possession – in short, what paradoxically at the time was known in England as the '*guerra di corsar*' (and what would later generally be referred to as *guerre de course*), precisely the sort of freebooter activity of which the Spanish accused the English! Sir Francis Drake's, Sir Walter Ralegh's and many other English sailors' enterprises and inclinations fall in this category.

As we shall see, all these options were tried, and all relied heavily on the navy; the majority relied on both navy and an army (what Julian Corbett would later call 'maritime' joint operations).

Spanish and English strategy in practice

As noted previously, by 1585 Spain was supporting an insurgency against Elizabeth's rule that broke out in Ireland. Throughout the entire Anglo-Spanish War, England also needed to make available forces to police Ireland, where the Fitzgeralds of Desmond (Munster) were staging an insurgency against English rule. At least, in the absence of any Irish navy or of a Spanish base in Ireland, English lines of communication across the Irish Channel were not threatened.

In the autumn of 1585, at the queen's command, one of her favourite pirate-captains, Sir Francis Drake, sailed off to the Caribbean, where he captured the Cape Verde islands belonging to Philip, and then attacked three other islands. He returned triumphant to England in the following summer. Arguably, he had succeeded in disrupting Spanish trade at the far end, although the booty he brought back scarcely paid for the entire expedition. One year later, he set off to do the opposite: to strike at the Spanish end of Philip's trade.

Economic pressures drove Elizabeth to see war as a means of securing revenue. She positively encouraged privateering – military enterprises by sea to capture booty to fill her empty coffers – by granting these naval enterprisers 'letters of marque', but would disavow any such potentially escalatory actions if her captains were caught. Typically, Elizabeth gave a string of contradictory orders before allowing Drake to set off on this voyage. Spain's most important harbour both for trade (mainly up the Guadalquivir River to Seville) and for men-o'-war was Cádiz. In 1587 Drake destroyed Spanish ships lying in its harbour, before repeating a similar raid on La Coruña, burning and plundering Spanish ships, bringing back £108,000 worth of booty. This campaign was boisterously referred to as his singeing the Spanish king's beard.

This strike against his ports clearly annoyed Philip no end, and indisputably contributed to his decision to take revenge, in 1588 sending his first armada to invade England. The Spanish fleet consisted of 140 ships in total that eventually set out from La Coruña with 8,000 sailors and 20,000 soldiers to invade England. It was famously defeated by the navy rustled up ad hoc by the English crown, and what was left of the armada was destroyed by storm and shipwreck en route home (the route chosen being that to the north around Scotland and then to the west around Ireland). While many Spanish survivors washed ashore in Ireland were killed by the locals, some 4,000 other survivors were welcomed and joined the Irish Catholic rebels.

In the following years, Philip was sufficiently diverted by his own campaigning in northern France and the Low Countries for him not to attempt any direct revenge campaign. England could thus follow the option of supporting allies on the Continent: English soldiers fought against the Spanish alongside the troops of Henri IV in Normandy, and alongside the Dutch in the Netherlands.

In 1589, in what might have been the most deadly of all the British strategies tried during this war, Sir Francis Drake and Sir John Norris with somewhere between 13,000 and 23,000 soldiers (who made up the majority) and sailors[20] set off to tear Philip's Iberian kingdom apart by overthrowing his rule in Portugal and putting a rival for the Portuguese crown, Dom Antonio, on the throne in Lisbon. Already in 1582, a French fleet had tried the same with another pretender, Dom Sebastian, and failed. For a number of reasons the English campaign also failed epically. Most crucially, the spontaneous uprising of the Portuguese, especially in and around the capital, Lisbon, which Dom Antonio had led the English to expect, failed to materialise. Other reasons included the paucity of artillery pieces taken along (only 8 of the 12 promised were delivered, it seems), and a great mortality that affected the soldiers. The reasons cited by eyewitnesses were that the English soldiers were not well enough provisioned with food and understaffed with surgeons, and showed extreme indiscipline: they gorged themselves on Portuguese wines in summer temperatures they were unused to. In short, this was an army that tried – and failed – to fight on a massive hangover.[21] The secondary campaign aim of trying to intercept the Spanish treasure fleet at the Azores (what one could call 'distant blockade') was not achieved either. (Map 4.1 shows the rough route of the Spanish treasure fleet and also the three ways in which Spanish forces moved to clash with English forces in Ireland, in the Channel, and in Flanders.)

The years 1590 and 1591 saw further naval campaigns aiming to intercept Spanish fleets at the Azores, one led by Sir John Hawkins and Sir Martin Frobisher, the other by Sir Walter Raleigh and Lord Thomas Howard. Together with Sir Francis Drake, Sir John Hawkins later pushed this option even further. Drake had participated in the Lisbon expedition of 1589, from where he had sought (and failed) to deviate some ships to the Azores. In 1595, Drake and Hawkins secured royal support for an even more daring venture, long proposed by Hawkins[22] – namely to intercept the treasure fleet at source, in the West Indies.

Meanwhile, a Spanish expeditionary force had attacked Brittany and Normandy, and held Rouen from 1590 to 1594. Henri secured his French crown only in 1593 as Henri IV after converting to Catholicism, while practising tolerance towards Protestants. Elizabeth sent English expeditionary forces to help Henri fight the Spanish, to Brittany 1591–1595, and to Normandy 1591–1593, one contingent being led by the Earl of Essex from 1591 to January 1592. But the alliance between Henri's and Elizabeth's forces was not untroubled; Henri used the presence of English troops in France to tie down Spanish forces there, while French forces took action against other enemy contingents elsewhere. Henri kept postponing the joint campaign to free Spanish-held Rouen in Normandy, which he had promised to

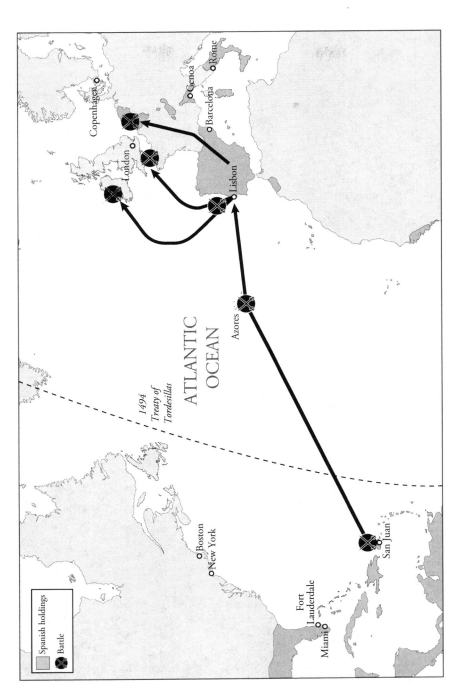

MAP 4.1 Atlantic and European routes of the Spanish navy and armies

Essex, and equally he did not honour his promise to pay some English troops.[23] Rouen was finally freed by Henri himself, not the English, in 1594.

At the same time, a rebellion was smouldering in Ireland under the Earl of Tyrone (Hugh O'Neill of Tír Eoghain), fully erupting again in 1594 (it was to continue until Elizabeth's death in 1603). In 1594 Philip once again authorised the dispatch of Spanish forces to Ireland in support of the rebels there. The situation was thus symmetrical: England helped anti-Spanish rebels in the Low Countries and backed the Protestants in France, while Philip backed the anti-English rebels in Ireland, and the Catholic, anti-Bourbon faction in France. From 1594, crushing Tyrone's Rebellion became England's priority second only to the direct defence of the English coast against a Spanish invasion. Even after Tyrone had agreed to a peace and to submission to England in 1603, Irish resentment of English over-lordship lived on and would become a major factor again in the War of the Three Kingdoms (1639–1651).

In 1595, the English helped Henri take back Calais temporarily from the Span-ish in the spring of 1595 (followed by Spain's attack on Cornwall). In the ensuing winter (1595/96), Drake, together with his cousin Hawkins, one of England's most adventurous naval entrepreneurs and earliest slavers, returned to the option of dis-rupting Spanish trade and intercepting the flow of American bullion at source. Their campaign took them to Panama and would have been successful, both militarily and in terms of the treasure they seized, had not the local climate and environment proved a more lethal enemy than the Spaniards: both leaders, and many of their soldiers and sailors, died of a locally contracted illness.[24]

The news of their death arrived in England at much the same time as the news that Calais had been recaptured by the Spanish. With the dynamic and enterprising Drake dead, the Earl of Essex now assumed the leadership of the 'war party' at court, but followed Drake's example of 1587 of setting out to hit Philip's main ports, while Henri IV of France was supposed to keep Philip occupied in the north.[25] Essex's plan had been not just to singe Philip's beard: it was to seize – *and hold* – the main ports of the Iberian Peninsula, Cádiz, but also Lisbon, according to the precedent of English monarchs' long-time possession of key French Atlantic and Channel ports. But after the successful capture of Cádiz and much booty, Essex's fellow command-ers overruled his plea to leave soldiers there (with himself as commandant). All the fellow commanders of Essex – the Lord High Admiral (Charles Lord Howard of Effingham, victor of the 1588 battle against the Spanish Armada), Lord Thomas Howard as his vice admiral and Sir Walter Ralegh – wanted to do was to return home with their booty as quickly as possible.[26]

After another Spanish invasion attempt had been foiled by adverse winds in the autumn of 1596, in the summer of 1597 Essex persuaded the queen to allow him to make a further – and as it turned out, last – attempt to attack the Iberian Pen-insula from the sea, to forestall the sailing of another Spanish Armada from Ferrol, where it was thought to be lying at anchor. Again, the queen insisted that Essex share command, this time only with Sir Walter Ralegh and Lord Thomas Howard. Ralegh wanted to repeat Drake's Caribbean campaigns in order to capture that year's Spanish treasure fleet, while the queen's instructions favoured Essex's plan. And yet the expedition ended up in the Azores in search of the Spanish merchantmen, whom they again failed to find. Luckily for England, as we have seen, the last Spanish attempt to invade England with a fleet in the autumn of 1597 was again frustrated by the unfavourable winds.

Philip II's death in the following year put an end to Spain's attempts to invade England directly, while Spanish support for the Irish rebellion continued. Under Philip's eponymous son and successor, a last attempt was made in 1601 to dispatch a fleet carrying soldiers to the south of Ireland, where the soldiers took part in the Battle of Kinsale, in which the Irish tried to put an end to English rule. Peace was made between the two countries only after the accession of Elizabeth's Scottish cousin James; no further attempt was made by either side to use a fleet for a direct attack on the other.

In the Anglo-Spanish War, what is interesting is not merely that a variety of strategic options involving navigation at great distances were identified and tested for the first time in human history but also that this set the pattern for many operations in the following centuries – repeated (unsuccessful) attempts to seize Spanish bullion fleets in the West Indies, or around the Azores or the Canaries, to blockade ports or to destroy Spanish fleets in Spanish harbours, and most ambitiously, to conquer and hold Iberian ports.[27]

The writers on strategy

As a whole series of long-range naval options were experimented with by the English for the very first time in history, there is plenty of evidence of lively debates about strategy in England at the time of the Anglo-Spanish War. One strategic option defended by some during the war was purely defensive. We find it summed up (only to be dismissed) by Matthew Sutcliffe (c. 1550-1629; see also Chapter 5), who attributed this position to a faction whom he described as the rich and well-established. These, he claimed, argued that

> wee have neither towne, nor port in Spaine to receive us: that the way thither is long, and uncertaine by reason of contrarietie of windes, and that it will be hard to remedie anie disorder that shall fall out in our army by reason of the distance of the place: they alleadge further that we have no friendes nor confederates in the countrey: and that it will be more difficult to subdoue the Spaniard in his countrey, then abroad, for every man doeth fight most valiantly when his wife and children, and his owne landes and goodes are in his fight. Lastly, they suppose that the number of the enemies will be such, as that an armie shall bee wearied with killing them. On the other side, if wee attend the Spaniardes comming hither (say they) they shall have all these things to mak against them; and wee all things favorable for us men, munitions, and victuals sufficient; our wives, children, and country in our sight, safe places to retreat unto.[28]

The other options for England were offensive. Even before the Anglo-Spanish rivalry turned fully violent, by a plan dated 12 August 1579, Sir John Hawkins, as treasurer of Queen Elizabeth's small navy, had begun to propagate a scheme for fighting Spain in her West Indian colonies to intercept their treasure fleet. He argued, 'There is to be stricken with this company' – referring to the fleet which he tried to persuade Queen Elizabeth to make available for this expedition – 'all the towns upon the coast of the Indies, and there need not be suffered one ship, bark, frigate or galley to survive untaken.' His biographer noted that Hawkins had had this idea long before Sir Francis Drake, whose last expedition and death at sea he shared. In 1579, the queen denied Hawkins the means to put his plan into practice.[29] Nevertheless, the chase after the Spanish treasure fleet was at the centre of his plans, which he once again pursued in 1587/1588. Alternatively to doing so in the West Indies at source, he argued that a mix of larger and smaller English ships might impose a distant blockade on the Spanish coast, there to intercept the Spanish treasure fleet.[30]

Hawkins's colleague Drake was a man of action rather than of the pen. Yet in one of the rare documents we have illustrating Drake's thinking we find that he strongly advocated a preventive strike against Spain, rather than waiting for a Spanish fleet to arrive in England's home waters: on 30 March 1588 – rumours of the impending Spanish campaign were rife – he wrote to the Queen's Council that for the expected invasion of England, Philip II probably intended to use troops currently deployed in the Netherlands under Alexander Farnese's, the Duke of Parma's, command. To transport them across the Channel, Philip presumably needed to bring a fleet north from Spain.[31]

> But if there maye be suche a staye or stoppe made, by any meanes, of this Fleete in Spaigne, that they maye not come throughe the seas, as conquerors (which I assure my selfe, they thincke to doe) then shall the prince of Parma have such a checke thereby, as were meett. . . .

To prevent a Spanish fleet from joining Parma,

> I thinke it goode, that theise forces here, should be made as stronge, as to your Honours' wisdoms shalbe thought convenyentt, and that for two special causes: Firste, for that they are like, to strike the firste blowe, and secondlie, it will putt great and goode hartes, into her Majesties loving subiects, bothe abroade and at home; For that they wilbe perswaded in conscience, that the Lorde of all strengthes, will putt into her Majestie, and her people, coraige, and boldness, not to feare any invasyon in her owne Countrie, but to seeke Gods enemyes and her Majesties, where they maye be founde: For the Lorde is one our side, whereby we maye assure our selves, our nombers are greater than theirs.

And he concluded, addressing the Council,

> I most humblie beseech your good Lordships to persever, as you have began, for that with feiftie saile of shippinge we shall doe more good upon their Coaste, then a great manye more, will doe here at home, and the sooner we are gone, the better we shalbe able to ympeach them.[32]

As we know, Drake's recommendation provided the rationale for England's 1589 campaign against Philip.

In chronological order, the next known paper on the subject is a 'Discourse . . . [on] the Voyage to Spaine and Portugall, 1589', by an author identified as 'Antonie Winkfield'. In the text itself, we encounter a 'Captain Antony Wingfield', written about, puzzlingly (given the presumed authorship) in the third person. An Ant[h]ony Wingfield,[33] born c. 1552 and deceased in or after 1611, nephew of Elizabeth, Countess of Shrewsbury (Bess of Hardwick), was first a pensioner, and then a scholar at Trinity College, Cambridge, and in the 1570s served as a Greek reader to Queen Elizabeth. He took leave of absence several times from his university post, first to go on diplomatic missions to Denmark and probably France, and again in 1589.[34] If he was indeed the author in question this would put him among the adventurers who embarked on the Lisbon campaign of which he gave an account.[35]

The account ends with a discussion as to whether, on balance, it would have been better to stick to the France-*cum*-Flanders campaign.[36] The author stressed 'what intollerable expenses' the prosecution of the land campaign in the Low Countries and north-western France required. English efforts in the Netherlands would not stop Philip from attacking England. By contrast, his energies might be deflected by an invasion of Spain, which had so many bays facilitating a landing.

> And having an armie of 20,000 royally furnished there, we shall not need to take much care for their payment: for shal not Lisbon be thought able to make so few men rich, when the Suburbs thereof were found so abounding in riches, as had we made enemie of them, they had largely enriched us all? . . . Or is not the spoyle of Sivil [Seville] sufficient to pay more then shall bee needful to bee sent against it . . .? And be there not many other places of lesse difficultie to spoyle, able to satisfie our forces?

If capturing Lisbon and Seville should prove too difficult, Wingfield identified extremely advantageous secondary effects of a naval campaign along the Iberian coast. Surprise attacks on the Spanish ports should force the Spanish to redeploy at least some of their soldiers from the Low Countries back to Spain for homeland defence. Wingfield rightly argued that that in itself would constitute a great success for England, as the same effect could be achieved in the Low Countries themselves only through the deployment of far more English soldiers, and even then, not with the same reduction of Spanish effectiveness. Even just running up and down the enemy's coast, in what would later be called a 'distant blockade', Wingfield thought an English fleet could intercept the Spanish treasure fleet, starve Lisbon and hunt down the Spanish royal navy. Even in the worst case scenario, in which England were able neither to secure a base nor to 'damnifie' the Spanish king at sea, she could tie him down in defence of his homeland. While the English had been very frightened when the Spanish invasion threatened, 'I wish that all England knew what terror we gave to the same people that frighten us, by visiting them at their owne houses.'[37] This is almost an early version of the 'fleet in being' argument that would be fully developed only at the end of the seventeenth century.[38]

In order to finance such a fleet, but especially the expeditionary force to go with it, Wingfield pleaded for the imposition of a special tax that would include the clergy. He lamented the 'idolatry to Neptune' and the decline in the respect for soldiers in England, as demonstrated by the inadequate preparations and strategy of the campaign he had just witnessed, which he thought could easily have achieved the capture of Lisbon: 'in this short time of our Adventure', which took less than two months in all,

> we have won a towne by escalade, battred & assaulted another, overthrown a mightie princes power in the field, landed our armie in 3 several places of his kingdom, marched 7 dayes in the heart of his country, lien three nights in the suburbs of his principall citie [i.e. Lisbon], beaten his forces into the gates thereof, and possessed two of his frontier Forts.[39]

The reasons he saw for the failure of the Lisbon voyage were the misguided strategic aim of bringing Dom Antonio to the throne through an insurgency which failed to materialise; the related decision to avoid living off the land, which made the English forces particularly vulnerable to the late arrival of the provisioning fleet which followed them to Lisbon; the inadequate provisions for the sick; and lack of discipline among the soldiers, which, as we have seen, led to excessive alcohol consumption. While on balance, it would seem that Wingfield underestimated the problems of securing the supply of English forces on the Spanish coast from England (the wind was a complete imponderable in all of this, and storms were a or even the major factor on which success or failure of operations depended in the 1580s and 1590s), Wingfield's argument deserved to be taken seriously. And this was done by Richard Hakluyt, who edited this account and had it printed within weeks of it being written.

Interestingly, Wingfield's account suggests that there were two factions, one devoted to the 'idolatry of Neptune' which pleaded for naval operations only, and another, which Corbett might later have called the 'maritime joint operations faction', as its members saw the navy as an instrument to take armies to the enemy's land to operate there.[40]

Sir Walter Ralegh retrospectively claimed to have advocated a more forceful and committed invasion of Spain rather than doing 'all by halves', of which he accused Queen Elizabeth.[41] In reality, as we shall see, he was a member of the faction whom Wingfield accused of the 'idolatrie of Neptune' – that is the naval faction who failed to recognise the importance of joint operations with the emphasis on what the army might do with the help of the navy. Thus for example he opposed Essex's strategy to seize *and hold* Cádiz in 1596 (see Chapter 5).

At the time, the queen's chief minister who had the function of secretary of state was Sir Robert Cecil, normally known for his reluctance to engage in war and for having countered many projects that seemed too risky to him. One of these was probably presented to him in the early 1590s — we do not know by whom. It was called 'A Project How to Make War upon Spain, Written in the Queen's Time, Presented to Sir Robert Cecil, by Her Majesty's Appointment', which proposed the following:

> First, and principally, we must keep employed two main fleets upon the coast of Spain eight months in the year, that is from March to November. Every fleet to consist of·forty-five ships to be divided into three squadrons; one to lie off the Rock [Cape Roca] to intercept all traders of Lisbon; the second at the South Cape [St Vincent], to stop all intercourse to San Lucar and Cadiz, and to and from the Indies; the third to the islands [Canaries], lest they should there stop and put their goods ashore, having intelligence of our being upon the coast of Spain . . . Perhaps the number of these ships will exceed the proportion her majesty is willing to employ. But if Holland will be drawn from the trade of Spain and join with us the number may be easily raised by them and our maritime towns in England, so that her Majesty need but employ six ships of her own in each fleet, to serve for the Admiral and Vice-Admiral of every squadron.[42]

While this option was apparently dismissed by Cecil as too costly, the need for alternative measures was apparent.

The most comprehensive strategic concept was put forward by the clergyman Matthew Sutcliffe in 1593 (see Chapter 5). Sutcliffe derived his strategic prescriptions for the war with Spain from first principles. He explained for example

> that it is farre better for the English nation, things standing as now they do, to inuade the Spaniard, or any other enemy in his owne country, than to receiue their assault, and inuasion here at home, or to stay untill we do see the enemy on our owne coast.

He dismissed the argument that the English should, out of a peaceful and defensive inclination, await another Spanish attack at home, where the English would have favourable conditions (see earlier). Instead he argued in favour of pre-emption, because 'He that first chargeth his enemie, hath many aduantages' as long as he is well provisioned and equipped with men and materiel. If the Spanish were to invade England, the English would not know 'where the enemie will land, all the coast must be furnished with souldiers.' This would require more men than an invasion of Spain, and it would be a great financial burden to keep them provisioned during all this time of waiting and uncertainty, while they would be removed from the workforce, as they could not be concentrated in time given the likely late intelligence of where the Spanish would choose to land. Moreover, English towns were no longer well enough walled to be able to fend off an invading force, once it set foot on English soil.[43] Therefore Sutcliffe extolled the importance of the navy, 'and diuers pointes to be considered of those that command at sea'.[44]

In the same spirit, the Earl of Essex in the 1590s tried to coax his sovereign lady into supporting his ambitious schemes for beating Europe's dominating power, Spain, through the use of sea power. He explained his position: ceaseless Spanish actions against England made it impossible to sit still and wait for Spain to launch its next attack at home or in Ireland.[45] Therefore, Essex pleaded for 'An offensive war at sea' which would be, to Philip,

> more annoyance because we shall not only impeach and interrupt his trafique with all other countryes of Christendom whereby we shall impoverish his merchants butt stop and divert his golden Indian streames whereby we shall cut his life vaynes and let out the vital spirites of his estate.[46]

This was to be achieved by seizing and permanently holding Philip's main ports – Cádiz, Lisbon and if possible also Ferrol and A Coruña.[47]

The alternative strategy, to seek to intercept the Spanish treasure fleet each time without a fixed territorial base to operate from (his fellow commander Sir Walter Ralegh's preference not only on the 1596 and 1597 campaigns but also throughout his freebooter career), was really 'fitter enterprise for some decayd private man then for a state, for yt savors of guerra di corsar'.[48] Essex thus proposed and defended a strategy formulatd on the basis of general principles of naval warfare, developing a more extensive notion than ever entertained before of what it meant to rule the ocean (see Chapter 6). It was presented as a distinct strategic option, the alternative to the *guerra di corsar* or commerce raiding,[49] then so popular among English naval enterprisers.

The writings cited earlier testify to the fact that Elizabethan England produced a revolutionary change in the thinking and arguing about the use of navies and the oceans, a change that went hand in hand with military naval operations on an unprecedented geographic scale, albeit carried out with what were still very small vessels and tiny fleets. The revolutionary change in thinking is reflected in the transition from mere ambitions to 'safeguard the sea' around the British Isles from invasion to active use of the seas – 'command of the ocean' well away from Britain.[50] We should not be too surprised at the trial-and-error nature of English strategy making in the Anglo-Spanish War: several of the strategic options, implying actions at such distances from home, were unprecedented and explored for the first time ever. Several strategic ideas were way ahead of the material ability to execute and sustain them. Nevertheless, we have here clear evidence of original and quite daring strategic thinking not only on the part of the Queen's Council and the queen herself but also on the part of a number of strategists and practitioners.

Later writing on naval warfare

Some of these thinkers and practitioners were still active under Queen Elizabeth's heir, King James I of England (and VI of Scotland). This, for example, was the period when Sir Walter Ralegh wrote his history of the world with its original strong naval interpretation of inter-polity relations.[51] From the mid-seventeenth century, however, writing on naval matters reverted to a concentration on technical and at best tactical matters, and curiously, as Britannia was ascending as a European and a colonial power, the British for two centuries seem to have lost their interest in any theoretical treatment of the subject that had any political dimension. This is true also for other European writers, who discussed the duties of naval officers, the problems of victualling of ships, 'The ordering of fleets in sailing, chases, boardings and sea-fights', orders of naval battle (now generally conducted in linear formations) and the construction of ships, rigging and manoeuvre. They showed little if any interest in the political ends of naval warfare and tended to think exclusively on a tactical level.[52]

We recall that Jacques Raymond Vicomte de Grenier wrote scathingly about previous authors on naval warfare, as they had, he claimed, written about little other than battles, not to grander aspects of naval warfare. In the view of his contemporary Audibert Ramatuelle, however, Grenier did not do much else himself. Ramatuelle in turn barely touched on greater political contexts in which navies might be used militarily: he stressed the need to protect French colonies against the objections of those who wanted to see the French navy focus on homeland defence.[53]

It was only in the late nineteenth century, commencing with the lectures of Vice Admiral Philip Howard Colomb, that political-strategic dimensions once again entered writing on naval warfare. Admiral Colomb paid particular attention to the concept of 'command of the sea', on which he elaborated extensively, elevating it to one of the main aims to be aspired to by naval strategy.[54] The term now experienced its second renaissance after that of the sixteenth century: soon it was gushing out of the pens of authors on both sides of the Atlantic.[55]

Writing on naval strategy took off with the works of Alfred Thayer Mahan, who sought his early inspiration in the English maritime campaigns especially of the late seventeenth, eighteenth and early nineteenth centuries.[56] His main competitor for the honour of having defined modern strategic concepts as they are with us still today was Julian Stafford Corbett (1854–1922). As he had private means, he could afford to abandon his employment as barrister, travel and try his hand at fiction writing. While researching the historical background – documents found in the British government archives – for a historical novel set in the late sixteenth century that he was writing, he became thoroughly fascinated by the exploits and writings of Sir Francis Drake and his successors.[57]

It is little wonder, then, that his great work of 1911, *Some Principles of Maritime Strategy*, by which he meant 'the principles which govern a war in which the sea is a substantial factor', should have been hugely influenced by the events and writings discussed earlier. With a particular focus on the naval element of maritime warfare, he wrote, 'The object of naval warfare must always be directly or indirectly either to secure the command of the sea or to prevent the enemy from securing it.'[58] The sea, Corbett argued, has the positive value of being a 'means of communication', but also a 'negative value' of being a barrier.

> By winning command of the sea we . . . [place] ourselves in position to exert direct military pressure upon the national life of our enemy ashore, while at the same time we solidify it against him and prevent his exerting direct military pressure upon ourselves.
>
> Command of the sea, therefore, means nothing but the control of maritime communications, whether for commercial or military purposes. The object of naval warfare is the control of communications, and not, as inland warfare, the control of territory.[59]

When Mahan and Corbett wrote, commerce raiding or the *guerre de course* was no longer an acceptable form of warfare. The Paris Declaration respecting Maritime Law of 1856 outlawed privateering and the retention of goods on neutral vessels (except if they were contraband, being supplied to the enemy). While economic warfare was very much an element of maritime strategy, privateering – and private gains arising from the interception of enemy vessels – was henceforth no longer as an acceptable form of naval warfare. Corbett therefore paid attention only to 'commerce prevention' by means of blockade rather than the enrichment of one's own economy by seizing the enemy's, so important a factor in Elizabethan warfare. Corbett defended blockades by arguing that wars have to be waged in such a way as to 'exert pressure on the citizens and their collective life' so as to bring them to an end.[60] Corbett differentiated between 'close' blockade – to keep the enemy ships in their port – and 'open' blockade – at a distance, more akin to economic blockade.[61] Corbett approved of the idea of 'seeking out' the enemy because of 'firstly, the moral value of seizing the initiative, and secondly, the importance of striking before the enemy's mobilization is complete'.[62]

Corbett dwelt also on how to secure command of the sea:

1. Methods of securing command:
   - (a) By obtaining a decision.
   - (b) By blockade.
2. Methods of disputing command:
   - (a) Principle of 'the fleet in being'.
   - (b) Minor counter-attacks.
3. Methods of exercising command:
   - (a) Defence against invasion.
   - (b) Attack and defence of commerce.
   - (c) Attack, defence, and support of military expeditions.[63]

All of this, with the exception of the late seventeenth-century concept of the 'fleet in being',[64] would have made perfect sense to Sutcliffe, Wingfield, Essex and even the Spanish strategists in Philip II's entourage.

Epilogue

One can look at these striking similarities between Corbett's concepts and the sixteenth-century English theory and practice of naval strategy in two ways. One is to note that Corbett deliberately couched his prescriptions for the early twentieth century in terms of conservative continuity with a traditional English/British way of war in order to counter divergent arguments from a very technically minded audience.[65] Corbett's approach and conceptualisation of maritime warfare were not unhelpfully conservative in themselves; in fact, there is general agreement that his ideas have weathered the changes of the last 100 years better than Mahan's.

The other way of looking at the remarkable parallels between arguments of English Renaissance naval thinkers and Corbett's writings is to doff one's cap to the prescience and modernity of the arguments of the former, even when in their own times, the technical limitations with which they had to contend made it impossible for England to defeat Spain in any of the ways proposed; all Elizabeth's naval and military commanders achieved – admittedly against a much more powerful adversary – was a defensive stand-off. One must admire the English authors discussed earlier for their innovative thinking, which they boldly attempted to put into practice at the risk of their lives, and the succinct and clear way they put their case and formulated their options – something strategists today would do well to imitate.

Several questions for further research arise from this. One is what concepts Spanish, Portuguese and Italian writers of the late sixteenth century brought to naval and maritime strategy. Another is why, at first viewing, the published literature on naval warfare that was written in the following century seems so lacking in strategic reflection, when clearly naval warfare became ever more important and in the histories of some countries, notably the British Isles, the Netherlands, Spain and also France, took centre stage. In any case, as we have demonstrated, it is clearly not true that there was an 'almost complete void' in writing about strategy before the French Revolution. And one suspects that many such treasures yet remain to be dug up in historical archives.

Notes

1 Jacques Raymond, vicomte de Grenier: *L'Art de Guerre sur Mer, ou Tactique navale, assujettie à de nouveaux principes et à un nouvel ordre de bataille* (Paris: Fermin Didot, 1787).
2 Amiral Raoul Castex: *Théories stratégiques*, Vol. 1 (2nd edn, Paris: SEGMC, 1937), pp. 31, and see also 37–39.
3 Beatrice Heuser: *The Evolution of Strategy* (Cambridge: Cambridge University Press, 2010), p. 208.
4 Chapter 19 of his *Tactica* deals with the *naumachia* or *de navalis proelio*.
5 Philippe Richardot: 'Y a-t-il une pensée navale dans l'Occident médiéval?', in Hervé Coutau-Bégarie (ed.): *Evolution de la Pensée navale*, Vol. 7 (Paris: Economica, 1999), pp. 13–23.
6 Alphonse Dain: *Naumachia* (Paris: Les Belles Lettres, 1943).
7 Hervé Coutau-Bégarie: 'L'émergence d'une Pensée navale en Europe au XVIe Siècle et au Début du XVIIe Siècle', in Hervé Coutau-Bégarie (ed.): *Evolution de la Pensée navale*, Vol. 4 (Paris: Economica, 1994), pp. 13–35; see also Philip Williams: 'The Strategy of Galley Warfare in the Mediterranean (1560–1630)', in Enrique García Hernán &

Davide Maffi (eds): *Guerra y Sociedad en la Monarquía Hispánica: Política, Estrategia y Cultura en la Europa Moderna (1500–1700), vol. I: Política, estrategia, organization y guerre en el mar* (Madrid: Ediciones del Laberinto, 2006), pp. 891–920; Enrique García Hernan: 'Tratadística militar', in Luis Robot (ed.): *Historia Militar de España III Edad Moderna* Part II *Escenario europeo* (Madrid: Ministerio de Defensa 2013), pp. 401–419.

8   Jean Pagès: 'Un traité de tactique navale du XVIe Siècle: le Libre III *Della Milizia Marittima* de Cristoforo da Canal', in Hervé Coutau-Bégarie (ed.): *Evolution de la Pensée navale*, Vol. 4 (Paris: Economica, 1994), pp. 37–64.

9   P.ᵉ Fernando Oliveira: *Arte da guerra do mar novamente escrita* (Coimbra: s.e., 1555, repr. in facsimile Lisbon: Edições 79, 2008).

10 Don Bernardino de Mendoza: *Teórica y práctica de la guerra* (Madrid: Pedro Madrigal, 1595); new impression (Madrid: Ministerio de Defensa, 1998), trans. into English: *Theorique and practise of warre*, trans. By Sir Edwarde Hoby (Middelburg: Richard Schilders, 1597).

11 Geoffrey Parker: 'Early Modern Europe', in Michael Howard, George J. Andreopoulos & Mark R. Shulman (eds): *The Laws of War: Constraints on Warfare in the Western World* (New Haven: Yale University Press, 1994), p. 56.

12 Enrique García Hernán: 'Planes militares de Felipe II para conquistar Irlanda, 1569–1578', in Enrique García Hernán, Miguel Ángel de Bunes, Óscar Recio Morales & Bernardo J. García García (eds): *Irlanda y la Monarquía hispánica: Kinsale 1601–2001: Guerra, Política, Exilio y Religión* (Madrid: Universidad de Alcalá, CSIS, 2002), pp. 185–204.

13 The 'Hulton MS', copy of a letter by Essex, written aboard the Dewrepulse [sic], 12 Aug [1596], BL Microfilm 2275, Fol. 149–152.

14 John Strype: *Annals of the Reformation*, Vol. 4 (originally 1735, repr. Oxford: Clarendon Press, 1824), p. 151; Reasons pro and con being a debate at the Council Table between the treasurer and the general for making peace or carrying on the war in the reign of Queen Elizabeth, wherein the force of the general's argument prevailed against the sophistry of the treasurer's (London: S. Popping, 1712), p. 8.

15 I am very grateful to Benjamin Redding for this reference to and his transcription of BL Add MS 18035, see id.: 'Divided by *La Manche*: Naval Enterprise and Maritime Revolution in England and France, 1545–1642' (MS PhD University of Warwick, 2016).

16 M. Oppenheim (ed.): *The Naval Tracts of Sir William Monson*, Vol. 1 (London: The Navy Records Society, 1902), p. 363.

17 Gustav Ungerer (ed.): *A Spaniard in Elizabethan England: The Correspondez on Antonio Pérez's Exile*, Vol. 1 (London: Thamesis Books, 1974), pp. 7f., 303–316.

18 Ibid., see correspondence especially for 1592 and 1596.

19 David Childs: *Pirate Nation: Elizabeth I and Her Royal Sea Rovers* (Barnsley: Seaforth, 2014).

20 'A True Discourse (as is thought) by Colonel Antonie Wingfield emploied in the voiage to Spaine and Portugall, 1589 . . .' in Richard Hakluyt: *The Principal Navigations, Voyages, Traffiques of Discoveries of the English Nation*, Vol. 6 (1589, repr. New York: Augustus M. Kelley, 1969), p. 314 gives 13,000; Wallace T. MacCaffrey: *Elizabeth I: War and Politics, 1588–1603* (Princeton: Princeton University Press, 1992), p. 88, gives the figure of 23,000.

21 'A True Discourse (as is thought) by Colonel Antonie Wingfield', p. 308f.

22 MacCaffrey: *Elizabeth I*, p. 82f.

23 Robert Lacey: *Robert Earl of Essex: An Elizabethan Icarus* (London: Weidenfeld & Nicolson, 1971), pp. 82–90.

24 James A. Williamson: *Sir John Hawkins, the Time and the Man* (Oxford: Clarendon Press, 1927), pp. 471–490.

25 Ungerer (ed.): *A Spaniard in Elizabethan England*, pp. 303–316.

26 Julian S. Corbett: *The Successors of Drake* (London: Longmans, Green, 1900), pp. 89–133.

27 For many such examples, see Paul M. Kennedy: *The Rise and Fall of British Naval Mastery* (1976, Amherst, NY: Humanity Books, 1983²); N.A.M. Rodger: *The Command of the Ocean: A Naval History of Britain, 1649–1815* (orig. 2004; London: Penguin, 2005).

28 Matthew Sutcliffe: *The Practice, Proceedings and Lawes of Armes* (London: Deputies of C. Barker, 1593), p. 96.

29 'A provision for the Indies fleet, drawn by Mr Hawkins, Admiralty', of 12 August 1579, see Williamson: *Sir John Hawkins, the Time and the Man*, p. 397.

30 Ibid., pp. 396–398.

31 Harry Kelsey: *Sir Francis Drake: The Queen's Pirate* (New Haven, CT: Yale University Press, 1998, repr. 2000), p. 302.

32 Ibid., pp. 312–315.

33 There were two eponymous cousins, however, one who died in 1605 and was the son and heir of a Sir Robert Wingfield, or a further eponymous cousin (dates of birth and death unknown), son of Sir Antony Wingfield (before 1488, d. 1552); see William Hervy: *The Visitation of Suffolk 1561*, Part II, transcribed by Joan Corder, *The Publications of the Harleian Society*, New Series, Vol. 3 (London: Harleian Society 1984), pp. 213, 219f.

34 Edward A. Malone: 'Wingfield, Anthony (*b. c.* 1552, *d.* in or after 1611)', in: *Oxford Dictionary of National Biography* (Oxford: Oxford University Press, 2004) [www.oxforddnb.com.idpproxy.reading.ac.uk/view/article/29734, accessed 17 Nov 2014].

35 'A True Discourse (as is thought) by Colonel Antonie Wingfield', pp. 517–526.

36 Ibid., pp. 517–526.

37 Ibid., pp. 520–522, 524.

38 See Heuser: *The Evolution of Strategy*, pp. 212f, 231.

39 'A True Discourse (as is thought) by Colonel Antonie Wingfield', p. 471.

40 Ibid., pp. 520–522, 524.

41 Quoted in Corbett: *The Successors* of *Drake*, p. 1.

42 David Loades: *England's Maritime Empire: Seapower, Commerce and Policy, 1490–1690* (Harlow: Longman 2000), p. 131.

43 Sutcliffe: *The Practice*, pp. 96f., 100.

44 Ibid., pp. 273–275.

45 The 'Hulton MS', formerly BL Loan 23(1), now Add.MSS 74286, Microfilm 2275, Fol. 157ᵛ–158ʳ.

46 Hulton MS, Fol. 163ᵛ.

47 Robert Devereux, 2nd Earl of Essex: *An Apologie of the Earle of Essex* (written 1598; printed London?, 1600), p. B1ᵛ.

48 Hulton MS, Fol. 165ʳ.

49 Or *guerre de course*, as it would be termed by later authors writing in English, with the sneering implication that it was an un-English, lily-livered French thing to do, when in fact it had been the preferred strategy in most sixteenth-century English naval operations.

50 As reflected in the titles of the two superb volumes on the subject by N.A.M. Rodger: *The Safeguard of the Sea: A Naval History of Britain, 660–1649* (originally 1997, London: Penguin, 2004); id.: *The Command of the Ocean: A Naval History of Britain, 1649–1815* (originally 2004, London: Penguin, 2005).

51 Sir Walter Raleigh: *The History of the World* (London: Walter Burre, 1614).

52 Nathaniel Boteler: *Six Dialogues about Sea-Services* (London: William Fisher & Richard Mount, 1688); Paul Hoste S.J.: *L'art des armées navales, ou Traité des Evolutions navales* (Lyon: Anisson & Posuel, 1697); id.: *Théorie de la Construction des Vaissaux* (Lyon: Anisson & Posuel, 1697); Michel Depeyre: 'Le père Paul Hoste, fondateur de la pensée navale moderne', in Hervé Coutau-Bégarie (ed.): *L'Evolution de la Pensée navale*, Vol. 1 (Paris: Economica, 1990), pp. 57–77; Sébastien-François, vicomte Bigot de Morogues: *Tactique navale, ou Traité des évolutions des signaux* (Paris: H.-L. Guérin & L.-F. de la Tour, 1763); John Clerk of Eldin, the Elder: *An Essay on Naval Tactics, Systematical and Historical* (London: T. Cadell, 1790); Michel Depeyre: *Tactique et Stratégies navales de la France et du Royaume-Uni de 1690 à 1815* (Paris: Economica, 1998), pp. 115–124, 195–205, 230–243; Bruno & Jean-Pierre Colson: 'Les Penseurs navals hollandais', in Hervé Coutau-Bégarie (ed.): *L'Evolution de la Pensée navale*, Vol. 4 (Paris: Economica, 1994), pp. 173–180.

53 Audibert Ramatuelle: *Cours élémentaire de Tactique navale* (Paris: Baudouin, Year X/1802), p. xii. On Ramatuelle, see Michel Depeyre: 'Audibert Ramatuelle ou des Enseignements perdus', in Hervé Coutau-Bégarie (ed.): *L'Evolution de la Pensée navale*, Vol. 1 (Paris: Fondation pour les Etudes de Défense nationale, 1990), pp. 79–88.

54 Philip Howard Colomb: *Naval Warfare: Its Ruling Principles and Practice Historically Treated* (London: W.H. Allen, 1891), pp. 25–70, 107–202.

55 Henry Spencer Wilkinson: *Command of the Sea and Brain of the Navy* (Westminster, London: Archibald Constable, 1894); C.E. Callwell: *Military Operations and Maritime Preponderance: Their Relations and Interdepenence* (originally Edinburgh: Wm Blackwood, 1905, repr. Annapolis, MD: Naval Institute Press, 1996), pp. 1ff., 170; Sir Cyprian Arthur George Bridge: *Art of Naval Warfare* (London: Smith, Elder, 1907), Chapter V (pp. 123ff.); Sir Julian Corbett: *Some Principles of Maritime Strategy* (1911, repr. Annapolis, MD: US Naval Institute Press, 1988), pp. 91–106.

56 See particularly Alfred Thayer Mahan: *The Influence of Sea Power upon History, 1660–1783* (Boston: Little, Brown, 1890); id.: *Sea Power in Its Relations to the War of 1812*, 2 vols. (Boston: Little, Brown, 1905).

57 Julian S. Corbett: *For God and Gold* (London: Macmillan, 1887); id.: *Sir Francis Drake* (London: Macmillan, 1890); id.: *Papers Relating to the Navy during the Spanish War 1585–1587* (London: Macmillan, 1898); id.: *Drake and the Tudor Navy* (London: Longmans, 1898); id.: *The Successors of Drake* (London: Longmans & Green, 1900).

58 Corbett: *Some Principles of Maritime Strategy*, pp. 91–106.

59 Ibid., p. 94.

60 Ibid., p. 97f.

61 Ibid., pp. 183–185.

62 Ibid., p. 174.

63 Ibid., p. 165f.

64 Ibid., p. 220f.

65 I am grateful to Professor Andrew Lambert for drawing my attention to this point.

5

A NATIONAL SECURITY STRATEGY FOR ENGLAND

Matthew Sutcliffe, the Earl of Essex and the Cádiz Expedition of 1596

A single-author comprehensive strategic concept applied in practice

While manuals on the art of war go back to antiquity, they rarely contain reflections on politics or make contributions to thinking about the political purposes of warfare, and thus of strategy.[1] There is at best a handful of comprehensive works on strategic theory before the nineteenth century. We do find occasional manuscripts surviving in which individuals inside state apparatuses – usually military officers – put forward strategic concepts for the next war.[2] But it is generally only from the eve of the First World War onwards that books provide an overall analysis of international configurations, including the danger of war affecting their own country and developing a grand strategy concerning everything from what sort of army to choose and how to recruit and finance it to where to deploy it and with what military aims, for which ulterior political purposes: in short, what one might call a comprehensive strategic concept for a given politico-military situation. Nowadays, such concepts are usually developed by committee within governments, kept very secret indeed, until they are put into practice – if ever they are put into practice. As the responsibility of collectives of decision-makers, they become the object of intense bureaucratic politics and inter-service rivalry, and end up full of compromises and contrdictions. Individuals could only dream of having a decisive impact on them – they are anything but single-authored concepts.

There is a case, however, in which a civilian, an 'armchair strategist', published a book containing a comprehensive concept for how to conduct a war with a specific enemy that was applied in practice. He was an Elizabethan clergyman and lawyer by the name of Matthew Sutcliffe, a commoner who otherwise wrote about theological issues. In 1593 he published his concept under the title *Practice, Proceedings and Lawes of Armes*. It was dedicated to Robert Devereux, second Earl of Essex, an Elizabethan aristocrat, soldier and courtier in his late twenties, who three years later, in 1596, attempted to apply it in war against Spain, in his famous Cádiz expedition. It is an astonishing work: in the light of the 1596 campaign, it can even be seen as the comprehensive strategic concept which Essex transformed into an operational strategy. As we shall see, Essex was prevented from implementing his strategy fully, which directly explains why the effects of this campaign were not as decisive and favourable to England as the original concept had assumed. This does not take away from the fact that with his book, Sutcliffe is an extraordinary example of the 'impact' which a scholar could in an equally extraordinary configuration have on his state's policies and on international events.

Sutcliffe and the second Earl of Essex

Matthew Sutcliffe (c. 1550–1629) was born as the second son of John Sutcliffe of Melroyd in the parish of Halifax, Yorkshire, and Margaret, his wife, née Owlsworth, originally of Ashley.[3] We do not know where he received his first education. He went up to Trinity College Cambridge like two of his brothers, in his teens (the records of Trinity, where he would spend about 12 years, suggest that he was first enrolled at Peterhouse, from where he moved to Trinity College in 1568 when he was elected a scholar of Trinity). Sutcliffe obtained a bachelor of arts degree in 1571 and was in the following year elected a minor fellow of Trinity, and a major fellow in 1574 – the elevation from minor to major occurring on the award of a master of arts, which Sutcliffe received in 1574. While Cambridge records suggest that he studied law and was awarded a doctorate in law (LLD) in 1581, at some stage he must have studied theology, among other subjects, as he later became an Anglican minister, and published extensively on theological issues, and styled himself as a doctor of divinity.[4] His last appointment at Cambridge was that of lecturer in the college for the academic year 1579–80. His last recorded payment as a fellow was in 1580.[5] At Trinity College Sutcliffe overlapped with Robert Devereux, who was already Earl of Essex, 15 years his junior. Young Essex went up to Trinity in 1577 at the age of 11, and stayed for four years, graduating with a master's degree in 1581. It is likely that he was tutored by Sutcliffe.[6] A student does not forget the fellows of his old college, and as we shall see, there is evidence that Essex stayed in touch with and furthered the careers of several other individuals connected with Trinity College. Sutcliffe's later career unfolded under the patronage of the young Earl.

Until 1585, Essex was merely a youth trailing after his eminent stepfather, Robert Dudley, Earl of Leicester, Elizabeth I's generalissimo and old favourite. In Leicester's military engagements on the side of the Dutch in the following three years, however, Essex emerged as a young hero and promising military commander. Leicester himself died in 1588 without a legitimate child of his own, but had been grooming his stepson as his heir to his position at court. The youth, three good decades younger than the queen, became her new preferred companion.

Youth, charm, beauty, noble birth and his close connection with Leicester alone would not have been enough to endear him to a monarch as erudite, refined and sophisticated as Elizabeth. Much less would he have been able to defend his position at Elizabeth's court and in her government vis-à-vis her male courtiers, less susceptible to his charms, if he had not had an outstanding intellect, and the ability to communicate his ideas effectively.

Paul Hammer has shown that Essex's intellectual seriousness was underestimated by his earlier biographers. Not only was the long period Essex spent at university exceptional for an aristocrat, but also at four and a half years it was twice as long as the sojourn at Trinity of the Bacon brothers – Francis the philosopher, and Anthony – who were to become his personal aides. As we have seen, Essex took an MA when he could have left with a lesser qualification. This suggests that he actually enjoyed study, even in his early teens. Essex described himself as 'bookishe, and given rather to contemplation then accion'.[7] The second statement was disingenuous, as Essex was a hotspur if anything, while the former statement was not: Essex definitely had periods when he withdrew from the court – usually after falling out with the sovereign – to read, meditate and write prodigiously. Even Essex's private correspondence suggests that he really believed in the practical applicability of scholarship, expressing his conviction that 'rules and patternes of pollecy are aswell learned out of olde Greeke and Romayne storyes as out of states which are at thys daye.'[8]

In the late 1580s and throughout the 1590s, Essex deliberately sought to balance his youth with *gravitas* derived from study and the counsel of old and young scholars who at once furnished him with weighty arguments and ideas, but were not rivals for power at court.[9] Moreover, he seems to have retained affection not only for his former tutors, including, besides Sutcliffe, the eminent scholar Robert Wright, but also for scholars in general. He strongly advised a friend, Fulke Greville, to follow his own example and employ a scholar, significantly from his own former college, Trinity, Cambridge, to serve him as a one-man think tank and secretary.[10] This was not a matter of merely seeking out spin doctors to help him with a better public presentation of aims he had espoused independently of any scholarly advice, as would be the pattern in any governmental consultation of academics in the twentieth and twenty-first centuries.[11] In turn, scholars of Essex's day and age seem to have known that they would find an open ear, and perhaps patronage of some sorts, if they brought good ideas to Essex's attention. Of 54 authors who dedicated works to Essex, there is evidence that 22 received some form of support from him.[12] Essex seems to have consulted experts – that is scholars from Oxford and Cambridge – on a whole host of issues. He himself stated, 'I profited more by some expert man in half a day's conference, than by myself in a month's study.'[13] He advised another friend to call upon such men to read *with* them – that is seek their guidance on what to read, just as he would have done formerly from his tutors.[14] 'To profit much by conference', he added, 'you must first chuse to confer with expert men, I mean expert in that which you desire to know.'[15] Much evidence can thus be found 'for real scholarly influence in the political domain',[16] what today would be called 'academic impact'.

Meanwhile, Sutcliffe had left Cambridge and became archdeacon in Taunton in Somerset in the winter of 1586–87,[17] which secured him a steady income, and the means to support a family: by now he had a wife and daughter.[18] It might have been William Bourchier, second Earl of Bath, to whom he owed this appointment, as Sutcliffe dedicated one of his first books to him.[19] Taunton was represented in Parliament in 1586 by Essex's future employee, the clever Francis Bacon, ten years younger than Sutcliffe, possibly also a previous tutee of Sutcliffe's at Trinity, Cambridge, and this might have revived their acquaintance.[20] In 1587–88, however, Sutcliffe was out of the country again, listed as judge martial (or advocate general) among the 'Officers serving in the Low Countries' of Elizabeth's army, receiving an income of 40 pounds. Perhaps it was due to Francis Bacon's intercession or direct contacts with Essex that, after this appointment came to an end in 1588, Sutcliffe was appointed dean at the Cathedral of Exeter, a position and income he retained until his death in 1629. He was simultaneously vicar of Welt Alvington in Devonshire, and had income from other ecclesiastic appointments, but cannot have spent much time there.

Why in 1593 did Sutcliffe at the age of about 43 dedicate his book to Essex, who was only 27 or 28? Although he was young, Essex was approaching the zenith of his influence and occupied what de facto amounted to the command-in-chief of Elizabeth's army on several expeditions. It is likely that Essex gave Sutcliffe more than moral 'encouragement' to write this 342-page book.[21] If this is what happened, why did Essex commission Sutcliffe to write this book? Essex's stepfather, the Earl of Leicester, had been the queen's chief general and as such had written a war manual containing ordinances, rules of behaviour for the armed forces.[22] Essex seems to have felt the need to update these, but not to have had the time to do so himself. He is likely to have asked Sutcliffe to take on this task for him.

Essex and Sutcliffe had in common a strong Hispanophobia, and Sutcliffe must have seen in Essex the chief advocate of war against Spain. Nor was their relationship a distant one once Essex had graduated in 1581. When he was judge martial, Sutcliffe seems to have taken part in the Flanders campaign in 1585/1586, where Essex won his first military glory. Sutcliffe claimed several times to have seen military action himself, in France, Italy, Flanders and Portugal, and he claims that Essex showed him 'singular fauour' in this last context.[23] One might speculate that he referred to Essex's Lisbon expedition of 1589. This set out from Plymouth, at a time when Sutcliffe was smugly established in Exeter, nicely placed along the route from London to Plymouth. So we can indeed assume that they spent time together in several contexts and occasions, to discuss politics and strategy. As we shall see, however, Essex was initially not wedded to Sutcliffe's central strategic argument, and only gradually came around to supporting it, after applying others without much success. It is thus possible to say where Sutcliffe's ideas begin and end, and where Essex's own ideas applied.

Strategic options

Sutcliffe's views on strategy

The *Practice, Proceedings and Lawes of Armes*[24] is one of a whole wave of books on the art of war published during this prolonged conflict between Spain and England, on both sides.[25] The great majority of these, however, are no more than field manuals, and Sutcliffe provided something quite different.

Sutcliffe seized the opportunity offered to him to produce a book which is probably the most comprehensive strategic concept written before the twentieth century, covering anything from recruitment and financing of wars to grand strategy. That Essex told Sutcliffe in detail what to write is unlikely: Sutcliffe prescribed an attack on Spain itself at a time when Essex's priority was to support Henri IV in France; Essex in mid-1595 was the last to abandon the policy of prioritising military help for Henri, somewhat prematurely, as the subsequent Spanish invasion of Normandy would show. Instead, Essex turned his support to an expedition to Panama planned by Sir Francis Drake and Sir John Hawkins in the hope for more loot (see Chapter 4). Essex began to warm to Sutcliffe's proposal – that is the direct attack on Spain along with a long-term seizure of at least one if not more Spanish ports – only in the winter of 1595/96, when there was a new scare of a Spanish invasion of England.[26] This means Essex did not yet share Sutcliffe's keenness on this option of seizing *and holding* Spanish land at the time of the publication of Sutcliffe's book, and came around to it only when there was new evidence of Spanish aggressiveness, after the Spanish raid on Mousehole in Cornwall in the summer of 1595. The strategic concept for the attack *and capture* of one or more Spanish ports was thus Sutcliffe's, before it became Essex's.

Preventive war

In his 'Epistle Dedicatorie', Sutcliffe professed a conviction that would please any modern 'realist' theoretician of international relations, one paradoxically shared with Catholic Church teaching, that war is an inescapable part of the world.

> [W]ere it, that neither we had warres with the Spaniard, nor others, nor stood in doubt of their attemptes or forces: yet can we not continue many yeeres without warres. Great countries and states cannot rest. If they haue no enemies abroad, yet restles heads seeke worke at home. Therefore can no time be thought vnseasonable, or to discourse of these matters. If we enjoyed peace, yet can we not assure vs of it without armes: if we doubt our enemies practices, there is no safer course then to arme. He that desireth peace, he must prepare for warres.[27] And long preparatiues of warre made in time of peace, giue speedy victorie in time of warres. Men doe not easily prouoke or attempt warres against a nation or country, that is ready to resist, & prouided

to prosecute iniuries. Contrariwise the peaceable and inconsideratiue are a spoile, and praye to their neighbours.[28]

And yet Sutcliffe strongly urged the pursuit of a peace, if it was a real option and could be accepted from a position of relative strength:

Although the joy and triumph that is made in victory be exceeding great, yet I accompt him not wise, that when al things hang in equal balance refuseth a reasonable peace with equal conditions, vpon hope of a doubtfull victory.

Thus two and a half centuries before Clausewitz, he emphasised the importance of chance in war:

All that we take in hand is subject to infinit chances, and successe of battell is common to both parties. . . .

Wherefore, seeing that peace is the end of warres,[29] and seeing that we take arms in hand not to do wrong, but that we may recover or obtaine our owne right: let no man refuse reason that may have it.[30]

Though a clergyman, Sutcliffe thus came down on the secular side of the argument about whether victory was obtained by divine intervention, human skill or chance.[31]

Sutcliffe the Anglican and fierce opponent of Catholicism paradoxically also subscribed to classical Catholic just war theory, rehearsing the reasons why a prince might without sin take up arms, adding to them that this could be done in defence of one's confession, and one's 'liberty'.[32] Further, war is just only if authorised by 'the sovereign' – a term that now in the literature on sovereignty which was spreading from the Continent replaced the earlier Catholic reference to God and His royal representative on earth.

As Sutcliffe expected a renewed Spanish invasion attempt on England any time, Sutcliffe counselled a pre-emptive war, or even a preventive war:[33] 'He that first chargeth his enemie, hath many advantages. . . . Victorie is obteined by prevention, and by the same warres are oft times diverted.'[34] The consequences of waiting for Spain to invade England would be more costly than waiting for the Spanish to attack:

not knowing where the enemie will land, all the coast must be furnished with souldiers. . . . [I]f any port be left open, as good all should be disarmed. But this would be double the charge of levying and furnishing an army for Spaine. And the longer the enemy holdeth us in breath, the greater would the charge arise. . . .

If the enemy should land, as well he may comming with great force, we neither have strong townes, nor many great rivers to stoppe his procedings, nor any way to resist, but by force of men in open fielde.[35]

Instead, England should 'assayle the enemy in his owne countrey'.[36]

Strategic aims in war and the strategy to reach them

Sutcliffe's comprehensive concept turned on what he saw as the grand strategic aim of England's security policy: decisively to disarm Spain, and to do so even to occupy Spanish territory. In a chapter entitled 'Wherein It Is Shown How the Victory Is to Be Used, and the Conquest Maintained, Once the Enemy Is Vanquished', Sutcliffe devoted extensive passages to how to pacify the conquered lands. We find most interesting humanistic ideas on warfare here. Unlike so many writers of the nineteenth and early twentieth centuries, Sutcliffe saw the enemy's army as equals, not some sort of *Untermenschen* to be butchered if defeated. Above all, he showed the clear recognition that military victory on its own did not signify the achievement of strategic war aims: an enemy force willing to retreat should be given a 'bridge of gold' – a reference to Plutarch's *Themistocles* – to do so. Once the enemy army had truly been defeated, or had fled,

> then the next task is to besiege their chiefe cities, and that presently while the smart of their woundes is yet fresh. . . . The terrour of a victorious armie, and sufficient to make any towne yeelde . . . There is no towne that dare holde out, without hope of succour.

In order successfully to conclude a siege, the country might have to be wasted. Once the provincial towns had fallen, the countryside would be controlled, and the army could move on 'to besiege the main city', presumably meaning the capital. '[T]he Generals care ought to be, howe to take away the enemies subjects from them, and to deprive them of the aide of their confederats.' This thought leads over to the next important issue,

> howe our conquest may be maintained, and assured. . . . To keepe our conquest, there are two principall meanes both necessarie; force and justice: for neither without force can those that are rebellious, and desirous of innovation be repressed, nor without justice can the peaceabul be defended, or contented. That Empire . . . is most firme and durable, which the subjects do willingly embrace, and gladly continue. And hard it is to keepe men discontent long in subjection by force. A countrey subdued is kept by the same meanes that it was subdued; that is . . . by fortitude, industrie, justice. . . .
>
> For no people can long like of a government, wherein they are spoyled, vexed, injuried, and to lay all in one worde, pilled, and tyrannised.[37]

In short, Sutcliffe effectively argued for winning over the population of the occupied region by good governance and justice, ultimately a hearts-and-minds campaign that would give them a stake in the new settlement, and no incentive to rise up in rebellion to bring their old masters back. This tallies with Sutcliffe's repeated injunction 'that no cruelty should be used', either in war or in the execution of justice in peace. He quoted from a work on military discipline by the Spanish author Sancho de Londoño: 'Women, children, and the elderly, by the order of war now observed in the Spanish camp, are exempt from the soldiers' fury in the sack of towns.'[38] The last part of his book contained the long list of self-denying ordinances which presumably were the main reason for this book to be commissioned along the model of the previous publication of such ordinances by Essex's stepfather, Leicester, and printed like his by Christopher Barker, by appointment to Her Majesty the Queen. These ordinances were rules to be obeyed by soldiers on pain of death, besides the call for discipline and obedience, rules against pillaging, murder and arbitrary executions, rape or any other unjust interference with the civilians in the theatre of war or the occupied territory, against scorched earth tactics, and especially massacres of either civilians or soldiers who had surrendered.[39] Like Londoño, Sutcliffe thus opposed all brutality against the local populations, of the sort that had been practised by the Duke of Alba in the Netherlands and indeed by Elizabeth's commander in Ireland in the 1560s.

The idea of capturing and holding Spanish port-cities was not absurd: for centuries, England had owned regions, later reduced to ports and their hinterland, in France. Although it had lost Calais in 1558, England in the 1590s still held the ports of Flushing and Brielle in the Netherlands by treaty with the Dutch. Venice still had an extensive maritime empire connected by sea routes, and military orders like the Knights Hospitaller controlled a network of strongholds, held together on naval lines of communication. A quarter of a century later, in 1620, an English fleet first took possession of Gibraltar.

Admittedly, the conquest of more extensive parts of Spain would have been an unattainable war aim for England at the time, as Napoleon would find out in 1808–1812 with a much greater population base for his own army and with superior logistics. On the other side of the Atlantic, however, the following decades would witness the first colonisation of amazingly large and ever increasing territories with their indigenous populations by the English, following the example set by the Spanish. In view of Sutcliffe's subsequent undertakings, one might read the first glimpses of such thinking into this book.

Sutcliffe devoted much space to the discussion of peace. As we have seen, he advocated choosing peace if it was at all a serious option, but not one that was disadvantageous, unreasonable, imposing 'unequal conditions' or that might not be honoured by the other contracting party or parties. He thought the French particularly slippery partners, able to outwit the English in their peace treaties even when defeated. With an echo of 'si vis pacem, para bellum', he wrote,

> in treating of peace wee must first see that wee slacke not our preparatives of warre, nor defer to take any advantage that is offered . . .
>
> For peace is not obtained with parley, or entreaty, unlesse wee also make ready our forces.[40]

He advocated circumspection both for peace treaties and truces, and taking securities of all forms to ensure the honouring of peace treaties – for example in the persons of hostages, or by appointing third parties as guarantors of the treaty.[41]

Financing war

The financial predicament of crown and nobility

While warfare was increasingly unaffordable for England's monarchs, another driver *towards* war both for the nobility and the crown was, paradoxically, again financial: the quest for booty. While the rulers of England until the 1640s managed to keep religious wars affecting all of Europe outside the boundaries of England (admittedly at times with swift and forceful suppression of the religious confession they did not favour), they did not manage the long-term financial crises that beset Europe. Had they succeeded in turning England into an absolutist state as Henri IV's successors would do with France, they might have secured the necessary tax revenues to create a standing army under the crown's exclusive control (creating a fiscal-military state).[42] The cost of the wars that had their origins in religious strife grew, as did the theatre of war, to encompass all parts of Europe plus the New World. Elizabeth's grandfather, Henry VII, had managed to control his finances through proverbial parsimony; Elizabeth's father, Henry VIII, had taken recourse to despoiling England's rich monasteries, an act that could as little be reversed as it could be repeated. Elizabeth had utterly inadequate resources and administrative machineries for the creation of armies or fleets: her own finances, either for buying and equipping ships or for paying, equipping and feeding soldiers, were too small compared with her growing needs. Her own and her chief counsellors' systematic attempts on the one hand to centralise control over the recruitment of soldiers and their deployment where needed were offset, on the other, by the decentralised relinquishment of the actual duty and expenses of recruiting and training militias to the counties, and to noblemen like Essex. Intimately linked with the problems of financing war in a state that was moving to establish some balance in government between crown, aristocracy and counties/nation was, thus, the debate about the recruitment and financing of soldiers, their provisions and their equipment (including of course, ships).[43]

As John Nolan has explained, this created slowly mounting tension between Elizabeth and her parliaments, both the House of Lords and the Commons, whom she expected to provide the forces she needed. While her father had *occasionally* needed large armies of around 20,000 soldiers, for campaigns on the Continent or against the Scots, Elizabeth's forces, which were continually deployed and active *every year*, averaged 15,700 for the years of 1585–1602, with a peak of almost 21,000 in the year after the 1588 armada, a peak of 19,000 in the year of Essex's expedition to Cádiz, and an *annual* average of 20,000 for the last five years of her reign.[44]

The international religious dimension of war meant that these forces could not, as in the days of Henry VIII, be concentrated in one theatre of war. The force levels were so high in relation to the entire population of England (variously estimated towards the end of Elizabeth's reign as having been between 3.5 and 4 million[45]) precisely because England had to fight on several fronts simultaneously. With a total population of perhaps four million, sending 6,500 soldiers and 5,000 sailors to Cádiz represented a great effort, not to mention supporting an army of 19,000 all told in several theatres; in the 2010s, Britain with a population of 62 million struggled to deploy 10,000 ground forces in Afghanistan, even after it had pulled out of Iraq.

As Sutcliffe would rightly note, there was a universal greed for money,[46] caused by the objective needs and wants of not only the Tudor monarchs but also the aristocracy, who often lived above their means, and all other strata of the growing English population. As a result, there were a number of thrusting – especially younger – aristocrats who eyed war as a possible way to fill their depleted pockets. All these problems in miniature affected the Earl of Essex. Between 1585 and 1592, he spent £28,500 out of his own pocket on the military campaigns in which he participated (a crucial reason he held high office when so young), and he wanted returns.[47] As much as it was concerned with knightly honour, Essex's interest in these campaigns was, much like primitive warfare and privateering, concerned with booty. As Essex explained before the Lisbon campaign of 1589, 'yf I speede well I will aduenture to be rich. Yf not I will not liue to see th'end of my pouerty.'[48] Historian Robert Lacey depicted Essex as a bad gambler, who constantly threw good money after bad, keenly hoping to recuperate the lot in one roll of the dice. In short, Essex, like the Tudor and Stuart monarchs themselves, was desperately short of the ready, and needed to mount another Viking-style raid. This is one explanation why the 1596 expedition against Cádiz ended up as a raid, rather than the first step towards a decisive move to strangle the military might of Spain lastingly, and to divert the flow of 'Indian treasure' more permanently towards England.

Sutcliffe's views on the war economy

Sutcliffe in this saw the enormous predicament of England in the light of the financial straits in which the crown found itself. This is a truly remarkable aspect of strategic concept. Unlike Machiavelli, Sutcliffe subscribed to Cicero's verdict that 'treasure' forms 'the sinews of war'.[49] Chapters 2 and 4 of his comprehensive national security concept deal exclusively with the problem of how this treasure could be found, and how it could be translated into muscle strength most economically. He urged an extension of taxation and customs tariffs on overseas commerce. Both Sutcliffe and Essex in his own writings proposed reforms in taxation and recruitment that would have allowed England to emulate the development of France to establish permanent taxes to finance military expenditure and a standing army, if accepted by Parliament.[50]

In keeping with his Hispanophobia, his ardent anti-Catholicism and his patriotism, Sutcliffe advocated hiring only English, Welsh or Irish men as soldiers. Foreigners, he argued, could not be trusted, and demanded more pay as mercenaries than the natives of his queen's realm.[51] Sutcliffe here oddly showed no awareness of the reservations which Catholic Irishmen might have felt at the time with regard to military service for Protestant England. Indeed, the whole Irish dimension is curiously absent from the picture of interstate relations he sketched for us. Nor did he fully examine different forms of military recruitment, from mercenaries or professional standing armies to county levies or the local militiamen. To be fair, these differences were in flux: 'pressed' men or county levies were sent abroad to fight, which was true even for the 'Trained Bands', originally created for the territorial defence of England.[52]

Sutcliffe emphasised that both foreign soldiers – that is mercenaries – and native soldiers needed to be paid, or they would resort to pillaging; he was less insightful in his prescriptions on how to find the necessary funds.[53] So 'that abuses of imprests, and false musters and accounts [be] taken away, loyall captaines might be chosen, and poore souldiers be well furnished'. Old codes of honour should be revived; for transgressions he urged 'sharpe punishment the mainteining of true militarie discipline, and orders'. 'Auditors and Commissioners' should identify and punish financial malpractices among the officers.[54]

Sutcliffe did understand that it would be hard to turn the wheel back to the Roman times he idealised, 'For inveterate customs are not easily rooted out; and desire of money has corrupted many men's minds.'[55] He attributed the problems of his age to 'the contempt for religion and true honour, and greedy desire for gain', a leitmotif in his writing,[56] but also to jealousy and vanity: 'Who wil adventure without praise, or reward?' Given this trait in human nature, he criticised that 'valiant captains and souldiers are slenderly considered.' Therefore, 'valiant deeds' should be rewarded.[57] Yet Sutcliffe's experience of Elizabethan warfare had been real enough for him to be aware that the problem of pay and rewards was intimately bound up with the distribution of booty, to which he devoted much space, explaining precisely which parts of any war spoils should go to the crown, which part to officers, and which to the soldiers themselves.[58] Sutcliffe did not, however, conceive of the option of instituting permanent taxation à la Française to pay for war.

The armed forces required

For an amphibious attack on Spain itself, or on the main body of the Spanish army in the Netherlands, England would need bigger armies. Sutcliffe attributed English setbacks in the Netherlands to Elizabeth's insufficient forces, which also created problems for her in alliance warfare.[59] In principle, Sutcliffe supported 'leagues' as force multipliers:

> Some nations for feare of their enemies do yeeld themselves into the protection of others with certaine covenants . . .
>
> In this case, as the receiver doeth binde himself to defend those that yeeld themselves into his armes: so they either binde themselves to pay money, or to do him service, or to deliver him by certaine townes. . . . [I]t is a dishonour not to protect those that are wrongfully oppressed, and much more to abandon those whom they have take upon them to defend.

He then spelled out the conditions which would render a rebellion against a prince's authority legitimate, articulating an early version of the social contract:

> Neither doe princes only and free states covenant ech with other, but also subjects with their princes, and princes with their subjects . . . But that the subjects should prescribe lawes to their soveraigne princes, and binde them to inconveniences, it savoureth rather of force, then loyaltie; and that princes

hestes should be obeyed against reason, proceedeth of tyranny, neither can any assurance be made of such agreements.[60]

Alliances as such he did not see as *panaceae*, if English forces were too slight to be preponderant within the alliance contingent. Invoking Roman precedent, he advised against excessive reliance upon allies. To benefit from an alliance, one should furnish the greater part of its forces, so as to be able to claim the supreme command.[61] Moreover, Sutcliffe wanted to see the English army engage the Spaniards in a decisive battle;[62] 'as a little water sprinkled on the fire doth make the same more to flame, and sparkle; so small supplies doe rather kindle, and nourish warres, then ende them, or extinguish them.'[63] Therefore, with an exaggerated estimate of England's total population ('many millions'), Sutcliffe wanted to raise armies of 30,000 or 40,000 men, numbers in excess of those which Elizabeth could afford for any one theatre of war.[64]

In all of this, Sutcliffe underscored the importance of the navy, with a much greater role in English and Spanish strategy of the late sixteenth century than in the military manuals and the art of war of the Italian authors who had dominated the genre until then.[65]

Sutcliffe implicitly criticised the queen for being so hesitant about putting her precious ships at risk, exhorting her to follow the example of her forebears, Kings Edward III and Henry VIII, who, he implied, had been less risk-averse.[66]

Subjects Sutcliffe was otherwise silent about included how to support a rebellion, but also how to subdue it, even though this, with its notable avoidance of pitched battles, was an important element in the conflicts both in the Netherlands and in Ireland.[67] He equally had no time for motivations in war such as chivalry or honour, which so drove Essex, not even national honour or pride. His comprehensive strategic concept was written in reaction to the perception of a vital threat to his country, not to further its glory or position in the world.

Essex's Hulton manuscript and his strategic concept for war with Spain

Sutcliffe's book must have been the conceptual foundation on which Essex in mid-1596 developed his own operational strategic concept for war with Spain. Admittedly, there is no actual passage in Sutcliffe's book that made its way verbatim into any of Essex's writing. But Essex was not one to stick to certain formulations; a comparison shows that he did not even repeat language from his own former writing.[68] The ideas, however, were the same.

In the preceding years, Essex had advocated and tried a number of other options. He had fought in Flanders alongside the Dutch. He had fought in France alongside or loosely allied with Henri Bourbon. He had joined the expedition bound for Lisbon in 1589 that attempted to put a pretender on the Portuguese throne to take the place of Philip. Now he was ready to try a new idea, Sutcliffe's idea: to seize and hold with an English garrison some of Philip's ports, even if no local uprising were to come to their aid. Cádiz with its riches, and its location at the end of a long island connected to the mainland by only one bridge, seemed most promising, although it was the furthest away from England among Iberia's Atlantic ports. But if England wanted to capture several such harbour cities, the element of surprise would be lost if it started with La Coruña in the North, and local defences could be strengthened in Ferrol, Lisbon and Cádiz, long before the English fleet might reach them. Essex therefore gambled on taking Cádiz first, and then working his way north along the other ports.

Essex himself later claimed that the idea for this expedition was that of Lord Howard of Effingham, who as the Lord High Admiral was commander of the fleet.[69] It is quite likely that Howard in turn was familiar with Sutcliffe's book, which after all had the status of an officially approved publication, printed by a publisher by appointment to Her Majesty the Queen. Nor is it inconceivable that Howard was positively disposed towards Sutcliffe's strategic proposal at some stage, even if he later argued against it as too ambitious. Essex's attribution of the idea to Howard, rather than Sutcliffe, is easy to explain in the context of his own bureaucratic battles – Howard the politician of course carried infinitely more weight than the Devonshire clergyman whom Essex had himself commissioned to write the proposal.

Essex's personal input can largely be ascertained from a letter to the Privy Council he had ordered to be handed over after the expeditionary force was well away, from the strategy he tried to impose during the Cádiz operation of 1596 according to witnesses, and from a fascinating manuscript identified by L. W. Henry in 1953 as a script in Essex's hand, the Hulton manuscript.[70] Paul Hammer has called this 'the most ambitious and comprehensive military strategy of the Elizabethan Era'.[71] It is a poorly structured, rough first draft and contains many deleted and amended passages and words, and it is barely decipherable even with good palaeographical skills.[72] A published document, known as 'Omissions of the Cales [= Cádiz] expedition', contains passages copied from this manuscript, redrafted in the interest of clarity. Manuscript and print versions list explanations on the part of Essex as to why his own strategic aims were not reached with the Cádiz expedition.[73] Altogether, published and unpublished parts, the manuscript is incomplete; there is no proper address, nor is there a conclusion, and half a page is destroyed. But we can make out what purpose it served. All the main commanders of the Cádiz expedition, sensing that what they needed to pass off as a great victory for the sake of their reputation had in fact been a pointless and wasteful expedition, rushed to get their own accounts to the queen and Privy Council.[74] Essex, too, sat down, still on board the *Due Repulse* that had taken him to Cádiz, to write such a representation of his side of the story, pre-emptively explaining actions and omissions that were already held against him by his fellow commanders: 'Now our actions are att an end, and we[']re all going home so as I have good lejsure to write in this time.'[75] (Indeed, Essex would continue to present the Cádiz campaign as his personal triumph, along with his later exploits in Ireland.)

The manuscript thus explains Essex's strategic concept for this operation, and how and why it was not fully implemented; that it was not fully implemented is the reason which Essex gave for its overall failure. We can deduce the following, even if it has to be handled with care in that it is a retrospective description of Essex's strategy.

In the text, Essex explored, and then dismissed, the option of peace with Spain, in view of 'Th' experience of tymes past', Spain's attempts at invasions, conspiracies against the queen's person, subversion and so forth.[76] Instead, in 1596, he advocated the Sutcliffe strategy – that is a naval attack on Spain itself – giving as arguments what reads like a summary of those put forward by Sutcliffe:

> First, that as wee are in warre so wee can nott in reson hope or disarme after peace, except by war we bring our . . . enemy very low. Secondly, that having war, yt is better for us in all imports to make yt offensive then defensive. Thirdly, that our offense shall more advantage us and hurte the enemy by sea then by a land warr. Fourthly, that yt is a better dession to make an offensive war by sea from the coste of Spayne and Portugall [than from the islands].[77]

An offensive war at sea would be, to the Spanish king,

> more annoyance because we shall not only impeach and interrupt his trafique will all other countryes of Christendom whereby we shall impoverish his merchants butt stop and divert his golden Indian streames whereby we shall cut his life vaynes and let out the vital spirites of his estate [the 'golden Indian streames' being the trade with America and the West Indies].[78]

Essex then discussed three theatres of war ('seates of warre') upon which such a sea offensive might concentrate – namely the American riches at their source in the Western Atlantic, or the Azores, or the coast of the Iberian Peninsula, then completely under Spanish control. Of these three, and in the light of Drake's and Hawkins's recent deaths, Essex thought an attack on the West Indies too ambitious. He also found arguments against directing an attack against the Azores (which he would nevertheless attempt in 1597): 'They are out of all such trades as are betwixt cuntry and cuntry in Europe or betwixt any of us and Africa' – that is an attack on the Azores would serve *only* to intercept the 'Indies' trade with Spain.[79] By contrast, directing an attack against the Spanish-dominated coast had multiple advantages, in cutting Spain off from its trade with the 'Indies', but also from the naval line of communication with the Low Countries, and depriving Spain of the opportunity of sending another armada against England. As the key ports that needed to be conquered *and held* by England, Essex identified Cádiz (Cales) and Lisbon:

> By a warr upon the coste of Spayne and [Spanish-held] Portugall yt is easy to cut of all entreecourse betwixt those 2 kingdoms and th'Indyes because the trafike is only from 2 places. Lisbone and Sevill [with Cádiz serving as Seville's port] are the cesternes that first receave the welth [from the Indies], and the Bay of Cales and the river of Tagus the portes wherby the king of Spayne's fleetes for th'Indyes ever go forth and to which they ever returne.

He then raised the question

> whether yf the king of Spayne had lost these two places, he might not renew
> his trafike in some other. I answer no, for yf he have any fitt place within the
> straytes [of Gibraltar], yet an English fleete lying in the Bay of Cales or any
> wher ther aboutes will still command the passage into the streights . . .
>
> So as I conclude that, as wee cut of the king of Spayne from trade to
> th'Indyes, if wee possess Cales and Lisbone, so yt is hard and almost impos-
> sible for him to make any new trade from any other porte of his dominions,
> whilst from those 2 places we make warres upon the rest of his coast. Allso,
> yt is as hard for him to have any trafike with the other cuntries of Christen-
> dom . . . And as one part of our fleete having Lisbone or some such place
> for ther retraict might range all the cost of Portugall, Galicia and Biskay: so
> another part of our fleete having Cales for succour might command all the
> costes of Algarve and Andolazia [Andalucía]: yea, within the Streigthes even
> to Marseilles.
>
> And now having barrd the Spaniard all entrecourse with the Indyes
> whereby he maintaynes his fleetes and warres by sea, and the trade of other
> countries from whence he is supplied with all the necessaries for his shippes
> and provisions for such services, yt is needless to prouve that, we may be the
> course sett downe, banish him [from] the Ocean: and yet thatt yt may appear
> that we shall disarm him by sea, I will add unto the 2 former mischeafes that
> he receaves this third, thatt we will leave him no shippes[80] [as the English fleet
> should also seek to] . . . take or burne any fleete in what porte of Spayne
> soever it be.[81]

Within this strategy of strangulating Spain by an attack on its own key ports,
Essex wanted to move tactically against Cádiz first:

> my end in going to Cales was not only because it was a principall port and the
> likeliest to be held by us, because of the seate and naturall strength of it: butt
> also for that it was the farthest good port southward, so as beginning with it,
> we might (yf some greater storme did not divert us) go to all the good portes
> betwixt that and the northermost portes of Biskaie: which was a better way
> then to have begon or given th'enemy the alarm in the midst of his cuntrie
> or the nearest partes to us, for so our attemptes, would have been more dif-
> ficile and our retrait att last from these farthest partes less safe considering the
> wants, infections and other inconveniences that for the most part to accom-
> pany the retraytes of our fleetes and armies in long iornyes.[82]

In any case, the English needed not only to *seize* the two ports but also to *hold* them
in the long term. In the aforementioned letter which Essex sent to the Queen's
Privy Council prior to his departure for Cádiz he had written, 'I doubt not but
after [the Spaniard] had once tried what it was to besiege 2,000 or 3,000 English

in a place well fortified and where [the English] had a port open, he would grow quickly weary of those attempts.'[83]

Of the several English expeditions of these years against the Iberian Peninsula, the Cádiz expedition was the only one that included a large army. This, and the appointment of Essex to lead the army, suggests that Essex had a considerable input into the strategic concept for this whole expedition, and had persuaded queen and Privy Council to go along with the plan for an attack also on Cádiz itself (not just the ships in its port). But the secretive way in which Essex dispatched this letter to the Privy Council, insisting it must be delivered only once the expedition could no longer be stopped, indicates that he had not found their consensus on the idea of *holding* the city, once conquered. Essex specifically wrote in the Hulton Manscript of taking an army large enough 'to conquer and *dwell*'.[84] This is confirmed also by his later *Apologie*, where he explains that the Cádiz campaign did not bring the Anglo-Spanish War to an end, as it failed to perform what Essex had intended: 'I purposed to dwell in a port of the enemies, and so to make a continual diuersion of the warres . . . And when I was possessed of *Cadz* [sic], I offered to stay with 3. or 4.000 men.'[85] Essex had also clearly failed to convince the queen and Privy Council of the viability of his plan to conquer Lisbon, as he noted in the Hulton manuscript that he was 'barred by name in my Instructions' from going to Lisbon.[86]

The overall outcome that Essex had aimed for was on a different plane from that any of his contemporaries developed, and was truly of strategic importance. The Hulton manuscript is thus not a mere restatement of Sutcliffe's strategic concept but a translation of the general concept into an operational plan. In this translation, Essex made original contributions, especially the choice of ports, and the idea of first conquering Cádiz, then working one's way North to Lisbon. In accordance with Sutcliffe's strategic concept, Essex did not merely want to deal Spain another blow; he wanted to establish English maritime supremacy. Elizabeth would be able to bring in riches from the Americas, and she would be 'Queene of the Ocean'[87] (see Chapter 6). Where Sutcliffe had only hoped with his strategic concept to safeguard England against Spanish-Catholic attacks and to further the Protestant cause in Europe, Essex was dreaming that England should rule the waves.

The strategic-political implication was lost on Ralegh, Essex's fellow commander. Ralegh's eyes were firmly set on the booty brought by wars, and he would oppose Essex's attempt to turn the Cádiz campaign into a decisive operation by holding the conquered city. Essex at that time still dismissed this focus on loot, saying that to waylay the enemy's merchant fleet was really 'fitter enterprise for some decayd private man [a swipe at Ralegh] then for a state, for yt savors of guerra di corsar'.[88] But, as Lacey rightly noted, 'The individual profit motive . . . inspired the formation of . . . every . . . English naval expedition' of the time,[89] and even Essex himself was mesmerised by the wealth transported by the seas at least as much as by the strategic power the command of the sea would bring.

There is also a point of disagreement between Sutcliffe's book and Essex's operational plan. Both Sutcliffe and Essex shared a preference for indigenous forces, but Essex was happy to take along Dutch contingents. Sutcliffe favoured large militia armies, while in his letters written at the outset of the Cádiz expedition[90] while in the post-Cádiz ruminations set down in the Hulton manuscript, Essex argued for a small force of professional soldiers, and not for a large army of native Englishmen raised in levies of militiamen for limited periods of time. Essex even opined that a small army ('An army well chosen of 3,000') of professional soldiers would be preferable for a larger army made up primarily of poorly trained local English levies of militiamen, whom Essex called 'for the most part . . . artificers and clownes'.[91]

Overall, Sutcliffe's was an offensive concept, set on conquest, but only in reaction to an analogous threat by Spain, and thus preventive. It was Essex who introduced pathos: he invoked 'the liberty of all Christendom',[92] and the dream of English rule of the sea. In practical terms, by contrast, Sutcliffe's aim of occupying land, not just the 'main city' (presumably Lisbon), was excessively ambitious, while Essex's more focused strategy of aiming to capture and hold two or three key ports (including Lisbon) might have stood some chance of success. At any rate, like the Italian Giulio Douhet in the early twentieth century with regard to air power, both men had a prophetic vision of the potential of naval power, while overestimating what it could achieve in their own day.

The Cádiz expedition of 1596

As we have noted, when Sutcliffe published his book, Essex was still intent mainly on helping Henri IV of France secure his kingdom against the Spanish operating from the Netherlands. Although Henri converted to Catholicism in July 1593, leading Sutcliffe to comment on France's unreliability, Essex continued from London to support Henri, which did not fit Sutcliffe's strategic concept (and his scepticism of alliances which one could not dominate). At the end of 1595, the Spanish forces withdrew from the north of France, leaving Calais in Henri's hands temporarily; only now did Elizabeth cease to give Henri financial and military support.

This allowed England's leading military minds to refocus their attention, but the financial straits of all sides were always part of the equation. As noted earlier, this was the point when Drake and Hawkins developed their plan to intercept Spanish trade near Panama, supported by Essex. That campaign's indirect approach, prioritising booty over the destruction of the Spanish men-o'-war and the capture of any stronghold in Spain, in no way fitted Sutcliffe's concept.[93] Due not least to the deaths of Drake and Hawkins but also to the fleet's inability to find much to plunder, the 1595 expedition proved an utter disaster.

Then in April 1596, Philip II's forces recaptured Calais, once again threatening the English coast at the narrowest part of the Channel. Now an English attack on Spain itself no longer had to be presented as a *preventive* war, as Matthew Sutcliffe had done, but a pre-*emptive* campaign.[94] For once, this clear and present danger united all the rivals at Elizabeth's court: her cautious civilian counsellors, Lord Burghley and his son Sir Robert Cecil, and the daredevils Sir Walter Ralegh and Essex agreed with Lord Howard of Effingham to send an impressive expeditionary fleet of 118 ships to strike pre-emptively at the Iberian Peninsula itself. This time, they would not merely aim to burn a fleet, as Drake had done in 1587; nor would they try to put a Portuguese prince back on the throne. This campaign, it was agreed, should have a more lasting and decisive effect. An army of 6,300 English recruits plus 2,000 experienced Dutch soldiers[95] was to be shipped to Spain, not merely a navy, which implied that something – a town, a fortress, land – should be captured. Somewhere between 500 and 1,000 English volunteers were party to this expedition at their own expense, hoping to reap honours and booty.[96] Essex was appointed to command the soldiers on this expedition, but besides the Lord Admiral, he had to accept Sir Walter Ralegh and Sir Francis Vere as military commanders alongside himself; decisions were made jointly within the terms of reference provided by the queen.

But there the agreement broke down. We have seen that Sutcliffe and Essex wanted Spanish territory to be seized *and held*, with a garrison of 2,000–3,000 men to be left in place, as Essex put it in his pre-Cádiz letter to queen and Council, as 'a continuall diversion and to have lefte (as it were) a thorne sticking in his [=Philip II's] foote'.[97] In the Hulton manuscript, we find a corresponding passage mentioning both a 'nayle' in a 'foote . . . and a thorne in his side'.[98] As the usual metaphor would have been 'thorn in his flesh' or 'thorn in his side', 'foote' could indicate either a reduction of Spain's (naval) mobility (which such an attack was indeed aiming at), or a target low down on the southern coast of Spain (which fits Cádiz beautifully), or both. Although it was supposedly the Lord Admiral who alone knew that the expedition that set out on 1 June 1596 was bound for Cádiz, and informed the other military leaders of this only after the fleet was out of harbour, the Hulton manuscript suggests that it might have been Essex who had proposed in the first place that Cádiz should be attacked *and occupied, along with Lisbon*, as the two largest ports of the Iberian Peninsula. But as we have seen, the very orders given to the expeditionary forces by the queen ruled out any attack on Lisbon.[99]

Thus in June 1596, the English expeditionary force sailed from Plymouth and managed to sail to Cádiz fast enough to take the Spanish by surprise, but not fast enough to capture a nearby Spanish merchant fleet, which its commander, the Duke of Medina Sidonia, preferred to burn rather than to let fall into English hands. The English-cum-Dutch force did indeed take Cádiz, and seized much plunder, with Ralegh, Vere and especially Essex engaging in childish rivalries and bravado in the process. The despoiling of the city and its population was central to the expedition. The contemporary Spanish historian Friar Pedro de Abreu recorded that the English

> robbed houses of everything they could find, carrying the plunder to the ships; they knocked down walls, roofs, and attics where they suspected that money or other goods could be hidden; they . . . drained the wells and even sewers and cesspools in order to remove as much silver, gold, and money as . . . they were sure to find. . . . They stripped women to see if they had anything hidden and if the dresses were expensive . . ., they would keep them, leaving the women in undergarments and some stark naked. And they did the same to the men.[100]

Inspired by Protestant fervour, the English and Dutch soldiers and sailors sacked the Catholic churches in Cádiz and destroyed Catholic images and statues, most famously a statue of a Madonna and Child, which was dragged out of the city's cathedral.[101] This was the only transgression against the female sex, however, if we discount the body search for hidden jewels or money imposed irrespective of gender. Impressively in keeping with Sutcliffe's great emphasis on discipline and good treatment of non-combatants, and with Essex's reputation as a very strict disciplinarian where his soldiers were concerned, there is no record of any rape or massacres of civilians in this raid.[102] The anonymous account of the campaign in the Yelverton manuscript notes that women were given permission to leave Cádiz, 'garded by men of reckoninge' to prevent any molestation by the English military,[103] prompting Philip II to comment later that 'such nobility has never been seen among heretics'.[104] The behaviour of the English and Dutch here was poignantly different from that recorded in Elizabeth's Irish campaigns of the previous decades.

After the capture of Cádiz, and in keeping with Sutcliffe's advice on how to reward soldiers and officers, Essex and Lord Howard between them proceeded to honour and knight 60 captains for good performance, more than had ever been knighted in any one year of the queen's reign.[105] The garrison which Essex wanted to install permanently in Cádiz would have had to be supplied from the sea; indeed, the option of doing so was negotiated with emissaries of the king of Morocco, who offered his services to supply Cádiz with victuals.[106]

All this was not enough, however, to win over all and sundry to Essex's project of turning Cádiz into an English stronghold with Essex as its governor. Essex's fellow leaders were staunchly opposed to this, obedient to the queen's instructions. Instead of being garrisoned and turned into an English stronghold, Cádiz was burned and abandoned on 1 July. The other leaders of the expedition all wanted to get home as soon as possible, and resisted further attempts on the part of Essex to persuade them to stop off either at the Azores to waylay a fleet of merchantmen on their way back from America, or at Lisbon, or at the Spanish ports in the north-west of the Iberian Peninsula. While the bulk of the fleet was already homeward bound, Essex himself just about managed to persuade a few vessels to check at Faro, on the south-western corner of the Iberian Peninsula, whether Spanish ships worth fighting or despoiling were at anchor there (there were none). After that, beset by unfavourable winds, he, too, headed back to England, missing the Spanish merchant fleet that was anchoring in Lisbon, laden with riches, and also missing the men-o'-war anchoring there, which Philip would unleash as a new armada against England barely three months later. Disappointingly, the booty which they brought home to Elizabeth barely covered the overall private and public investment in this military operation.[107]

Sutcliffe's and Essex's strategic concept had been to strangle Spanish power by cutting off its American trade and its military lines of communication right where they entered Spain. The consequence would have been a big step in the direction of an English predominance on the Atlantic, and domination of the trade with America, but also a perhaps fatal weakening of the Spanish grip on the Netherlands.

One can only agree with Paul Hammer that this 'grand conception of war against Spain . . . remained untested', or more accurately, it was applied only in small part.[108]

The reason for this was what would today be called bureaucratic politics and inter-service rivalry. From the beginning, Essex's leadership was disputed: he had to share the command of this expedition with three other men: the Lord High Admiral, the vice admiral and Sir Walter Ralegh. Collectively, they saw it as their mission to rein in the ambitious Essex, the youngest of them, who was given command of the soldiers who were sent on this expedition.

Even before the fleet was launched, Essex's strategic plan had been truncated, amputated of vital elements – the establishment of a permanent garrison, the double attack on Cádiz and Lisbon – by the orders it received from the queen and Privy Council, and thus deprived of any chance of lasting success. When Essex tried to persuade his fellow commanders on the expeditionary force's war council to go against these express orders and to implement his strategic plan in its entirety, they refused to disobey their queen's express instructions.[109] The resounding record of rivalry and antagonism among Elizabeth's foremost leaders is traced by Paul Hammer to her peculiar style of government. This he sees as the understandable result of the quandary in which she, as a woman and unable to assume military command, found herself when faced with the potential solidarity against her springing from male military bonding.[110] As we can see from this example, Elizabeth managed to dominate her servants with the notable exception of the Earl of Essex, who would pay dearly for his insubordination.

In the campaign of the following summer (1597), the queen again insisted that Essex share command, this time only with Ralegh and the younger Howard. As a result her wars were conducted on the basis of incoherent strategies resulting from bureaucratic compromise reflecting the greatest common factor among the views of her closest counsellors, not a logically coherent plan. Some years later, Sir Walter Ralegh would complain that 'If the late queen had believed her men of war as she did her scribes, we had in her time beaten that great empire in pieces . . . But her majesty did all by halves, and by petty invasions taught the Spaniard how to defend himself.'[111] In reality, it had been her ministers and military commanders who had done all by halves, by disagreeing among themselves on the strategy to follow. No wonder Sutcliffe had devoted much time to stressing the desirability of putting any campaign under one, and only *one*, supreme commander.[112]

As to the origins of the strategic concept underlying the Cádiz campaign, its novelty in taking the war to Spain's soil and not merely to its navies, and the 'sheer scale of its conception', it can be traced to Sutcliffe, not Essex,[113] although it was Essex who worked out the detail of how to translate it into a concrete strategic plan of action. This latter point is also demonstrated by the quick subsequent abandonment of the concept by Essex, when he might have persevered, trying to put it into practice once more. (As we have seen in Chapter 5, even in 1597, ever open to new ideas, Essex allowed himself to be persuaded to venture on the *guerra de corsar* which he had dismissed as below his dignity only one year earlier.) Essex, whose only constancy lay in his commitment to war, booty and the quest for personal martial 'fame',[114] would during his career experiment with just about all the possible options. Besides those he tried before 1596, he would later plead for an *English* re-conquest of Calais in early 1597,[115] for an attempt to intercept Spanish trade at the Azores later that year, for war against the Irish rebels, and later for peace with those same rebels. With the Cádiz campaign of 1596, Essex gave Sutcliffe's capture-and-hold strategy a try. But that the concept in all its coherence and magnitude, a quantum leap away from all the others that Essex tried, was Sutcliffe's, not Essex's, is demonstrated by the *à la carte* approach to the pursuit of England's security that Essex showed.

Epilogue

Had the success of Sutcliffe's strategic plan been a real possibility? Even with a navy that for its time was big, and even without their personal priorities of acquiring loot, Essex and the other members of the war council of the Cádiz expedition could not have translated their successful strike into a disabling defeat for Spain, if they left the Spanish war fleet in Lisbon untouched. Had they carried out a supplementary raid against Lisbon and also Spain's northern ports of La Coruña and Ferrol, they might have struck the naval weapon out of Philip's hands and thus lastingly disarmed him at sea. This would not have ended Spanish control of the Low Countries instantly, but it would have reduced Spanish communications with the Low Countries to the '*camino español*', the land route across the Pyrenees through Burgundy, or via Genoa, Milan and on over the Alps, which might have brought on Dutch independence much sooner.

Essex's assessment was that the English fleet had sufficient provisions to execute at least the double campaign against Cádiz and Lisbon, or even to hold them. One must keep in mind that England had a long experience with holding on to ports on the Continent, when the hinterland was hostile, and with supplying them by sea if necessary. Cádiz was the furthest from the British Isles where this had ever been tried in Europe, but meanwhile, even bolder attempts to create settlements in similar ways in North America were tried and failed: famously with the Roanoke colony in 1586, in what later became North Carolina (abandoned in the following year). Yet this was all a matter of evolving naval power. By 1607, the Virginia Company of London founded Jamestown, Virginia, a colony that *would* survive. A century later, in 1704, an Anglo-Dutch fleet captured another promontory of the Iberian Peninsula, Gibraltar, and Britain has managed to hold onto it ever since. So why were Sutcliffe's plans for the seizure of Iberian ports not realised?

As we have seen, already at the outset of the 1596 expedition, orders had been to concentrate on a short, sharp strike against Cádiz, to the exclusion of all other endeavours, without committing forces for any length of time. The other principal commanders of this enterprise, unlike Essex, were too obedient to their instructions to take the risk – proposed by Essex – of confronting her with the *fait accompli* of Cádiz's capture and garrisoning. They were unwilling to wait for new orders from the queen in reaction to a request to approve such a change of plan. They had a point: Lord Howard of Effingham for one would be rewarded for his services by becoming Earl of Nottingham, and he would die in his bed, while Essex, too fond of pursuing his own strategies against Elizabeth's express orders, would yield to hubris and claim the crown for himself, ending with his head on the block at the Tower in 1601.

What of Sutcliffe? We still find Sutcliffe taking an interest in military matters in 1598: 'Mr. Dean Sutlyf is made captain' of some horsemen raised for military service in his diocese – that is he presumably trained them for military service.[116] Thereafter we find no further evidence of any military exploits: his other publications in English and Latin concerned theological disputes, illustrating his garrulous nature and visceral hatred of Catholicism.[117] As neither Sutcliffe's own nor his wife's families could have done much to further his career through connections, Sutcliffe owed most of his success to his own scholarly achievements, and more still to patronage, especially Essex's. Sutcliffe was not, however, tainted by Essex's rebellion, indictment and execution as a traitor. At the downfall of his patron, Sutcliffe hastened to ingratiate himself with Essex's long-standing rival, Sir Robert Cecil, Elizabeth's trusted adviser, by dedicating a book to him only a year after Essex's rebellion and execution.[118] Sutcliffe retained his offices throughout the rest of Elizabeth's reign.

After her death, under the patronage of the new monarch, Sutcliffe founded King James' College at Chelsea, a 'polemical college', a sort of think tank and propaganda institution, which had the mission for 'learned divines' to 'study and write in maintenance of all controversies against the papists'. James I as the patron laid the first stone in 1609. Sutcliffe was the first provost, and had 19 (research) fellows under him, mostly clerics. The building of Chelsea College was never completed, however, and it seems that the fellows of this anti-Catholic think tank made little contribution to the solution of the problems of their time. Eventually, Chelsea College went under with Sutcliffe's death.

But Sutcliffe was not quite without principles. When the Stuart dynasty sought to improve relations with Spain through a royal marriage between crown prince Charles and a Habsburg princess, Sutcliffe's fierce opposition landed him in prison along with other opponents of the match, and his income was suspended for a year. Sutcliffe, Hispanophobe and arch-Protestant, was not the only one to oppose a union with Europe's foremost Catholic family, and the match came to naught.

Apart from this, Sutcliffe took a great interest in the settlement of Virginia and New England, in keeping with his lasting conviction that England should conquer *and hold* territories, and he is said to have encouraged John Smith in his exploits.[119] While it seems that Sutcliffe never again turned his hand to military writing, his *Practice, Proceedings and Lawes of Armes* merits the title of the most coherent and comprehensive, and even influential, strategic concept published in Western Europe between classical antiquity and the Age of Enlightenment.

Notes

1 For definitions of Strategy, see Beatrice Heuser: *The Evolution of Strategy: Thinking War from Antiquity to the Present* (Cambridge: Cambridge University Press, 2010), pp. 1–28.

2 For an overview of early literature on strategy, see Beatrice Heuser: 'Introduction', in id. (trans. & ed.): *The Strategy Makers: Thoughts on War and Society from Machiavelli to Clausewitz* (Santa Barbara, CA: ABC Clio for Praeger, 2010), pp. 1–31.

3 The sources for this biographic sketch are Sidney Lee (ed.): *Dictionary of National Biography*, Vol. 55 (London: Smith, Elder, 1898), pp. 175–177; Nicholas W.S. Cranfield, 'Sutcliffe, Matthew (1549/50–1629)', in H.C.G. Matthew & Brian Harrison (eds): *Oxford Dictionary of National Biography 53* (Oxford: Oxford University Press, 2004), pp. 351–353.

4 Matthew Sutcliffe, Doctor of Diuinitie: *The Blessings on Mount Gerizzim, and the Curses on Movnt Ebal: Or, the Happie Estate of Protestants Compared with the Miserable Estate of Papists vnder the Popes Tyrannie* (London: Printed for Andrew Hebb, 1625).

5 This information was gleaned from the archives of Trinity College, Cambridge, by Jonathan Smith, Archivist and Modern Manuscript Cataloguer, and recorded in a letter to the author, 10 June 2011.

6 Paul E.J. Hammer: *The Polarisation of Elizabethan Politics: The Political Career of Robert Devereux, 2nd Earl of Essex, 1585–1597* (Cambridge: Cambridge University Press, 1999), p. 239 footnote 216.

7 Essex in the Yelverton MS, Paul Hammer, 'New Light on the Cadiz Expedition of 1596', *Historical Research*, Vol. 70 No. 172 (June 1997), p. 200; see also Robert Devereux, 2nd Earl of Essex: *An Apologie of the Earle of Essex* (written 1598; printed London?: for J. Smethwick?, 1600), p. A1ᵛ.

8 In a letter to Robert Naunton, printed in full in the appendix to Paul E. Hammer: 'Essex and Europe: Evidence from Confidential Instructions by the Earl of Essex, 1595–6', *English Historical Review*, Vol. 111 No. 441 (April 1996), p. 378.

9 Paul E.J. Hammer: 'The Uses of Scholarship: The Secretariat of Robert Devereux, Second Earl of Essex, c. 1585–1601', *English Historical Review*, Vol. 109 No. 430 (Feb. 1994), pp. 26–51.

10 Paul E.J. Hammer: 'The Earl of Essex, Fulke Greville, and the Employment of Scholars', *Studies in Philology*, Vol. 91 No. 2 (Spring 1994), pp. 167–180.

11 Sir Michael E. Howard: *Captain Professor: A Life in War and Peace* (London: Continuum, 2006), p. 162.

12 George Leonard Bird: 'The Earl of Essex, Patron of Letters' (MS PhD University of Utah, 1969), cited by Alzada Tipton: '"Lively Patterns . . . for Affayres of State": Sir John Hayward's *The Life and Reigne of King Henrie IIII* and the Earl of Essex', in *Sixteenth Century Journal*, Vol. 23 No. 3 (Autumn 2002), p. 789.

13 Quoted in Hammer: 'Uses of Scholarship', p. 49.

14 Such a tutorial-type discussion is described as a means of understanding by Richard Mulcaster: *Positions wherein Those Primitive Circumstances Be Examined . . .* (London, 1581), p. 254f., summarised in Lisa Jardine & William Sherman: 'Pragmatic Readers: Knowledge Transaction and Scholarly Services in Late Elizabethan England', in Anthony Fletcher & Peter Roberts (eds): *Religion, Culture, and Society in Early Modern Britain* (Cambridge: Cambridge University Press, 1994), p. 106.

15 Quoted in Tipton: '"Lively Patterns"', p. 790.

16 Jardine & Sherman: 'Pragmatic Readers', p. 105. See also Hammer: *Polarisation*, pp. 309–313.

17 As the older English calendar still counted January as belonging to the previous year.

18 Sutcliffe married Anne, the daughter of John and Frances Bradley of Louth in Lincolnshire. Her maternal grandfather was one John Fairfax of Swarby. They had only one child, a daughter, who according to Matthew and Harrison predeceased them without ever getting wed. See Matthew & Harrison (eds): *Oxford Dictionary of National Biography 53*; Lee: *Dictionary of National Biography*, 55.

19 Matthew Sutcliffe: *A Treatise on Ecclesiastical Discipline . . .* (London: George Bishop & Ralph Newberie, 1590).

20 Robert Lacey: *Robert Earl of Essex: An Elizabethan Icarus* (London: Weidenfeld & Nicolson, 1971), p. 94.

21 Sutcliffe: *Practice*, p. C[1]ʳ.

22 Robert Dudley, Earl of Leicester: *Lawes and Ordinances* [for the English forces in the Low Countries] (London: Christopher Barker, 1586).

23 Matthew Sutcliffe: *The Practice, Proceedings and Lawes of Armes* (London: Christopher Barker, 1593), pp. B4ᵛ, 136.
24 For excerpts from the book in modernised English, see Heuser (ed. & trans.): *The Strategy Makers*, Chapter 4: 'Matthew Sutcliffe', pp. 62–86.
25 Maurice Cockle: *A Bibliography of Military Books up to 1642 and of Contemporary Foreign Works* (London: Simpkin, Marshall, Hamilton, Kent, 1900).
26 Hammer: *Polarisation*, pp. 240–264.
27 Quoting Flavius Vegetius: *De Re militari*, III.1.
28 Sutcliffe: *Practice*, A3.
29 Reference to Aristotle: *Nikomachian Ethics*, X.7.
30 Sutcliffe: *Practice*, p. 288.
31 Paul A. Jorgensen: 'A Formative Shakespearean Legacy: Elizabethan Views of God, Fortune, and War', *Proceedings of the Modern Language Association*, Vol. 90 No. 2 (Mar. 1975), pp. 222–233.
32 Sutcliffe: *Practice*, p. 3.
33 'Preventive war' is taken to mean a war to prevent the other side, imputed to have an intention of attacking and to be making general preparations in that direction, from getting to the point of launching it one day. 'Pre-emptive war' refers to action taken on confirmed notification that the enemy is actually on the point of launching an attack now.
34 Sutcliffe: *Practice*, p. 97.
35 Ibid., pp. 101–2.
36 Ibid., p. 103.
37 Ibid., pp. 203–207.
38 Sancho de Londoño, *El discvrso sobre la forma de redvcir la Disciplina militar, à meyor y antigvo estado* (1589, repr. Madrid: Ministry of Defence, 1992); Sutcliffe: *Practice*, p. 12. See Heuser (ed. & trans.): *The Strategy Makers*, pp. 87–102.
39 Sutcliffe: *Practice*, pp. 316–342.
40 Ibid., p. 288.
41 Ibid., pp. 288–295.
42 Jan Glete: 'Warfare, Entrepreneurship, and the Fiscal-Military State', in Frank Tallett & David Trim (eds): *European Warfare, 1350–1750* (Cambridge: Cambridge University Press, 2010), pp. 300–321.
43 John S. Nolan: 'The Militarization of the Elizabethan State', *Journal of Military History*, Vol. 58 No. 3 (July 1994), p. 399, lists some literary contributions to this debate.
44 Ibid., pp. 418, and 391–420 *passim*.
45 Ibid., p. 403.
46 Sutcliffe: *Practice*, p. 291.
47 Lacey: *Robert Earl of Essex*, p. 85.
48 Hatfield House: 'Cecil Papers 18/82, Robert Devereux, Earl of Essex, to Vice-Chamberlain Sir Thomas Heneage' (ca. 1 April, 1589), quoted in Michele Margetts: 'Stella Britanna: The Early Life (1563–1592) of Lady Penelope Devereux, Lady Rich (d. 1607)' (MS PhD Yale, 1992).
49 Sutcliffe: *Practice*, p. 16.
50 Neil Younger: 'The Practice and Politics of Troop Raising', *English Historical Review*, Vol. 127 No. 526 (2012) pp. 566–591.
51 Sutcliffe: *Practice*, pp. 70–73.
52 Nolan: 'The Militarization', p. 402.
53 Sutcliffe: *Practice*, pp. B4ᵛ f., 75.
54 Ibid., pp. B4ʳ, 77.
55 Ibid., p. B1ʳ.
56 Ibid., p. 290.
57 Ibid., p. 301f.
58 Ibid., pp. 13–15, 338.

59 Ibid., p. 21.
60 Ibid., pp. 294ff.
61 Ibid., pp. 29–34.
62 Ibid., pp. 148–152.
63 Ibid., p. B4^r.
64 Ibid., p. 76f.
65 Sutcliffe: *Practice*, pp. 273–279; Heuser: 'Introduction', pp. 3–6.
66 Sutcliffe: *Practice*, p. 284f.
67 G.A. Hayes-McCoy: 'Strategy and Tactics in Irish Warfare, 1593–1601', *Irish Historical Studies*, Vol. 2 No. 7 (Mar. 1941), pp. 255–279.
68 See for example the 'Hulton MS', formerly BL Loan 23(1), now Add.MSS 74287, Microfilm 2275, below, and Essex: *Apologie*.
69 Essex: *Apologie*, p. A4^r; see also Walter B. Devereux (ed.): *Lives and Letters of the Devereux, Earls of Essex, in the Reigns of Elizabeth, James I, and Charles I, 1540–1646*, Vol. 1 (London: John Murray, 1853), p. 351, and see also R.B. Wernham: *The Return of the Armadas: The Last Years of the Elizabethan War against Spain, 1595–1603* (Oxford: Clarendon Press, 1994), p. 55.
70 This MS was identified as written by Essex and is discussed in detail with long excerpts by L.W. Henry: 'The Earl of Essex as Strategist and Military Organizer (1596–7)', *English Historical Review*, Vol. 64 No. 268 (July 1953), pp. 363–393; see also Paul Hammer: 'Myth-Making: Politics, Propaganda and the Capture of Cadiz in 1596', *The Historical Journal*, Vol. 40 No. 3 (1997), pp. 621–642.
71 Hammer: *Elizabeth's Wars*, p. 200.
72 For a photographic reproduction of one page, see Hammer: *Polarisation*, p. 256.
73 Henry: 'The Earl of Essex'. The 'Omissions' are printed inter alia in Josiah Burchett: *A Complete History of the Most Remarkable Transactions at Sea from the Earliest Account of Time to the Conclusion of the Last War with France in Five Books* (London: J. Walthoe & J. Walthoe Jr, 1720), pp. 361–363.
74 Hammer: 'New Light', pp. 182–202.
75 Hulton MS, Fol. 154^v-Fol. 155^v; see also Burchett: *A Complete History*, pp. 361–363.
76 Hulton MS, Fol. 157^v–158^r.
77 Hulton MS, Fol. 157^v.
78 Hulton MS, Fol. 163^v.
79 Hulton MS, Fol. 165^r.
80 Hulton MS, Fol. 168^r f.
81 Hulton MS, Fol. 169^r.
82 Hulton MS, Fol. 156^r f.
83 Quoted in Henry: 'Essex as Strategist', p. 370.
84 Hulton MS, Fol. 164^r.
85 Essex: *Apologie*, p. A4^v.
86 Hulton MS, Fol. 156^v.
87 Essex: *Apologie*, p. B1^v.
88 Hulton MS, Fol. 165^r.
89 Lacey: *Robert Earl of Essex*, p. 179; see also Robert W. Kenny: *Elizabeth's Admiral: The Political Career of Charles Howard Earl of Nottingham 1536–1624* (Baltimore, MD: Johns Hopkins Press, 1970).
90 Quoted in Henry: 'Essex as Strategist', p. 370.
91 Hulton MS, Fol. 161^r f.
92 Hulton MS, Fol. 159^r.
93 Hammer: *Polarisation*, pp. 243–248, 258–260.
94 Lacey: *Robert Earl of Essex*, pp. 137–150.
95 Hammer: *Elizabeth's Wars*, p. 195.
96 Ibid., p. 195.
97 Quoted ibid., p. 194.

98 Hulton MS, Fol. 155^v.

99 Hulton MS, Fol. 2^r, quoted in Henry: 'Earl of Essex as Strategist', p. 368, Note 2.

100 Quoted in Anne Cruz: 'Vindicating the *Vulnerata*: Cádiz and the Circulation of Religious Imagery as Weapons of War', in Anne Cruz (ed.): *Material and Symbolic Circulation between Spain and England, 1554–1604* (Aldershot: Ashgate, 2008), p. 43f.

101 Cruz: 'Vindicating the *Vulnerata*', *passim*.

102 Hammer: *Polarisation*, p. 229f.

103 Hammer: 'New Light', p. 197.

104 Cruz: 'Vindicating the *Vulnerata*', pp. 43, 48–60.

105 Hammer: 'New Light', p. 198.

106 Stephen Usherwood & Elizabeth Usherwood: *The Counter-Armada 1596: The Journal of the Mary Rose* (London: Bodley Head, 1983), p. 85, entry for 24 June 1596, Thursday.

107 Lacey: *Robert Earl of Essex*, pp. 161–172.

108 Hammer: *Polarisation*, p. 267.

109 Hulton MS, Fol. 155 ^{v}.

110 Hammer: *Elizabeth's Wars*, pp. 1–8.

111 Quoted in Hammer: *Elizabeth's Wars*, p. 1.

112 Sutcliffe: *Practice, Proceedings and Lawes*.

113 Hammer: *Polarisation*, pp. 260, 267.

114 Notwithstanding his protestations in his *Apologie* of 1600, which in its entirety belies this claim in being a plea for war with Spain: Essex: *Apologie*, p. A1^v.

115 Hammer: *Polarisation*, p. 254.

116 Quoted in Henry Webb: 'Dr. Matthew Sutcliffe', *Philological Quarterly*, Vol. 23 (1944), p. 86.

117 These included Matthew Sutcliffe, *An ansvvere to a certaine libel supplicatorie* . . . (London: The Deputies of C. Barker, 1592); id.: *An ansvvere vnto a certaine calumnious letter* published by M. Iob Throkmorton . . . (London: the Deputies of C. Barker, 1595); id.: *An abridgement or suruey of poperie* . . . (London: Melchisedech Bradwood for Cuthbert Burbie, 1606); id.: *A Briefe Examination, of a Certaine Peremptorie Menacing and Disleal Petition* . . . (London: W. Cotton, 1606); id.: *Apologia pro christiano batavo* (London: s.n., 1610); id.: *The Blessings on Mount Gerizzim, and the Curses on Movnt Ebal* (London: Andrew Hebb, 1625?).

118 Matthew Sutcliffe: *A Challenge concerning the Romish Church, Her Doctrine and Practises* (London: A. Hatfield, 1602).

119 Glyn Redworth: *The Prince and the Infanta: The Cultural Politics of the Spanish Match* (Newhaven, CT: Yale University Press, 2003), pp. 100–111.

6

COMMAND OF THE SEA

The origins of a strategic concept

In 1609, the Dutch jurist Hugo Grotius noted that 'because the sea is fluid and ever changing, it cannot be possessed.'[1] This statement has lost nothing of its plausibility. How then could anyone ever argue that a state could aspire to 'command of the sea' or to 'rule the oceans'? This chapter seeks to explore the origins of a concept which was always an overstatement of ambitions, to the point that it is difficult to understand how it ever came into being.

The dual roots of the command of the sea

In his great work on the Peloponnesian War, Thucydides let the Athenian ruler Pericles muse, 'Μέγα γαρ το της θαλάσσης κράτος,' a phrase difficult to translate elegantly, roughly meaning, 'The rule' or 'command of the sea is indeed a great matter,' or 'of great importance'.[2] This work was translated into Western European languages by the sixteenth century.[3] Anglophone students who struggled with Greek or indeed those who had none were helped by the fact that the *Peloponnesian War* was translated into English for the first time in 1550 – admittedly via French and thus not very satisfactorily, but well enough to serve students as a crib. Significantly, as we shall see, the library of Trinity College, Cambridge, still holds a copy of this translation, presumably acquired soon after its publication.[4] Thucydides's account of Athens's naval exploits could thus influence English elite thinking about the possibilities offered by navies, even if not all members of this elite were accomplished Greek scholars. And this happened just as sail was winning the competition over oar, and oceans were ever more extensively navigated.[5] Admittedly, English and British claims to rule the sea predate the impact of Thucydides. They were more modest, however, until naval technological innovation with the admixture of Thucydidean notions of 'thalassokratia' resulted in a revolution in strategic thinking *before* Britain, from the seventeenth to the nineteenth centuries, rose to become the world's leading naval power.

Medieval feudal roots of English claims to overlordship of the sea

The medieval roots of claims to sovereignty or overlordship of the sea lie in the struggle of medieval monarchs to assert their superiority over their noble vassals. While they were first documented for England by an early seventeenth-century antiquarian and archivist, John Selden, with great political ambitions for himself and for his monarch, these early documents reflect medieval monarchs' gradual construction of a royal monopoly of the use of force, their assertion of supremacy over their own barons and local chieftains, and their concern about equality with other monarchs.[6] Digging through the royal records of England, Selden found a charter dating from as early as 964, in which the Anglo-Saxon king Edgar had granted land to Worcester Cathedral, where we read, 'Ego Edgardus Anglorum Basileus omniumque Regum insularum, Oceanique Britanniam circumjacentis . . . cunctarumque nationum quae infra eam includuntur Imperator et Dominus.'[7] Edgar in this document is thus styled king, emperor and lord of all the islands of the kingdom, of their populations and of the oceans surrounding Britain. The terms used – *basileus, imperator, dominus* – all reflect medieval concerns about prestige and rank. Two centuries later, a legal text promulgated by his Norman successor, King Richard I, referred to the 'antiquam Superioritatem maris Angliae', England's old superiority (sovereignty) of the sea; it emphasised, incidentally, that English kings had claimed this sovereignty even before possessing Normandy, so not only on the grounds of ruling over land on both shores of the Channel.[8]

Over a century later, in 1336, King Edward III, about to launch his bid for the French crown, reminded his naval commanders '*quod progenitores nostri reges Angliae Domini Maris Anglicani circumquaque* et etiam defensores contra hostium invasiones ante haec temporar extiterint'[9] – that his forebears, the kings of England, had been Lords of the English sea and defenders against army invasion even before that time. Four years later, Edward III won a naval victory over French ships at the Battle of Sluys on the coast of Flanders. To celebrate this triumph, he had a 'noble', a gold coin, minted which showed him aboard a ship, carrying his sword as a sign of domination,[10] much as previously kings and other rulers had shown themselves either on thrones or horseback, sword in hand (Figure 6.1).[11]

A century later, a little book presenting political advice in the form of a long poem, known as the *Libelle of Englyshe Polycye* (line 1436ff.), commented on the 'noble':

> Ffor iiii [=four] thynges our noble sheueth to me,
> Kying, shype, and swerde, and pouer of the see.[12]

This 'power of the see' was crucial in assuring communications of Plantagenet rulers, first, of the Angevin Empire, and then of the areas claimed and conquered by Edward III and Henry V in the Hundred Years' War.

FIGURE 6.1 Edward III's noble[13]

. . . *Now do something about it*

There are documents of non-English provenance seemingly recognising this claim to the rule of the sea by the English monarchs. Ironically, these are mainly in the forms of petitions to the king of England to do something about pirates[14] in the area supposedly under his control. Thus a petition of Montreuil-sur-Mer, dating from 1306, pleads with both the kings of France and England to redress damages done to the merchants of this town. Especially King Edward II was addressed, because the kings of England, since time immemorial, had 'the peaceful possession of the sovereign lordship of the Sea of England and the isles within it', with the right to 'establish laws, statutes, and defences' of all sort, 'and to keep the peace . . . among all sorts of people, both under their own lordship as those who pass through, and through the sovereign guard over all manner of knowledge and justice, high and low.'[15] A few years later, in 1320, Flemish envoys asked King Edward II to prosecute robberies of Flemish ships by English sailors, calling him 'lord of the sea'.[16] In 1372, the Commons submitted a petition to his son, urging him to restore a previous situation when 'all countries held our aforesaid lord to be and called him "King of the

Sea".'[17] Half a century later, the Commons made a similar petition to King Henry V to redress new grievances, on the basis that he and all his ancestors had 'at all times been lords of the sea', especially seeing that the king was now 'lord of the coasts of both sides of the sea'. Henry V replied with what the historian William Fulton called 'the usual formula of refusal' – namely that he would consider it ('soit avise par le Roy'), but apparently never acted upon it.[18]

For a long time English monarchs had more bark than bite even when they were directly challenged by others on this issue. The English kings were by no means the only ones to make such claims to sovereignty over territorial waters. Eric of Pomerania, who was king of Denmark as Eric VII, king of Norway as Eric III and later counted as King Eric XIII of Sweden, claimed overlordship over the Sound (as he like his adoptive mother, Queen Margaret I, before him ruled the lands on either side). In 1429, Eric turned this into practical policy by instituting a Sound Duty which ships passing through this area had to pay until 1857. Castles constructed or fortified in his reign ensured Danish ability to enforce these duties.[19] When Queen Mary I of England lost Calais, her last possession on the Continental mainland, to the French crown in 1558, the French kings could not help gloating about this, as the English monarchs had claimed sovereignty over their coast for so long. Henri II and Henri III paid them back in kind, and in 1555 and 1584 respectively insisted that vessels strike their sails to French ships when they met them at sea.[20] By the seventeenth century if not earlier, the Russian tsar forced all fishermen 'within his seas, though it may be many Leagues from the Maine, to pay him tribute', as Sir John Boroughs recorded, and he claimed that such dues were also exacted by the Duke of Medina Sidonia in Spain, all princes of Italy whose territories bordered the Mediterranean, and the Dutch with respect to their own fishermen.[21]

A charming example of such competition for naval pre-eminence is the *The Debate betwene the Heraldes of Englande and Fraunce*, written in the late fifteenth century, in which the allegorical figure of Dame Prudence is asked to settle a dispute as to which of the two countries deserves pre-eminence. This was translated into English in the mid-sixteenth century, with appropriate contemporary additions, and in the English translation we read, about a third into the text, that 'the most puyssaunt kyng of England is Emperour within his owne Realmes, and holdeth of no man, he is supryme hed of his church of England & Irland, weryng a diademe Imperiall,' a formula traditionally employed by the king of France to ward off imperial or papal attempts to meddle in domestic French affairs. This needled the French herald who, speaking 'of the feates of the sea', appealed to Dame Prudence to concede that 'the kyng of Fraunce is very kyng and lorde of the sea' because of France's harbours, ships and trade. To this the English herald answers,

> I woll proue that the kyng of England is kyng of the narowe sea and not you, for a kyng that wolde be lorde of the sea, must haue thre thinges necessary, that is to say, great and perfounde waters and Hauyns to kepe his shyps in, secondarely plenty of shyps, & thirdly marchaundises to exercise them.

He claimed that England could beat France in all three points – a classic Annie-get-your-gun argument.[22]

Practical implications

There were practical implications of the English monarchs' claim to overlordship in their territorial waters. Foreign ships were required to lower their single sail, or, if they had several, their topsail, and strike their flag to greet English ships. We find this in the Angevin Empire, in an ordinance of King John of 1201. He commanded that any ship was to be seized if it refused 'at sea' to lower its sail(s) when ordered to do so by an English ship. The point of this was that if it lowered its sail (at the time usually only one), it could not get away fast and could be searched. At the same time, King John promised that all merchantmen would be allowed to pass unmolested.[23] In 1368, King Richard II issued an ordinance whereby all ships 'de quelque passage qui passe par la mere' should be taxed, according to their tonnage.[24] Exemptions from such duties (and thus the right to non-taxed fishing) were granted to French fishermen in an ordinance of Henry IV, and by Henry VI with regard to the fishermen who were subjects of the Duchess of Burgundy (by implication confirming that others still had to pay these dues).[25]

A record dating from 1402 – that is the reign of Henry IV – illustrates the practical implications: we are told that the English insisted that foreign vessels – including especially fishery vessels – salute the English flag. That year two foreign vessels were captured and towed away by English ships, even though the former were unarmed and had lowered their sails but not their flag.[26] From then until the mid-sixteenth century, Fulton seems to have found no further example of enforcement. Even though Henry VIII had called himself 'Lord of these [English] seas', it was only in 1549, under his son, that we have records of English ships firing at Flemish men-of-war to force them to salute the English ships. When in 1552 Sir Henry Dudley, commanding several English vessels, asked the Council how he should react if French men-of-war should refuse to salute him ('touching the pre-eminence of honour to be given'), the Council replied that 'in respect of thamitie and that the sayd Baron is stronger then he upon the sees sume tymes yelde and sume tymes receive thonnour', so he should use 'such discression that the same yelding of the preeminence may be interpreted to be of curtesy rather than to the derogacion of the Kinges honour.'[27]

Only two years later, however, there is a record of an impressive act of bravado when the English elite was torn apart over the marriage of their Queen Mary, who had restored Catholicism in England, to her Catholic cousin, the king of Spain: in 1554, when King Philip II came to England to join his wife, with his personal flag flying unlowered on the Spanish admiral's ship, the English admiral Lord William Howard gave orders to open fire on the Spanish fleet. This was an insult which would continue to rankle with the Habsburg monarch. Again, the English antagonised Philip, when in 1570, after the death of Mary, his new bride Anne of Austria's ships drew into Plymouth when she was *en route* for her wedding.[28] Again, the English fired at her ships as they did not strike sails in the requested fashion.

It is worth examining a little closer to what seas English monarchs laid claim.

What seas?

As historian Sebastian Sobiecki has pointed out, the seas referred to are really what would later become known as 'territorial waters'. He shows that in the twelfth century, a glossator on Roman law[29] at the leading law European university, Bologna, emphasised that the sea was common to all to be used by all (a line that would later be taken by Grotius in the early seventeenth century). He added, however, that it fell under 'Caesar's' jurisdiction. In the fourteenth century, another Bologna lawyer, Bartolus da Sassoferrato (1313 or 1314–1357), writing for Emperor Charles IV, defined that '*Mare dicitur illius Domini sub cuius terrirorio comprehenditur*' – the sea is said to belong to that lord to whose territory it belongs.[30]

In fact, the claims of English monarchs did not extend beyond territorial waters. In a compendium of laws of the sea dating from the fifteenth century, we find reference to a document dating from the reign of Henry I (1100–1135) containing the expression la 'mer appartenant au roi dAngleterre'.[31] Subsequently, Fulton has identified documents dating from the reign of Edward I referring to '*in mari nostro*', and of Edward II using the phrase '*partibus maris infra regnum nostrum Angliae*'. From the thirteenth century, we find references to the 'Four Seas of England' or the 'Four Seas'. Queen Elizabeth I spoke about 'our seas of England and Ireland'. The 'Narrow Sea/s' usually mean the Straits of Dover – as for example in the *Libelle of Englyshe Polycye*. James I (1603–1625) laid claim to control only of 'his seas' and 'streams' and the 'chambers' (bays) along the coasts of Britain; his successor, by contrast, was pushed by writers of the period (especially John Selden) to use the term 'Sovereignty of the Seas' in more extensive fashion, and pompously called one of his ships *Sovereign of the Sea*.[32]

Thus the English tradition of claiming sovereignty over the sea sounded grander than it was. At best the English claimed overlordship or mastery in general over the seas immediately surrounding England's shores or the British Isles collectively, and over the Channel in particular. This is of course a far cry from laying any claim for the rule of the oceans of the world, or a Thucydidean command of the sea, unsurprisingly, given its different ideational roots.

The rediscovery of Thucydides and *Thalassokratia*

Thomas Arne's eighteenth-century call for Britannia to rule the waves, which rings in our ears annually during the Last Night at the Proms, thus hails from earlier limited and quite reasonable claims of medieval English monarchs to control the Channel only, or the waters immediately around England or at best the British Isles. Indeed, N.A.M. Rodger has argued persuasively that subsequent English naval ambitions probably stemmed in large part from the very recognition of English weakness as a land power. In 1511, King Henry VIII of England was urged by unnamed counsellors to abandon ideas of reconquering the lost territories in France, with the argument that

> The natural situation of islands seems not to consort with conquests of that kind. England alone is just an empire. Or, when we would enlarge ourselves,

let it be that way we can, and to which it seems the eternal Providence hath destined us, which is by the sea.[33]

The confrontation with Philip II's Spain in the last two decades of the sixteenth century catalysed on the part of enterprising Englishmen developed greater ambitions for their monarch and their country, and introduced the quantum leap in the interpretation of the 'command of the sea'. And this was inspired by the rediscovery of Thucydides and his idea of '*thalassokratia*'.

It seems that educated Spaniards were just as aware of the Thucydidean term in its various possible translations as were their English contemporaries. A manuscript translation into Spanish had been in circulation since the fourteenth century, and a printed translation into Spanish since 1564.[34] Given Philip's ambitions, we are not surprised to find Spaniards citing the concept of rule of the sea. For example Don García de Toledo, Philip's viceroy for Sicily, wrote to him six years before the epic showdown in Lepanto that such a battle for the Mediterranean seemed inevitable, 'for as Your Majesty claims the dominion of the sea, and the Turk claims it, it is not possible to exclude that this dominion will come to be proven by naval battle.'[35]

It is probably no coincidence, given his experience at the English court, that Don Bernardino de Mendoza, Philip's one-time ambassador to London and conspirator to put Mary Stuart on Elizabeth's throne (for which he was expelled as *persona non grata*), would advise Philip's eponymous son and successor, then still crown prince, that empires such as his father's and his were held together by 'being Lordes of the sea'.[36] The command of the sea was thus also introduced into Spain's strategic thinking, while Spaniards recognised that several powers could claim it. Mendoza went on to outline all the advantages of naval power, proffering the interesting view that empires were more likely to survive if they consisted of 'sundry Prouinces' connected only by the sea than

> in one bodie, where corruption once entring causewth a farr greater ruyne, then in the deuided, and distant, being seldome times all infected at once with one morion [*violencia* in the original], as it may fall out where they stande vnited.[37]

But in the context of Philip's greater — indeed global — aspirations (see Chapter 1), his strategic ambitions were never limited to a mere pre-eminence on the seas.

In England, however, the idea of *thalassokratia* would gain a particular weight. Under Queen Elizabeth, we find a quantum leap upwards, a revolutionary change in the use of the notion of command of the sea in all its semantic variants, inextricably linked to an early blooming of writing about strategy more generally (see Chapter 4). One can trace this to a number of individuals connected with Trinity College Cambridge. Not only did Trinity College produce advocates of an aggressive or rather pre-emptive strategy towards Spain, like Antony Wingfield (see Chapter 4), but also it produced Matthew Sutcliffe (see Chapters 4 and 5), whose time at Trinity overlapped with that of not only Wingfield but also Anthony and Francis Bacon, and the young Earl of Essex. As we have seen, in the context of the Anglo-Spanish

War, Sutcliffe extolled the importance of the navy, 'and diuers pointes to be considered of those that command at sea' [!]. Sutcliffe elaborated further:

> Those Nations and Cities, that haue the commaundement of the sea, howsoeuer they are foiled at land: yet can neuer be thoroughly vanquished, before they be beaten from yᵉ Sea. . . . Contrariwise howe strong soeuer a Nation is by land, yet cannot the same mainteine itself long, nor continue in reputation without sufficient power at Sea. . . .
>
> The use of yᵉ nauy is great in peace, greater in warres. Thereby traffic, & entercourse betwixt friends is maintained: victuals yᵉ goe to the enemies are stopped; our wants of victuals, armes, munitions, & other necessaries are supplied: the enemies coast is spoiled, our owne defended: the coast townes of the enemiess country, that liue upon the sea are brought to great extremities, our own mainteined. Without yᵉ same neither can the trade of merchandize be mainteined, nor yᵉ sea townes of yᵉ enemie be besieged, nor their country spoyled, nor can we understand yᵉ enemies proceedings, nor helpe, or wel defend our friends, or our selves.[38]

Sutcliffe's patron, the Earl of Essex, waxed even more lyrical in his pleas for action against Spain. He tried to win Her Majesty's support for his strategies by arguing that a campaign to seize and occupy Philip's main Atlantic ports would make Elizabeth 'an absolute Queene of the Ocean'.[39] Or, as he put it elsewhere, in following his strategy, 'our souverayn shallbe trewly Regina maris and the trafike of th'Indyes and all things els that belong to one that commands the seas will be certainly, and only, her's.'[40]

A further proponent of a bid for naval power was an equally colourful character, Dr John Dee (1527–1608/9), who in his life had taught at universities from Cambridge to Prague as a Greek scholar, a mathematician specialising in navigation, but also as an astrologist and alchemist, and who found himself, towards the end of the century, as an adviser to Queen Elizabeth I.[41] As the first fellow for teaching Greek at the newly established Trinity College Cambridge (1546–1548), Dee would have read his Thucydides in the original Greek, of course. The term 'command of the sea', the translation of 'thalassokratia', was thus in circulation among the English elite who sought to advise Her Majesty on where to put her strategic priorities.

On 8 September 1597, Dr John Dee wrote a letter to Sir Edward Dyer (a fellow adventurer and courtier, with whom Dee had dabbled in alchemy in Bohemia), inscribed 'Thalattokratiá Brettanikē' (Dee's transcription of 'Θαλασσοκρατία Βριταννική', the British rule of the sea). In it Dee argued that the seas all around England, up to the very coast of Picardy, Normandy and Brittany, should be under the queen's 'sea-jurisdiction and sovereignty absolute'; the queen should have jurisdiction also of the seas to the west of England and Ireland, and indeed Scotland (as that country had in olden times been tributary to the English kings), all the way to 'that famous and very ancient Platonicall or Solonicall Atlantis'. Finally, the queen should rule over the North Sea up to the coasts of Norway and Denmark, or 'at least to the mid-sea', and again 'half seas over' towards Denmark, Friesland and Holland.[42]

Around this time, Dr Dee also proposed the creation of what at the time would have been an enormous royal fleet of 60 ships, which he oddly described as 'Petty Navy Royal', to protect the 'British Impire' – by which he meant mainly the region around the British Isles and the trading routes.[43] Such an expense was way beyond the means of the English crown then, or even after the union of England and Scotland. (The British navy could reach such figures only in the mid-seventeenth century under Oliver Cromwell's Commonwealth.[44])

Egged on by Spanish ambitions and the shock created by the threatened Spanish invasion of 1588 and the triumph over the Spanish Armada, Englishmen thus developed much grander ideas than their medieval predecessors. The armada painting of Queen Elizabeth I in its several versions shows that Elizabeth's leading artists and larger entourage of courtiers and aristocrats were well aware of this programme, subtly expressed pictorially: in this painting, the elegant right hand of the Tudor monarch reposes lightly on the globe, or to be precise, on the Atlantic and North America, the very region which the Spanish monarchs sought to claim as taboo for their European peers and their adventurous explorers and colonisers (Figure 6.2).

Queen Elizabeth herself did not take up those of her advisers who tried to blandish her into assuming the role of Regina Maris and lay claim to a larger sovereignty of the seas than mere dominion of 'our seas of England and Ireland'.[45] Yet her own

FIGURE 6.2 Queen Elizabeth I's armada portrait[46]

strategy – regardless of whether coherent – also aimed to challenge the Habsburg bid for global predominance. Queen Elizabeth refused to accept Pope Alexander VI's bestowal of the non-European world upon Spain and Portugal. Elizabeth had a quarrel with King Sebastian of Portugal about this, and thus allowed Drake a free hand in North America. In 1580 when Ambassador Mendoza complained about Drake and his adventures in the 'Indian' seas, Elizabeth told him that making part of the oceans a national *chasse gardée* was contrary to the Law of Nations, especially as she did not recognise any jurisdiction of the bishop of Rome. In her view, 'the use of the sea and air is common to all; neither can any title to the ocean belong to any people or private man, forasmuch as neither nature nor regard of the public use permitteth any possession thereof.' Elizabeth thus, well before Grotius, opposed any claim to a *mare clausum* and insisted that the seas were free for all.[47]

The result, however, was – if anything – the absence of a grand strategy unless it was a purely defensive, prudently conservative one: conservative of scarce resources, crown income and manpower. Both eyewitnesses and historians have accused Queen Elizabeth of lacking a coherent plan to build an empire, to colonise new territories, to increase her sphere of power. Elizabeth did not fully espouse the colonisation idea, and the colony named after her (Virginia) initially foundered and the settlement was discontinued in 1599, supposedly because Elizabeth 'did everything by halves' (see Chapter 5) and did not do enough to support the private entrepreneurs who espoused colonial plans.[48] From a postcolonial twenty-first-century perspective, this looks less worthy of criticism than it looked to the entrepreneurs like Sir Walter Ralegh or Dr John Dee or Matthew Sutcliffe, who having invested their private fortune in colonial projects, felt let down by the queen.

From Thalassocracy to command of the sea

How Britannia came to rule the waves under the Stuarts and the Hanoverians

We find the concept of 'command of the sea' employed and pondered under James I and VI as well. Both Bacon brothers in the 1580s and 1590s worked for the Earl of Essex. Sir Francis Bacon was later credited with the possibly apocryphal dictum that 'He that commands the sea is at great liberty and may take as much and as little of the war as he will'.[49] When Bacon urged King Charles I in the 1620s to go to war against Spain, all the arguments and strategic options he mustered were nothing but a reiteration of those that had been proposed and in part implemented in the Anglo-Spanish War.[50] Sir Walter Ralegh in his *History of the World*, which he began to write in 1607 while a prisoner in the Tower under James I, and which therefore was published only in 1614, pondered the strength of the Phoenicians, who were 'absolute kings of the Mediterranean Sea', and their main city of Carthage, which was 'invincible while it commanded the sea', and how Rome wrested the 'absolute masterie of the sea' from it.[51] The saying is attributed to him that 'Whosoever commandeth the sea commandeth trade; whosoever commandeth trade commands the riches of the world,' and thus the world itself.[52] (As we have seen in Chapter 4, however, Ralegh was not set on such high ideals when he urged the premature termination of the Cádiz expedition of 1596 and the return to England with what booty they had seized, rather than the permanent occupation of the city.)

Thenceforth, strategic-theoretical reflections all but disappeared. On the whole the term 'command of the sea' was now relegated to contexts of legal claims and British attempts to assert authority over the waters surrounding the British Isles. James I tried to uphold the 'saluting of the flag', repeatedly greatly offending neighbours (including well-wishers, ambassadors and ships from more remote lands), but did not manage systematically to collect the fishery taxes on the Dutch which he imposed in theory. As he stopped issuing letters of marque to English privateers, he has been portrayed as falling behind the French and Swedes in joint venture naval commerce raiding while these continued to back their own privateers; ships from both countries also tried to avoid saluting English ships if at all possible.[53] From 1631 the Stuart navy stepped up its insistence upon this ritual. Foreign ships were even expected to pass English ships leeward only, to mark their submission. If foreign ships did not 'do their duty', they would be hailed by the English, and then a shot might be fired across their bows, or over the poop, and then between the masts or at the flag. The insubordinate captain's vessel might be captured and towed into an English port.[54]

In 1609, Grotius published, anonymously, his *Mare Liberum* in Leyden. This created a lasting framework of thinking about international law and the seas, built on Grotius's assertion that the ocean cannot be turned into private property (see earlier). One of the important points of consensus between him (who is usually quoted on this matter) and many other writers of his age was that the sea could not be owned as land is owned, and that total 'command of the sea' could never be more than an ideal.

Grotius was answered for Scotland and King James by William Welwod, a professor of law at the University of St Andrews, in a little book presenting a short guide to the customary laws of the sea. Title XXVII contains a response to Grotius's *Mare Liberum*: here Welwod argued with his fourteenth-century Italian colleague Baldus de Ubaldis, '*Videmus, de iure gentium, in mare esse regna distincta, sicut in terra arida*' – the sea, too, can be divided up. He further argued that fishery in the territorial waters of one country should be freely open to the citizens of that state, but not just to anybody. He claimed that the fish shoals around Britain had become scarce because of the Dutch busse fishing. His bottom line was that the territorial waters around land should be under the sovereignty of that country, but concedes that 'that part of the maine Sea or great Ocean, which is farre remoued from the iust and due bounds aboue mentioned, properly perteyning to the nearest Lands of euery Nation. *Atq; ita esto mare vastum liberrimum*', and that vast sea is most free.[55]

In an even smaller book of handy pocket size, Sir John Boroughs, keeper of His Majesty's Records in the Tower, showed that by 1633 (the time of writing) the debate seemed by no means settled. Boroughs claimed

[t]hat Princes may have an exclusive property in the Soveraigntie of the severall parts of the Sea, and in the passage, fishing & shores thereof, is so evidently true by way of fact as no man that is not desperately impudent can deny it.

He goes on to say that some – by implication desperately impudent characters – still did.[56] The absence of such laws and 'correcting and securing power in case of wrong, or danger', however, would 'make men of the like condition with the fishes that live [in the sea], of which the greater doe usually devoure, and swallow the lesse'.[57] He claimed that the English kings had held 'the Superiority of the Seas of England derived and confirmed upon him by immemorable prescription, and continued possession even until this very yeare 1633', on which basis he had the right to impose taxes on passing ships and fishermen, and to close English waters to ships.[58] And he concluded,

[T]herefore the Soveraignty of our Seas being the most precious Jewell of his Majesties Crown, and (next under God) the principall meanes of our Wealth and Safetie, all true English hearts and hands are bound by all possible meanes and diligence to preserve and maintaine the same, even with the uttermost hazard of their lives, their goods, and fortunes.[59]

Next came John Selden, whom we introduced at the beginning, and who argued for an extension of the bounds of the maritime dominion of Britain up to

the very Shores or Ports of the Neighbor-Princes beyond-Sea, are Bounds of the Sea-Territorie of the *British* Empire to the Southward and Eastward; but that in the open and vast Ocean of the North and West, they are to bee placed at the utmost extent of those most spacious Seas, which are possest by the *English, Scots*, and *Irish*.[60]

With this, like Dr Dee before him, he claimed the Atlantic Ocean up to the borders of North America.

Cromwell's republican government maintained the Stuart insistence that other navies, passing through the Channel, must strike their flags to British ships. Meanwhile, the Danes continued levying their Sound Duty, and the outcome of the Thirty Years' War led Christina, queen of Sweden, to claim sovereignty over large parts of the Baltic, as the Westphalian Peace Treaties had confirmed Swedish entitlement to lands conquered that formed part of the Holy Roman Empire.[61] Moreover, the kingdoms of Denmark-Norway and Sweden competed for superiority over the Baltic Sea.[62] Nearer home, the monarchs of England and Scotland found themselves once again challenged by the French, who in a tit for tat tried to force the English to strike their flags to French ships. Charles I stubbornly revived the Plantagenet claim to the sovereignty over the entire Channel, *in pace Domini Regis*, prohibiting the passage of foreign men-of-war.[63]

But the worst were the contests on this point of honour and sovereignty with the Dutch. On 12 May 1652, Captain Anthony Young and his flotilla of two warships and one merchantman encountered a convoy of seven Dutch merchantmen and three warships, commanded by Commodore Huyrluyt. Young followed orders to insist on the procedure of the foreigners striking the flag in salute and not approaching the British vessels from the windward side, and the ensuing scuffle, with only partial compliance by the Dutch, triggered the Anglo-Dutch War, one in a series of three, in each of which the British insistence on foreign vessels striking their flag would be an aggravating factor.[64] At the end of the Third Anglo-Dutch War in 1674, Charles II imposed on the Dutch that they would salute the English flag, but as a matter of courtesy and honour, rather than obligation. In the peace treaty, signed at Westminster on 9 February 1674, the article concerning the flag confirms that the Estates General of the United Provinces of the Netherlands acknowledge that they have to honour the British 'flag called the *Jack*, in any of the seas from the Cape called *Finisterre*, to the middle point of the land called *van Staten*, in Norway' by 'striking their own flag and lowering their topsail'. Fulton observes that this clause was inserted in Anglo-Dutch treaties as late as 1784, but as a mere formality and precedent.[65]

British-Dutch hostilities were for some time transformed into the most perfect peace, of course, through the marriage of the heir to the Orange dynasty, William III, with Mary II, the oldest daughter of the Stuart king James II, who would jointly seize power and depose her father in 1688 as he had openly converted to Catholicism and the prospect of a Catholic succession through Mary's newly born half-brother, also named James, arose. The couple would rule over England, Scotland, Wales, Ireland and the United Provinces of the Netherlands, ushering in an era of peace between the two countries, united in their opposition in war to Louis XIV's expansionist France.

In the eighteenth century, it became the practice for countries to claim domination over the sea along their coastlines within cannon shot, or in the words of Cornelius van Bynkershoek (1673–1763), '*terrae dominium finitur ubi finitur armorum vis*', which in turn became part of the Law of Nations. Later this distance was agreed to be about three miles from shore.[66] Fishery rights continued to be a bone of contention, and when the daughters of James II were succeeded by the Hanoverian rulers of Britain, the eighteenth century once again saw incidents of clashes between the Dutch and indeed the Danes on the one hand and the British on the other, over who had fishing or trading rights in the North Sea, towards Iceland. But when France ceded Newfoundland and Nova Scotia to Britain with the Treaty of Utrecht of 1713, the treaty allowed French fishermen to fish in that area. When in 1740 Thomas Arne composed the music to the poet James Thomson's lyrics for their opera on King Alfred, Britannia's rule of waves well beyond those surrounding the British Isles was well established, although still periodically challenged, especially by the French Royal Navy. But as Britain's power grew, it could afford to become more conciliatory. In 1763 Canada as a whole was ceded by France to Great Britain; in turn, as a part of this settlement, however, fishery rights for France in the oceans around Canada were confirmed.[67] Fulton records that the clause insisting on the saluting of British ships was 'quietly dropped out of the admiralty instructions' on their dealings with other nations' ships after the British victory at Trafalgar in 1805.[68] Nicholas Rodger observes shrewdly that 'There was no more need of it, now that Britain had incontestably gained the real command of the ocean.'[69]

Epilogue

The expression 'command of the sea', however, would continue to haunt naval and maritime strategists, even though its absolute interpretation was never a realistic one, as Grotius had already argued soberly. Fascinated by the term, subsequent strategists would struggle to make sense of it and to find ways of integrating it into a viable strategy for their country. In the late nineteenth century, Vice Admiral Philip Howard Colomb claimed that since Elizabethan times, 'The struggle [of naval strategy] was for the mastery at sea, whether territorial conquest was or was not to follow success in this respect.' He recognised grudgingly that this could not be an end in itself, but must be ultimately the means to the end of staging an invasion on land, but 'the dividing line between attempts to gain the command of the sea in order to facilitate a descent upon the land, and descents upon the land with an admitted want of command of the sea, is an exceedingly fine one.'[70] Less subtly, Henry Spenser Wilkinson postulated that any war between Britain and its major rivals – he was thinking of France –

> must begin by a fight for the command of the sea – that is, the two navies will fight until one has destroyed the other or broken its force so that it must withdraw from the contest and retire to its fortified harbours. The winning side will then take means to prevent the weaker defeated fleet from doing any further harm, will endeavour to destroy the enemy's merchant shipping, or to shut it off from the sea, and will be at liberty to move armies across the sea. The losing side will do all that it can for the destruction of the commerce of the victor. Probably, from the beginning, there will be a chase of merchant ships by cruisers. . . . But until the decisive battles have been fought the protection of trading ships is a secondary matter.

Indeed, he argued, 'The command of the sea is to be had only by destroying or crippling the hostile navy. Until this has been done the transport of troops by sea is a dangerous operation.'[71] Or, as Sir Cyprian Bridge put it,

> The aim in naval warfare is to obtain command of the sea, . . . which means control of maritime communications – that is to say, of the ocean paths which connect one part of an extensive empire with another, which sea-borne commerce must traverse, and along which belligerent expeditions must proceed. The Power that obtains this control can attack its enemy where it pleases, and

evidently the control must be obtained before a great military expedition can be sent across the sea.[72]

In America, Alfred Thayer Mahan also made pronunciations suggesting the inescapable need to achieve 'command of the sea'.[73] One sees here the deleterious notion of the inescapable decisive battle at sea creeping into naval thinking, one that would haunt navies until the Second World War and later.

It was perhaps not surprisingly a general, Charles Callwell, who pleaded for the abandonment of the term 'command of the sea' and the substitution of the more modest 'maritime preponderance'.[74] But the key thinker who tried to break with this adulation of the 'command of the sea' whom Callwell followed was Sir Julian Corbett, who had written earlier, 'The object of naval warfare must always be directly or indirectly either to secure the command of the sea or to prevent the enemy from securing it.' While conceding this, he argued that 'one of the commonest sources of error in naval speculation' is

> the very general assumption that if one belligerent loses the command of the sea it passes at once to the other belligerent. The most cursory study of naval history is enough to reveal the falseness of such assumptions. . . . it ignores the power of the strategical defensive.[75]

> 'Command of the Sea' is not identical in its strategical conditions with the conquest of territory. You cannot argue from the one to the other, as has been too commonly done. Such phrases as the 'Conquest of water territory' and 'making the enemy's coast our frontier' had their use and meaning in the mouths of those who framed them, but they are really little but rhetorical expressions founded on false analogy. . . .
>   The analogy is false for two reasons . . . You cannot conquer sea because it is not susceptible to ownership, at least outside territorial waters. You cannot, as lawyers say, 'reduce it into possession', because you cannot exclude neutrals from it as you can from territory you conquer. In the second place, you cannot subsist your armed force upon it as you can upon enemy's territory.[76]

The sea has the positive value of being a 'means of communication', but also a 'negative value' of being a barrier.

> By winning command of the sea we remove that barrier from our own path, thereby placing ourselves in position to exert direct military pressure upon the national life of our enemy ashore, while at the same time we solidify it against him and prevent his exerting direct military pressure upon ourselves.
>   Command of the sea, therefore, means nothing but the control of maritime communications, whether for commercial or military purposes. The object

of naval warfare is the control of communications, and not, as inland warfare, the control of territory.[77]

And finally he added,

> If the object of the command of the sea is to control communications, it is obvious it may exist in various degrees. We may be able to control the whole of the common communications as the result either of great initial preponderance or of decisive victory. If we are not sufficiently strong to do this, we may still be able to control some of the communications; that is, our control may be general or local. . . .
> Finally, it has to be noted that even permanent general command can never in practice be absolute.[78]

Following Corbett, later twentieth-century maritime strategists would go out of their way to disassociate themselves from any call for the 'command of the sea', proposing a further series of terms signalling more modest ambitions, such as Herbert Richmond's term 'sea power', a vague concept if ever there was one.[79] The term did not entirely disappear, but could no longer sustain the lofty ambitions projected onto it by strategists from the Earl of Essex to Mahan. Geoffrey Till summed up that today,

> Being 'in command of the sea' simply means that a navy in that happy position can exert more control over the use of the sea than can any other. The degree of command varies greatly and is primarily illustrated by the extent to which it covers the capacity to use the sea for one's own purposes and prevent the enemy using it for his.[80]

Notes

1 Hugo Grotius: *De Jure Belli ac Pacis*, trans. by Louise R. Loomis (Roslyn, NY: Walter J. Black, 1949), p. 80f.
2 Thucydides I.143, 20.
3 Laurentius Valla's translation into Latin was printed in 1483. Half a century later followed the oldest translation into French: *L'histoire de Thucydide athenien, de la guerre qui fut entre les Peloponesiens et Atheniens*, trans. by Claude de Seyssel, bishop of Marseille and the archbishop of Turin (Paris: Josse Badius, 1527), went through several corrected re-editions; for the earliest Italian edition, see *Gli otto libri di Thucydide atheniese, delle guerre fatte tra popoli della Morea, et gli Atheniesi*, trans. by Francesco di Soldo Strozzi Fiorentino (Venice: Vincenzo Vaugris, 1545), in the Vatican Library.
4 *The hystory writtone by Thucidides the Athenyan of the warre, whiche was betwene the Peloponesians and the Athenyans*, trans. from French by Thomas Nicolls (London: William Tylle, 1550).
5 See also Andrew Lambert: 'Sea Power', in George Kassimeris & John Buckley (eds): *The Ashgate Research Companion to Modern Warfare* (Farnham: Ashgate, 2010), pp. 73–88.
6 Ioannis Seldeni: *Mare Clausum sev de Dominio Maris Libri dvo* (London: William Stanesbeius for Richard Meighen, 1636), published subsequently in English: John Selden: *Of the Dominion, or Ownership of the Sea, Two Books* (London: William Du-Gard, 1652).
7 Selden: *Mare Clausum*, p. 337. See also Thomas Wemyss Fulton: *The Sovereignty of the Sea* (Edinburgh: William Blackwood & Sons, 1911), p. 27.

8 Quoted in Fulton: *Sovereignty*, p. 51f.

9 Full text also in Josiah Burchett: *A Complete History of the Most Remarkable Transactions at Sea, from the Earliest Accounts of Time to the Conclusion of the Last War with France* (London: W.B. for J. Walthoe, 1720), p. 33.

10 Clifford J. Rogers: *War Cruel and Sharp: English Strategy under Edward III, 1327–1360* (Woodbridge: The Boydell Press, 2000).

11 See for example the seals of King Edward the Confessor, and Henries I and II, Stephen, Richard I, John, and Henry III of England, dating from the eleventh to the thirteenth centuries, www.historicseals.net/sealLists.php?cat=66&order=date, consulted on 18 XI 2014.

12 Sir G. Warner (ed.): *The Libelle of English Polycye* (1436–8, revised 1438–41, Oxford: Oxford University Press, 1926). Fulton points out that The *Libelle* also claims it was struck after Edward III captured Calais, but that makes no sense as the noble was issued in 1340, and Calais was taken in 1347; see *Sovereignty*, p. 37.

13 ©The Trustees of the British Museum. All rights reserved.

14 On the use of the term 'pirates', see N.A.M. Rodger: 'The Law and Language of Private Naval Warfare', *The Mariner's Mirror*, Vol. 100 No. 1 (Feb. 2014), pp. 5–16.

15 '*come les roys Dengleterre par raison du dit roialme, du temps qil ny ad memoire du contraire, averoient este en paisible possession de la sovereigne seigneurie de la meer Dengleterre et des isles esteans en ycele par ordinance et establisement de loiz, estatuz et deffenses communes et privees a garder pees et droiture entre tote manere des gentz tant dautri seignurie come de leur proper par illeqes passantz et par sovereign garde* ove tote manere de cognisance et justice haute et basses.' Text in Pierre Chaplais (ed.): *English Medieval Diplomatic Practice*, Vol. 1 Pt. 1 (London, 1975), document 206, pp. 367–369, here p. 367, partly quoted in N.A.M. Rodger: *The Safeguard of the Sea: A Naval History of Britain, 660–1649* (1997, London: Penguin, 2004), pp. 78, 525.

16 'Et prierent que le Roi, de sa seignurie et poer real, fait sente dreit et punissement del dit fait, de siccome il est *seigneur de la mer*, et la dite roberie fut fait sur la mer dans son poer, sicomme dessus est dit.' Text in Fulton: *Sovereignty*, p. 55.

17 Rodger: *The Safeguard of the Sea*, pp. 114, 530, quoting from *Rotuli Parlamentorum* II, p. 311.

18 Fulton: *Sovereignty*, p. 35.

19 Palle Lauring: *A History of Denmark*, trans. by David Hohnen (Copenhagen: Høst & Son, 1995³), p. 110f.

20 Fulton: *Sovereignty*, pp. 117, 277.

21 Sir John Boroughs: *The Sovraignty of the British Seas, Proved by Records, History, and the Municipall Lawes of this Kingdome, Written in the Yeare 1633* (London: Humphrey Moseley, 1651), p. 83f.

22 Jhon Coke: *The Debate betwene the Heraldes of Englande and Fraunce, compyled by Jhon Coke, clarke of the kynges rcognysaunce, or vulgerly, called clarke of the Statutes of the staple of Westmynster, and fynyshed the yere of our Lorde MDL* (1550), pp. 30ff., 62ff.

23 Quoted in Fulton: *Sovereignty*, p. 40.

24 Boroughs: *The Sovereignty*, pp. 65–67.

25 Ibid., pp. 74–78.

26 'omn es tamen inermes, et velum suum, ad primum clamoren Anglicorum declinantes'; see Fulton: *Sovereignty*, pp. 43, 207.

27 Ibid., p. 116f.

28 Ibid., p. 117.

29 Justinian's *Corpus Iuris Civilis*.

30 Sebastian Sobiecki: *The Sea and Medieval English Literature* (Cambridge: D.S. Brewer, 2008), pp. 140, 141, 143.

31 Sir Travers Twiss (ed.): *The Black Book of the Admiralty*, Vol. 1 (London: Longman etc. for *Monumenta Juridica*, 1871), p. 58.

32 Fulton: *Sovereignty*, pp. 9–11, 16f., 28, 118.

33 Rodger: *Safeguard of the Sea*, p. 176.

34 Guido delle Colonne: 'Discursos sacados de la Historia de la guerra del Peloponeso', MSS/10801 (second half of fourteenth century); *Historia de Thucydides: que trata de las guer-*

ras entre los Peloponesos y Athenieses: la qual allede las grandes y notables hazañas por mar y por tierra, delos vnos y delos otros, y de sus aliados y cōfederados, esta llena de oraciones y razonamiētos prudentes y auisados a proposito de paz y de Guerra, trans. by Diego Gracian (Salamanca: Iuan de Canoua, 1564).

35 'porque pretiendo V.M. el señorío de la mar, y pretendiéndolo el turco, no es posible excusar que no se venga á conocer esta superioridad por batalla de mar.' Letter of 31 May 1565, in Marquis of Pidal & Miguel Salvá (eds): *Colección de Documentos Inéditos para la Historia de España,* Vol. 29, Pt. 1 (Madrid: Imprenta de la Viuda de Calero, 1856), p. 167.

36 Mendoza: *Teórica y práctica,* p. 128, Hoby (trans.): *Theorique and Practise,* p. 148.

37 Ibid., p. 148.

38 Matthew Sutcliffe: *The Practice, Proceedings and Lawes of Armes* (London: C. Barker, by appointment to H.M. the Queen, 1593), pp. 273–275.

39 Robert Devereux, 2nd Earl of Essex: *An Apologie of the Earle of Essex* (written 1598; printed London?, 1600), p. B1ᵛ.

40 'Hulton MS', formerly BL Loan 23(1), now Add.MSS 74287, Microfilm 2275, fol. 167ᵛ.

41 R. Julian Roberts: 'Dee, John (1527–1609)', in *Oxford Dictionary of National Biography* (online edn, May 2006, Oxford: Oxford University Press, 2004), www.oxforddnb.com. idpproxy.reading.ac.uk/view/article/7418, accessed 7 Dec. 2014.

42 Fulton: *Sovereignty,* p. 104.

43 David Loades: *England's Maritime Empire: Seapower, Commerce and Policy, 1490–1690* (Harlow: Longman 2000), p. 111.

44 Rodger: *Command of the Sea,* p. 607.

45 Fulton: *Sovereignty,* pp. 104, 107f.

46 From the Woburn Abbey Collection. © His Grace the Duke of Bedford and the Trustees of the Bedford Estates.

47 Ibid., pp. 104, 107f.

48 David Armitage: 'The Elizabethan Idea of Empire', *Transactions of the Royal Historical Society,* 6th series, Vol. 14 (2004), p. 277.

49 Quoted in David H. Olivier: *German Naval Strategy 1856–1888: Forerunners of Tirpitz* (London: Frank Cass, 2004), p. 38. John Evelyn in his *Navigation and Commerce, Their Origin and Purpose* of 1674, and later French military writers paraphrased this; see Hervé Coutau-Bégarie: 'L'émergence d'une Pensée navale en Europe au XVIe Siècle et au Début du XVIIe Siècle', in Hervé Coutau-Bégarie (ed.): *Evolution de la Pensée navale,* Vol. 4 (Paris: Economica, 1994), p. 34.

50 Francis [Bacon] Lo. Verulam Vi. St Alban: *Considerations tovching a Warre with Spaine* (s.l.: s.e., 1629).

51 Sir Walter Ralegh: *Historye of the World* (London: Walter Bvrre, 1614), pp. 314, 360, 696.

52 Quoted in Olivier: *German Naval Strategy,* p. 38.

53 Paul M. Kennedy: *The Rise and Fall of British Naval Mastery* (1976; 2nd edn, Amherst, NY: Humanity Books, 1983), p. 39.

54 Fulton: *Sovereignty,* pp. 204f., 207f., 276.

55 William Welvvod [Welwood]: *An Abridgement of All Sea-Lawes: Gathered Forth of All VVritings and Monuments, Whih Are to be Found among Any People or Nation, Vpon the Coastsof the Great Ocean and Mediterranean Sea* (London: Humfrey Lownes for Thomas Man, 1613), pp. 61–72.

56 Boroughs: *The Soveraignty of the British Seas,* p. 1f.

57 Ibid., p. 3.

58 Ibid., pp. 6, 65–67.

59 Ibid., p. 164f; see also Fulton: *Sovereignty,* p. 365.

60 John Selden: *Of the Dominion, or Ownership of the Sea, Two Books* (London: William Du-Gard, 1652), p. 459.

61 Instrumentum Pacis Caesareo-Suecicum Osnabrugense: *Instrumenta Pacis Westphalicae: Die Westfälischen Friedensverträge 1648* (Bern: Herbert Lang, 1949), Article X.

62 Jan Glete: 'Naval Power and Control of the Sea in the Baltic', in John Hattendorf & Richard Unger (eds): *War at Sea in the Middle Ages and the Renaissance* (Woodbrige: Boydell Press, 2003), p. 217.

63 Fulton: *Sovereignty*, pp. 117, 263, 277.

64 Roger Hainsworth & Christine Churches: *The Anglo-Dutch Naval Wars 1652–1674* (Stroud: Sutton, 1998), p. 3.

65 Fulton: *Sovereignty*, p. 508f.

66 Ibid., p. 21.

67 Ibid., p. 531.

68 Ibid., p. 15.

69 N.A.M. Rodger: *The Command of the Ocean: A Naval History of Britain, 1649–1815* (London: Penguin, 2005), p. 583.

70 Philip Howard Colomb: *Naval Warfare: Its Ruling Principles and Practice Historically Treated* (London: W.H. Allen, 1891), pp. 32, 107–202, 203.

71 H.S. Wilkinson: *Command of the Sea and Brain of the Navy* (Westminster: Archibald Constable, 1894), pp. 31–33.

72 Sir Cyprian Arthur George Bridge: *Art of Naval Warfare* (London: Smith, Elder, 1907), p. 123.

73 Alfred Thayer Mahan: *Naval Strategy Compared and Contrasted with the Principles and Practice of Military Operations on Land* (Boston: Little, Brown, 1918), p. 165.

74 C.E. Callwell: *Military Operations and Maritime Preponderance: Their Relations and Interdependence* (originally Edinburgh: Wm Blackwood, 1905, repr. Annapolis, MD: Naval Institute Press, 1996), p. 1f.

75 Sir Julian Corbett: *Some Principles of Maritime Strategy* (1911, repr. Annapolis, MD: US Naval Institute Press, 1988), p. 91.

76 Ibid., p. 93.

77 Ibid., p. 94.

78 Ibid., p. 103f.

79 Admiral Sir Herbert Richmond: *Sea Power in the Modern World* (London: G. Bell & Sons, 1934); Anthony E. Sokol: *Seapower in the Nuclear Age* (Washington: Public Affairs Press, 1961), p. 213; Captain Stephen Wentworth Roskill: *The Strategy of Sea Power: Its Development and Application* (London: Collins, 1962); Bernard Brodie: *A Guide to Naval Strategy* (5th edn, New York: Frederick A. Praeger, 1965), p. 2.

80 Geoffrey Till: *Maritime Strategy in the Nuclear Age* (London: Macmillan, 1982), p. 16.

7

LAZARUS SCHWENDI, RAIMONDO MONTECUCCOLI AND THE TURKISH WARS

Peaceful coexistence or rollback?

Lazarus Schwendi and Raimondo Montecuccoli's lives are separated by roughly a century, and their lifetimes span the period of Europe's religious wars and continuing Turkish expansion into Europe. Emblematically, the latter can be evoked by the two sieges of Vienna, that of 1529 and that of 1683, which ushered in the slow decline of the Ottoman Empire. The steep fall in the number and scope of confessional wars among the Christian polities of Europe after 1648 furnishes perhaps the most important explanation as to why Schwendi's approach to fighting the Turks differed so greatly from that of Montecuccoli. The relative religious peace in Europe, added to the growth of the military establishments in Europe in the second half of the seventeenth century,[1] could make the latter more optimistic about defeating the Turks, with his strategic concept successfully implemented, arguably, by his successors.

Schwendi and Montecuccoli were born on either side of the Alps, which formed a linguistic barrier at lower levels of society. Despite this, and despite the cumbersome means of communication which had not changed substantially since Roman times, the Alps were not a political divide: both men grew up in the Holy Roman Empire. The Austrian branch of the Habsburg dynasty ruled it from Vienna and Prague, and the elite were entirely accustomed to its multicultural, multilingual character. Schwendi and Montecuccoli were both members of this elite from birth as they were of noble descent. They wrote with ease in their respective and each other's native languages, German and Italian, and Schwendi also wrote in Latin, which Montecuccoli at least understood and read fluently.

Both authors have previously received a good deal of attention, mainly in Austria and, in the case of Montecuccoli, also in Italy. But on the whole attention has been paid to dimensions other than that of strategy: authors wrote about their interest in tactics and weaponry, about their thoughts on recruitment and the military recruitment and finance system as a whole.[2] Lazarus Schwendi has attracted interest in particular because of his tolerant religious attitudes.[3] Surprisingly, Azar Gat in his impressive collection of essays on early strategists focused little on Montecuccoli's strategic thinking, and instead on his less rationalist interest in the occult.[4] As both have left copious literary traces, their thinking is amply documented, and a great deal is known about their adult lives which took place in the context of complex wars.

The wars of Lazarus Schwendi's and Montecuccoli's times

As noted in Chapter 1, Christendom in general and the Holy Roman Empire in particular were torn apart by religious wars during both Lazarus Schwendi's entire and Montecuccoli's early lifetimes (they lived during 1522–1583 and 1609–1680 respectively). Schwendi witnessed the confessional Wars of Religion of the middle part of the sixteenth century, which involved especially the western and north-western areas of the Holy Roman Empire, and Montecuccoli's military career took off during the Thirty Years' War that engulfed Central Europe and was at least in part a war caused by confessional differences among the Christians. The big difference was that the Peace Treaties of Westphalia of 1648 led to the decline of confessional differences as a cause of major civil or interstate war within Europe, although they would continue to be a factor in domestic uprisings and civil wars, such as the Hungarian uprisings against Habsburg overlordship that would preoccupy Montecuccoli in the last decade of his life.

In general this meant that during Schwendi's entire life, Christendom was deeply divided and weakened by this strife as it simultaneously confronted the dynamic expansionism of the Ottoman Empire on its eastern and south-eastern borders, on land and at sea. By contrast, from 1648 onwards, Montecuccoli's Holy Roman Empire could concentrate its efforts on turning back the Turks as they resumed their battering assaults on its frontiers after having concentrated for a substantial period on defending and reconquering their own eastern provinces from the Persians. As we shall see, this in large part explains why, imbued with a strong sense of realism, Schwendi would propose a strategy of appeasing the Turks, while Montecuccoli could advocate an offensive rollback strategy.

Another difference in their experience also helps explain their divergent strategic visions. Schwendi's Europe experienced confessional conflict not only along interstate or at least inter-ethnic borders but also within polities, communities and indeed within families. Putting oneself in his place one can see how arriving (as he would, and as the emperor and the authorities of the Holy Roman Empire did at Augsburg in 1555) at the conclusion that peaceful coexistence was the best solution to this strife might make it possible to contemplate similar arrangements with the expansionist Muslims. Schwendi would see for himself that it was a tolerable burden to come to an arrangement with the Ottoman Empire – which was going through a particularly tolerant phase itself at this point – by agreeing to pay the sultan a tribute and accept the ritual self-abasement that went along with acknowledging him as overlord. How was this fundamentally different from serving a Christian lord whose confession one thought sinfully misguided?

By Montecuccoli's times, and due not least to the Thirty Years' War and its outcome, confessional lines in Europe were more neatly drawn between communities and polities, rather than being fought over within them. Catholic Schwendi's second wife was and remained a Protestant; in Montecuccoli's times, such inter-confessional marriages among aristocrats or princes would be possible only if one spouse (usually the wife) converted to the other spouse's religion. In areas of the Holy Roman Empire not directly controlled by the Habsburgs, among lesser people, a pattern established itself and largely held until the Second World War that people from Protestant villages X, Y, Z would not intermarry with people from the Catholic villages A, B, C, even if the villages were interspaced like the white and black squares on a chess board. In the Habsburg hereditary lands, by contrast, as the outcome of the Thirty Years' War, Catholicism was imposed uncompromisingly. Analogously, in a world as seen from Montecuccoli's perspective, the idea of submitting to the Ottomans and coexisting peacefully rather than fighting them had become less acceptable.

Meanwhile, the Ottoman threat to the Holy Roman Empire and the Habsburg possessions to the east and south-east of the empire was ever-present and skirmishing along whatever was the frontier region of the times never quite ceased. Indeed, it had become a form of life for the *Grenzer* and the *gazi*, the soldier-farmers on both sides of the border. But the century and a half between the two sieges of Vienna included long periods of stand-off, such as 1568–1593 and 1606–1660, when no major Ottoman campaign took place against the Habsburg possessions in Central-South-East Europe.[5] Unbeknown to contemporaries, in 1541, the Ottoman Empire had reached its maximum extension in Europe, having established client states in Transylvania and most of what is now Hungary and direct imperial rule in all the other areas of South-East Europe (see Map 7.1). In the following century and a half, it was mainly preoccupied with conquest in the east (up to the Caspian), and counter-insurgency in all its other possessions, from what is now Crimea and Ukraine in the north to the Arab peninsula in the south, and around the southern coast of the Mediterranean.[6]

In Europe, in the years of Ottoman campaigns of expansion, they followed a fairly constant pattern of beginning in the spring and ending in the autumn, and of assembling and then moving the bulk of the army from around Constantinople to the theatre of operations, and then taking them back home for the winter.[7] The overall numbers of soldiers whom the Sublime Porte would send on a campaign stayed relatively constant over this entire period, numbering on average 50,000 for a lesser campaign, and 80,000 for one led by the sultan in person.[8] On exceptional occasions, the Ottoman force numbers could soar to 100,000, such as at the occasion of the siege of Raab (Győr) – the crucial city blocking the passage to Vienna – in 1594.[9] The Ottoman Empire could muster far more soldiers than this, but they, too, were often campaigning on two fronts, and the size of their empire at this stage was greater than all the European Habsburg possessions taken together. Even on one front, therefore, the numbers of soldiers the multi-ethnic Ottoman host could field exceeded those that could be fielded by the Holy Roman Empire and its allies to counter them. While rituals of proclaiming that a campaign was coming would be performed in Constantinople and/or Edirne (Adrianople) in advance of such a campaign, allowing Western

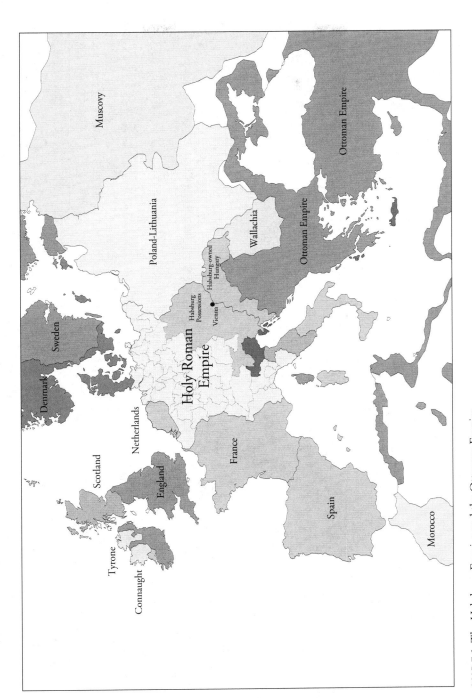

MAP 7.1 The Habsburg Empire and the Ottoman Empire

spies to report the immanency of the campaign in time for the Holy Roman Empire to call to arms, the emperor would take a long time to persuade his empire's constituent entities to make available the troops necessary for defence.[10] Even towards the end of Montecuccoli's career, the emperor could count only 25,000 imperial soldiers *on paper*, not all of whom could be deployed in time. To imperial troops paid from the empire's collective coffers one would have to add loaned troops and additional forces mustered from the Habsburg family lands. So it was an extraordinary challenge to match the Ottoman host numerically, one in general not accomplished. At the relief battle for Vienna in 1683, besieged by the Turks three years after Montecuccoli's death, the Christians managed to put together an allied army composed of 26,000 Poles and Lithuanians, 11,000 Bavarians, 10,000 Saxons, 9,000 Waldeckers and only 21,000 imperial soldiers, thus totalling 70,000–75,000 men. They were confronted with the sultan's army of around 100,000, an exceptionally large number, warranted by the coveted prize: the 'golden apple' of Vienna.[11]

Yet the religious fervour of Ottoman expansionism of the fourteenth to fifteenth centuries had given way in most of the sixteenth and seventeenth centuries to an expansionist logic more centred upon sultan, empire and his glory than, as in previous centuries, on the imperative of spreading Islam by the sword. By now the Ottoman Empire had many subject peoples who had for centuries resisted conversion to Islam, but who, through the added taxation of the infidel (*giaour*), consistently brought good revenue to the empire. Religious tolerance in return for heavier taxation was a compromise acceptable to both sides; indeed (as eight to nine centuries earlier when the Byzantine Empire was imposing Orthodoxy) heterodox populations, such as the Lutheran Protestant 'Saxons' of Transylvania or the mainly Calvinist Protestants of Hungary, the Orthodox or Unitarian Rumanians, the Armenians and Jews, preferred to submit to Muslim rule – in its tolerant phases – rather than risk persecution by Christians intolerant of other confessions. Moreover, in several areas, Hungarians were taxed both by the Ottomans and by their traditional Christian lords, and could see both as equally burdensome. Meanwhile, the Ottomans became less disliked as they gradually allowed occupied towns to exercise their own jurisdiction and to pursue marauders and other criminals.[12] Also, over the one and a half centuries of Ottoman occupation of Hungary and the Balkans, the percentage of locally recruited soldiers in the permanent garrisons grew steadily, until up to 90 per cent of the permanent Ottoman occupation forces in Hungary could be described as stemming from the Balkans (even if the large majority had converted to Islam).[13]

All these factors came together to make the idea of peace treaties and peaceful cohabitation with the infidel more acceptable to a good Christian than it would have been in the age of the Crusades, or when Constantinople was besieged and fell.[14] Indeed, in 1547 Emperor Charles V concluded an armistice with the Ottoman Empire, which contained a clause that obliged the Holy Roman Empire to make an annual payment to Constantinople, a payment which could be interpreted as a tribute.[15] By 1551 this payment had ceased, but the precedent thus existed of buying off the Turks, much as the Byzantines had bought off their respective assailants for centuries before ultimately succumbing to the expansionist fervour of Mehmet II. As we shall see, Lazarus Schwendi would favour such chequebook diplomacy as the bloodless alternative to a hopeless confrontation.

Lazarus Schwendi's life[16]

Lazarus Schwendi was the son of a local nobleman, Rutland/Rudland/Ruland Schwendi von Hohenlandsberg (c. 1485–1525), who in turn was the younger of two sons and thus not the heir to his father's fortunes, a castle of the same name in Swabia. Rutland never married; Lazarus, apparently his only child, was illegitimate, the mother, Apollonia Wencken, a commoner from the nearby village of Mittelbiberach, where Lazarus was born around 17 December 1522. Amazingly, two years after his birth, at Rutland's request, little Lazarus was recognised as his legitimate heir by the emperor himself; none too soon, as Rutland died in the following year, having charged the mayor and council of the nearest small town of Memmingen with the wardship of his son. The town of Memmingen sympathised with Protestantism, and when Lazarus was 13, the town councillors sent Lazarus to Basle for his further schooling, where he was taught by the humanist Protestant Simon Grynaeus. Subsequently he went on to Strasbourg, where he received a classical education, again by a Protestant humanist, Johann Sturm, who had recently set up a grammar school in one of Strasbourg's former monasteries that numbered well over 300 pupils. The basic curriculum – containing a strong element of Latin – took six years, followed by two more years in philosophy and theology.[17] In testimony to this classical education, in his later life, he would use quotations from Thucydides (such as the Melian dialogue), Plato, Horace, Seneca and Vergil, often slightly distorted and thus probably written down from memory. He also travelled to France and read and wrote in French – this was how he would correspond with Emperor Charles V.[18] We know that in 1548/49 he read Machiavelli's *Discorsi* in a French translation, and one of his biographers sees a strong influence of Machiavelli's ideas on Schwendi. Schwendi seems to have been inspired by Machiavelli's patriotism and even proto-nationalism, which Schwendi applied to all things *teutsch* – and referred to the Holy Roman Empire both as the *'hailige Reich, unser liebes vaterland'* (the holy empire our beloved fatherland) and the *'teutsche Reich'* (German empire), to which the other peoples should look up.[19] Schwendi agreed with Machavelli on the priority of the wellbeing of polity and state over religious issues, but also the emphasis on Machiavelli's idea of *virtù*, that might be summed up as the positive strengths and talents of the polity. Schwendi talked of its components, virtues such as honesty (*biderkheit*), strength, order, unanimity and one law for all (*gleychmessige gesatz*), all 'manly virtues'.[20]

We do not know what Lazarus did immediately after his graduation from Strasbourg, but at the age of 23 he returned to Memmingen, demanding to be recognised as having come of age and to claim what was left of his father's inheritance. The town council, who in the past had defended Lazarus Schwendi's rights and inheritance against the claims of other Schwendis who wanted to dispute the inheritance of Ruland's bastard, now took against Lazarus, accusing him of having employed the services of a madam to consort with a '*beschreite Frau*' – that is a prostitute. A row ensued in which Lazarus said that, as a bachelor, he could do as he wished, and he in turn accused the town of having squandered much of his heritage; the council, in turn, put him in prison for several days for his rude behaviour.[21]

This local scandal apparently did not prevent Lazarus Schwendi from offering his services to Emperor Charles V, on whose staff he first appears at the meeting of the Imperial Diet in Ratisbon in the following year. And apparently the skills he had acquired in Strasbourg served him well. Very soon he was dispatched on diplomatic missions on behalf of the emperor, including negotiations with some of the leaders of the Schmalkaldic league who had risen against the emperor to defend the Protestant cause.

The only other scandal attached to his name occurred in the following year, when the emperor sent him on a most problematic mission that must have tested his loyalty severely. With the support of the Imperial Diet meeting in Ausgburg in 1547/1548, Charles V prohibited military service for a foreign potentate on pain of death. On the basis of this prohibition, he dispatched Schwendi to arrest one captain Sebastian Vogelsberger, who had led a unit of German mercenaries into the service of the king of France; Vogelsberger was at the time on leave in his home town within the empire, and Schwendi persuaded him to come to Augsburg, perhaps in the sincere belief that the emperor would sentence but pardon Vogelsberger. Instead, Charles had Vogelsberger executed; from the very scaffold, Vogelsberger denounced Schwendi as 'arch-villain' for this unchivalrous behaviour; Schwendi himself saw the need to circulate a reply for his exoneration.[22]

Until 1558, he served Charles V as loyal emissary and diplomat, and after Charles's abdication, passed into the service of Philip II of Spain, and that of his half-sister, Margaret of Parma, governess of the Netherlands (1559–1567 and 1578–1582). The general background of European politics was one of religious strife, and both Charles and Philip were most troubled by the religious wars and Protestant challenges to their powers, a situation not aided by their often uncompromising opposition to Protestantism (despite the religious peace that had been agreed at the Diet of Augsburg in 1555). Schwendi was sent on a number of missions to negotiate with rebellious town councils, such as that of Magdeburg, or other Protestant dignitaries. In these years he vociferously defended the Habsburg ambition to restore some unity to Christendom.

Besides the diplomatic career, he also developed a military one. In 1552 he commanded a unit at the siege of Metz, after which he was knighted and was made 'imperial counsellor'. Proudly, he had a medal struck which described him as '*Lazarus a Sevendi, Caroli V Imperatoris et Regis Philippi filii Consiliarus et legatus Germanicae militiae Praefectus. Aetatis XXXIV*' (Lazarus von Schwendi, Counsellor of Emperor Charles V and his son King Philip, and emissary and prefect of the German military. Aged 34). On the reverse one sees seven mythological figures blowing upon waves with his own motto, '*Durat et lucet*' (he endures and shines). From 1553, Lazarus Schwendi was the Burgvogt (commander) of the fortifications of Breisach in the Breisgau.[23]

On such missions on behalf of King Philip, Schwendi became acquainted with Count Egmont, then still leading Habsburg forces into battle against the French (Schwendi was present with Egmont at the victories of the Imperial Army at St Quentin in 1557 and Gravelines in 1558), and William of Orange, with whom he would form a strong attachment. Both taught him the art of war, and by 1561 Ferdinand I, who had succeeded Charles as emperor in 1558, summoned him to his court in Prague and asked him to inspect the defences of Hungary, over which he ruled as king due to his marriage with its Jagellonian heiress.

This is where Schwendi's military career took off, as he detached himself from Philip II and went over entirely to the service of the Austrian Habsburgs, Ferdinand and, after his death in 1564, Maximilian II. Both bestowed great trust in him and even allowed him to speak out increasingly against the uncompromising policies of Philip's chief agent in the Netherlands, Cardinal Antoine de Granvelle; in fact both shared his critical attitude towards the brutally repressive counter-insurgency strategy which Philip II and his successive emissaries applied in the Netherlands.[24] In the early 1560s, Schwendi supported the efforts of Counts Egmont and Horn, and William of Orange to get rid of Granvelle and later of the Duke of Alba, whose brutality would become legendary. The execution of Egmont and Hoorn in 1567, which truly got the Dutch Revolt going (it would last for 80 years), must have further shaken Schwendi's sympathy for Catholic repressions under Habsburg rule.

Schwendi seems to have been eager to accept a new mission against an external foe as, commissioned by Maximilian II, he in 1565 joined the Imperial Forces in Northern Hungary to fight the Ottoman sultan and his client, John Zapolya, the prince of Transylvania. In the winter of 1565/1566, as an Ottoman attack loomed, Schwendi in his quarters at Caschau wrote a memorandum for the emperor, outlining his comprehensive strategy for the war.[25]

The ensuing campaign was a relative success; Schwendi freed the famous wine-growing area of Tokaj and the town of Szerencs and a number of fortresses. The war went on until February 1568, with victories in the Battles of Szatmár, Erdöd, Kövar, St Martin and Muncas.[26] He was rewarded by being made hereditary Baron of Hohenlandsberg in Alsace.[27] Buda, however, remained under Turkish control. Even so, Schwendi returned as celebrated victor from this campaign; his unflattering portrait in his splendid coat of armour, both of which are preserved at the Hofburg in Vienna, probably dates from this period. It shows him as a confident and assertive man with a curiously long horizontal black moustache, raised eyebrows and short black hair with a widow's peak.

In the following years, Schwendi tried to curb the radically repressive policies of Catholic Spain and to move Maximilian II to assume a more tolerant posture, and to reform the empire. He criticised the popes for fomenting strife, and advocated religious tolerance.[28] He was horrified throughout by the excesses not only of the Spanish in the Netherlands but also of the French Religious Wars – he commented that the French were 'washing their hand in their own blood'. Throughout his career, his chief worry was that the Holy Roman Empire would be torn apart and would disintegrate entirely under the impact of religious strife.

He blamed not only religious extremism on both sides and the machinations of the pope in particular but also poor statecraft – 'For when the coach gets stuck or falls over, the driver has driven badly.'[29]

Against this background, it can be understood why Schwendi showed great activism in promoting better governance with regard to the military, with a concern for the wellbeing of the soldiers, and for the dangerous effects of arrears in their payments. In 1570 he prepared a document for Emperor Maximilian II in which he urged a comprehensive reform of the defences of the empire. In the same year he was asked to work out the best way to raise money to fight the Turks, whom he did see as the 'most dangerous enemy', and proposed an annual levy of *Türkensteuer* for the defence especially of Hungary, the *antemurale* or glacis of the Holy Roman Empire.[30] Finally, he continued working on a script that he began in 1571, his *Discourse on War*.[31] Neither of these works on war was published within his lifetime.

Schwendi's own ideas of Christianity took him closer to Calvin's than befitted a loyal servant of the ultra-Catholic Habsburgs, but as we have seen, Schwendi believed that politics and statecraft should take priority over private religious preferences.[32] Disgusted by his experience of the politics of the religious wars, but also by court politics (as two pieces headed 'gratitude at court' and 'life at court' suggest), Schwendi retired to his possessions on both sides of the Rhine, in Breisgau and Alsace. In 1552, aged 30, he had married Anna, the daughter of an 'imperial counsellor' called Wilhelm Böcklin von Böcklinsau, with whom he had one son, William, who survived him (d. 1609). He had long been estranged from Anna, who died in 1571, but it was only after her death that Schwendi married a second time, a woman 32 years younger than himself, Eleonore, one of several daughters of the late Froben Christoph Count Zimmern. Eleonore was a Protestant, and her confession was tolerated by her husband. In 1583, aged 61, Schwendi died in his manor house in Kirchhofen in the Breisgau, and was buried with an impressive funerary monument in the Catholic Church of Our Lady in Kientzheim in Alsace, on the other side of the Rhine, where he also had possessions. Perhaps the priest there did not mind the details of Schwendi's beliefs as much as the priest in Kirchhofen. Eleonore survived him (and would marry again); a son born to them and christened Maximilian (presumably after the emperor) did not.

Schwendi's *Discourse on War* and his advice on fighting the Turks

The *Discourse on War* was dedicated to Charles of Zerotin, Lord of Namiest and Rossitz in Moravia, a rich scion of the Protestant nobility at the Imperial Court in Prague. If the title evokes Machiavelli's *Discorsi*, this is not altogether accidental. While the black-listed works of the Florentine were not referred to openly by Schwendi, there are multiple echoes of his writing in Schwendi's. Unlike Machiavelli, however, but like most other early modern authors, Schwendi was very concerned about the justice or injustice of a war (the *ius ad bellum*), the observation of rules in the conduct of war (the *ius in bello*) and the disciplining of soldiers so they would spare civilians and abstain from pillaging. Despite Schwendi's humanist education, this is not a work of a cleric or scholar who takes pride in listing all the classical examples and references he can recall or find. Just occasionally one finds a learned reference, such as when he talks about 'the nerves of war – that is money'.[33] Instead, probably because of his experience in keeping texts short to impress their contents on the emperor or his advisers, the text consists of nothing but statements, at best underpinned with appeals to 'reason' and 'the teachings of nature'.

The work thus starts with an implied plea for good governance, by defining as good heads of state those who are 'instruments for the creation of prosperity and good order in the world, and the preservation of peace and quiet', while wicked heads of state are those inciting 'secession, disorder, change, war, tyranny, foreign power and slavery'. The latter are ruled by 'pride, miserliness, lust, and [a passionate pursuit of] revenge'.[34] Just wars of self-defence and unjust wars of aggression flow from the quality of the rulers. In keeping with the age, we find considerable hostility to 'change', but also resonances of Schwendi's classical education, which was a world away from an uncritical servant of an absolute monarch: Schwendi saw the monarch as subservient to the welfare of the polity, not as an untouchable sovereign who must not be judged by his subjects.

Other themes in the *Discourse* are not unusual in the literature of the time, such as Schwendi's warnings against gambling on luck:

> Who in war entrusts his case exclusively to fortune and daring rarely lasts long. It is generosity and seriousness, skill and advantage which normally cause fortune and the good result of a war. Yet fortune in war is like a die: it contains all sorts of chances. The great advantage is to play safe and even when good chances present themselves, not to wager too much.[35]

A bearable peace to him was always preferable to war with its uncertainty. War – and battle – should be avoided lest the outcome was near certain to be favourable for one's own side. Schwendi definitely belonged to the school of those who, in the tradition of Vegetius, preferred to avoid battle, instead recommending starving an enemy into surrender, or waiting patiently for him to give up, or using ruses or any possible means rather than the pitched battle to decide the war. He recognised, however, that there might be opportunities to seize that if passed up would cede victory to the enemy. Unconsciously echoing Sun Tsu – whose *Art of War* would not be introduced to Europe before the eighteenth century – Schwendi wrote, 'Where the enemy is weakest, one should seek him out most; and where he is strongest, one should defend oneself best.'[36] He conceded that battle was at the core of war,[37] but he formulated 'the general rule in war that one never accept battles with their uncertain and unfavourable outcome unless there is extreme need or a great and almost certain advantage.'[38] On this point he agreed with the earlier writing of Raymond de Beccarie de Pavie, Baron de Fourquevaux, published in French in 1548.[39] This put him on the side of the Fabian school of strategists named after the Roman general Fabius Maximus, known as 'Cunctator', the hesitant, the predominant school of thought before Napoleon.[40] It also distinguishes him from Montecuccoli, as we shall see.

Schwendi favoured taking a campaign into the enemy's land, rather than waiting, defensively, for the enemy to attack.[41] Logically, however, one would find it difficult to mobilise militias composed of peasants for such a campaign; Schwendi advocated using professional soldiers, and feeding, clothing and paying them well to secure their loyalty.[42] Given the motley mix of ethnicities and loyalties in South-Eastern Europe, it is surprising neither that Schwendi emphasised the importance of good intelligence nor that he thought one should never trust the enemy.[43]

Schwendi also included a section on sieges, where we find a remarkably humanitarian approach to taking a city by force. It had been accepted as normal since antiquity that a besieged city that refused to surrender could be destroyed at will as well as sacked, its citizens taken into slavery, killed or raped.[44] The practice of his age does not seem to have deviated much from this long-standing convention. In 1512, when the Gaston de Foix, Duke of Nemours, took the Italian city of Brescia by force after it had resisted the French, it was sacked and pillaged, and the population who resisted were killed, others taken prisoner, several raped. Only the paragon of knightly virtue, the French Chevalier de Bayard, who was himself wounded, protected the family in whose house he was quartered; this corroborated his outstanding fame as 'knight without fear and without reproach'.[45] In general, authors urged that the populations be treated clemently after a siege *only if the town had surrendered* of its own will.[46] In Schwendi's *Discourse*, by contrast, we find this remarkable passage concerning how to take a besieged town *by force*, which foreshadows the humanitarian concerns of the eighteenth-century author Santa Cruz de Marcenado:[47]

> Before storming [a town], the commander in chief should have it announced, that churches, women and virgins and the children and undefended should be spared. Item: the town must not be burnt down. The commander must not allow the pillaging to take long, but must soon order the soldiers out of the town again and order a garrison to move in, to clear the fortifications and to lock them up, if he intends to keep them. If not, one razes them or burns them down. If, however, one decides to keep the fortifications, and if this is an important town, the commander should soon lay down law and order for those he places there [his garrison], so that they cohabit peacefully and well with the citizens. And then he should establish among the citizens a régime of the sort that they would have a good heart [disposition] and will towards their new master, and do not dwell on treason and worse thoughts against him. If, however, there are some among them which are so suspect and treacherous, the safest thing to do is to punish them or to get them out of the town.[48]

This prescription of a hearts-and-minds campaign may again echo Fourquevaux, but again was fairly standard among authors of his period.[49]

The whole *Discourse* was written very much with the Turkish wars in mind. Schwendi certainly did not underrate the danger emanating from the Turks: he exhorted his readers to bear in mind the fate of the Byzantines (the 'Greeks', as he called them) and of their miserable downfall, 'for the same reasons and dangers with which otherwise Germany is now confronted'.[50] But he also showed impressive humility and unusual resignation: against the backdrop of Christendom tearing itself apart over its religious quarrels, Schwendi was all too conscious of the weakness of the Occident in the face of the challenge posed by the Ottoman Empire. His prescription was that of appeasement, for peace is preferable to disastrous war:

> Reason and nature teach us that we should humble ourselves somewhat before those who are stronger [than us], and we see this even among the irrational animals. Powerful and strong kingdoms and regimes have always eventually vanquished and subjected the weaker, just as we now see with the Turks and others. Therefore peace is much better, in such cases, if it can be obtained in a bearable way, and to humble oneself and cede, rather than running headlong towards one's own perdition. The Christian countries and princes who could not withstand the Turk have done better if they agreed in time to pay him tribute and render him other services, while preserving their own régime and a little freedom, than those who, albeit weaker, opted for unwarranted resistance and were exterminated or came under the Turk's yoke.[51]

In his 'Counsel on War and Considerations' on how to counter the Turks, written in or shortly after 1576, Schwendi took the same line. Seeing the Turks as God's scourge sent to punish the sins of the Christians, he pointed out that hitherto no people, no emperor, king or prince had been able to withstand their onslaught, and had either been forced to submit to the sultan and come to some arrangement by paying tribute, or had been forced to suffer the destruction of their polity and descent into slavery. Given the divisions within Christendom, Schwendi saw no chance of the degree of Christian solidarity that would be needed to change this pattern. He described the Turks as greatly superior to Christendom in terms of power, money, manpower and opportunity, and in terms of military commanders, order and discipline, and continuous armed exercises. They seemed to him almost undefeatable in open battles; if occasionally they were vanquished, they would return with a much larger force.[52]

Tactically also, the Turks were superior to the Westerners, even if the latter had a superior cavalry. But the Turks were more numerous, more disciplined, faster and more patient, kept better order in battles, and were inclined to use ruses. Often enough, he had seen Turkish cavalry yield to an onslaught by the Christians, only to reconfigure and launch a stronger counter-offensive. Turkish infantry would set up their wagons to form a defensive barrier (wagon fort), reinforced by moats and walls if necessary, protected by the janissaries and their best cavalry. These wagon forts were virtually unassailable. Moreover, the Turks operated with the greatest agility. They would forage day and night and hardly ever fall short of provisions.

By contrast, the German (*teutsch*) cavalry was too heavy to be able to keep up with the light Turkish cavalry, and neither the former nor the German infantry could keep such order as would be necessary to pull their weight in this context. They were far less flexible, less able to withstand heat, thirst, hunger or sorrow, or being mounted for several successive days. Thus the Christians must avoid an open battle, or else they would come to grief as several kings had done, including in 1526 the famous defeat and death of King Louis (Lajos) II of Hungary at the Battle of Mohacs, which had led to the loss of most of his lands to the Turks.[53] Moreover, in his proposals on how better to defend against Turkish attacks, Schwendi clearly advocated learning from the adversary, bringing much more discipline to the Imperial Forces who weakened themselves by excessive drinking (of course, the Islamic host abstained from alcohol!), and training the infantry to move in disciplined tandem with the cavalry in engagements, but always in units large enough not to be surrounded and cut off by the Turks.[54]

Schwendi was aware that the Turks had not made much progress since 1526, as the Christian forces, once established in their defensive fortifications, were difficult to oust. The Turks would content themselves with assaults on individual fortified 'places', but be obliged to withdraw again – they tended to 'go home' for the winter. He pondered how to get intelligence of Turkish offensive plans. He designed responses on the part of the empire that would allow further increasing defences in the areas most likely to be affected. He was not averse to seizing chances if they presented themselves – for example if the Turkish host was affected by illness or famine. In this case one might, after all, seek to defeat them locally, and win back some areas or fortifications from them.[55]

Strategically, Schwendi thus counselled firmly against going to war against the Turks, and instead argued for negotiating the best possible peace settlement in the circumstances (even if he warned against putting too much trust in the Turkish observance of its terms). At the same time, he recommended profiting from any period of peace to fortify the empire's frontiers and to improve existing fortifications (e.g. those of the vital town of Raab/Györ), and especially in those areas of Hungary still under Habsburg control, which he saw as a glacis for the empire: they were largely fortified, and the population was already hardened by past sufferings at the hands of the Turks. These would have to be defended by the local populations, forming a militia and doing military service for two or three years,[56] while in an emergency, a (professional) army would have to be sent, paid for by the '*Stände*' (Estates) of the empire (its polities, including duchies, archbishoprics and imperial towns and cities). Recruitment to the professional army should be open to anybody, noble or commoner, German or Hungarian or from any other ethnic group. In an emergency, the entire nobility should go to war, and every fifth or tenth man among the empire's subjects should be mobilised. He went on to explain that the militia, too, would have to be provided for by regular payments and provisioning, with money for this coming to the individual provinces from the imperial funds.[57] He also suggested that the Teutonic Knights should move their bases to the Hungarian frontier, somewhere around Nagykanizsa, as the defence of Christendom against the infidel had been their raison d'être; moreover, were not the Maltese knights doing a good job in defending Malta and Italy? To this end, the revenues of the Teutonic Knights should be increased. (This would have given the order a new mission after its grand master, Albrecht of Prussia, had converted to Lutheranism, and had turned the order's Prussian possession into his personal duchy.)

Meanwhile, the suburbs of all potentially endangered towns and cities which had grown up outside the medieval walls should be torn down and replaced by a defensive glacis, or else be treated as new towns and given their own fortifications. The work should be carried out by locals, who should be obliged to take charge of it. All these payments for the empire's defence should stem from *permanent* contributions from the Estates (rather than the taxes for the defence against the Turks agreed ad hoc by the Imperial Diet whenever an acute threat arose), based on tithes collected from the population, and supplemented by payments from the Imperial Treasury.[58] One can presume here knowledge of the French state's permanent taxation that financed its standing army. All this would encourage the Turks to channel their expansionist tendencies towards the Mediterranean (and by implication, this would then be the business for the Spanish Habsburgs; the Christian triumph in the Battle of Lepanto of 1571 made this a promising option).[59]

Further, he recommended paying tribute to the Turks regularly and fulfilling the acts of self-abasement of Western emissaries on which the Turks insisted; avoiding any measures that would irritate the Turks, yet driving back any small frontier incursions by the Turks.[60] (If such incursions took place despite the formal agreements made with the Sublime Porte, Schwendi recommended writing post haste to the local Turkish potentates and even to Constantinople to explain that this was not a breach of the peace settlement by the empire, but that the skirmish had been occasioned by Turkish transgressions – the contemporary equivalent of installing the red telephone between Washington and Moscow during the Cold War to avoid escalation to major war arising from military misunderstandings.[61])

Schwendi counselled his emperor to keep his hands off Poland – Maximilian II had made an unsuccessful attempt to have himself elected king of Poland in 1576. Instead, he counselled the emperor to wait for the new king, Stephen Báthory, who was also prince of Transylvania, to put out peace feelers to the Habsburgs, once he had noticed that Turkish support against the Habsburgs would turn out to be dangerous for him.[62]

To complete his recommendations for an organisational overhaul of the defence system, Schwendi advised the emperor to set up a War Council (*Kriegsrath*) in an emergency, which was to reside in Vienna and deal with the day-to-day administration of a campaign, overseeing the finances, the work of engineers, architects and recruitment agents, the communications network and supplies in terms of both food and munitions, but also to identify and arrest enemy spies. The War Council would have to work closely with an Imperial Cabinet (*Kammer* or *Reichskammer*), which was to head the peacetime government and administration of the empire.[63]

Kriegsrath and *Reichskammer* were indeed created later, and they were still in existence when Montecuccoli entered the picture.

Raimondo Montecuccoli's life[64]

On 21 February 1609, Raimondo (Figure 7.1) was born to Galeotto IV Count Montecuccoli and his wife, Anna Bigi, from Ferrara, at the castle of Montecuccolo, in the foothills of the Apennines. On both sides, his ancestors were noblemen. Raimondo's mother had been lady-in-waiting of Virginia de' Medici, wife of Cesare d'Este, Duke of Módena. His father died when he was ten, by which time

RAIMONDVS COM. MONTECVCVLI. S.C.R$_q$M.
CONS. BEL. CAM. MARESCHAL. LOCVMTENENS.

Graf Raimondo Montecuccoli.

FIGURE 7.1 Peter Aubry: Raimondo Montecuccoli, c. 1650

Raimondo was the oldest surviving child. His paternal uncle, Ernesto Montecuccoli, an officer in the imperial armed forces, took charge of his fortunes from this point. Raimondo and his younger brother Massimiliano received their first education in Módena, enabling them to read and write in Italian and Latin. When he was 11 years old, Raimondo was put into the service of Cardinal Alexander d'Este. Despite his succession to his father's possessions, he now seemed destined for the church, and received a tonsure; his younger brother would follow the same path and would indeed become a cleric. But when Cardinal Alexander died in March 1624, this career was discarded for Raimondo. His academic schooling was cut short and, at the insistence of Uncle Ernesto, he enlisted with the Imperial Army at the age of 16 – by which time, in 1625, the Thirty Years' War was well underway. Until its end in 1648, Raimondo would be learning on the job, working his way up through the ranks; he would always be a supporter of meritocracy, arguing that 'virtue and vice must be judged according to merit, not according to . . . noble birth.'[65]

He had plenty of military experience and the participation in every year's campaigns took him to the Netherlands and to Northern and north-eastern Germany. He took part in the Battles of Breitenfeld (1631, after which he was briefly made prisoner of war) and Lützen (1632). He was promoted to colonel after showing particular bravery and competence at the Battle of Nördlingen in 1635. In 1639 he was wounded in the fighting around the Imperial Forces' investment of the towns of Melnik and Brandeis and again made prisoner of war by the Swedes. He was packed off for two and a half years, first to Stettin (today Szczecin in Poland) and then to Weimar. He took advantage of this involuntary time for reflection, aged 30–32, to do some thinking, reading and writing, and the result of this would be a first draft of his *Discourses on the Battle*[66] and of his *Treatise on War*.[67] In writing the preface, he grumbled that not enough had been written about the theory of war, which is more a reflection of the paucity of literature available to him in Stettin and Weimar than a justified comment on the actual state of affairs. Even then, Montecuccoli mentioned[68] works of Basta,[69] Melzi,[70] Rohan[71] and la Noue[72]; meanwhile, he explicitly acknowledged his own debt to the works of the Dutch humanist Justus Lipsius.[73]

He rejoined the Imperial Forces in 1642, gained further combat experience in the Habsburgs' East European possessions, and was then loaned to the Duke of Módena – we see here the hand of his mother and her old connections – for campaigns in Italy concerning the disputed possession of the Duchy of Castro. This gained him further promotion, but Montecuccoli returned to the main theatre of the Thirty Years' War in 1644, henceforth deployed in Silesia, Bohemia and Moravia. In countering the Hungarian insurgency under George I Rákóczi, Montecuccoli practised what would later be called 'small war' tactics. He would encounter a further generation of the rebellious Rákóczi clan again in battle in the 1660s, when Francis I Rákóczi jointly with his father-in-law, the Banus of Croatia, Miklós (Nicholas) Zrínyi, made new troubles for the Austrian Habsburgs.

Laying down the sword and picking up the diplomatic valise, he turned to writing again, producing a tactical manual headed *On the Military Art*, of purely tactical interest, which need not retain us here.[74] Perhaps it was also in this period that he began writing the texts in a collection called the Zibaldone, which have not yet been published, and which concern alchemy, the occult and magical natural philosophy, but which do not seem to have influenced his very rational ponderings on how to conduct war.[75] He travelled much, acting as imperial emissary on several occasions, and ingratiating himself with Catholic queen Christina of Sweden, who thought him sufficiently spiritual to have asked Pope Alexander VII to grant Montecuccoli a cardinalship. Montecuccoli declined and instead, at the age of 48, married an 18-year-old countess, Margarete of Dietrichstein. She was a lady-in-waiting and favourite of the empress, and the daughter of Prince Dietrichstein and the sister of the prince of Liechtenstein, and thus combined 'rare beauty, virtue and angelic grace' with the opportunity to marry into 'the first families of Austria'. It does not seem to have bothered Montecuccoli much that she did not speak any Italian.[76] The couple would have a son (Leopold Philip, born in 1663 and named after the emperor) and three daughters (Anna Aloisia, Carlotta Polizena and Ernestina). Initially he saw little of his wife, as he was now promoted to field marshal, thus being given the supreme command of the Imperial Army, seeing action above all against the Swedes in northern Germany.

In 1660 he was appointed governor of the fortified town of Raab (Győr). As we have seen, Raab had already been identified as a strategic stronghold by Schwendi as it controls the confluence of River Raab and Danube, and the gap in the foothills of the Alps on the western side and the foothills of the Carpathian mountains to the east, which allowed – or obstructed – the passage from the Ottoman-controlled Buda in the Hungarian plains to Vienna. Meanwhile, the Ottoman Empire under Sultan Mehmet IV Avcı ('the Hunter', ruled 1648–1687) and his Grand Vizier Mehmet Köprülü Paşa had embarked on a new phase of expansionism in Europe. In 1663, Montecuccoli failed to stop a Turkish incursion that reached the borders of Moravia to the north and Styria to the west. In the winter of 1663/1664 he wrote a strategic concept for war with the Turks,[77] which he put into action in the summer of 1664, when on 1 August he managed to defeat them in an open pitched seven-hour battle at St Gotthardt (Szentgotthárd, today in Hungary on the Austrian border), a small town that commands the access to Graz and thus Styria. This would be Montecuccoli's most famous and most celebrated victory, as it led to a new peace treaty with the Ottomans, the Peace of Vasvár, which would last for two decades (until the second and final Ottoman attempt to conquer Vienna in 1683).

Meanwhile, Montecuccoli was brought back to Vienna, where he was made supreme director of the imperial artillery and president of the War Council. It was mainly in this period that Montecuccoli managed to introduce reforms of the imperial armies, remodelling them on the example of the Swedish Army, which he had got to know all too well in the Thirty Years' War.[78] In the late 1660s he worked on his *Military Memoirs*,[79] which contained an important section, 'On Fighting the Turks in Hungary',[80] and a new version of 'On Battles'.

In the mid-1670s, he was given a last military commission, this time to fight Louis XIV's expansionist France, against which Austria could turn all its forces as its eastern borders were now protected by peace with Constantinople. This time, Montecuccoli's main adversary was not the Ottoman Empire but the celebrated French general

Henri de la Tour d'Auvergne, Viscount Turenne, whose forces had penetrated well into imperial territory and had reached the rivers Main and Tauber. In 1675, without giving battle, Montecuccoli managed to drive Turenne's forces back to the Rhine and join the Spanish-Dutch forces near Bonn. This became a famous campaign that was characterised by an indirect approach of battle avoidance and manoeuvre, later alluded to frequently as an exemplar of this form of war. Only on 25 July 1675 did Turenne manage to force Montecuccoli to present his forces for battle at Sasbach (or Salzbach), where the hills of the Black Forest border on the Rhine – not far from Schwendi's possessions. But the encounter ended with a first exchange of fire, which killed Turenne, and after this Montecuccoli's forces forced the French to retreat. The campaign was eventually decided by the Dutch forces at a battle further to the north, at the Konzer Bridge, but Montecuccoli faced fire one last time at Altenburg.

After this, aged 66, he felt unable to take to the field again, and instead once more tackled the bureaucratic politics at the Court of Vienna energetically, still as president of the War Council. In this context he complained strongly to Emperor Leopold about the institutional rivalry between the War Council and the Imperial Cabinet.[81] During this period, his attention had to be focused mainly on the recurrent Hungarian uprisings (inevitably involving the Rákóczis) and issues over the extent to which imperial intervention was welcome in Transylvania (which was at once a client state of the Ottoman Empire, but beset by succession quarrels that triggered Tatar and Turkish intervention), and more generally on further improvements of the military apparatus, including fortifications and issues of recruitment and garrisoning, and military taxation. The two subjects overlapped greatly: Montecuccoli is one of the rare writers on strategy and military issues many of whose works were directly considered for implementation, and indeed were often translated into practice. While some of his writings – his 'Aphorisms' and other pieces later published in his *Memoirs* – summarised his experiences, others, such as the script he now turned to, headed 'On Hungary in 1677', were prescriptions for action, and one can see that some of his recommendations were directly applied.[82]

Most of his writings were treated as internal government documents, and would thus be published only posthumously. Montecuccoli died at the age of 71 in Linz, where he was staying with Emperor Leopold I, agonising for 30 days, probably after being hit by a falling beam.[83] He was buried, curiously without any monument, at the Jesuits' Church next to the imperial palace in Vienna. But unlike Schwendi, who was all but forgotten outside the imperial lands, Montecuccoli passed into legend as one of the greatest military commanders of modern times.

Montecuccoli on battle, war and peace

From our perspective, Montecuccoli's works fall into three sections: one concerning regular warfare with Christian princes of equal standing, which we shall deal with first; one concerning insurgencies; and a third, concerning the particular challenge of warfare against the sprawling Ottoman Empire, which was still extending its tentacles in the direction of the 'golden apple' of Vienna.

Large parts of his treatises on war followed classical patterns that can be traced back to Vegetius.[84] Montecuccoli was more concerned than Schwendi to turn out the classical scholar, self-consciously drawing attention to his learned sources.[85] He thus began by defining war, following in the footsteps of Cicero and Hugo Grotius, as a quarrel with the admixture of violence; he himself added the definition that 'war is an action aimed at harming each other in every possible way, and its aim is victory.'[86] He covered the classical sections on offensive and defensive war, sieges, battles and deployment. In the classic Catholic tradition, he accepted the need for arms and war:

> No State can enjoy peace without arms, avenge insults, and defend laws, religion and freedom. God Himself honoured arms by calling himself 'Lord of Hosts'. Majesty is not honoured without them, neither among the subjects, as without them there will be insurgencies, nor among strangers, for without them there will be war.[87]

Whatever the practice of his times – the Thirty Years' War is of course famous for its atrocities and inhumane treatment of soldiers and civilians – we find Montecuccoli time and again advocating restraint, clemency and moderation, albeit not to the extent that we found it with Schwendi. Montecuccoli thus advocated in an offensive war to 'Treat those well who surrender and ill [those] who resist' (he liked punchy maxims). He was also more willing to leave some things to chance, and to seize advantageous opportunities, but favoured extensive reflection over chance.[88]

To him, the choice between an offensive or a defensive strategy depended on a number of assessments. Was one's own side objectively stronger or weaker than an adversary? Could one take advantage of factional strife in the adversary's camp? In any case, one should spread false rumours about one's own superior strength.[89]

Similar musings should underlie the decision as to whether to give battle (and here, we find him showing off his classical knowledge by praising the Roman general Fabius Maximus Cunctator).[90] Montecuccoli emphasised the importance of motivating soldiers before a battle, whether this was by giving them alcohol or promising them riches or pretending to believe in dreams and portents (as long as they could be interpreted favourably). Prayers and mass he also listed among the *useful* preparations for battle.[91]

Montecuccoli's attitudes to victory and defeat were particularly sober: in case of victory, one should thank God, he wrote, bury the dead, exaggerate one's victory by proclaiming it triumphantly in the hope that this would affect other adversaries psychologically, incite insurgencies against the enemy, devastate the country, deny the enemy time to regroup, and persuade his allies to change sides.[92] In case of defeat, one should not be despondent as the fortunes of war can change any time. One should withdraw one's forces, round up refugees and arm them and the local population, fall back on the nearest fortifications, secure passes, frontiers and strong points, cut down forests, destroy bridges and flood land to create barriers for the enemy's advance and secure auxiliary forces (while ensuring that one's own forces remained numerically the stronger).[93] Thus one should change one's strategy, and one should wait for some time to pass after the unfortunate event, ensuring that one's forces recovered before resuming the offensive, rather than taking any risks.[94]

Montecuccoli's treatment of the subject of how to end wars is particularly original. It is easy, he argued, to start a war, but difficult to end it; 'beginning and end do not lie in the power of the same person.'[95] Negotiations with the adversary were crucial for a good peace, but he was clear about this being a process that would be affected by each side's needs.[96] Nevertheless, under the influence of Lipsius's writings, he emphasised that the peace one made should be 'honourable and sincere'.[97] He elaborated:

> A peace is honourable when it is useful, and if on has achieved the purpose with glory for which one has started the war; if one secures advantageous conditions, such as, if one is the victor, [he counselled] that each side should keep what he has, that the enemy lays down his arms and swears not to support any of our other enemies either directly or indirectly; . . . or if one retains some important fortifications, receives a sum of money, and that hostages are given to us.
>
> A peace is sincere if it is safe and does not cover some intrigue, such as the intention to recruit the other side's soldiers, or to recuperate important prisoners, or to make the world believe that the other side is implacable and the only cause of all the unrest and miseries of war.

In any case, Montecuccoli urged caution, as an armistice might well be broken, and he believed in the honesty of the adversary only if he could see that the adversary had an interest in establishing this peace.[98]

When dismissing troops at the end of a campaign, he cautioned that one should be careful to pay them their full wages, lest they go over to the enemy or in other ways create unrest, or one should pass them on to another friendly prince who is at war and might need them. He thought that one must never in such circumstances dismiss the entire army but retain some forces for emergencies, and to keep down rebellions. One should keep cadres who are experienced in the science of war, both in theory and practice. They should be able to train new recruits and bring them up to standard within two months.[99]

By this time, these strategic choices were made not by the emperor alone but through decision-making processes involving his ministers and other individuals. It is here particularly that experience of the court in Vienna resonates in his later works, where he formulated an early version of the theory of path-dependency. Drawing on ideas from medicine, he argued that a small mistake made by a high-ranking civil servant at the beginning of a campaign cannot be corrected and will determine the rest of the campaign.[100] Time and again he therefore urged lengthy reflection and steadiness in execution, or as he put it elsewhere, 'One should deliberate slowly and execute fast.'[101]

Like Matthew Sutcliffe before and many strategists after him, he emphasised the need to have one sole commander in charge of a campaign, cautioning against the competition that would arise in the co-leadership among equals.[102] He was clearly scarred by bureaucratic battles and clashing competences when he made the afore-mentioned appeal to the emperor to intervene in tensions that had been building up between the War Council, seated at the court in Vienna, and the Imperial Cabinet. Previously, he reminded Leopold, it had been the convention for the president of the War Council (himself) to be consulted by the councillors of the Imperial Cabinet in all matters pertaining to the military, such as alliances, subsidies and military pro-curement. Now, however, he was left in the dark about subjects of vital concern to his work.[103] Dysfunctionality in policy and strategy making was thus rampant also at the Imperial Court of the seventeenth century.

Clearly, as president of the War Council, Montecuccoli had priorities other than those of the councillors, who he noted were making savings all round (he was less sure that the savings actually benefitted the Imperial Treasury rather than lining the councillors' pockets). Montecuccoli thought that 'the wellbeing of the army' should be 'regarded as the supreme law' – a maxim for the prioritisation of the imperial finances with which Schwendi would largely have agreed.[104]

Montecuccoli was aware of how difficult it was to persuade subjects to pay taxes. Therefore, one had to explain the need to them, and promise tax relief for a more distant future. Taxation had to be equitable and geometrically rising according to income. It should be levied without undue coercion and without private gains. The same should apply if one took substitutes in kind, such as cloth or victuals. As the very feeding of an army caused the local population so much suffering, this was good reason to take one's army into enemy territory or any other foreign country as soon as possible, where one should conquer enough land to feed the army fully or partly off it.[105]

Already in 1641 he argued strongly for a standing army, as it 'secures the survival of the State, retains the loyalty of its citizens and the friendship of foreigners; insur-gencies can be nipped in the bud. Moreover, there is a great difference between an army of veterans and a newly established one.' In other words, a professional soldier was preferable for his discipline and his experience. Montecuccoli was aware of arguments to the contrary: 'One might argue that the army might rise up, that its general might overthrow the prince, that this army corps is a commonwealth unto itself.' To this he replied that

> One might distribute the soldiers so that they do not know each other and do not rebel, and quarter them in different towns; but then the towns may not be safe, as the soldiers would not have exercised joint action, and the towns would lose the advantages of a standing army.[106]

He conceded that large standing armies would be noxious in times of peace, but that the garrisons should be kept up. The other half of the professional army should at all times follow the prince. A soldier should spend half the year at home, the other half in the military camps. Thus the army would not be large enough to stage an insurrection, nor would soldiers be away from their military duties for long enough to forget their military habits. It was crucial to pay them regularly to stave off rebellions, but in turn, discipline must be enforced rigorously, and raucous behaviour and theft should be punished severely.[107]

Montecuccoli on insurgencies and counter-insurgency

Montecuccoli well understood soldiers' grievances and the temptation to rise up against those in authority. Very impressively, in his captivity in Stettin, with no loyalties to his captors and being far from his emperor, Montecuccoli also contemplated the questions of how to prepare for civil war, how to conspire against a tyrant, and conversely, how to prevent or quash a rebellion, and how to secure the loyalty of a conquered people.[108] Here is how Montecuccoli in his early thirties analysed the politics of uprisings: given factionalism at home,

> The party which fears to be the weaker in this domestic strife will rather side with foreigners than cede to the opposite party in its own country. It seeks support from and contacts with foreign lands; it seeks to strengthen its own ranks by contacting other opponents of its own adversaries, drawing them to itself and emphasising the need for a decision brought about by force.[109]

A classic measure would be to bring somebody from the dynasty of the deceased or exiled prince over to your side and use him as a figurehead for the uprising. Against such a background of conspiracies and revolts, the insurgents would be well advised to keep their allies in line by taking their families hostage or by giving them offices and presents. Moreover, Montecuccoli left us an early prescription of propaganda warfare: standard measures would be to slander adversaries, bribe priests so that they preach in your interest, and distribute flyers and leaflets.[110]

He also seemed in great sympathy with those who felt the need to conspire and rise up against a tyrant. He is possibly the earliest author to have written actual prescriptions on how to organise an insurgency. He recommended killing off those members of the tyrant's dynasty still commanded widespread support. One should, he argued, have people who at the outbreak of the rebellion would occupy fortresses and other places useful for defence, man gateways and call the people to rise up and take arms for the sake of freedom. 'If a prince or the authorities are not entirely hated . . . the appreciation that a discontented crowd will follow us in this dangerous enterprise and will join us often turns out to be false. Thus it is necessary to have our own forces and our own places of refuge' in case the insurgency fails.[111]

Even-handedly, however, Montecuccoli also paid attention to the means of dealing with unrest among the population, in a long passage which must have been known to the later writer Santa Cruz de Marcenado.[112] Montecuccoli listed the following: one should, to start with, practice good governance so as not to give rise to rebellions and insurgencies. Therefore one had to curtail luxury, avoid tyranny and keep an eye on governors so they did not enrich themselves (they should not stay more than three years in any one place). One should employ spies who report on public opinion.

In case these measures should fail, one ought to be prepared at any time to quash an incipient early on, with small forces; the earlier one took action, the easier it would be to turn the forces of an insurgency around through good counsel. One should dispatch an eloquent negotiator with a good reputation who warns the potential rebels of the consequences of their plans. Sometimes the prince himself should go to meet the disaffected, displaying boldness, generosity, majesty and fearlessness.

The longer the insurgency had been going on, the more forces one would need to suppress it. Yet one should do so slowly, 'so as to give the wicked time for repentance, the good time to negotiate'. One should use all sorts of devices: 'one offers hope, one increases fear,' one divides to rule, one corrupts some rebels by giving them presents, and one infiltrates an agent of influence into the midst of the insurgent forces who pretends to be on their side and gives them destructive advice. One promises in ambiguous words to concede what they demand; it is better to cheat them than to force them to submit and lose face. While this is a dirty trick, one can wash this sin away by showing generosity in other ways. If the insurgents come to terms and get back to business as usual, he argued, one must not use them cruelly. If all were guilty, one should nevertheless punish only the main leaders, and not investigate their supporters too closely. If the prince decides to have the chief leader of the insurgency assassinated, he should write a formal letter to his chief minister to let the insurgent leader go (presumably so that the prince can later deny involvement in the assassination). Then the prince should charge somebody else with the assassination by impressing upon him the importance of this mission, but take the assassin's brothers or children as hostages, and urge him to act quickly, so that rumours of these plans do not precede the action.[113] Montecuccoli had heard that Wallenstein, prince of 'Friedland, head of a conspiracy against the emperor, was removed in almost the same way.'[114]

Crucially, one should make peace with the rebels, and urge them to go their separate ways, for once dispersed, they are less likely to assemble again. 'If at all possible', wrote Montecuccoli, 'it is better to put down internal unrest through treaties and wisdom than with arms and victory.'[115] Nevertheless, he thought that

> one should not conclude peace lightly with rebels, lest others take them as example. [Yet] One should not be moved by the advice of those who do not want to settle for a compromise because unrest brings them more honour and gains than a quiet life. The best time to negotiate a peace is thus when one has the military advantage, for then one can lay down the conditions and does not need to accept the adversary's.[116]

In a later section that in part also concerned the prevention of discontent and uprisings, Montecuccoli dealt with how, after a victorious conquest, one should maintain the lands thus won. He conceded that no nation enjoyed being ruled by foreigners, and that one would gain nothing but hatred if one brought in foreign soldiers and heaped honours and benefits upon them in return for their services in keeping the local population down. Thus, to hold on to conquered lands, he defined as the main tasks 'to deprive those whom one has subjected of the will to rise up, and of the means to do so'. This was more easily done with a people who had been used to living under a ruler than one who had lived in freedom; even in the former case, the population would want to live under whichever ruler, former or present, (had) treated it better.[117] Montecuccoli added the following:

1   It is thus always necessary first to try clemency, and to create for those whom one has overcome conditions under which they would be sure of their lives and property. Therefore the prince must practice punctilious justice, help the oppressed to his rights, and himself shun all transgressions by force concerning the honour of women or property. Otherwise it will be impossible to win a subjected people for oneself.
2   One must also, as far as possible, maintain the customary form of government, and also open the way for some locals to such appointments, dignities and honours as they may occupy without endangering security.
3   Or else one can leave everything as it is and content oneself with annual tributes in form of people and money.

Here he was clearly referring to what was the Ottoman practice in South-Eastern Europe.

4   If possible, the conqueror-prince should live in the conquered land, as the presence of the prince prevents much disorder, while the splendour of the court creates a certain form of admiration in the hearts of the people and benefits craftsmen and citizens in the vicinity of the court. Even if the place is merely entrusted to a governor, he should appear in splendour, as the people are more attached to appearances than to reality.
5   One wins the benevolence of the people if one suspends tribute payments for two or three years, and frees them of the obligation of military service. In order to gain standing, one will destroy temples, statues and monuments of the previous lords of the conquered country, so that no name is worthy of greater veneration than that of the conqueror.
6   Under the pretext of attendance of a public school and special favours, the children of the higher aristocracy should be retained as hostages in a town under our control.[118]

Further recommendations included to hold down each of the conquered provinces with garrisons and administrators recruited in other provinces, so that they could keep watch on each other, and to encourage intermarriage. In short,

> You will deprive these countries of the will to rise up by treating them in a humane way, and if cruelty becomes necessary, by applying it well . . .

thereafter calming the spirits with benefactions and depriving them of all fears that further cruelty will follow. For no-one can be fully loyal to him whom he has to fear always.[119]

When as president of the War Council he was variously put in charge in the 1660s and 1670s of putting down the Rákóczi-led uprisings in Hungary, Montecuccoli can be seen to have argued for applying his own prescriptions. Yet he also seems to have despaired, at times, of the Hungarians and also the Transylvanian Saxons and their willingness to come to arrangements with the Turks. One can almost see him fuming as he described the Hungarians in his paper 'Hungary in the Year 1677' as

> proud, restless, inconstant and unpacifiable. . . . They strive for unbridled liberty and in that way, unwittingly, they turn themselves into slaves of vices and injustice, to which everybody contributes with all their forces. In the past they caused the division of [their] kingdom and a part of them, under János Szapolyai, sought the protection of Sultan Süleyman [I the Magnificent] in order to be able to lead a more unfettered life, but in that way they inflicted the yoke [of slavery] upon themselves.

(The other king of Hungary was of course Ferdinand of Habsburg, whom we have encountered earlier as Emperor Ferdinand I.) Montecuccoli, utterly intolerant of other religions and other confessions, thus added the prescription that one should raze the private castles of aristocrats, expel untrustworthy individuals from fortified towns and vigorously pursue the Counter-Reformation – the Rákóczi clan were Calvinists until the 1660s.[120]

Montecuccoli's new strategic concept for fighting the Turks

Montecuccoli's strategic concept for war with the Turks was greatly inspired by his experience of warfare among Christian entities. He thus departed from Schwendi's strategy of appeasement and defence, and instead applied to the Turks most of what he had already prescribed for warfare among the European powers.

Montecuccoli had an amazing strategic concept to defeat the Turks.[121] With a relatively smaller mobile army of 50,000 men (28,000 infantry, 2,000 dragoons, 17,000 heavy cavalry, 3,000 light cavalry) he wanted to go after the Turkish army of 300,000. He wanted to use surprise and mobility (the Turks were slow because they brought all their food and supplies up to the borders of their empire), but put off battle: the Turks usually withdrew to Konstantinyya/Constantinople for the winter, and that might allow the Imperial Forces to hold out for longer. He wanted to push into Ottoman-controlled territory using the main rivers – Danube, Raab, Drava – the flow of which favoured the Habsburg side. Key to his plan was to establish a reliable supply system and a network of well-provisioned fortresses so as to be able to counter Ottoman scorched earth tactics. The latter usually ended up harming the sultan's forces themselves, as they, too, needed to live off the land at some stage. Montecuccoli even toyed with the idea of going all the way to Konstantinyya, which even his victorious successors did not dare.[122]

The Italian historian Raimondo Luraghi argues persuasively that – leaving aside the ambition of going all the way to the Bosphorus – Montecuccoli's strategy was essentially also that adopted by Charles of Lorraine in his campaign of 1684–1688, and by Prince Eugene of Savoy in the early eighteenth century. Indeed, one biographer of Prince Eugene attributed the Imperial Army's spectacular victories in these campaigns to the reforms introduced by Raimondo Montecuccoli.[123] Under Charles of Lorraine and then Prince Eugene, they ultimately led to the liberation of Raab/Györ, and then of Budapest and Belgrade. It ushered in the long yet halting rollback of the Turkish Empire until the Ottoman Empire's final demise in 1918.[124]

Conclusions

While neither Schwendi nor Montecuccoli wrote a strategic concept of the comprehensiveness of Sutcliffe's, we can piece together from their several works that they did see strategy in the round. Their thinking on war included reflections not only on the standard topics of how to recruit troops, how to prepare for battle and whether an offensive or a defensive strategy was generally preferable. Both reflected on how the Holy Roman Empire could raise the money to pay for a standing army, and must have looked at France with no little envy.

Each came up with his own grand strategy on how to deal with 'the Turk', a strategy of appeasement and, as much as possible, peaceful coexistence on the part of Schwendi, and a strategy of rollback on the part of Montecuccoli. It must be said that each made good sense in the context of his respective times. Moreover, explicitly or implicitly, Schwendi's strategy was followed by the Holy Roman Empire until the Ottoman Empire turned its energies once more to further expansionism in Europe. Montecuccoli's strategy was partially applied in his own lifetime, and fully applied in the decades after his death. Both were thus strategists whose ideas where applied – and successfully, one might say. Not only that, but also as we have seen, their writings contained thoughts and recommendations many of which are of lasting persuasiveness, or which foreshadow ideas with which later strategists would be credited.

Notes

1 David Parrott: *Richelieu's Army: War, Government and Society in France, 1624–1642* (Cambridge: Cambridge University Press, 2001), and id.: *The Business of War: Military Enterprise and Military Revolution in Early Modern Europe* (Cambridge: Cambridge University Press, 2012).

2 This applies also to what little has been written in English on Montecuccoli: Thomas M. Barker: *The Military Intellectual and Battle: Raimondo Montecuccoli and the Thirty Years' War* (Albany, NY: State University of New York Press, 1975); Gunther Rothenberg: 'Maurice of Nassau, Gustavus Adolphus, Raimondo Montecuccoli, and the "Military Revolution" of the Seventeenth Century', in Peter Paret, Gordon A. Craig & Felix Gilbert (eds): *Makers of Modern Strategy: From Machiavelli to the Nuclear Age* (Princeton, NJ: Princeton University Press, 1986), pp. 56–63.

3 Kaspar von Greyerz: 'Lazarus von Schwendi and Late Humanism in Basle', in Kaspar von Greyerz (eds): *Von Menschen die glauben, schreiben, und wissen* (Göttingen: Verderhoeck & Ruprecht, 2013), pp. 53–67.

4 Azar Gat: 'Montecuccoli: The Impact of Proto-Science on Military Theory', in Azar Gat (ed.): *The Origins of Military Thought from the Enlightenment to Clausewitz* (Oxford: Oxford University Press, 1991), pp. 13–24.

5 Rhoads Murphy: *Ottoman Warfare, 1500–1700* (New Brunswick, NJ: Rutgers University Press, 1999), p. 144f.

6 Mehrdad Kia: *The Ottoman Empire* (Westport, CT: Greenwood Press, 2008), pp. 59–94.

7 Murphy: *Ottoman Warfare*, pp. 16–25.

8 Ibid., p. 41.

9 Ibid., p. 32.

10 Andrew Wheatcroft: *The Enemy at the Gate: Habsburgs, Ottomans and the Battle for Europe* (London: Pimlico, 2009), p. 13f.

11 Isabella Ackerl: *Von Türken belagert – von Christen entsetzt: das belagerte Wien 1683* (Vienna: Österreichischer Bundesverlag, 1983), pp. 134–138; Johannes Sachslehner: *Wien Anno 1683: Ein europäisches Schicksalsjahr* (Vienna: Pichler Verlag, 2004), p. 308.

12 Gabor Ágoston: 'La frontière militaire ottomane en Hongrie', in Marie-Françoise Vajda-Saudraix & Olivier Chaline (eds): *L'Hongrie ottomane, XVIe-XVIIe siècles*, Special Issue of *Histoire, Economie & Société*, Vol. 34 (Sept. 2015), pp. 36–54, esp. 51–54.

13 Klára Hegyi: 'Les origines ethniques et la confession des soldats de l'armée turque servant dans les châteaux forts en territoire hongrois', in Marie-Françoise Vajda-Saudraix & Olivier Chaline (eds): *L'Hongrie ottomane, XVIe-XVIIe siècles*, Special Issue of *Histoire, Economie & Société*, Vol. 34 (Sept. 2015), pp. 54–64.

14 Murphy: *Ottoman Warfare*, pp. 146f.

15 Halil İnalcik: 'The Heyday and Decline of the Ottoman Empire', in P.M. Holt, Ann Lambton and Bernard Lewis (eds): *The Cambridge History of Islam*, Vol. IA (Cambridge: Cambridge University Press, 1970, repr. 1985), p. 328.

16 Most of the details here are taken from August von Kluckhohn: 'Schwendi, Lazarus Freiherr von', *Allgemeine Deutsche Biographie*, Vol. 33 (1891), pp. 382–401, and Thomas Nicklas: 'Schwendi, Lazarus Freiherr von', *Neue Deutsche Biographie*, Vol. 24 (2010), pp. 65–66.

17 Theobald Ziegler: 'Sturm, Johann', in: *Allgemeine Deutsche Biographie*, Vol. 37 (1894), pp. 21–38.

18 Thomas Nicklas: *Um Macht und Einheit des Reiches: Konzeption und Wirklichkeit der Politik bei Lazarus von Schwendi (1522–1583)* (Husum: Matthiesen Verlag, 1995), pp. 74, 78. It was only when the centre of gravity of the Holy Roman Empire moved east to Prague and Vienna that Schwendi started corresponding with the imperial court in German and Latin. As we shall see, Montecuccoli corresponded in Italian throughout.

19 In his *Discurs und bedencken über den jetzigen stand und wesen des hailigen Reichs, unsers lieben vaterlands* (1570).

20 Nicklas: *Um Macht und Einheit des Reiches*, pp. 22–25, 40–50.

21 Ibid., p. 39.

22 *Mein Lazarus vonn Schwendis etc. Warhaffter und unwidersprechlicher Bericht, was ich, die niderwerffung und fengknus, weyland Sebastian Vogelsperger belangend, weyland und gethon habe* (repr. ReInk Books, 2016).

23 Eugène Papirer: *Kientzheim en Haute-Alsace: La Ville de Lazare de Schwendi* (Colmar: Editions d'Alsace, 1982), p. 130ff.

24 Peter Rauscher: 'Kaisertum und hegemoniales Königtum: Die kaiserliche Reaktion auf die niederländische Politik Philipps II. von Spanien', in Friedrich Edelmayer (ed.): *Hispania-Austria II: La época de Felipe II (1556–1598)* (Vienna: Verlag für Geschichte und Politik, 1999), pp. 57–88.

25 Lazarus von Schwendi[0]: 'Kriegsraht und Bedencken des Freyherrn Lazarus von Schwendi weiland Römischer Kais. Majstaet tapfern und glückseligen Kriegs-Obersten', in [Erasmus Francisci?]: *Türckischen Staats und Regiments Beschreibungen; Das ist: Gründliche Nachricht von der Ottomannischen Monarchi Ursprung, Wachsthum, derselben Form zu regieren, Landschafften, Städten, Vestungen, [et]c. Item was vor Potentaten auf dasselbe Reich zu praetendiren: Diesen sind beygefügt etliche der berühmtsten so woln alten als neuen Weissagungen, Muthmassungen und Erklärungen, von gedachten Türckischen Reichs Tyranney und Untergang* (s.l.: Nürnberg?, 1664).

26 Papirer: *Kientzheim en Haute-Alsace*, p. 141.

27 For the liberation of Tokay, Schwendi was given the privilege of importing annually the famous Hungarian Tokay wine, and to plant the grape in his Alsatian properties.

28 Eugen von Frauenholz: *Des Lazarus von Schwendi Denkschrift über die politische Lage des Deutschen Reiches von 1574* (München: Beck, 1939); also Lazarus von Schwendi: *Consilium, Oder: Bedencken An Kaiser Ferdinanden, wie deß Bapsts in Rom Pij V unbillichen anmassen wider Ihrer Kays. Majest. ordentliche Wahl durch die Churfürsten des H. Römischen Reichs ohne des Bapst Consens und Bewilligung geschehen, zu begegnen sey. . . . II. Bedencken An Kaiser Maximilian den Andern, von Regierung deß H. Römischen Reichs . . .* (Frankfurt: Kopf, 1612).

29 Quoted in Nicklas: *Um Macht und Einheit des Reiches*, p. 138.

30 Ibid., pp. 120, 122.

31 Lazarus von Schwendi & Freyherr zu Hohen Landsperg etc: *Kriegsdiscurs, von Bestellung deß ganzen Kriegswesens unnd von den Kriegsämptern* (Frankfurt/Main: Andree Weichels Erben Claudi de Marne & Johan Aubri, 1593).

32 Nicklas: *Um Macht und Einheit des Reiches*, p. 21f.

33 Schwendi: 'Kriegsraht und Bedencken', p. 166. A reference to Cicero *Philippics*, V, ii, 5. This was a popular subject in political philosophy since the mid-fifteenth century; see Frédérique Verrier: *Les Armes de Minerve: L'Humanisme militaire dans l'Italie du XVIe Siècle* (Paris: Presses universitaires de Paris-Sorbonne, 1997), p. 40f.

34 Schwendi: *Kriegsdiscurs*, p. 3.

35 Ibid., p. 11.

36 Ibid., p. 45f.

37 Ibid., p. 46.

38 Ibid., p. 47.

39 Anon. [Raymond de Beccarie de Pavie, baron de Fourquevaux]: *Instructions sur le faict de la Guerre extraictes des livres de Polybe, Frontin, Végèce, Cornazan, Machiavelle* (Paris: Michel Vascosan, 1548), p. 132, translation in Beatrice Heuser: *The Strategy Makers: Thoughts on War and Society from Machiavelli to Clausewitz* (Santa Monica, CA: ABC Clio, 2010), pp. 32–49.

40 Heuser: *The Strategy Makers*, Chapter 1.

41 Schwendi: *Kriegsdiscurs*, p. 12.

42 Ibid., p. 15f.

43 Ibid., p. 14.

44 Heuser: *The Strategy Makers*, Chapter 1.

45 Symphorien Champier: *Les gestes ensemble la vie du preulx Chevalier Bayard* (Lyon: Gilbert de Villiers, 1525), ed. Denis Crouzet (Paris: Imprimerie Nationale, 1992), pp. 164, 170ff.

46 See for example Count Giacomo/Jacopo di Porcia: *Clarissimi viri Jacobi Pvrliliarvm comitis de re militaris liber* (Venice: Joannis Tacuinus di Tridino, 1530), Chapter 138.

47 Heuser: *The Strategy Makers*, Chapter 7.

48 Schwendi: *Kriegsdiscurs*, p. 84.

49 Fourquevaux: *Instructions sur le faict de la Guerre*, p. 217, translation in Heuser: *The Strategy Makers*, pp. 47–49.

50 Quoted in Nicklas: *Um Macht und Einheit des Reiches*, p. 121.
51 Schwendi: *Kriegsdiscurs*, p. 6.
52 Schwendi: 'Kriegsraht und Bedencken', p. 166.
53 Ibid., p. 177f.
54 Ibid., p. 179.
55 Ibid., pp. 177–179.
56 For this reason, Schwendi has been hailed as the father of universal military service in Austria; see Eugen von Frauenholz: *Lazarus von Schwendi: der erste deutsche Verkünder der allgemeinen Wehrpflicht* (Hamburg: Hanseatische Verlagsanstalt, 1939).
57 Schwendi: 'Kriegsraht und Bedencken', pp. 171f., 174.
58 Ibid., pp. 172f., 175f.
59 Ibid., pp. 167–170.
60 Ibid., p. 170.
61 Ibid., p. 181.
62 Ibid., p. 170.
63 Ibid., p. 180f.
64 For most of the biographic data, see Helmut Neuhaus: 'Montecuccoli, Raimund Fürst von', in: *Neue Deutsche Biographie*, Vol. 18 (1997), pp. 44–47, and Schzl. [sic]: 'Montecuccoli, Raimund Fürst von', in: *Allgemeine Deutsche Biographie*, Vol. 22 (1885), pp. 183–189, and Giampiero Brunelli: 'Montecuccoli, Raimondo', *Dizionario Biografico degli Italiani*, Vol. 76 (2012). For a biography based on his surviving correspondence, see Gerhard Schreiber: *Raimondo Montecuccoli: Feldherr, Schriftsteller und Kavalier* (Graz: Verlag Styria, 2000).
65 *Trattato della guerra* (MS in Italian written in Stettin, 1641), trans. into German in Hauptmann Alois Veltzé (ed.): *Ausgewählte Schriften des Raimond Fürsten Montecuccoli*, Vol. 1 (Vienna: Wilhelm Braumüller, 1899), p. 44.
66 Raimondo Montecuccoli: *[Discorso] Sulle Battaglie* (1639–1642?), ed. & trans. by Barker: *Military Intellectual and Battle*.
67 Montecuccoli: *Trattato della guerra* (1641/1899), pp. 3–387.
68 Ibid., p. 5.
69 Giorgio Basta, Conte d'Host, Generale per l'imperatore nella Transiluania: *Il mastro di campo Generale* (Venice: s.e., 1603).
70 Francesco Ludovico Melzi: *Regole militari sopra il governo e servitio della cavalleria* (Venic: Deuchino, 1626).
71 Henri Duc de Rohan: *Le Parfaict Capitaine, Autrement l'abrégé des guerres de Gaule des commentaires de César* (Paris: Iean Hovzé, 1636).
72 *Discovrs politiqves et militaires du Seigneur de la Noue* (2nd edn, Bâle: François Forest, 1587).
73 Montecuccoli: *Trattato della Guerra* (1641/1899), pp. 4, 6.
74 *Del arte militare* (MS K. und K. Hof-Bibliothek zu Vienna, Cod 10.966; written at Hohenegg, 20 März 1653), trans. into German in Hauptmann Alois Veltzé (ed.): *Ausgewählte Schriften des Raimond Fürsten Montecuccoli*, Vol. 2 (Vienna: Wilhelm Braumüller, 1899), pp. 27–117.
75 Gat: 'Montecuccoli', pp. 17–19. In my view Gat wrongly claims that there was an 'impact of proto-science on military theory' in his works; the only traces of impact I can see are classical and humanist writings on war and politics.
76 Letters of Montecuccoli to Father Massimiliano Montecuccoli, in Alois Veltzé (ed.): *Ausgewählte Schriften des Raimond Fürsten Montecuccoli*, Vol. 4 (Vienna: Wilhelm Braumüller, 1900), pp. 272–275.
77 Raimondo Montecuccoli: *Discorso della Guerra contro il Turco* (Vienna, 1 March 1664).
78 Derek McKay: *Prince Eugene of Savoy* (London: Thames & Hudson, 1977), p. 28.
79 Montecuccoli: *Memorie Militari* (1668[1]), printed in Ugo Foscolo & Giuseppe Grassi (eds): *Memorie militare di Raimondo di Montecuccoli*, 2 vols (Torino: Tipografia Economica, 1852).

80 Raimondo Montecuccoli: *Della Guerra col Turco in Ungheria* (1670), trans. into German in Hauptmann Alois Veltzé (ed.): *Ausgewählte Schriften des Raimond Fürsten Montecuccoli*, Vol. 2 (Vienna: Wilhelm Braumüller, 1899), pp. 195–563.

81 Raimondo Montecuccoli: 'Mal governo della camera aulica' (7 August 1670), trans. into German by Alois Veltzé (ed.): *Ausgewählte Schriften des Raimond Fürsten Montecuccoli*, Vol. 3 (Vienna: Wilhelm Braumüller, 1900), pp. 385–389.

82 *L'Ungheria nell'anno 1677.*

83 Alois Veltzé: 'Introduction', in Alois Veltzé (ed.): *Ausgewählte Schriften des Raimond Fürsten Montecuccoli*, Vol. 1 (Vienna: Wilhelm Braumüller, 1899), pp. xix–xxii.

84 For such patterns and standard topics covered, see Heuser: 'Introduction', in *eadem: The Strategy Makers.*

85 For example Montecuccoli: *Della Guerra col Turco in Ungheria* (1670/1899), p. 250. The Austrian editor of his works has traced citations of Herodotus, Thucydides, Xenophon, Polybius, Cicero, Caesar, Aeneas Tacticus, Aelian, Frontinus and, of course, the inevitable Vegetius.

86 Montecuccoli: *Della Guerra col Turco in Ungheria* (1670/1899), p. 206.

87 Ibid., p. 250f.

88 Ibid., p. 258f.

89 Montecuccoli: 'Aforismi dell' Arte Bellica' (1668/1852), Vol. 1, pp. 152–155.

90 Montecuccoli: *Della Guerra col Turco in Ungheria* (1670/1899), pp. 243–246, 257–260.

91 Ibid., p. 276.

92 Ibid., p. 355.

93 Ibid.

94 Ibid., p. 258.

95 Montecuccoli: *Trattato della guerra* (1641/1899), p. 51.

96 Ibid., p. 373.

97 Ibid., p. 374, see Justus Lipsius: *Politica*, Cap. 19, 20.

98 Montecuccoli: *Trattato della Guerra* (1641/1899), p. 374f.

99 Ibid., p. 378f.

100 Montecuccoli: *Della Guerra col Turco in Ungheria* (1670/1899), p. 255.

101 Ibid., p. 273; Demost., exord., 22; Arist., 6. ethic. Cap. 9; Lips., Pol.

102 Montecuccoli: *Della Guerra col Turco in Ungheria* (1670/1899), p. 274.

103 Montecuccoli: 'Schwierigkeiten, welche beim Hof-Kriegsrathe unterlaufen', p. 386.

104 Montecuccoli: *Della Guerra col Turco in Ungheria* (1670/1899), p. 253.

105 Ibid., p. 250f.

106 Montecuccoli: *Trattato della Guerra* (1641/1899), p. 378.

107 Ibid., pp. 378–380.

108 Ibid., pp. 23–60, 381–387.

109 Ibid., p. 28.

110 Ibid., pp. 29–33.

111 Ibid., pp. 33–37.

112 Excerpts in Heuser: *The Strategy Makers*, Chapter 7.

113 Montecuccoli: *Trattato della guerra* (1641/1899), pp. 37–42.

114 Ibid., p. 41f.; See also Raimondo di Montecuccoli: *Dalla relazione della congiura del Wallenstein* (Italian, 1634), trans. into German in Hauptmann Alois Veltzé (ed.): *Ausgewählte Schriften des Raimond Fürsten Montecuccoli*, Vol. 3 (Vienna: Wilhelm Braumüller, 1901), pp. 3–8.

115 Montecuccoli: *Trattato della guerra* (1641/1899), pp. 42, 50.

116 Ibid., p. 373.

117 Ibid., pp. 381–387.

118 Ibid., p. 382f.

119 Ibid., pp. 384, 386.

120 Raimondo Montecuccoli: 'L'Ungheria nell'anno 1677', in Hauptmann Alois Veltzé (ed.): *Ausgewählte Schriften des Raimond Fürsten Montecuccoli*, Vol. 3 (Vienna: Wilhelm Braumüller, 1899), pp. 423, 459–472.

121 Austrian State Archive, War Archive: Montecuccoli papeers: 'Discorso sulla guerra contro il Turco', written mainly 1664, completed 1671.
122 Raimondo Luraghi: 'Montecuccoli's Plans for a General War against the Turks', in Johann Christoph Allmayer-Beck (ed.): *Beiträge zum Internationalen Congress für Militärgeschichte* (Vienna: 6.-10. Juni 1983, gedr. durch Österreichische Komission für Militärgeschichte), pp. 71–78.
123 Derek McKay: *Prince Eugene of Savoy* (London: Thames & Hudson, 1977), p. 28.
124 Luraghi: 'Montecuccoli's Plans'.

8

GUIBERT

Prophet of total war?

'The god of war is about to reveal himself, for we have heard his prophet.' Thus wrote the French strategist Jean Colin in his book on the military education of Napoleon (styled the 'god of war' by contemporaries), and the prophet he had in mind was Jacques Antoine Hippolyte, Count de Guibert, a prolific writer of the eighteenth century.[1] Indeed, the connection between Guibert and Napoleon is supported by historical evidence. Napoleon was made to read Guibert's works at the Ecole Militaire in Paris, the military school he attended. He later called Guibert's principal work, the *Essai général de Tactique* (*A General Essay on Tactics*), 'a book fit to educate great men'. He took it on campaign with him and bestowed a pension on Guibert's widow 'in consideration of the works of M. de Guibert and of the advantages which the French Army has drawn from them'.[2] George Washington is also reported to have read Guibert and to have said, 'The works of M. de Guibert are my companions of war.'[3]

The influence of Guibert's writings on the warfare of the French Revolution, however, was at best indirect. To be sure, his *Essai général de Tactique* was so widely read and so frequently and thoroughly studied that several authors wrote entire books as commentaries on his views – usually to take him to task over his views with regard to marching in columns, his preferred length for the bayonet and the deep order or the shallow order for shooting volleys.[4] But Guibert was not among the authors of the great *Encyclopédie*, even though the *encyclopédistes* writing on military matters had read and referred to his *Essai*. As Kathleen Hardesty Doig has found, the *encyclopédistes* were fairly conservative where military technology, doctrine and concepts of recruitment and training were concerned,[5] and Guibert, in his earlier writings, was more revolutionary than they when it came to his ideas about the need for citizens to identify with and defend their country as citizen-soldiers.

Looking at war more generally, however, the *encyclopédistes* and *philosophes* were more radical than Guibert. Some philosophers, most notably Voltaire, hoped to abolish warfare altogether and did not think that the creation of mass armies would be helpful for this purpose. When he was in his thirties, Guibert distanced himself from this position of the *philosophes*, professing his belief that war was an eternal human phenomenon but it could be made rarer and less bloody if waged in the way he advocated.[6] When the revolution erupted, the revolutionaries, while borrowing here and there from his ideas, regarded Guibert as not radical enough, associating him with the monarchy's failed reforms. Guibert therefore cannot be said directly to have played a part in the thinking of the great actors of the revolution, the Dantons, Robespierres or Carnots. And yet some of the ideas he set out in his *Essai général de Tactique* – 'tactics' being used by Guibert, prior to the introduction of the word 'strategy' into French, as meaning something like 'comprehensive approach to defence' – especially on the need for all citizens to defend their country, seem to have found their echo in revolutionary rhetoric and practice.

One believer in Guibert's prophetic gifts was the French anthropologist Roger Callois. Commenting on the way of war of the French Revolution, he argued that it is a misperception and misrepresentation to think of the *levée en masse* as a 'desperate expedient' or 'that the tactics of the armies of the Year II were only a function of the inexperience of the generals and the soldiers'. Callois argued,

> A reading of Guibert shows that both fit a doctrine which was already 20 years old, worked out by one of the most admired theoreticians of the century, and doubtless the object of impassioned discussions. . . . In advance [of its time], [the doctrine] analyzed the conditions of a new form of recruitment, it developed a new strategy, it sketched the mind-set of the future combatant. It foresaw the violence of war, the mobility of troops, the disdain for conventions, the boldness of manoeuvres, the conscription of recruits, the frequency and the fierceness of battles, the[ir] decisive character.[7]

And for Lucien Poirier, the Fifth Republic general turned philosopher of strategy, there is no doubt that 'Ahead of his times by thirty years, [Guibert] announced the furies of nationalism.'[8] The Gaullist politician and intellectual Léo Hamon commented on Guibert's later writings that they reflected the fear with which he had discovered the slippery slope leading to the politics of the Romantic era and to apocalyptic conflicts.[9]

There is thus broad agreement that Guibert was indeed the prophet of French revolutionary and Napoleonic warfare.[10] But was he also the prophet of 'total war'?

The young Guibert

Jacques-Antoine Hippolyte de Guibert was born in 1743 as the only son of Jean-Bénoît Guibert, a member of the minor nobility and an officer in the French army. The boy was only 13 when his father first took him on campaign at the outbreak of the Seven Years' War. Jacques-Antoine was to witness that war in its entirety, fighting on the side of the French against the Prussians under Frederick II, 'the Great'.

In the course of the war, the adolescent rose to the rank of captain, while his father became a brigadier. Together, they took part in several battles, including those at Rossbach and Minden, which Frederick famously won. Against the backdrop of these experiences, which he must have discussed in great detail with his father or have heard his father discuss with other officers, Jacques-Antoine became a great admirer of Frederick, as he reckoned that Frederick had revolutionised warfare.[11] And yet he recognised shortcomings even in Frederick's conduct of warfare and dreamt of even more intensive, comprehensive and decisive campaigns.

Jacques-Antoine de Guibert wrote down his thoughts on the subject of the art of war and society in his two-volume *Essai général de Tactique* when he was in his early twenties, towards the end of several years of independent study in Paris, where he had followed his father, who was now employed at the Ministry of War. The *Essai* thus deals with much more than what we today would call tactics. He included a great *tour d'horizon* of France's relations with many other countries as well as a most impressive sketch of a utopian state. Like Kant's later ideal non-aggressive republic, Guibert's ideal state would have no territorial ambitions and wage only defensive wars. It would be open to commerce and the arts, and it would thus in every possible way serve as an example to other countries. Kant, it is worth emphasising, wrote his *vom Ewigen Frieden* only in 1795, a quarter of a century after Guibert. Perhaps a copy of his *Essai général* had found its way to Königsberg, or else these ideas were in the air, engendered at much the same time in different places by the reading of Montesquieu, Voltaire and others.

As Guibert took some of his basic ideas on the *ius ad bellum* from Montesquieu, it is imperative to outline these briefly. Montesquieu's *Esprit des Lois* (1748) was frowned upon by French patriots because of its approval of the British system, just as Guibert was criticised 30 years later for his admiration for Frederick II of Prussia. Unlike Voltaire, Montesquieu accepted war as an inherent part of human relations and saw it as justified above all in the case of self-defence.[12] The types of states Montesquieu admired most – democracies, oligarchies and constitutional monarchies – were those he thought most likely to wage only defensive wars. In Books 9 and 10 of the *Esprit des Lois*, Montesquieu reflected upon the relationship of the law with the defensive use of force, and he opined, 'The spirit of monarchy is war and aggrandizement; the spirit of the republic is peace and moderation.'[13] He refined this argument by pointing to dictates of size. A monarchy of middling size would be inclined to surround itself by fortresses à la Vauban to strengthen its defences. (Despotic régimes, however, would not dare build fortresses on their own territory, as they would trust no guardian of such a fortress to be loyal to them.)[14] A smallish state, by contrast, might be tempted to wage a preventive war in the fear that a neighbour might grow to become a threat.[15] A republic would contradict its own ideals of liberty if it ever waged aggressive wars with the aim of lasting conquest (as opposed to an offensive campaign aimed at neutralising a neighbouring territory for a limited time), let alone the enslavement of a conquered people.[16] We will see several of these views taken up by Guibert in his *Essai général de la Tactique*.

Writing after the Seven Years' War, from which France emerged with much shame and dishonour, Guibert vented his dissatisfaction with the customs of waging war in his age, which he blamed in part for France's defeat. Here is his description of warfare under the Ancien Régime: 'Today, all of Europe is civilized,' he proclaimed.

> Wars have become less cruel. Outside combat, blood is no longer shed. Towns are no longer destroyed. The countryside is no longer ravaged. The vanquished people are only asked to pay some form of tribute, often less exacting than the taxes that they pay to their sovereign. Spared by their conqueror, their fate does not become worse [after a defeat]. All the states of Europe govern themselves, more or less, according to the same laws and according to the same principles. As a result, necessarily, the nations take less interest in wars. The quarrel, whatever it is, isn't theirs. They regard it simply as that of the government. Therefore, the support for this quarrel is left to mercenaries, and the military is regarded as a cumbersome group of people and cannot count itself among the other groups within society. As a result, patriotism is extinct, and bravery is weakening as if by an epidemic.[17]

For this reason, the majority of military thinkers under the Ancien Régime were, Guibert contended, working within limited parameters. They usually had the practical knowledge of experienced soldiers, and their interests were limited to organisational and operational matters, such as the recruitment of troops, training and discipline, patterns of deploying troops and composing armies (infantry, cavalry, artillery), logistics and other truly tactical considerations (e.g. how to besiege a fortified place and how to fortify places to withstand sieges, or how to cross rivers without becoming excessively vulnerable to enemy attacks). These are the main subjects addressed in the military writings of Henry Lloyd, Frederick II, Maurice de Saxe, Jean de Folard (whom Guibert despised whole-heartedly)[18] and most of their contemporaries. They operated in a political context in which the political aims of commanding princes were as clear as they were simple: the self-preservation of ruling dynasties and the defence or aggrandisement of their lands, as we read in the political testament of Frederick the Great.[19] Jean-Jacques Rousseau put it similarly: 'The business of kings or of those who discharge their duties has only two aims: extend their domination abroad and to render it more absolute internally.'[20] As war aims were thus fairly straightforward in this period, when religion featured much less than at any time since antiquity, and when all princes essentially wanted to uphold the existing social order, hardly any military thinker considered the possibility of extending wars, of making them more decisive, more brutal or more far-reaching. They thought and wrote about how to make battles technically more efficient and armies more disciplined, how to deploy forces more effectively, not how to revolutionise warfare as such. On the whole, the eighteenth century produced limited thinking about limited wars.

Guibert was the crucial exception to this rule. He paired military experience and the quest for a more decisive victory with a politico-philosophic approach.

In the *Essai général de Tactique*, the young Guibert set out his reflections on the wars of his age he had witnessed or read about, against the background of the societies he knew.

> Now that all the peoples of Europe are, so to speak, mixed . . . because of the similarity of the principles of their governments, by . . . their morals, by politics, travel, literature, the national prejudices which used to separate them no longer exist. . . . Today indeed all the nations of Europe model themselves on one another. . . . Today all the troops of Europe have, with small differences, the same constitutions, which is to say . . . constitutions . . . which are based neither on honour nor on patriotism.[21]

It was not only the ways of conducting war and the 'military constitutions' that determined the nature of warfare under the Ancien Régime. Guibert also identified deep structural patterns in macroeconomics and demographics which played crucial roles. 'Today', wrote Guibert,

> the States have neither treasure, nor a population surplus. Their expenditure in peace is already beyond their income. Still, they wage war against each other. One goes to war with armies which one can neither [afford to] recruit, nor pay. Victor or vanquished, both are almost equally exhausted [at the end of a war]. The mass of the national debt increases. Credit decreases. Money is lacking. The fleets do not find sailors, armies lack soldiers. The ministers, on one side and on the other, feel that it is time to negotiate. Peace is concluded. Some colonies or provinces change hands. Often the source of the quarrels has not dried up, and each side sits on the rubble, busy paying his debts and keeping his armies alert.[22]

In Guibert's description of the situation in the eighteenth century, we see where Clausewitz drew his inspiration for his passages on civil-military relations:[23] Guibert described eighteenth-century Europe as full of

> tyrannical, ignorant or weak governments; the strengths of nations stifled by their vices; individual interests prevailing over the public good [common wealth]; morals, that supplement of laws which is so often more effective than them, neglected or corrupted; . . . the expenses of governments greater than their incomes; taxes higher than the means of those who have to pay them; the population scattered and sparse; the most important skills neglected for the sake of frivolous arts; luxury blindly undermining all states; and governments finally indifferent to the fates of the people, and the peoples, in return, indifferent to the successes of governments.[24]

We hear here echoes of Tacitus and Suetonius deploring Rome's abandonment of the republican virtues that made it the greatest power in the known world. And, indeed, Guibert was setting eighteenth-century Europe in contrast to Republican Rome, the Rome whose *citizens* had conquered many kingdoms and whose pride in their citizenship made them feel superior to the kings they defeated.[25] Applying this model to the ideal state of his own times, Guibert did not use the term 'citizen-soldiers' but spoke of a 'national militia', in principle tasked only with the defence of their country. But if attacked, this militia, these 'happy citizens, interested in defending [their own] prosperity' could not be defeated by the sort of *stipendiaires* (mercenaries, professional soldiers) that constituted the European armies of his own age. Indeed, if attacked, such a state would fight back 'with all the efforts in its power', it would go over to the offensive, to conquer, but not to retain its conquests, only making 'expeditions' into enemy territory. If

> one has come to insult this happy and pacific people, it will rise up [*il se soulève*], it leaves its home. It will perish, up to the last [man] if necessary, but it will obtain satisfaction, it will avenge itself, and it will assure, with the explosion of this vengeance, its future peace [*repos*].[26]

As no professional army fighting alongside this 'militia' is mentioned, and as this force is contrasted with the *stipendiaires* of a potential aggressor, Guibert has probably rightly been interpreted as calling, in his *Essai*, for a citizen army.[27]

Guibert did not, however, at this stage call for the constitution of a full-fledged democracy, and he certainly did not come down entirely against monarchy. He described France, his fatherland, as composed of the king *and* the three estates of citizens. This was not merely paying lip service to the monarchy to get past the censors: Guibert felt obliged to publish the *Essai général de Tactique* abroad – in London in 1772 and in Leiden a year later – for fear of censorship. At the very least, we have here a clear shift from the old loyalty to the king only – regnalism, as defined by Susan Reynolds[28] – to a new reverence for the entire polity, the country and its citizens. He thus dedicated the *Essai* to his *patrie* (fatherland), not his king, even though he saw his king as father of his fatherland.

Yet this patriotism was mixed with a universalist, humanist approach, as he defined his patriotism as free from pride as well as from hatred or disdain for other peoples. 'I can thus be useful for my fellow citizens, while not displeasing foreigners. I can write for France, and be read by the rest of Europe.'[29] (This attitude can still be found in his writings a decade later, when he contended, 'I am not writing only for France; I am addressing also those foreign armies who practice what we discuss.')[30]

What, then, was it that Guibert wanted for France? A new military rooted in a new society, a military able to deal with enemies decisively. 'Imagine', he wrote,

> that a people will arise in Europe that combines the virtues of austerity and a national militia with a fixed plan for expansion, that it does not lose sight of this system, that, knowing how to make war at little expense and to live off its victories, it would not be forced to put down its arms for reasons of economy. One would see that people subjugate its neighbours, and overthrow our

weak constitutions, just as the fierce north wind bends the slender reeds. . . . Between these peoples, whose quarrels are perpetuated by their weakness [i.e. they cannot fight to the finish], one day there might still be more decisive wars, which will shake up empires.[31]

It is impossible to read this passage without thinking of the *levée en masse* during the French Revolution and of the Napoleonic achievements. It is as if Napoleon had consciously set out to be the *aquilon*, the fierce north wind that swept across Europe, bending the slender reeds of the old monarchies. Guibert, however, merely dreamt about this; he did not prophesy it.

What would be the strategy of Guibert's ideal state? He imagined it to be defensive in a Montesquieuian sense: it would wish for peace and fight only defensive wars. Here, Guibert injected a strong dose of mercantilism. The overarching policy of the government of his ideal state would be to engender prosperity on every level through internal growth of production turned into riches through trade. It would open its ports, let its commerce flow, and trade with as many other countries as possible. That, in turn, dictated this state's foreign and defence policy. To secure copious and free trade, this state's arms had to be feared but 'never its ambitions'. This state 'would not fear that [foreigners] visit its arsenals, its ports, . . . its troops' because it would have nothing to hide.[32] To the contrary, 'the view of its resources would make [others] wish for its friendship, and fear its arms.'[33] Negotiations between the states of his new world would be conducted in good faith, while in the actual world of his times,

> It is the weakness of our governments which puts into their negotiations so much obliquity and bad faith. It is that which foments the divisions between the peoples, which . . . corrupts reciprocally the officials of all [state] administrations.[34]

The motto of Guibert's ideal state would be 'Liberty, Security, Protection'.

> This state, vigilant to avenge its injuries, will politically be the ally of no people; but it will be the friend of all. It will bring them, without cease, words of peace. It will be, if it can, the mediator in all its quarrels, not because of its interests, not in order to profit from its mediation, not because of any chimerical balance of power calculations. . . . It will propose its arbitration, because peace is a good, and [the State] knows its price; because war interrupts the communications which should exist between the peoples and it harms also neighbouring countries. . . . [This state] would say to its neighbours: 'O peoples! O my brothers! Why are you tearing each other apart? What false politics are separating you? Nations are not born as enemies. They are the branches of the same family. Come benefit from the spectacle of my prosperity. . . . I do not fear that my neighbours become happy and powerful – the more they do, the more they will cherish calm. It is from public happiness that universal peace will be born.'[35]

The reader is left to wonder who in Guibert's view stood in the way of creating this paradise – and cannot quite shake off the feeling that it is the selfish, the incompetent, the uncaring monarch and his supporters. Indeed, later on in the *Essai*, Guibert expressed doubts that one individual alone could rule over a country without making it suffer from his whims.[36] But then there was the enlightened Frederick the Great, who served as the inspiration for Guibert's vision of a vigorous prince who would bring about 'that great revolution' of rekindled patriotism, virtue and morale – a revolution, in short, in state, society and strategy.[37]

It was the Roman spirit, not Roman tactics, which according to Guibert we should copy. This in his view was where Maurice of Nassau and Gustavus Adolphus of Sweden (and indeed Folard,[38] still seen as the greatest teacher of the art of war in France at the time) had gone wrong. Technology had changed, Guibert noted, and it was pointless to try to copy Roman and Greek battle formations – phalanxes and all the rest – when you had firepower. It was pointless, he argued for example, to have more than three lines of troops with firearms, as any further line cannot fire. Rather than advocate a slavish copying of the Ancients where tactics were concerned, Guibert in the *Essai* called for imaginative innovation and explored a variety of new tactical approaches.

If the Roman Republic offered a useful model for the modern day, it was above all, Guibert thought, in civil–military relations. Like Machiavelli before him, he wanted a return to the Roman system of organising citizens to defend their own country, of mobilising the population. That would reduce the cost of waging war by reducing dependence on foreign mercenaries – seen by Guibert as expensive and unenthusiastic about the country they fought for. Citizen armies, driven by patriotism, would be 'invincible', Guibert believed.[39]

In this view Guibert was as much the successor of Machiavelli as of the French philosophical discourse into which he had been born. Perhaps the single most important area in which French thinkers – including Guibert – now began to distinguish themselves from other European military thinkers was the subject of the recruitment of soldiers and their relationship with state and society.

We recall that in the fifteenth century, the French royal state under Charles VII was the first in Europe to develop the political postulate that only the crown, only the central government of the budding state, only the king had the right to have an army and, further, that this army should be a standing army ready for action year round. Centralising and monopolising the right to a standing army were perhaps the most crucial step on the way to the assertion of the authority of the monarch in France. It was that monopoly that enabled one of Charles VII's successors, Louis XIV, to claim to *be* the state, a claim the great Francophone philosophers of statehood would have endorsed.[40]

This meant that France abandoned limited, seasonal military service by the peasantry, who by definition could not provide a standing army, for the professional army that came to be associated with the monarchic state system and absolutism. Against this stood the spirit of the Enlightenment and its ideas about statehood and society, which were rooted in classical models and the idea of a social contract. Periodic revivals of Roman Republican ideals – in the Swiss cantons during the thirteenth and fourteenth centuries, in the writings of Machiavelli around 1500, and under the Nassaus in the sixteenth century and Gustavus Adolphus in the seventeenth – had linked pre-modern practices of military service owed to one's lord and neoclassical calls for the defence of the *res publica* by all citizens, and thus for universal male military service. The thinkers of the French Enlightenment also made this connection, linking the citizen-soldier, the people that would rise up to defend itself and its values (as Guibert had written in the *Essai*, '*il se soulève*'!), the *levée en masse*, and the French revolutionary ideals of equality and universality.

Under the Ancien Régime, France had both a professional army and a militia, whose members, scattered all over the country, had to perform two to six years' seasonal military service. In peacetime, this service consisted only of annual exercises of 8–15 days. In 1775, the French militia was changed into a simple reservoir of recruits for the main professional army. Wars under the Ancien Régime were fought mainly by professional – in part mercenary – soldiers, as was true for most parts of Europe. This meant that the armies of the eighteenth century, like those that fought the Hundred Years' War and the Thirty Years' War, consisted of soldiers from many different countries. Within the individual armies, they were usually grouped together by country of origin even though these groups were rarely homogeneous ethnically. The wars of the eighteenth century were not national wars, fought with the nations' armies: they were princes' wars, fought with the princes' armies.

Guibert, by contrast, wanted to develop an army of citizen-soldiers. He thus advocated a certain degree of militarisation of society. He wanted to see the education of youngsters in a martial spirit and of the entire society in a spirit of rigor, discipline and patriotism.[41] This would make a really strong defensive campaign possible, he wrote enthusiastically in his *Essai*, a defensive war that could be fought to the finish. And this is what, as a young man writing in his twenties, he regarded as desirable: a truly decisive war that mobilised the entire citizenry, not the lukewarm affairs of his day.

The world of limited battles and indecisive warfare so deprecated by Guibert was to be profoundly shaken by the introduction of new values, values for which the people of France were prepared to fight not only against their own government, their monarchy, but also against all other countries. The French Revolution, with its ideals of liberty, equality, fraternity, was the fierce northerly wind that swept away the luxury and the indulgence and the peace of this relatively calm age. The young Guibert, like many thinkers of his time, had craved this change. But he had not thought about the bloodshed, the pain and the destruction which those who set the revolutionary fire to the rococo palaces of France would unleash. The twentieth-century French strategist Lucien Poirier has called the young Guibert the sorcerer's apprentice who conjured up these devastating flames in a society built entirely of very dry wood, with the tinder of social grievances everywhere: 'The *Essai* appears very ambiguous to us today,' he noted.

Nothing allows us to say that [Guibert] preferred offensive war to the defensive, which is moreover more in keeping with the project of happiness and the political system he asked for. But his remarks about an offensive strategy, the axiom of a decisive battle calling, by mental continuity, for a war of annihilation, the references to the nation in arms which packed off the rules of the game [of war] into the museum of history, all this allows a polarised reading: that of a strategy . . . of annihilation.[42]

And this was the reading of Guibert's work that the Convention, Carnot and Saint-Just preferred, as well as Napoleon with his quest for the decisive battle.

The mature Guibert

As with Clausewitz, we find that Guibert changed his views about war over time, and as with Clausewitz, it was particularly on the issue of limited or absolute war. Only Guibert saw this distinction a good half century before Clausewitz had his sudden revelation on this subject.[43] Unlike Clausewitz, Guibert had since his youth understood the existence of both these forms of war. And what is most amazing is that Guibert understood this distinction *before the French Revolution had created the levée en masse*. In fact, Guibert predicted a form of war almost 20 years before it was practised in Europe; indeed his ideas contributed to its creation.

Guibert had gone through alternating periods of success and disappointment in the decades between his service in the Seven Years' War and the storming of the Bastille. In 1769, after completing the *Essai général* but before its publication in 1772, he saw active service again in France's short campaign to subdue the newly acquired Corsica. In 1773, he embarked on a self-financed tour of Central Europe, mainly to study the military systems of Prussia and the Habsburg Empire.[44]

Thereafter, Guibert had a roller-coaster career, marked by peaks of fame and influence and deep valleys of depression and self-imposed exile from the world on his family estate. Through his father, who had risen to the rank of lieutenant general but served mainly as an administrator in Paris, Guibert, still nominally an officer with an infantry regiment, periodically worked for the War Ministry himself. He rose to the rank of brigadier at the age of 38, but he never rose as far as his father had done. He had two periods in influential positions at the War Ministry. He worked for Count Saint-Germain (minister of war from 1775 to 1777), Marshal de Ségur, Count Brienne as minister of war and archbishop of Toulouse, and Loménie de Brienne (older brother of Count Brienne) as minister of finances, whom he advised on a cost-effective restructuring of the French military forces in 1787–88, and on the creation of a War Council to coordinate decision-making.[45] In each case, Guibert was involved in fundamental reforms of the French military, which were very much in the spirit of his views and writings.[46] He was also seen as very influential by jealous competitors, who turned into political enemies when Guibert became principal rapporteur of the War Council. They not only spread venomous criticism about him but also attacked him fiercely to his face.[47] In 1779, during a lull between his two periods of government service, Guibert published a *Défense du Systême de Guerre moderne* (defence of the modern system of war), to which we shall return shortly, encapsulating much of the advice he had been giving his ministers.

At the outbreak of the French Revolution, the revolutionary Military Committee that succeeded the War Council overthrew practically all the reforms Guibert's Council had instigated.[48] In March 1789, Guibert unsuccessfully tried to have himself elected to the Estates-General. On 14 July 1789, Louis XIV closed down the War Council, and Guibert's involvement came to an end. Frustrated, Guibert sat down to write a new book on civil-military relations. *De la force publique considérée par tous ses rapports* (which roughly translates as 'on the public use of force in all its dimensions') was published in 1790; shortly after it appeared, Guibert was seized by the fatal illness that carried him off at the age of 46.

Taken together, the *Défense* and *De la force publique* make clear that Guibert the nobleman had changed his mind about the role and constitution of the armed forces in the years since writing the *Essai*. By the time he was writing *De la force publique*, the sorcerer's apprentice who had played with fire now threw away his matches, smelling the first smoke rising up where the sparks had caught. Guibert now sought to contain the fury of the forces of human nature that his very own earlier writing had contributed to unleashing, the 'laws of nature' he had so light-heartedly invoked in his *Essai*.[49] The *Défense* and *De la force publique* are, in Jean Klein's words, 'an appeal for moderation' prompted by his vision of imminent conflagration.[50] Once again, Guibert was cast in the role of prophet.

In the *Défense*, Guibert took leave of advocating a militia that would be raised ad hoc as principal means of the defence of France. Instead, he now argued for the creation of an even larger standing army, ideally a professional army of 200,000 men. A militia might supplement this force,[51] but, in an age of what Guibert regarded as high-technology warfare, mobilising and training one would take too long to be of much use if the country were attacked. Interestingly, Guibert continued to hope that his country's armed forces would serve only to defend it. He argued at length that war had become very rare in the course of the eighteenth century and less bloody and cruel than in previous ages – but now he wanted to keep it that way! The best deterrent to enemy attack, he was now convinced, was a large professional army.[52]

Domestic political reasons also figured in Guibert's change of mind about the desirability of a citizen army. He stated blandly in the *Défense* that republics were not the best political system for all countries and argued that France was best served by a monarchy.[53] (To escape French censorship, Guibert had this book was published in Neuchâtel in Switzerland, which was under Prussian rule at the time. Again, this statement therefore cannot be interpreted as a bow in the direction of the French crown, but at best a nod to Frederick the Great. There is nothing to indicate, however, that this was not Guibert's sincere opinion at the time and until the end of his life.) He devoted some space to the argument about whether a large standing army was a prop to a tyranny. It was not, he decided, but rather a check on tyrannical tendencies as well as the greatest support for a legitimate government.[54] He had clearly abandoned his great faith in the citizen-soldier and was rapidly moving into the camp of the champions of law and order who feared the consequences of putting a weapon into every peasant's hands.

Ten years later, when he was writing *De la force publique*, Guibert sent a letter to the National Assembly under the pseudonym of Abbé Raynal, warning against the passions that the appeal to the whole nation and universal military conscription would unleash. He pleaded urgently for the recreation of a professional army and against the unleashing of the forces of human nature.[55]

While he was a supporter of the ideals of liberty inherent in the French Revolution, and of the transfer of a good portion of sovereignty from the king to the National Assembly and the provincial assemblies, Guibert was not and had never been in favour of eliminating the monarchy altogether.[56] More important for our purposes, he no longer regarded the limitations on war under the Anciens Régimes as decadent and had come to regard them as thoroughly positive. In *De la force publique*, which contained complete passages also found in his letter to the National Assembly, he displayed conservative inclinations and took a moderate position on political reform.[57] Where earlier he had been the advocate of a citizen army, of the type of army that would be created under the French Revolution, he now praised professional armies. He seems to have taken some of the criticism levelled against his *Essai* to heart, particularly that by General de Warney, who had written at length to refute the idea of the possibility of a citizen army.[58] Guibert partly took up the general's arguments and added stimulating considerations of his own. In the eyes of the mature Guibert, the soldier and the civilian citizen were two opposites who have little in common.

> So that training and discipline may prevail in the army, the army has to make them its occupation, its habit, and its glory. But the principles which are at the basis of discipline, and the dispositions which make up the military spirit, are necessarily and naturally in opposition with all the principles of the spirit of the [civilian] citizen. Soldiers have to be hungry for war, citizens must love peace. Equality and liberty are the rights of the citizen. Subordination and passive obedience are the duties of the soldier. Soldiers cannot have the same tribunals, nor the same punishments [e.g. for murder] . . . as citizens. Soldiers have to have an *esprit de corps* and a professional feeling. Citizens should only have public and national feelings. In the present state of Europe and of military art, to want a citizen army is to aim to bring very disparate principles and elements together.[59]

It was with these arguments that Guibert advocated a professional army: 'we need men who will commit themselves by a voluntary contract of some years or months.'[60] Several further reasons that he gives are again still of relevance today. Guibert, back in 1790, pointed out that a militia, a conscript army, an army of citizens, cannot easily operate outside its own country. But that was needed, as

Today, the hostilities between the great peoples, through commercial relationships and through the colonies, can have as their theatre all parts of the world.[61]

He went on to argue,

If the task at hand is only to defend one's fields, one's house, one's family, every man becomes soldier or at least a combatant. Every man can, animated by these great interests, give his life or take a life. But in a vast empire, can you persuade all inhabitants that all the provinces of that empire should be equally valuable to them? Can you make the people from the South of France defend Flanders or Alsace, or those of the inner provinces of France defend the shores of the Mediterranean or of Gascony?[62]

This question would haunt conscript armies until this day.

Discipline was another problem that Guibert saw with militias. How could you make the masses obey properly, how could you bring them to act like a well-trained professional force? What the young man in his twenties had thought so desirable – a bloody war fought with the total mobilisation of the population – horrified the mature Guibert of 46. During the eighteenth century, civilians usually experienced war indirectly, through increased taxation. Creating vast citizen armies, Guibert warned, would not only make warfare more expensive but also make citizens direct participants in warfare and envelop them in all its horrors.

Even those that are defeated, even those whose countries become the theatres [of war], hardly experience disastrous calamities. Blood is only shed by the armies, and generosity and humanitarian feelings halt further blows, once one side has won. One always respects the life and often also the property of prisoners. One exchanges them or trades them for a small ransom. One never puts fire to or ravages the country. The population works and sows in the middle of the [military] camps. And discipline glories in the preservation of what does not need to be destroyed.

But if the nations themselves will be involved in the war, all that will change. The inhabitants of a country having become soldiers will be treated as enemies. The fear of having them against you, the fear of leaving them behind will make you destroy them. At least one will seek to confound them and intimidate them by ravages and desolation. Think back to the barbarism of ancient wars, to those wars where the fanaticism and the spirit of taking sides has armed the people. That is what you will give birth to once again.[63]

Having given this warning, the mature Guibert went on to praise the happy bygone age of limited war.[64]

In what again sounds today like a very modern argument, Guibert called for a small, well-trained, well-equipped and highly mobile army. Already in his *Essai* of

20 years earlier, he had criticized the tendency of the governments of his time to go for quantity rather than for quality and expressed his conviction that this quantity was achieved at the expense of mobility and really good training. This was one of the points that Guibert admired about Frederick the Great, who he thought was the only ruler who understood the importance of training (drill) and, through new tactics (which others failed to develop), of manoeuvre. Guibert understood that Frederick only ever won by out-manoeuvring his enemies. Of Frederick's army itself, Guibert thought little, initially dismissing it as 'a motley crowd of stipendiaries, vagabonds, foreigners'.[65] But in *De la force publique*, Guibert calls for just the sort of army Frederick had commanded.

At the same time, the mature Guibert recognized that a standing army would, through the sheer power it commanded, always pose a threat to civilized society. Once again, he was prophetic in his insight, as the history of military-civil relations in France from Napoleon to de Gaulle or the experiences of any number of other countries attests. He argued in *De la force publique* that the public force, the civilian government, has to be particularly careful to assert its own predominance over the standing professional army, which 'could become dangerous for public freedom, if all the forces of the nation are not the brake and the counterweight to it'.[66]

Conclusion

To take up the question posed at the beginning of this essay, did Guibert's thinking presage 'total war'? There are many definitions of this term. After burrowing deeply into the subject, Stig Foerster and Joerg Naegler have defined 'total war' as follows:

> Total war, at least theoretically, consists of total mobilization of all the nation's resources by a highly organized and centralized state for a military conflict with unlimited war aims (such as complete destruction of the home front, extermination and genocide).[67]

The term 'total war' has been used in two separate fashions. It was first used by two Frenchmen, Alphonse Séché, who wrote about the 'totalization of the national strength' during the First World War,[68] and Léon Daudet, who called that war a 'total war'.[69] They both referred mainly to the total mobilisation of populations and the economies on both sides in that conflict. (This is usually the meaning associated with 'total war' in the English-language literature on the subject as well.) Leaving the economic dimension aside, mobilisation on this scale can be associated less with Napoleon than with the revolutionary *levée en masse* of 1793. We have seen that such a mobilisation followed logically from Guibert's thinking as a young man in his *Essai*.

As popularized by Erich von Ludendorff in 1935, however, the term 'total war' added a crucial aspect to the idea of a total mobilisation of economy and population: total war would include a fight to the finish. The objective of such a war would be nothing less than the total enslavement or, better still, extermination of the enemy's population, while trying to 'breed' more 'Aryans'.[70]

This genocidal dimension of total war, encompassed in Foerster and Naegler's definition of the term, is nowhere to be found in Guibert's writings. It could have crept in via his reading of the Ancients, or the discussion of their practices by Montesquieu, but it did not. The total mobilisation of the population of a social entity – from tribe to city to kingdom – can be found in many historical periods and in many places. The Melians did their utmost to fend off the Athenians, and the Romans rallied around with a society-wide war effort to withstand the onslaught of the Celts and other invaders.

Genocidal persecutions had also been known long before Raphael Lemkin coined the term in 1944. It was known to the Ancients in the total destruction of Melos or Carthage; to the Dark Ages in the devastating raids of the Huns and later the Magyars; to medieval Europeans in the merciless persecution of heretics and non-Christians, as in the sack of Jerusalem, the Albigensian Crusade and the anti-Jewish pogroms; and to early modern people through the St Bartholomew's massacre of the Huguenots in France and episodes of the Thirty Years' War, most famously with the sack of Magdeburg, to which Guibert alluded in his *Défense*. This is how Montesquieu wrote about war aims, or what a state might intend to do with a conquered country:

> A State which has conquered another treats it in one of the following ways: the former continues to govern the latter according to the latter's laws, and does not [even] take for itself the exercise of political and civil; or [the conqueror] gives [the conquered] a new political and civil government; or [the conqueror] destroys the society, and disperses it among others; or, finally, it exterminates all the [conquered] citizens.
>
> The first fashion is the one that conforms to the law of nations that we follow today; the fourth corresponds furthest with the law of nations of the Romans; I leave it to others to judge to what degree we have become better. Here we have to render homage to our modern times, to the reason which is present, to the religion of today, to our philosophy, to our morals.[71]

Clearly, then, the 'extermination of all the citizens' of the conquered state was something known to the philosophers of the Enlightenment from classical antiquity but was seen by Montesquieu as incompatible with the ideals and values of his times. Even the enslavement of a conquered population was acceptable to Montesquieu only as a temporary expedient towards re-establishing the security of one's own state's security. He saw it as 'contrary to nature' that such slavery should be 'eternal'.[72] Total war in the genocidal sense in which the term was defined by Ludendorff and practised by the National Socialists against the Jews, the Gypsies and the Slavs was thus an idea with which Montesquieu and, at the very least through reading him, Guibert were familiar. And yet this is clearly a line of thought completely absent from Guibert's writings. It did not fit into either his or Montesquieu's system of values and ideals. Nor did the extermination of the aristocratic class that was espoused as a politico-social aim by the French Revolution fit the world as they wanted it; they were no more at the origin of totalitarian democracy than they were at the origin of total genocidal war.[73]

To conclude, then, the young Guibert prophesied and wished for something like the *levée en masse*, the total mobilisation of one's own side in a defensive war but not for 'total war' à la Ludendorff with the aim of annihilation of an enemy nation. The older Guibert, by contrast, disassociated himself even from the former. The latter's works were rarely read beyond his own lifespan, and are quite at odds with what happened in the French Revolutionary and Napoleonic Wars; the older Guibert was more a counter-revolutionary than anything else. Jonathan Abel has argued forcefully that there was continuity or resurrections of several of Guibert's tactical reforms of the 1770s and early 1780s by the French Revolution and even Napoleon.[74] When it comes to his political views, however, one wonders whether Guibert might not have ended his life under the guillotine had he not died from natural causes in 1790.

Notes

1 Jean Lambert Alphonse Colin: *L'Education militaire de Napoléon* (Paris, 1901), quoted in Matti Lauerma, *Jacques-Antoine-Hippolyte de Guibert (1743–1790)* (Helsinki: Suomalainen Tiedeakatemia, 1989), p. 25.

2 Lucien Poirier: *Les voix de la stratégie* (Paris: Fayard, 1985), p. 124.

3 So Guibert's widow claimed in the first posthumous edition of the *Essai*: see Jean-Paul Charnay: 'Portraits de Guibert', in Centre d'études et de recherché sur les strategies et les conflicts (ed.): *Guibert ou le Soldat Philosophe* (Paris: CERSC, 1981), p. 16.

4 Anon. [Marquis de Silva]: *Remarques sur quelques articles de l'Essai général de Tactique* (Turin: Frères Reycends, 1773); Le G[énéral Charles Emmanuel de] de W[arner]y: *Remarques sur l'Essai général de Tactique de Guibert* (Warsaw: s.n., 1781); see also the works of François-Jean Mésnil-Durand.

5 Kathleen Hardesty Doig: 'War in the Reform Programme of the Encyclopedie', *War and Society*, Vol. 6 No. 1 (May 1988), pp. 1–9.

6 Guibert: *Défense du Système de Guerre Moderne, ou Réfutation complette du Système de M. de M. . . . [Ménil] D. . . . [Durand]* Par l'Auteur de l'Essai général de Tactique, 2 vols (Neuchâtel: s.n., 1779).

7 Roger Caillois: *Bellone ou la pente de la guerre* (Brussels: La Renaissance du Livre, 1963), pp. 84, 101, quoted in *Guibert ou le Soldat Philosophe*, p. 115.

8 Poirier: *Les voix*, p. 139.

9 Léo Hamon: 'Guibert devant la politique', in *Guibert ou le Soldat*, p. 164.

10 See also Guglielmo Ferrero: *Aventure: Bonaparte en Italie, 1796–1797* (Paris, 1936), p. 85f., quoted in *Guibert ou le Soldat*, p. 112.

11 *Défense du Système de Guerre Moderne*, Vol. 2, p. 228.

12 Montesquieu: *De L'Esprit des lois*, Vol. 1 (Paris: Garnier, 1990), book 10, Chapter 2, p. 273.

13 Ibid., Vol. 1, book 9, Chapter 2, p. 267.

14 Ibid., Vol. 1, book 9, Chapters 1 and 5, pp. 265–269.

15 Ibid., Vol. 1, book 10, Chapter 2, p. 273f.

16 Ibid., Vol. 1, book 10, Chapter 6., p. 278ff.

17 Jacques-Antoine-Hippolyte de Guibert: *Essai général de tactique* (London: Librairies associés, 1772), reprinted in Guibert: *Stratégiques*, ed. by Jean-Paul Charnay and Martine Burgos (Paris: Herne, 1977), p. 187f.

18 *Défense du Système de Guerre Moderne*, Vol. 1, Part 1.
19 Iselin Gundermann (ed.): *Das Politische Testament Friedrichs des Grossen* (1768, repr. [Vienna]: Archiv-Verlag, c. 2000).
20 Jean-Jacques Rousseau: 'Jugement sur la Paix perpetuelle' (1756, publ. 1782. MS. Neuchâtel, 7859 1), para. 1175, http://oll.libertyfund.org/index.php?option=com_ staticxt&staticfile=show.php&title=710&search=extend+their+domination&layout=ht ml#a_2011872, accessed 14 Sept. 2008.
21 Guibert: *Essai général de tactique*, p. 186f.
22 Ibid., p. 137f.
23 Carl von Clausewitz: *Vom Kriege*, Book 8, Chapter 3B, ed. by Werner Hahlweg (19th edn, Bonn: Dümmler, 1991), p. 967.
24 Guibert: *Essai général de tactique*, p. 135.
25 Loc. cit.
26 Ibid., pp. 137, 148, 149.
27 Jonathan Abel's otherwise excellent biography of Guibert gets itself tangled on this point, and Abel even contradicts himself: *Guibert: Father of Napoleon's Grande Armée* (Norman, OK: University of Oklahoma Press, 2016), p. 190.
28 Susan Reynolds: *Fiefs and Vassals: The Medieval Evidence Reinterpreted* (Oxford: Oxford University Press, 1994).
29 Ibid., p. 132.
30 Guibert: *Défense du Système de Guerre moderne*, p. 4.
31 Guibert: *Essai général de tactique*, p. 138.
32 Ibid., p. 148.
33 Ibid., p. 149.
34 Ibid., p. 145.
35 Ibid., p. 149f.
36 Ibid., p. 143.
37 Ibid., p. 150.
38 Jean Charles Chevalier de Folard: *Nouvelles découvertes sur la guerre, dans une dissertation sur Polybe* (Paris: Jean-François Josse & Claude Labottière, 1724).
39 Guibert: *Essai général de tactique*, p. 135.
40 Above all François Hotman & Jean Bodin: see Julian Harold Franklin: *Jean Bodin and the Rise of Absolutist Theory* (Cambridge: Cambridge University Press, 1973).
41 Guibert: *Essai général de tactique*, p. 188.
42 Poirier: *Les voix*, pp. 289, 292.
43 See Beatrice Heuser: *Reading Clausewitz* (London: Pimlico, 2002), pp. 33–41.
44 Lauerma: *Guibert*, p. 116f.
45 Jonathan Abel: *Guibert - Father of Napoleon's Grande Armée* (Norman, OK: University of Oklahoma Press, 2016).
46 As Lauerma shows convincingly: *Guibert*, pp. 98, 175–211. Guibert's influential career for the French Council of War, under successive secretaries for war, is best explained by Abel: *Guibert*, passim.
47 Samuel Anderson Covington: 'The Comité militaire and the Legislative Reform of the French Army, 1789–1791' (PhD dissertation, University of Arkansas, 1976), pp. 1–17.
48 Ibid., pp. 18–27.
49 Guibert: *Essai général de tactique*, p. 149; Jean Klein: 'Guibert et les Relations internationals', in *Guibert ou le Soldat Philosophe*, p. 171.
50 Klein: 'Guibert et les Relations internationales', p. 173.
51 Guibert, *Défense*, Vol. 2, p. 238.
52 Ibid., Vol. 2, p. 271f.
53 Ibid., Vol. 2, pp. 221–223.
54 Ibid., Vol. 2, p. 220f.
55 'Lettre à l'Assemblée nationale publiée sous le nom de l'abbé Raynal' (10 Dec. 1789), in Guibert: *Stratégiques*, pp. 667–675.

56 Guibert: *Projet de Discours d'un Citoyen aux trois orders de l'Assemblee de Berry* (n.p., 1789).

57 Guibert: 'De la Force publique', in *Stratégiques*, p. 589.

58 de W . . . y, *Remarques sur l'Essai général de Tactique de Guibert*, pp. 189–193.

59 Guibert: 'De la Force publique', p. 574.

60 Ibid.

61 Ibid., p. 573f.

62 Ibid., p. 612f.

63 Ibid., p. 613f.

64 Ibid.

65 Guibert: 'Essai general de la Tactique', p. 162.

66 Guibert: 'De la Force publique', p. 590.

67 Stig Foerster & Joerg Nagler: 'Introduction', in Stig Foerster and Joerg Nagler (eds): *On the Road to Total War: The American Civil War and the German Wars of Unification, 1861–1871* (Cambridge: Cambridge University Press, 1997), p. 11.

68 Alphonse Seché: *Les Guerres d'Enfer* (Paris: Sansot, 1915), p. 124.

69 Léon Daudet: *La Guerre Totale* (Paris: Nouvelle Librairie, 1918), p. 8f.

70 Erich von Ludendorff: *Der Totale Krieg* (Munich, 1935), trans. by A.S. Rappoport: *The Nation at War* (London: Hutchinson, 1936).

71 Montesquieu: *L'Esprit*, Vol. 1, book 10, Chapter 3, p. 274f.

72 Ibid., p. 275.

73 J.L. Talmon: *The Origins of Totalitarian Democracy: Political Theory and Practice during the French Revolution and Beyond* (New York: Praeger, 1952).

74 Abel: *Guibert*, especially pp. 175–189, 191–193.

9

WHAT CLAUSEWITZ READ

On the origins of some of his key ideas

Clausewitz is often referred to as though his opus magnum, *On War*, had been created ex nihilo, without precedent or notable tradition of thinking or writing about war. He is treated as though he were a prophet, who through divine inspiration or genius articulated some eternal truths, ideas nobody before him had ever thought of. A genius he certainly was, and many things he wrote are indeed original. But his genius lay perhaps most in pulling together, in original ways, or in fresh wording, ideas that had been around, some of them for centuries. It is the purpose of this chapter to trace the origins of some of Clausewitz's most fascinating and important ideas. This undertaking is not designed to lessen his standing as the giant of polemology or of the 'Philosophy of War' (in the words of his contemporary Otto August Rühle von Lilienstern). Much to the contrary, it is hoped that we will gain better insights into Clausewitz's own ideas by tracing their genealogy to the works of other writers.

Clausewitz's education

To get a better picture of what Clausewitz could draw upon, he himself indicated that he did not come from a very educated household, despite the fact that his grandfather had been a professor of theology; his father was a retired minor officer and his home was frequented by his father's old comrades-at-arms, whose conversations apparently did not fly high intellectually.[1] Clausewitz went to the local school in his small home town of Burg near Magdeburg, where he would have started schooling at the common age of six. He probably proceeded to the local grammar school at the age of ten, but two years later, like two of his three brothers before him, he was sent off to become an officer cadet. It is unlikely that Clausewitz was exposed to any Greek or Latin before joining the army, as he never used any expressions in either language, and we find hardly any references to Greek or Latin authors in his works. He referred to Vegetius only once, for example, in a most banal context: on how partisans should avoid camping out in the open.[2] On the down side, the result was that concepts he would have found very congenial – such as Vegetius's 'if you want peace, prepare for war' – were apparently not known to him, and he missed out on a considerable treasure of wisdom and case studies, from Thucydides to many sixteenth-century authors writing in Latin or Italian. Nor, with the exception of Machiavelli, whom he must have read in translation, did Clausewitz read later Italian or Spanish authors. On the upside, this gave his *On War* much originality and great longevity, in contrast for example to Santa Cruz de Marcenado's multi-volume work on war, published a century before Clausewitz's, the great reference work of its time, but one crammed with examples and wise tenets taken from previous authors.[3]

Clausewitz's education only really took off when, at the age of 21, he joined the first promotion of the newly founded War Academy that had just been opened by General Gerhard von Scharnhorst (1755–1813), a rather homespun outfit, as one can gather from Scharnhorst's lecture notes.[4] His teachers there included the philosopher Johann Gottfried Kiesewetter, himself a student of Immanuel Kant's, some of whose ideas can be said to resonate in Clausewitz's writings even though not directly quoted.[5] Scharnhorst himself was an artillerist, and more concerned with teaching his students the complex mathematics necessary to calculate the trajectory of cannon balls than with anything else; the smattering of history which the attendees of the Academy were taught seems to have consisted mainly of the establishment of chronologies and the compilation of facts and figures, not interpretation, if Clausewitz's own early writings on historical events are anything to go by.[6] Students seem to have learned French, which Clausewitz had the opportunity to improve during his time in France as a gentleman-prisoner of war after the Prussian defeat of 1806. Somewhere around that time, Clausewitz clearly read some French literature. Given Clausewitz's language skills – limited to German and French – we must look mainly to works originating in these two literary cultures, and to translations into German and French for inspirations for his own writing.

War as business of the people

A small number of French authors' influence on Clausewitz is probably the most important, despite his personal dislike of all things French. We find evidence that he read the work of Antoine de Pas, Marquis de Feuquières (1648–1711),[7] Jacques de Chastenet, Seigneur de Puységur (1655–1743),[8] Count Lancelot Turpin de Crissé (1682–1759)[9] and General Matthieu Dumas (1753–1837),[10] all authors whose works he may well have found in the Prussian royal library that was accessible to him when he was the companion of Prince August of Prussia, and definitely when he accompanied the prince to his French exile. They might well also have been in the library of the *Allgemeine Kriegsakademie*, the General War School, the administrative director of which Clausewitz was from 1817 to 1830.[11]

Above all, the very form and level of argument that Clausewitz aimed for in writing *On War* were modelled on 'the way in which Montesquieu has treated his subject matter', as Clausewitz noted in the preface of *On War*.[12]

As far as content was concerned, it was most crucially Count Guibert (1743–1790) who had a key influence on Clausewitz's thinking. If Clausewitz had not already encountered Guibert's writing during his time as prisoner of war in France, he would have heard about it on his way back to Prussia through Switzerland, where he spent time in the house of Germaine de Staël, formerly a close friend of Guibert's.[13] It is conceivable that Clausewitz was introduced to Guibert by de Staël. Guibert in his *Essai général de Tactique* analysed the wars of his own times, the mid-eighteenth century, in a passage immediately preceding that which Clausewitz translated in his 'Confession Memorandum'. Guibert explained the limited financial, economic and human resources, the limited political aims and indecisive outcomes of these wars, later often referred to as 'Cabinet wars'. In his eyes, European governments resembled each other in all ways, being corrupt and detached from the interests of their populations.

We find Guibert's thoughts paraphrased and elaborated further by Clausewitz in *On War*, who then added that the French Revolution changed all this, making war 'suddenly once again . . . the business of the people' (see Appendix). Shorn of its 'limits', war was brought to 'perfection', militarily, by Bonaparte.[14] If war was the business of the people, however, then war was fought by the people: the logical step was for Clausewitz, just like young Guibert before him,[15] to call for an army of citizen-soldiers. Thus despite his animosity towards France and Napoleon, he embraced Guibert's and the French revolutionaries' idea of the nation in arms. That he was acquainted with the ideas of Carnot, one of the key instigators of the *levée en masse*, is apparent from his correspondence with Gneisenau.[16] Indeed, it is in his writings to Gneisenau that he most openly took a position in favour of conscription, even criticising one of Gneisenau's other protégés, Karl Anton Andreas von Boguslawski (1758–1817), director of the General War School in Berlin (whom Clausewitz would succeed upon his death 1817): Boguslawski had opposed conscription on the grounds that he considered it a setback in terms of human civilisation and progress (with the latter based on the division of labour).[17]

Small war

Guibert's idea of the citizen army that would defend its state to the end against any external aggression is also at the basis of Clausewitz's idea of the people's war or insurgency (uprising) that we find in Book 6 of *On War*. To contextualise Clausewitz's reading and writing on 'small war' – in its two forms, as will become apparent presently – one has to start with the fact that until about 1810, military literature on irregular or asymmetric warfare assumed that it consisted of special operations conducted by special forces or 'parties' who in their activities prepared and complemented operations by regular forces. Both 'parties' – whose leader alone was originally called 'the partisan' – and regular forces were in the employment of states.[18] There were of course ample historical accounts of civil wars, uprisings, insurgencies and other forms of asymmetric wars (e.g. tribal raids for booty). These were not, however, defined in Europe as conventionally accepted forms of warfare between states. Ergo, they were not taught at military academies.

At the age of 30, in 1810–1811, Clausewitz was tasked, at the Prussian War College, to lecture on small war. The result was a rather run-of-the-mill job, not particularly noteworthy in any respect, and hardly indicative of what genius Clausewitz would later display in his opus magnum. The lectures covered a broad spectrum of things that one could do with 'parties', which he variously called '*Partheigänger*', '*détaschemens*' (sic!), '*Posten*' (*Vorposten* or *Avant Garde*, *Defensiv-Posten*) and *Patrouillen* and in a specific case he referred to the operations of regiments of hussars. This variation in terminology for the special forces or detachments themselves reflects the different developments in various parts of Europe, but all came under the umbrella term of *guerrilla/petite guerre/Kleiner Krieg* – the title of his lecture series – that is small war. Unsurprisingly, as a lecturer with this newly assigned task of holding a series of lectures on this topic, Clausewitz built on existing literature on the subject. For once, in these lectures, as Clausewitz was still relatively young and modest and had a particular educational task to perform, he himself listed the literature he had consulted and which he recommended to his students.[19] Loyally, he began with the field manual of his mentor General Gerhard von Scharnhorst, who headed the reforms of the Prussian army at the time.[20] Secondly he drew on the works of Johann von Ewald, a Hessian who had fought for the British in the American War of Independence and had then made good in the Danish army.[21] Thirdly, he cited the German classic at the time, the Prussian officer Georg Wilhelm von Valentini's work, reprinted in 1810.[22] He then referred to an anonymously published book on *Vorposten* (avant-garde) that has been identified as the work of one Captain von Süssmilch.[23] Another Hessian who had fought in America, Andreas Emmerich, was also cited;[24] Emmerich had been executed in 1809 for organising an uprising in Hesse against Napoleon's brother Jerome, whom Napoleon had made king of Westphalia. Clausewitz would have been acquainted with Hoyer's translation of Emmerich's work, and elsewhere demonstrated his awareness of Hoyer's writings.[25] Beyond these authors, Clausewitz cited a number of military journals.[26] All these works, as even their titles suggest, dealt with the employment of 'parties', special forces, in special operations complementing the campaigns of regular armies.

★

But in the very years when Clausewitz was giving these lectures, a different sort of irregular war was underway in Tirol, in Spain and indeed in Prussia.[27] In Tirol, peasants rose up against the new Bavarian regime that had been granted the region by Napoleon in return for Bavaria's support in his wars against Austria. In Spain and Prussia, there was direct resistance against Napoleon's own armies; Clausewitz followed these events with great interest, as a treatise written by him in 1811 on '*la guerre en Espagne et en Portugal*' (curiously in French) shows. Such uprisings were of course by no means unprecedented in European history, and they were what today we would call insurgency against foreign occupation. The Romans had known them all too well, as had subsequent empires. Over the centuries, they had been described in a variety of terms, usually a function of who won: if it was the insurgents, then the conflict would retrospectively be described by the historians of the victorious party as a liberation war (or words to that effect); if the counter-insurgency forces prevailed, then historians loyal to their regime would refer to them as a rebellion (revolt, mutiny, . . .). Interestingly, when Clausewitz wrote about what was happening in Spain, he nowhere referred to this as a 'small war', and nowhere described it in terms other than regular warfare, focusing in his description exclusively on the actions of the regular forces on both sides.[28]

These uprisings against Napoleon and his allies, however, tended to blend together several forms of fighting. Already the two major insurgencies of the late eighteenth century – the American War of Independence of the 1770s, and the 1790s uprising in the Vendée against the French revolutionary regime and the policies it imposed – had consisted of operations of regular forces alongside operations by militia-type irregular forces. These irregular forces consisted in large part of locals who had organised themselves for acts of sabotage and ambushes and supported the regular forces by providing intelligence and reconnaissance, acting as messengers and foragers. The latter activities to any contemporary observer were nothing other than what the special forces or 'parties' did, and would simply be described as such. If anything, contemporary observers therefore conceptualised these late eighteenth-century uprisings, and subsequently those against the French and their allies in Spain, in the Tirol and elsewhere in Europe, in terms of 'partisan warfare' or 'small war'. In Spain in particular, the resistance against the French took the form of a mix of special forces–type operations by disbanded units of the previous royal forces, gangs of bandits-turned-patriotic-rebels and spontaneous uprisings by peasants, all in co-operation with the regular army of Wellington.[29] In Prussia, some regiments of light troops (*Freikorps*; again one might think of them as special forces) seized the initiative without orders from above and tried – unsuccessfully – to initiate a popular uprising. Frederick William III, the Prussian king, and his advisers saw this as potentially very dangerous and belatedly granted their half-hearted support, too late, however, to save one famous and popular regiment under Ferdinand von Schill. It was defeated in 1809 by Danish and Dutch units of the Napoleonic forces when attempting to liberate Stralsund on the Baltic Sea from their occupation. Schill was hacked down in the fighting, whereas his officers were tried and subsequently executed.[30]

Clausewitz, full of *Sturm und Drang* himself as a great fan of the poet and writer Friedrich von Schiller, wanted to plan and organise such a mass uprising of the people. He worked out a concept for this purpose which forms the larger part of a document known as his 'Confession Memorandum' or 'Testimonial' (*Bekenntnisdenkschrift*) that he sent to his patron (then General) August Neidhardt Count Gneisenau in 1812. Written only one year after his lectures on 'small war' in the sense of special operations, Clausewitz's concept dealt with quite distinct a subject: the organisation of a government-controlled uprising that would mobilise all Prussian adult men, using what remained of the regular army but also by creating a

Landwehr (literally defence of the land) or *Landsturm* (literally, land assault), a militia of all adult able-bodied men recruited primarily from the land – that is among the peasantry. The élan that he hoped could be created among these forces to drive out the French paradoxically owed much to French ideas: again Clausewitz was directly inspired by Guibert, from whose *Essai général de Tactique* he quoted verbatim in the memorandum the epic passage on a people that might one day arise in Europe,

> with genius, with power, and a happy form of government, that combines the virtues of austerity and a national militia with a fixed plan for expansion, that it does not lose sight of this system, that, knowing how to make war at little expense and to live off its victories, it would not be forced to put down its arms for reasons of economy.[31]

Guibert hoped that this would be the French; Clausewitz presumably saw this as applying to the armies of the French Revolution, but in the same spirit, he imagined a people's uprising against foreign invaders. For such a purpose, following Guibert's early views on the need for all male citizens to defend their country,[32] Clausewitz wanted to conscript all adult able-bodied men to fight against the French. Clausewitz and the other leading Prussian military reformers thus paradoxically wanted to emulate the French model of the *levée en masse*, the one point on which they agreed with the French revolutionaries, but in order to fight *against* the French.

Later in *On War* Clausewitz returned to the subject of the mobilisation of the male population to resist an invading army, if the regular forces had failed to fend it off. Unfortunately he left us no direct references to the works he had read since the early 1800s, but they can be inferred through comparing them with published works to which he would have had access. These include the works of the adventurous Prussian officer Heinrich von Brandt (1789–1868),[33] who, nine years younger than Clausewitz, had fought alongside the French forces in the Peninsular War. Nevertheless, after the defeat of Napoleon, he was admitted to the Prussian officer corps thanks to the intervention of Gneisenau. In 1819, he became an instructor for officer cadets, and in 1823 he published his own eyewitness account of the Peninsular War, an outstanding source for the Spanish *Guerrilla* that would also be translated into English, in which he described the Spanish uprising as a 'people's war'.[34] At the end of the 1820s, he moved to the General War School, then directed by Clausewitz, where he published a field manual in 1829, a large part of which was devoted to the question of how to stage a popular uprising against a foreign occupying forces, what he again called a 'people's war' or *Volkskrieg*.[35] He was thus Clausewitz's junior colleague or even subordinate, and Clausewitz clearly liked him, and suggested to Gneisenau that he should be one of the men on a general staff for the operation in Poland in 1831.[36] It is thus inconceivable that Clausewitz had not read Brandt's two books. In *On War*, presumably under the influence of Brandt, Clausewitz used the term 'people's war' for such a general mobilisation of men for the defence of the country.[37] Brandt continued to differentiate conceptually between 'small war' in the modern sense of special operations and 'people's war' in the sense of a nationwide, prepared insurgency to resist foreign occupation forces: six years after Clausewitz's death, Brandt would publish a book on small war (in the sense of special operations), the content of which does not differ significantly from the lectures Clausewitz had given in 1810/1811 and the eighteenth-century literature on small war.[38]

In the same year in which Brandt published his Spanish memoirs, another eye-witness of the Peninsular War, the Frenchman Jean-Frédéric Auguste Le Mière de Corvey (1770–1832), published a work on partisans and irregular forces which also drew on his experiences of the Spanish *Guerrilla*. Other than describing the operations of irregular units, in this book, Le Mière de Corvey laid out ways in which the French might in future defend themselves against a foreign invasion of French soil, and against foreign occupation. His answer was that they should 'spontaneously rise up *en masse*', echoing of course the *levée en masse* of the French Revolution.[39] Like Brandt, Le Mière de Corvey eschewed the term 'small war' both for what he had witnessed in Spain and for what he prescribed for his own country in case its regular army might be defeated by foreign forces (as it was in 1813 and 1815), using instead '*guerre nationale*' for a popular resistance to invading forces, and '*soldats-partisans*' for the locally mobilised defenders of their homeland. That '*guerre nationale*' under his pen really seems to have much the same meaning as the German '*Volkskrieg*' or 'people's war' can be deduced from the fact that Le Mière still used the French word '*nation*' in the older sense of tribe or people – he wrote of the 'nations' of the Normans, Lorrainers, Alsatians and Angevins, who should be prepared to rise up and defend their *respective* regions (*pays*).[40]

It is difficult to imagine that Clausewitz had not read Le Mière's book. Reading it side by side with Book 6, Chapter 23 of Clausewitz's *On War*, one sees many parallels, not least in the respect both works express for the popular uprising of the 1790s in the Vendée.[41] Le Mière also covered issues such as the formation of partisan units, the wider mobilisation of volunteers to back up the regular army, the defence of towns, and resistance against enemy occupation in the mountains.[42]

War as a duel

Symmetric conflicts by contrast had long been the core subject of writing on war, as was their perception as something like a duel, which according to a fourteenth-century jurist goes back to Germanic perceptions of war.[43] Clausewitz would have been very surprised had he been told that he would later be cited as the original source of the wisdom that war resembles a duel. By the time he was writing, this observation – found at least since the fourteenth century in the writings of Giovanni da Legnano, Francisco Suárez, William Fulbecke, Samuel Pufendorf and Rühle von Lilienstern – had long become a commonplace.[44]

It is implausible to suggest that Clausewitz at the General War School would have been unfamiliar with the field manual used by Prussian officers. The first version had been written by Clausewitz's teacher and mentor Scharnhorst, but in 1817/1818 Clausewitz's former fellow student in the War Academy, and after Clausewitz himself the best student in their first promotion, Otto August Rühle von Lilienstern (1780–1847) wrote and published the successor volumes.[45]

Rühle and Clausewitz clearly were not the closest of friends, but their paths crossed often.[46] One can assume that they saw but respected each other as competitors. Peter Paret has conjectured that Rühle and Clausewitz disagreed massively over what military education should entail when the former chaired the Committee of Military Studies, which overruled Clausewitz's proposals for reforms when Clausewitz became director of the General War School in 1819.[47] Rühle's extremely sympathetic review of Clausewitz's posthumously published *On War* in the journal *Allgemeine Militär Zeitung* would suggest otherwise.[48]

And yet Rühle must have raised an eyebrow when reading Clausewitz's *On War*: for one, already the title was taken from one of Rühle's own publications, a pamphlet similar to or even worse in tone than Clausewitz's 'Confession Memorandum'.[49] A number of other ideas expressed in Clausewitz's *On War* are already found, usually in greater detail, in Rühle's work, and as noted, one of them is that of war as a duel. Rühle's handbook dealt with this commonplace in an original way, in that it discussed conflict from its smallest manifestation in the duel via the clashes of armed gangs to warfare between organised armies, to establish what united and what distinguished each level.[50] Clausewitz used Rühle's analogy of the duel-wrestling match as a starting point in *On War*.[51] Nevertheless, Rühle passed up the opportunity of this posthumous book review to draw attention to the origins of Clausewitz's ideas in his own works. Instead, he generously accorded full honours to Clausewitz for putting them together in a new and original way. Moreover, as we shall see presently, Rühle in this review drew attention to a methodological approach of Clausewitz's work which he, Rühle, fully supported and in which *both* men had clearly been overruled by views on the matter prevailing among their colleagues.

Clausewitz's debt to Rühle is greater still when it comes to the treatment of the relationship between *die Politik* and war (as I hope to elaborate elsewhere). This is not to deny that Clausewitz had an original take on the subject: while Rühle in his field manual reflected on the relationship between war aims, victory, the professed quest for justice and the use of war,[52] Clausewitz had no interest whatsoever in the justice of war. This omission is noteworthy, as it heralded a new era of writing on war by military men in which the justice of the cause was not discussed. Moreover, curiously, although Clausewitz has become so famous for his dictum that war is the continuation of *die Politik* by other means, unlike Rühle – and unlike Henri Baron de Jomini (1779–1869)[53] – Clausewitz did *not* explore the different forms wars might take as a function of particular political war aims. The most he implied was that the particular nature of the individual war's aims prevented war from achieving its 'absolute perfection'.[54]

The centrality of battle

Jomini was convinced that Clausewitz owed him an unacknowledged debt by having appropriated the idea of the enemy's centre of gravity, and that concentrating one's forces on it in battle would be the key to victory.[55] There is no doubt that Jomini articulated this much before Clausewitz: Jomini first wrote about this in 1804, and in 1808 published an article expounding on the subject in the journal of statecraft and military art *Pallas* – with the help of Rühle von Lilienstern, its editor![56] But one could also see the idea growing organically out of Scharnhorst's writings about the concentration of forces, and of course Napoleon's practice of moving his columns separately but bringing them together in battle.[57] Clausewitz first tackled the subject in his teaching of the crown prince in 1810–1812.[58] In *On War*, we find only one small reference to Jomini when Clausewitz alluded to Jomini's emphasis on the advantages of 'inner lines'.[59]

One can only speculate that Clausewitz did not include any reference to Rühle because the whole of *On War* is devoid of footnote references and contains only a few allusions to anybody else's work (clearly, Clausewitz's ambition was not to satisfy some scholarly standards but to establish a body of thought). Meanwhile we find no indication that Clausewitz disagreed with anything Rühle had written.

By contrast Clausewitz tended to be quite explicit when he *disagreed* with somebody. One such disagreement concerned Maurice de Saxe, who had famously said – reinventing Sun Tsu's idea about the avoidability of battle, shortly before Sun Tsu was first introduced to Europe – that the skilful general might manage to avoid battle altogether.[60] Already in 1804, Clausewitz in his early sketch on strategy had quoted Montecuccoli's dictum (in French translation!): 'to imagine that one can make great conquests without fighting is a chimera.'[61] Presumably of the opinion that this thinking had led Prussia into its defeat of 1806 and its status as semi-vassal of France in the subsequent seven years, Clausewitz begged to differ strongly with this approach, saying,

> We do not want to hear about commanders-in-chief who win without shedding human blood. If bloody battles are a horrible spectacle, this must only lead us to respect war all the more, not, however, to allow swords to be blunted by humanitarian qualms, until there is once again a sharp sword among us which will hack off our arms at our shoulders.[62]

Battle was thus essential to Clausewitz's concept of war, and a theme that already preoccupied him in 1811. On 17 June 1811 he wrote to his new mentor General Neidhardt von Gneisenau, with a swipe against the colourful military author Dietrich Heinrich Freiherr (Baron) von Bülow (1752–1807):[63]

> What boundless folly it is in my view that Bülow could write, twelve years ago, that nowadays, battle decides little and strategy almost everything; I think what we have experienced since has proved Bülow almost as hugely wrong. Battle equals money and goods; strategy is the commercial transaction. The latter only gains its importance through the former. If somebody squanders this property (i.e. who does not know how to fight) he might as well give up trading, as he is about to go bankrupt imminently.[64]

Methodological disputes

Also in his lectures on small war, Clausewitz could not refrain from ranting against Bülow's 'immature and stale ideas',[65] and in his 'Confession Memorandum' of 1812 he alluded to Bülow's childish writings that could hardly be termed 'military wisdom'.[66] Again, Clausewitz's teacher Scharnhorst had been interested in the relationship between theory and its application in warfare.[67]

Under Scharnhorst's influence, Clausewitz studied the mathematics of Leonard Euler (1707–1783), whose legacy Clausewitz clearly admired; we find two references to him in *On War* alone, along with one to Newton.[68] Euler had coined the term 'function', and invented the concept of one thing being a function of another, simply expressed in the formula y = f(x), where 'y' is a function of 'x'. By the time Clausewitz pursued his studies, the idea of functions with several *inter*dependent variables was not yet being taught in classrooms, but the logical step could be easily taken. To put it in Eulerian terms, Clausewitz's idea of the trinity of factors influencing the nature of warfare could be recast as warfare being a function of all three, and indeed all three factors (or variables) must be seen as mutually *inter*dependent. Clausewitz saw dozens of other factors – also variables – also influencing warfare, so that he saw no way of creating one single formula that could contain them all.[69] Crucially, Clausewitz thus rejected the pretension of Bülow that warfare could be reduced to mathematical formulae.[70] He equally rejected the more generally held claim that warfare could be reduced to positivist *Lehrsätze* – that is the very 'principles of war' which would make Jomini's work so widely read and popular, as a century later the work of J.F.C. Fuller and other authors until this day.

We know from Rühle von Lilienstern that Clausewitz was at odds with the rest of the staff of the General War School, and that even as its (administrative) director, he did not have the influence to fight against this excessively positivist tendency that wanted to make warfare a calculable, predictable subject that could be taught with the help of formulae, principles or omnibus prescriptions. Clausewitz had dismissed this categorically: 'All these attempts to base the conduct of war upon arithmetic and geometrical principles are to be discarded, as the application of the rule excludes the genius [probably better translated as 'judgement'] and limits the activity of intelligence.'[71] Instead of such a positivist-mathematical approach (as Rühle rightly explained in his review of Clausewitz's *On War*), Clausewitz proposed a 'Philosophy of War'.[72] (Rühle himself agreed strongly with this approach, and noted that 'Theory must be contemplation and not a positivistic doctrine.'[73]) In his 'Abstract Principles of Strategy' of 1808/1809, Clausewitz wrote further about theory:

> The more I think about this part of the Art of War [Strategy], the more I become convinced that its theory can posit few or even no abstract rules [*Sätze*]; not, as is commonly thought, because the matter is too difficult, but because one would drown in trivia.

On the one hand, he argued,

> In war, there are so many circumstances which contribute to affect action that if one wanted to include them appropriately in his abstract rules, one would appear as the biggest pedant, trivialising everything to a repulsive degree.

Clausewitz repeatedly rejected the possibility of drawing up a comprehensive formula or theory that would take into account the many factors influencing war, and

their interrelationship, as this would be 'pedantic'. On the other hand, to ignore the many factors would be unrealistic. Thus he criticised Jomini's 'scientific theory', because it took into account too few factors.[74]

Clausewitz developed similar scepticism with regard to *Vorschriften* or prescriptions, rules to be obeyed by soldiers. In a short essay on *Kunst* (a skill) and on *Kunsttheorie* (the theory behind this) he differentiated between law – for example law of physics – and prescription; he argued that a prescription had to depend on the purpose and the means available, and could thus not aspire to general applicability beyond specific cases. Again, this line of argument went against the notion that a set of prescriptions (or principles of war) could pretend to general applicability.[75]

Clausewitz himself believed in educating future commanders[76] by letting them study historical case studies, or in the words of Clausewitz, they should study 'examples', rather than be presented with formulae, prescriptions or principles of war:

> Example and formula are of quite different natures. An *example* is a living case; a *formula* is an abstraction. If in formulating an abstraction one does not lose anything in the process, as is the case in mathematics, it fully achieves its purpose. But when abstraction must constantly discard the real-live [example] in order to focus on the dead form, which is easiest to turn into abstraction, then the result is a dry skeleton of dull truths and commonplaces, shoehorned into doctrine [*eine Schulform*]. It is really astonishing to find people who waste their time on such conceptualizations, if one considers that the very factors that are the most important in war and Strategy – what is special, singular, and local – most elude abstractions and scientific systematisation.[77]

With his praise for the study of concrete examples, Clausewitz was in every way an empiricist, and in this he followed a centuries-old tradition. Writers on war from Christine de Pizan to Santa Cruz de Marcenado had cited historical examples from which they deduced general statements about war and warfare.[78] Like them, Clausewitz himself over time studied a large number of diverse modern historical examples to understand war and warfare, and added to this collection – much as Christine de Pizan or Machiavelli or Santa Cruz de Marcenado had done before him – analyses of warfare in his own times. Concomitantly, he dismissed all claims and theories that were not firmly rooted in historical reality. This was a criticism that he levelled even against Fichte.[79]

Clausewitz's approach and assumptions about what the study of war could and could not do, which today we must call 'methodology', remained sterile in his own time and were not integrated into the syllabus of the General War School. It has often been assumed wrongly that there was a link between its supposedly excellent teaching and the ascent of the Prussian military, focusing especially on the person of Helmuth von Moltke the Elder who attended the school while Clausewitz was still its director. There was no such link, at least not between Clausewitz and Moltke, as Clausewitz's approach clashed with 'the prevailing military-absolutist views' among his colleagues and the military leaders of Prussia. Rühle von Lilienstern emphasised this in his 1833 review of *On War*, and he continued: 'It must be noted that General von Clausewitz did not have sufficient influence to clear the way for a better form of instruction, as the prevailing syllabus depended on the Superior Committee of Military Studies, and not on him.'[80] Clausewitz's approach would become accepted by other writers only long after his death.

Equally, Clausewitz's approach to what can be gleaned through study and how to draw out lessons (i.e. his 'methodology') is at odds with the same schools that attack strategic studies today: on the one hand, he thought Bülow's mathematic formulae approach – which would today be the approach of scholars coming from operational research or economics who employ mathematical formulae, seeking to quantify strategy – overly reductionist. On the other hand, he dismissed those who reduced warfare to a series of principles which today would equate the univariate, monocausal theorisers and those who would put the 'testing of such-and-such a theory' with one independent variable and one dependent variable at the centre of all their work. Both approaches would produce nothing but 'trivialities' of the sort that God sides with the bigger battalions, and neither could make due allowance for the multiplicity of – interdependent! – factors that in reality influence warfare.

Instead of formulae, we find Clausewitz stressing, time and again, that the whole purpose of educating the military commander is not to give him a series of answers for the task he will face (the complexities of which cannot be foreseen) but to educate him about different aspects of what will face him so as to let him evaluate the situation facing him for himself, and develop his own strategy.

With this latest point, Clausewitz also made enemies of those scholars of later generations who would argue that nothing could be learned from history, and that nothing could be taught to officers – in short, those dismissing positivist approaches, as scholars of critical security studies would today. Like any practitioner, Clausewitz understood the need for judging a situation and taking action on the basis of this judgement. The very inaction of the Prussian king on the highest political level, the hesitation and the deferring of action had, after all, led to Prussia being caught out and left without allies when Napoleon chose to ignore Prussia's attempts to stay neutral and to throw his war machine against Prussia in 1806. On a lower level, that of military operations, again the almost passive stance of the Prussian military commanders of 1806 when they ceded all the initiative to the French compounded the crushing defeat at Jena and Auerstedt. For the practitioner, mere contemplation and the rejection of positivism are not an option.

Clausewitz and the state

Another key idea of Guibert's writing that we find spelled out in Clausewitz's work is that warfare changes over time, and that its changes are related to the character of the state waging it; this is of course a key contribution of Guibert's entire reflection in his *Essay général de Tactique*. The idea that warfare changed over time in more than its technological development is already present, albeit not expressly articulated, in the history of warfare by Georg Heinrich von Berenhorst, formerly Prussian officer and chamberlain of Frederick II. This was first published in 1797–1799, and Clausewitz would have encountered it in his education two years later. Berenhorst was highly sceptical of dogma and doctrines. His book was reprinted in 1827, when Clausewitz was working on *On War*, and Clausewitz could not have ignored it or even been indifferent to it, even if he did not refer to Berenhorst explicitly in *On War*.[81] The idea that warfare was culturally dependent was a commonplace for all those writing about the history of wars and warfare since antiquity.[82]

Guibert's more original contribution was to examine explicitly the relationship between the political setup of the state and its *système de guerre*, the recruitment and configuration of the armed forces, the financing of war and the purposes for which such an army of citizen-soldiers could be used. Guibert's ideal was that of a constitutional monarchy that put the interest of the entire polity above that of the royal family. Indeed, shockingly in the context of his times, Guibert dedicated his *Essai général* to his fatherland rather than only to his monarch (see Chapter 8).[83] Clausewitz never went as far as to come down in favour of a constitutional monarchy. But the idea that the interests of the polity itself should stand above those of the royal family (and especially, a king excessively willing to compromise with an aggressive adversary), equally implicit in Guibert's *Essay*, was entirely in keeping with Clausewitz's views. Moreover, Clausewitz was one of those who thought the German-speaking nation as a whole should be seen as this polity, not just the Prussians. In this respect, King Frederick William III of Prussia was right in harbouring suspicions about Clausewitz's critical views.[84]

Peter Paret in his political biography on Clausewitz has already done sterling work on establishing and fully tracking Clausewitz's early intellectual encounter with Niccolò Machiavelli, his correspondence with Johann Gottlieb Fichte, his personal meeting with Madame de Staël in Switzerland and, through her, his contacts with the poets August and Friedrich Schlegel and the Swiss educator Johann Heinrich Pestalozzi.[85] For influences of these authors on Clausewitz, it is sufficient here to summarise Paret's findings.

Clausewitz apparently had already read Machiavelli's *Discorsi, Arte della Guerra* and *Prince*, presumably in a French translation, sometime before or in 1807. References to Machiavelli's writing can be found in his sketches on strategy dating from 1804 to 1809.[86] These are mostly of a technical-tactical nature – for example whether it is a good idea to bring in fresh troops after an enemy has been partly victorious (referring to *Discorsi* II.22), or on the appointment of a commander. One point which Machiavelli made in the *Discorsi* III.9 and Clausewitz liked very much was that measures must suit the particular situation and circumstances. In a fragment dating from c. 1807, however, Clausewitz waxed lyrical about the Florentine, noting that 'No book in the world is more necessary for the politician than Machiavelli,' and he thought those who scorned his work pathetic. While Clausewitz conceded that some of Machiavelli's ideas on the political relations between prince and subjects were outdated, others 'will remain valid forever', especially where 'external relations' are concerned.[87] Paret argues plausibly that Clausewitz followed Machiavelli's example in his deliberate silence on the subject of the morality of war. More still,

Paret sees Clausewitz's pan-German patriotism as inspired by Machiavelli's hope for an eventually united Italy.[88]

It is through Clausewitz's and Fichte's shared admiration of Machiavelli that Fichte became of real interest to Clausewitz. In 1809, he read Fichte's article 'On Machiavelli as Author', published two years earlier. Before that, Clausewitz wrote to Marie that he had read some Fichte but did not find it sufficiently practical or based in empiricism (Fichte did not use historical examples or draw comparisons with the present). In 1809, however, an epistolary exchange between Clausewitz and Fichte ensued, but their common interests seemed to stop there.[89]

Clausewitz drew on the aesthetic theories and art criticism of the German Enlightenment, including Kant's writings on the subject, which we find reflected not least in his conceptualisation of warfare as something that should aspire to a 'harmonious combination of elements', and his use of the word 'beautiful' for examples that well illustrate certain aspects of warfare.[90] Sibylle Scheipers has explored further Clausewitz's interest in Immanuel Kant and art criticism, explaining how Clausewitz (in a letter to Fichte) could describe people's war as 'the most beautiful' form of 'war', something we would find very odd today. But inspired by Kant, Clausewitz used the term 'beauty' as linked to morally good, as people's war would mean the liberation of the individual.[91] Peter Paret also claims to have found echoes to thoughts on this subject matter of Gotthold Ephraim Lessing, Moses Mendelssohn, Johann Georg Sulzer and even more indirectly through them of the third Earl of Shaftesbury.[92]

We have no evidence, by contrast, that Clausewitz read Hegel. Andreas Herberg-Rothe has gone through all surviving evidence with a fine-tooth comb, and has come to the conclusion that there are many similarities in thinking and approach, but it is impossible to demonstrate that these are due to Hegel's influence on Clausewitz, rather than to shared ideas and approaches typical of Berlin's intelligentsia at the time.[93] Prominent among them is what Hegel referred to as *Dialektik*. Clausewitz's emphasis on the *interaction* between two belligerent parties – something that to my knowledge had not been stressed by any writer other than Rühle von Lilienstern – was thus probably less a debt to Hegel than to Rühle and the *Zeitgeist* more generally. Either way, it constitutes a very important step forward in our thinking about war, as it is a step away from mechanistic views of war to which certain prescriptions (*Vorschriften*) can apply, irrespective of special circumstances and above all the reactions of an intelligent enemy constantly out to thwart our plans, as soon as he recognises them.

Conclusions

Clausewitz certainly built on more literature than has been discussed here. There are more authors he mentioned, especially in his early works, such as his sketches on strategy of 1804 and 1808/9. These include von Lindenau,[94] Johannes Müller and General Karl Ludwig Phull,[95] but he mentioned them mainly in order to disagree with them, or show (in the case of Müller) that he had derived his ideas from

Machiavelli.[96] Clausewitz also mentioned Colonel Carl von Decker[97] (Rühle von Lilienstern's co-editor of a later military journal[98]), the bellicose Constantin von Lossau (1767–1848)[99] and the Saxon Friedrich Wilhelm von Zanthier (1741–1783),[100] who had translated into German an abridged version of Santa Cruz's work,[101] but without any indication that their works had made an impact on him. Elsewhere, Clausewitz drew on arguments of Adam Smith's.[102] Perhaps he read Turpin de Crissé's translation into French of the Habsburg general Raimondo Count Montecuccoli's work (1608–1680), but again Clausewitz no more than alluded to him.[103]

We have therefore thought it useful in this chapter to concentrate on some of Clausewitz's more famous ideas that can be traced, at least in part, to other authors: first, the idea that Cabinet wars were wasteful and counterproductive, and that one should not seek to avoid battle, as Prussia had learned at its cost; second, that the war of his age was and had to be 'the business of the people', and that the mobilisation of all (male) citizens should be envisaged and if necessary executed in extremis. And third, we have explored his methodological reflections, which are extremely relevant to the question of how and what officers should be taught. Indeed, they are an earlier version of methodological debates which are taking place in our own times, and which by now apply to far more than military education.[104]

As noted initially, pointing in this way to the sources that Clausewitz used can in no way lessen his genius. It can, however, help us to fathom the working of his mind and his ideas a little better. Moreover, it should prevent us from treating him like deus ex machina, who descended upon the scene ex nihilo, and caution us against treating his dicta as eternal truths, unconditioned by the circumstances of his or all subsequent times.

APPENDIX

Clausewitz and Guibert

Guibert: Essay général de Tactique	Clausewitz: 'Bekenntnisdenkschrift'	Clausewitz: Vom Kriege
Today the States have neither treasure, nor a population surplus. Their expenditure in peace is already beyond their income. Still, they wage war against each other. One goes to war with armies which one can neither [afford to] recruit, nor pay. Victor or vanquished, both are almost equally exhausted [at the end of a war]. The mass of the national debt increases. Credit decreases. Money is lacking. The fleets do not find sailors, armies lack soldiers. The ministers, on one side and on the other, feel that it is time to negotiate. Peace is concluded. Some colonies or provinces change hands. Often the source of the quarrels has not dried up, and each side sits on the rubble, busy paying his debts and keeping his armies on alert [in preparation for the next campaign].		[Under the Ancien Régime] Armies were paid for from the treasury, which princes treated almost like their privy purse or at least as the property of the government, not of the people. Apart from a few commercial issues, relations with other states concerned the treasury or the government, not the people. . . . War thus became the business exclusively of the governments to the extent that these were isolated from their peoples and behaved as if they were themselves the state. Governments conducted war by means of the dollars in their coffers and of idle vagabonds recruited in their own or neighbouring provinces. Consequently the means available to all of them had certain limits, which their adversaries could in turn calculate both in terms of size and available time.

Guibert: *Essay général de Tactique*	Clausewitz: *'Bekenntnisdenkschrift'*	Clausewitz: *Vom Kriege*

[All European nations are] corrupt and resemble each other. They have all of them forms of government that are inimical to every sentiment of virtue and patriotism. When corruption has made such progress . . . it is then next to impossible to hope for regeneration; for the place from whence it would come would be the very focus of that evil.		War was thus deprived of its most dangerous side – its tendency towards the extreme . . . One had an approximate idea of the financial means, the treasure, the credit of one's adversary; one knew the size of his army. Significant increases in times of war were unlikely. As one knew the limits of the hostile forces one could feel safe from total ruin oneself, and as one felt the limits of one's own forces, one was forced to adopt limited aims. Protected from extreme outcomes, one did not need to take extreme risks oneself. . . .
If Europe no longer fears . . . blood and ignorance; if the vices, which undermine all governments, seem to create a kind of balance between them, her countries . . . weak and corrupted as they are, do not enjoy greater tranquillity. For such are their miserable . . . Politics, that they are continually divided by fallacious interests of trade or ambition. Despite treaties which pacify them, there remain ever amongst them some seeds of altercation, which, after a certain periodical truce, cause them to rise again in arms against each other. . . . The fancies and ingenuity of ministers, the vain and silly etiquette, the petty intrigues [of] our negotiations, will soon provide them with a pretext. In short, such is the kind of war adopted by all nations, which consumes their forces, and never puts an end to their quarrel. Conqueror or conquered each in peace returns to his former boundaries. Thus war, hardly fearful to governments, is more frequent. They are affrighted champions, covered with wounds, and always in arms, they exhaust their strength in watching each		War thus essentially became a real game . . .; its meaning was only a stronger form of diplomacy, a more vigorous way of negotiating, in which battles and sieges were the main démarches. Even the most ambitious only aimed to acquire a limited advantage that they could use [as a negotiating chip] in the peace negotiations. . . .

Looting and devastation of enemy territory, which had played such an important part in the warfare of the . . . ancients and even in the middle ages, were no longer regarded as acceptable to the spirit of the Age [of Enlightenment]. One rightly regarded them as pointless brutality which could easily lead to reprisals and which affected the inimical subjects more than the inimical |

(Continued)

Guibert: Essay général de Tactique	Clausewitz: 'Bekenntnisdenkschrift'	Clausewitz: Vom Kriege
other's motions, now and then attacking . . ., rendering battles ineffectual, like themselves; they lie down when they bleed, and agree on a truce to wash the blood from their wounds.[105]		government, and thus remained without [political] effect but only served eternally to thwart the peoples in their cultural development. War was thus limited more and more to the armed forces themselves, not only in terms of its means but also aims. . . . only when a battle became unavoidable was it sought and given.
Imagine that a people will arise in Europe, with genius, with power, and a happy form of government, that combines the virtues of austerity and a national militia with a fixed plan for expansion, that it does not lose sight of this system, that, knowing how to make war at little expense and to live off its victories, it would not be forced to put down its arms for reasons of economy. One would see that people subjugate its neighbours, and overthrow our weak constitutions, just as the fierce north wind bends the slender reeds.[106]	Imagine that a people will arise in Europe, with genius, with power, and a happy form of government, that combines the virtues of austerity and a national militia with a fixed plan for expansion, that it does not lose sight of this system, that, knowing how to make war at little expense and to live off its victories, it would not be forced to put down its arms for reasons of economy. One would see that people subjugate its neighbours, and overthrow our weak constitutions, just as the fierce north wind bends the slender reeds.[107]	This was the situation when the French Revolution occurred. . . .[Now] war had suddenly once again become the business of the people, in this case a people of thirty million [the French], all of whom regarded themselves as citizens. . . . With its participation in the war, the whole people threw its weight into the scales, not merely the cabinet and the army. The means that could be used, the effort that could be made, no longer knew limits; the energy with which the war itself could be waged was no longer checked, and consequently the danger for the adversary was extreme. . . .
		[I]n Bonaparte's hand all this was brought to perfection, and this force of war, based on the entire strength of the people, wrought havoc upon Europe.[108]

Notes

1 Clausewitz: "Nachrichten über Preußen in seiner großen Katastrophe" (written 1824/25), in Hans Rothfels (ed.): *Carl von Clausewitz: Politische Schriften und Briefe* (Munich: Drei Masken Verlag, 1922), p. 213f.
2 Werner Hahlweg (ed.): *Carl von Clausewitz: Schriften, Aufsätze, Studien, Briefe*, Vol. 1 (Göttingen: Vandenhoek & Ruprecht, 1966), p. 392.
3 Don Alvaro de Navia Ossorio y Vigil, Vizconde de Puerto, Marques de Santa Cruz de Marcenado: *Reflexiones Militares* 11 Books in 5 volumes, of which vols. 1–5, i.e. Books 1–10 (Turin: Juan Francisco Mairesse, 1724–1727), Vol. 6 i.e. Book 11 (Paris: Simon Langlois, 1730). There is no evidence that Clausewitz bothered even with the abridged German translation of Santa Cruz's magnificent but ponderous work.
4 Michael Sikora & Johannes Kunisch (eds): *Gerhard von Scharnhorst, Schüler, Lehrer, Kriegsteilnehmer (Kurhannover bis 1795)* (Cologne: Böhlau, 2002).
5 Peter Paret: *Clausewitz and the State* (Oxford: Clarendon Press, 1976), p. 161.
6 We know that Clausewitz drew on the works of Prussian general cum military historian Georg Friedrich Tempelhoff (1737–1807) on the campaigns of Frederick the Great, but otherwise we know little about his sources. See Carl von Clausewitz: *On War*, ed. & trans. by Peter Paret & Michael Howard (Princeton, NJ: Princeton University Press, 1976), pp. 195, 315, 511, 536, 555.
7 Werner Hahlweg (ed.): *Carl von Clausewitz: Schriften, Aufsätze, Studien, Briefe*, Vol. 2 (Göttingen: Vandenhoek & Ruprecht, 1990), pp. 25, 27, 674, 714, 717. See Marquis de Feuquières: *Mémoires sur la Guerre où l'on a rassemblé les Maximes les plus nécessaires dans les operations de l'Art Militaire* (Amsterdam: Francois Changuion, 1731) trans. into German as *Geheime und sonderbare Kriegsnachrichten des Marggrafen von Feuquieres, Königl. Französischen General-Lieutenants* (Leipzig: Im Weidmannischen Buchladen, 1738) and *Historische und Militärische Nachrichten, verfasset von dem Herrn Marqvis de Feuqvieres, General-Lieutenant der Königl. Französischen Armeen, zum Unterricht seines Sohns*, ed. by Anderer Theil (Leipzig: Im Weidmannischen Buchladen, 1738).
8 Clausewitz: *On War*, Book I, Chapter 3; see Puységur or Puysegur: *Les Mémoires et Instructions Militaires* (originally Paris, this edition Amsterdam: chez Abranahm Wolfgang, 1690); id.: *Art de la Guerre, par principes et par règles* (Paris: Charles-Antoine Jombert, 1748).
9 Clausewitz: *Schriften*, Vol. 2, p. 27; see Turpin de Crissé: *Essai sur l'Art de la Guerre*, 2 vols (Paris: Prault & Jombert, 1754).
10 Clausewitz presumably referred to Matthieu Dumas: *Précis des événemens militaires, ou Essai historique sur la guerre présente, avec cartes et plans . . .*, 2 vols (Paris: Treuttel et Würtz, 1800–1801).
11 Unfortunately for our purposes, the holdings of this latter library have been scattered and my research has been unable to track down its catalogue, if it still exists.
12 Montesquieu's *De l'Esprit des Lois* (1748) had been translated into German as *Vom Geist der Gesetze* (Altenburg: Richter, 1782). Clausewitz had read Montesquieu before his involuntary time in Paris; see Rothfels (ed.): *Clausewitz: Politische Schriften*, p. 4.
13 Jonathan Abel: *Guibert: Father of Napoleon's Grande Armée* (Norman, OK: University of Oklahoma Press, 2016), pp. 147f., 200.
14 Clausewitz: *On War*, trans. Paret & Howard, VIII.3, pp. 589–592. On the genesis of *On War*, see Paul Donker: *Aphorisumen über den Krieg und die Kriegführung as the first version of Clausewitz's masterpiece* (Breda: Publications of the Netherlands Defence Academy, 2016).
15 Guibert later changed his mind about this; see Chapter 8 of this book.
16 Clausewitz: *Schriften*, Vol. 2, pp. 182, 1108, 1114.
17 Carl von Clausewitz: *Schriften, Aufsätze, Studien, Briefe*, Vol. 1 (Göttingen: Vandenhoek & Ruprecht, 1966), p. 622. Vol. 2 (Göttingen: Vandenhoek & Ruprecht, 1966 1997), pp. 300 Fn, 301, 336 Fn.
18 On the terminology, see Beatrice Heuser: 'Exploring the Jungle of Terminology', *The Origins of Small Wars: From Special Operations to Ideological Insurgencies*, Special Issue, *Small Wars and Insurgencies*, Vol. 25 No. 4 (Aug. 2014), pp. 741–753.

19 Christopher Daase and James W. Davis (eds & trans.): *Clausewitz on Small War* (Oxford: Oxford University Press, 2015), p. 167f.

20 Gerhard [later: von] Scharnhorst: *Militärisches Taschenbuch zum Gebrauch im Felde* (1793, 2nd impression 1793, 3rd impression Hanover: Helwigsche Hofbuchhandlung: 1794).

21 Johann Ewald: *Abhandlung von dem Dienst der leichten Truppe* (Flensburg: Schleswig & Leipzig, 1790 & 1796). Clausewitz preferred this to Ewald's later: *Belehrungen über den Krieg, besonders über den kleinen Krieg, durch Beispiele großer Helden und kluger und tapferer Männer* (Schleswig: J.G. Röhß, 1798), which Clausewitz curiously describes as two separate books. Clausewitz seems not to have known Ewald's, *Abhandlung über den kleinen Krieg* (Cassel: Johann Jacob Cramer, 1785), trans. into English by Robert A. Selig and David Curtis Skaggs: *Treatise on Partisan Warfare* (New York: Greenwood Press, 1991) or his anonymously published earliest work: *Gedanken eines Hessischen Officiers über das, was man bey Führung eines Detaschements im Felde zu thun hat* (Cassel: Johann Jacob Cramer, 1774).

22 Georg Wilhelm Freiherr von Valentini: *Abhandlung über den kleinen Krieg und über den Gebrauch der leichten Truppen mit Rücksicht auf den französischen Krieg* (3rd edn, 1799, Berlin, 1810).

23 Hahlweg (ed.): *Carl von Clausewitz: Schriften – Aufsätze – Studien – Briefe*, p. 447.

24 Andreas Emmerich had originally published his book in English as *The Partisan in War or the Use of a Corps of Light Troops to an Army* (London: H. Reynell, 1789); his treatise was then translated into German by J.G. Hoyer, *Der Partheygänger im Kriege, oder Gebrauch der leichten Truppen im Felde* (Berlin: Voss, 1791).

25 Clausewitz: *Schriften*, Vol. 1, pp. 306, 308, 449.

26 *Bellona, Neue Bellona, Neues Milit[airisches] Journal, Milit[ärische] Monatsschrift, Magazin der Merkwürdigsten Kriegsbegebenheiten, et al.*

27 Beatrice Heuser: 'Small Wars in the Age of Clausewitz: Watershed between Partisan War and People's War', *Journal of Strategic Studies*, Vol. 33 No. 1 (Feb. 2010), pp. 137–160.

28 Hahlweg (ed.): *Carl von Clausewitz: Schriften*, Vol. 2, pp 604–611.

29 Charles J. Esdaile: *Fighting Napoleon: Guerrillas, Bandits and Adventurers in Spain, 1808–1814* (New Haven: Yale University Press, 2004); id. (ed.): *Popular Resistance in the French Wars: Patriots, Partisans and Land Pirates* (Basingstoke: Palgrave Macmillan, 2005).

30 On the German resistance to Napoleon, see Martin Rink: 'The German Wars of Liberation 1807–15: The Restrained Insurgency', *The Origins of Small Wars: From Special Operations to Ideological Insurgencies*, special issue, *Small Wars and Insurgencies*, Vol. 25 No. 4 (Aug. 2014), pp. 848–842.

31 Guibert: *Essai général de Tactique*, excerpts in Beatrice Heuser (ed. & trans.): *The Strategy Makers* (Santa Monica, CA: ABC-Clio, 2010), p. 151f. In this passage, Guibert can be said to have prophesied the *levée en masse* of the French Revolution; see Heuser: 'Guibert: Prophet of Total War?', and see Clausewitz's: 'Confession Memorandum' or 'Testimonial', in Daase & David (eds & trans.): *Clausewitz on Small War*, p. 188f.

32 On Guibert's change of heart in later life, see the excerpts of his later works in Heuser (ed. & trans.): *The Strategy Makers*, pp. 163–170, and Chapter 8 in this book.

33 For Brandt's biography, see Kurt von Piersdorf: 'Brandt', in: *Soldatisches Führertum*, Vol. 6 (Hamburg: Hanseatische Verlagsanstalt, 1938), p. 575.

34 Heinrich von Brandt: *Ueber Spanien mit besonderer Hinsicht auf einen etwaigen Krieg* (Berlin: Schüppel'sche Buchhandlung, 1823); translated as *The Two Minas and the Spanish Guerrillas: Extracted and Translated from a Work 'On Spain'* (London: T. Egerton, 1825).

35 Heinrich von Brandt: *Handbuch für den ersten Unterricht in der höhern Kriegskunst* (Berlin: 1829[1], repr. Wiesbaden: LTR Verlag, 1981).

36 Clausewitz: *Schriften*, Vol. 2, p. 618.

37 Clausewitz: *On War*, Book VI, Chapter 23.

38 Heinrich von Brandt: *Der kleine Krieg in seinen verschiedenen Beziehungen* (Berlin: Herbig, 1837).

39 J.F.A. Le Mière de Corvey: *Des Partisans et des corps irréguliers* (Paris: Anselin & Pochard et al., 1823), p. xivf.

40 Le Mière de Corvey: *Des Partisans et des corps irréguliers*, pp. 108–111.

41 Clausewitz also wrote an undated, very technical-quantitative chronological account on the civil war in the Vendée: *Hinterlassene Werke des Generals Carl von Clausewitz über Krieg und Kriegführung*, Vol. 10 (Berlin: Ferdinand Dümmler, 1837), pp. 321–348. The similarity in style and structure to his treatise on the war in Spain and Portugal of 1811 suggests that it might have been written at the same time.

42 Le Mière de Corvey: *Des Partisans*, Part II, Chapters V and VI.

43 Giovanni da Legnano: *Tractatus de Bello, de Represaliis et de Duello* (1360), ed. by Thomas Erskine Holland, trans. by James Leslie Brierly (Oxford: Oxford University Press for the Carnegie Institute, 1917), Chapter 78ff.

44 Stephen Neff: *War and the Law of Nations* (Cambridge: Cambridge University Press, 2005), p. 140.

45 Otto August Rühle von Lilienstern: *Handbuch für den Offizier zur Belehrung im Frieden und zum Gebrauch im Felde*, Vol. 1 (Berlin: G. Reimer, 1817), and Vol. 2 (Berlin: G. Reimer, 1818).

46 Clausewitz: *Schriften*, Vol. 2, pp. 165, 305 Fn, 306, 386, 407, 434, 584.

47 Paret: *Clausewitz and the State*, pp. 272–274.

48 *Allgemeine Militär-Zeitung*, Vol. 8 Nos. 1–3 (1833).

49 Otto August Rühle von Lilienstern: *Apologie des Krieges* (1813), reprinted as *Vom Kriege: ein Fragment aus einer Reihe von Vorlesungen über die Theorie der Kriegskunst* (Frankfurt/Main: Wenner, 1814).

50 Lilienstern: *Handbuch*, Vol. 1, p. 114ff.

51 *On War*, I.1.2.

52 Rühle: *Handbuch*, Vol. 2, for excerpts in translation, see Heuser: *The Strategy Makers*, pp. 178–181.

53 Baron de Henri Jomini: *Tableau analytique des principales combinaisons de la guerre, et de leurs rapports avec la politique des Etats, pour servir d'introduction au Traité des grandes opérations militaires* (Paris: chez Anselm, successeur de Magimel, 1830), pp. 5–37.

54 *On War*, VIII.2, p. 580.

55 Crane Brinton, Gordon A. Craig & Felix Gilbert: 'Jomini', in Edward Mead Earle (ed.): *Makers of Modern Strategy: From Machiavelli to Hitler* (Princeton, NJ: Princeton University Press, 1943), p. 80.

56 *Principes fondamentaux de l'art de guerre* (written in 1804, first printed in Glogau in 1807); Baron de Henri[0] Jomini: 'L'art de la Guerre' (the Art of War), *Pallas: Zeitschrift für Staats- und Kriegskunst*, No. 1 (1808), pp. 31–40.

57 Eberhard Kessel: 'Zur Genesis der modernern Kriegslehre: die Entstehungsgeschichte von Clausewitz' Buch "Vom Kriege"', *Wehrwissenschaftliche Rundschau*, Vol. 3 No. 9 (1953), p. 408.

58 'Über die sr. königl. . . .', in Carl von Clausewitz: *Vom Kriege*, ed. by Werner Hahlweg (19th edn, Bonn: Ferdinand Dümmler, 1989), p. 1053f.

59 Clausewitz: *On War*, VI.30, p. 516.

60 Maurice de Saxe: *Rêveries sur l'Art de la Guerre* (written 1732, published posthumously in The Hague, 1756), p. 298f.

61 "Strategie aus dem Jahre 1804", p. 35.

62 *On War*, IV.11, p. 260.

63 Dietrich Heinrich Frhr von Bülow: *Geist des neuern Kriegssystems aus dem Grundsatze einer Basis der Operationen* (1st edn, Hamburg: Benjamin Gottlieb Hoffmann, 1799); id. (Ein ehemaliger preußischer Offizier): *Geist des neuern Kriegssystems aus dem Grundsatze einer Basis der Operationen* (2nd edn, Hamburg: Benjamin Gottlieb Hoffmann, 1802); Dietrich Heinrich Frhr von Bülow: *Leitsätze des neuern Krieges oder reine und angewandte Strategie* (Berlin: Heinrich Frölich, 1805).

64 Clausewitz: *Schriften*, Vol. 1, p. 647. Clausewitz also published a diatribe against him in a military journal: 'Bemerkungen über die reine und angewandte Strategie des Herrn von Bülow oder Kritik der darin enthaltenen Ansichten', *Neue Bellona*, Vol. 9 No. 3 (1805), pp. 252–287.

65 Clausewitz: *Schriften*, Vol. 1, p. 568.

66 Ibid., p. 718. For further swipes against Bülow, see Clausewitz: *Schriften*, Vol. 2, pp. 38f., 67f., 80, 96.

67 Azar Gat: *The Origins of Military Thought: from the Enlightenment to Clausewitz* (Oxford: Clarendon Press, 1989), p. 166f.

68 In the Paret & Howard edition, pp. 112, 146.

69 On Euler's influence on Clausewitz, see also Andreas Herberg-Rothe: 'Theory and Practice, the Inevitable Dialectics: Thinking with and beyond Clausewitz's Concept of Theory', *Militaire Spectator*, Vol. 184 No. 4 (2015), pp. 160–172.

70 "Strategie aus dem Jahre 1809", in Werner Hahlweg (ed.): *Carl von Clausewitz: Verstreute kleine Schriften* (Osnabrück: Biblio Verlag, 1979), p. 47.

71 Quoted in Rühle's review of *On War* in the *Allgemeine Militär Zeitung*, Vol. 8 No. 3 (1833), col. 22–24. and Clausewitz: *On War*, II.2.

72 See Rühle's review of *On War* in the *Allgemeine Militär Zeitung*, Vol. 8 No. 1 (1833), col. 6, including Footnote, col. 8.

73 *Allgemeine Militär Zeitung*, Vol. 8 No. 3 (1833), col. 23.

74 "Strategie aus dem Jahre 1809", in Hahlweg (ed.): *Carl von Clausewitz*, p. 46f. Jomini's principles were published in his *Résumé des principes généraux de l'art de la guerre* (1807), which in turn became the final chapter of Jomini's *Traité des grandes operations militaires*.

75 Clausewitz: "Über Kunst und Kunsttheorie" (which was written some time between 1807 and 1812), in Walther Malmsten Schering (ed.): *Kleine Schriften: Geist und Tat – das Vermächtnis des Soldaten und Denkers Carl von Clausewitz in Auswahl aus seinen Werken, Briefen und unveröffentlichten Schriften* (Stuttgart: Alfred Kröner Verlag, 1941), pp. 158–162.

76 Thomas Otte: 'Educating Bellona: Carl von Clausewitz and Military Education', in G.C. Kennedy & K. Neilson (eds): *Military Education: Past, Present and Future* (New York: Praeger, 2001).

77 "Strategie aus dem Jahre 1809", in Hahlweg (ed.): *Carl von Clausewitz*, p. 60.

78 Beatrice Heuser: 'Introduction', in Beatrice Heuser (ed. & trans.): *The Strategy Makers: Thoughts on War and Society from Machiavelli to Clausewitz* (Santa Monica, CA: ABC Clio for Praeger, 2010), pp. 1–31, esp. pp. 7–9.

79 Karl Linnebach (ed.): *Karl u. Marie v. Clausewitz: Ein Lebensbild in Briefen und Tagebuchblättern* (Berlin: Martin Warneck, 1917), p. 154.

80 Rühle von Lilienstern: 'Review of Carl von Clausewitz: On War, Books I–II', *Allgemeine Militär-Zeitung*, Vol. 8 No. 1 (Jan. 1833).

81 Georg Heinrich von Berenhorst: *Betrachtungen über die Kriegskunst, über ihre Fortschritte, ihre Widersprüche und ihre Zuverlässigkeit* (1st edn 1797–1798, enlarged 3rd edn, Leipzig, 1827, repr. Osnabrück: Biblio Verlag, 1978).

82 See Beatrice Heuser & Patrick Porter: "Guerres asymétriques: l'orientalisme militaire contre la Voie de la guerre en Occident", in Albert Galvany & Romain Graziani (eds): *La Guerre en perspective: Histoire et culture militaire en Chine* (Paris: Presses universitaires de Vincennes, 2014), pp. 207–218.

83 See Chapter 8.

84 Paret: *Clausewitz and the State*, p. 256f.

85 Linnebach (ed.): *Karl u. Marie v. Clausewitz*, p. 138ff.

86 For example "Strategie aus dem Jahre 1804", in Hahlweg (ed.): *Carl von Clausewitz*, p. 9f.

87 Rothfels (ed.): *Clausewitz: Politische Schriften*, p. 63.

88 Paret: *Clausewitz and the State*, pp. 169–173.

89 In Hahlweg (ed.): *Carl von Clausewitz: Verstreute kleine Schriften*, pp. 157–166.

90 Paret: *Clausewitz and the State*, p. 160, and *On War*, Book I.3. Stemming from this tradition, the use of the expression 'beautiful example', although also occurring in English (but usually with the element of actual admiration, as in 'a beautiful example of sportsmanship'), is still very current in modern German as an analytical description:

for example 'a beautiful example of measles in their first stage of the illness' — that is an example that matches all descriptors in the book.

91 Sibylle Scheipers: '"The Most Beautiful of Wars": Carl von Clausewitz and Small Wars', *European Journal of International* Security, Vol. 2 No. 1 (February 2017), pp. 47-63.

92 Paret: *Clausewitz and the State*, p. 162.

93 Andreas Herberg-Rothe: 'Clausewitz und Hegel — ein heuristischer Vergleich', *Forschungen zur Brandenburgischen und Preussischen Geschichte*, Vol. 10 No. 1 (2000), pp. 49–84.

94 "Strategie aus dem Jahre 1804", p. 3.

95 Ibid., p. 17f.

96 Ibid., p. 10.

97 Clausewitz: *Schriften*, Vol. 1, p. 201; Clausewitz: *Schriften*, Vol. 2, pp. 418, 420, 422, 1152, 1161f.

98 *Allgemeine Militär Zeitung*.

99 Clausewitz: *Schriften*, Vol. 1, p. 208; Anon. (Constantin von Lossau): *Der Krieg: Für wahre Krieger* (Leipzig: W. Engelmann, 1815).

100 Clausewitz: *Schriften*, Vol. 1, p. 27.

101 For excerpts in English, see Heuser: *The Strategy Makers*, pp. 124–146.

102 Clausewitz: *Schriften*, Vol. 1, p. 735.

103 Ibid., Vol. 2, p. 24. See also Hans Rothfels (ed.): *Carl von Clausewitz: Politik und Krieg. Eine Ideengeschichtliche Studie* (Berlin: Dümmler, 1920), p. 29f.

104 The genesis of his most famous dictum on the link between war and politics deserves a chapter of its own, but that, too, needs to be contextualised.

105 Guibert: *Essai général de Tactique*, excerpts in Heuser (ed. & trans.): *The Strategy Makers*, p. 152f.

106 Ibid., p. 151f.

107 Clausewitz's: '"Confession Memorandum" or "Testimonial"', in Daase & David (eds & trans.): *Clausewitz on Small War*, p. 188f.

108 My translation; see also Clausewitz: *On War*, trans. Paret & Howard, VIII.3, pp. 589–592.

BIBLIOGRAPHY

Sources – manuscripts

Guibert, Comte de: 'Observations sur la constitution militaire et politique des armées de S. M. prussienne, avec quelques anecdotes de la vie privée de ce monarque' (probably 1775), Bibliothèque Mazarine, MS 1888, p. 135.

The 'Hulton MS', Copy of a letter by Essex, written aboard the Dewrepulse [sic], 12 Aug [1596], formerly BL Loan 23(1), now Add.MSS 74286, BL Microfilm 2275.

Montecuccoli, Raimondo: *Trattato della guerra* (Biblioteka Estense, Módena, MS italiano 21 α.P. 9.15, 1641), trans. into German in Hauptmann Alois Veltzé (ed.): *Ausgewählte Schriften des Raimond Fürsten Montecuccoli*, Vol. 1 (Vienna: Wilhelm Braumüller, 1899).

Sources – printed

Actas de las Cortes de Castilla, Vol. 3 (Madrid: Imprenta Nacional, 1863), pp. 16–24.

Actas de las Cortes de Castilla, Vol. 10 (Madrid: Los Hijos de J.A. García, 1886), p. 244f.

Alava y Viamont, Diego de: *El Perfecto Capitán instruido en la Disciplina Militar y nueva ciencia de la Artillería* (originally Madrid: Pedro Madrigal, 1590, repr. Madrid: Ministerio de Defensa, 1994).

Alberti, Leo Baptista: *Leonis Baptista Alberti De Re Aedificatoria Libri X* (Florence: Laurentius Alamannus, 1485).

Anon.: *Dessein perpétuel des Espagnols à la monarchie universelle avec les preuves d'iceluy* (s.l., 1624), trans. into English by Robert Gordone (?): *The Spaniards perpetvall Designes to an Vniversall Monarchie* (s.l., 1624).

Anon.: *The Libelle of English Polycye* (1436–8, revised 1438–41) ed. by Sir G. Warner (Oxford: Oxford University Press, 1926).

Anon.: *Reasons Pro and Con Being a Debate at the Council Table between the Treasurer and the General for Making Peace or Carrying on the War in the Reign of Queen Elizabeth, wherein the Force of the General's Argument Prevailed against the Sophistry of the Treasurer's* (London: S. Popping, 1712).

Anon. [Marquis de Silva]: *Remarques sur quelques articles de l'Essai général de tactique* (Turin: Frères Reycends, 1773).

Anon. [Raymond de Beccarie de Pavie, baron de Fourquevaux]: *Instructions sur le faict de la Guerre extraictes des livres de Polybe, Frontin, Végèce, Cornazan, Machiavelle* (Paris: Michel Vascosan, 1548), p. 132, trans. in Beatrice Heuser: *The Strategy Makers: Thoughts on War and Society from Machiavelli to Clausewitz* (Santa Monica: ABC Clio, 2010), pp. 32–49.

Bacon, Francis, Lo. Verulam & Vi. St Alban: *Considerations tovching a Warre with Spaine* (s.l.: s.e., 1629).

Barret, Robert: *The Theorike and Practike of Moderne Warres, Discoursed in Dialogue Wise* (London: William Ponsonby, 1598), p. 2.

Basta, Giorgio, Conte d'Host, Generale per l'imperatore nella Transiluania: *Il mastro di campo Generale* (Venice: [s.e.], 1603).

Bellona, Neue Bellona, Neues Milit[airisches] Journal, Milit[ärische] Monatsschrift, Magazin der Merkwürdigsten Kriegsbegebenheiten, et al.

Berenhorst, Georg Heinrich von: *Betrachtungen über die Kriegskunst, über ihre Fortschritte, ihre Widersprüche und ihre Zuverlässigkeit* (1st edn, 1797–1798, enlarged 3rd edn, Leipzig: 1827, repr. Osnabrück: Biblio Verlag, 1978).

Berenhorst, Georg Heinrich von: *Betrachtungen über die Kriegskunst, über ihre Fortschritte, ihre Widersprüche und ihre Zuverlässigkeit* (Leipzig: Gerhard Fleischer, 1827, facsimile repr. Osnabrück: Biblio, 1978), pp. 18–27.

Bigot de Morogues, Sébastien-François, vicomte: *Tactique navale, ou Traité des évolutions des signaux* (Paris: H.-L. Guérin & L.-F. de la Tour, 1763).

Bingham, John (trans.): *The Tactiks of Aelian. . .; the Exercise Military of the English by the Order of That Great Generall Maurice of Nassau Prince of Orange . . .* (London: Laurence Lisle, 1616).

Bonet, Honoré: *The Tree of Battles*, trans. & ed. G.W. Coopland (Liverpool: Liverpool University Press, 1949), p. 118f.

Boroughs, Sir John: *The Soveraignty of the British Seas, Proved by Records, History, and the Municipall Lawes of This Kingdome, Written in the Year 1633* (London: Humphrey Moseley, 1651).

Boteler, Nathaniel: *Six Dialogues about Sea-Services* (London: William Fisher & Richard Mount, 1688).

Botero, Giovanni: *Della Ragion di Stato Libri Dieci* (Venezia: Giolitti, 1589).

Brandt, Heinrich von: *Der kleine Krieg in seinen verschiedenen Beziehungen* (Berlin: Herbig, 1837).

Brandt, Heinrich von: *Handbuch für den ersten Unterricht in der höhern Kriegskunst* (Berlin, 1829[1], repr. in Wiesbaden: LTR Verlag, 1981).

Brandt, Heinrich von: *Ueber Spanien mit besonderer Hinsicht auf einen etwaigen Krieg* (Berlin: Schüppel'sche Buchhandlung, 1823); trans. as *The Two Minas and the Spanish Guerillas: Extracted and Translated from a Work 'On Spain'* (London: T. Egerton, 1825).

Bueil, Jean de: *Le Jouvencel* (1466, first printed Paris: Antoine Verard, 1493); Léon Lecestre (ed.): *Le Jouvencel par Jean de Bueil* (Paris: Renouard, 1887).

Bülow, Dietrich Heinrich Frhr von: *Geist des neuern Kriegssystems aus dem Grundsatze einer Basis der Operationen* (1st edn, Hamburg: Benjamin Gottlieb Hoffmann, 1799).

Bülow, Dietrich Heinrich Frhr von (Ein ehemaliger preußischer Offizier): *Geist des neuern Kriegssystems aus dem Grundsatze einer Basis der Operationen* (2nd edn, Hamburg: Benjamin Gottlieb Hoffmann, 1802).

Bülow, H. Freiherr von: *Leitsätze des neuern Krieges oder reine und angewandte Strategie* (Berlin: Heinrich Frölich, 1805).

Burchett, Josiah: *A Complete History of the Most Remarkable Transactions at Sea from the Earliest Account of Time to the Conclusion of the Last War with France in Five Books* (London: J. Walthoe & J. Walthoe Jr, 1720).

Bynkershoek, Cornelius: *De Dominio Maris Dissertatio* (1703), facsimile ed. by Ralph van Deman Magofin, James Brown Scott and Herbert F. Wright (New York: Oxford University Press, 1923).

Callwell, Charles Edward: *Military Operations and Maritime Preponderance: Their Relations and Interdepenence* (originally Edinburgh: Wm Blackwood, 1905, repr. Annapolis, MD: Naval Institute Press, 1996).

Champier, Symphorien: *Les gestes ensemble la vie du preulx Chevalier Bayard* (Lyon: Gilbert de Villiers, 1525), ed. Denis Crouzet (Paris: Imprimerie Nationale, 1992), pp. 164, 170ff.

Clausewitz, Carl von: *Hinterlassene Werke des Generals Carl von Clausewitz über Krieg und Kriegführung*, Vol. 10 (Berlin: Ferdinand Dümmler, 1837).

Clausewitz, Carl von: *Vom Kriege* (1832), trans. by Michael Howard and Peter Paret: *On War* (Princeton, NJ: Princeton University Press, 1984).

Clerk, John, of Eldin, the Elder: *An Essay on Naval Tactics, Systematical and Historical* (London: T. Cadell, 1790).

Coke, Jhon: *The Debate betwene the Heraldes of Englande and Fraunce, compyled by Jhon Coke, clarke of the kynges rcognysaunce, or vulgerly, called clarke of the Statutes of the staple of Westmynster, and fynyshed the yere of our Lorde MDL* (s.l.: s.e., 1550).

Corder, Joan: *The Publications of the Harleian Society*, New Series, Vol. 3 (London: Harleian Society, 1984).

Daase, Christopher & James W. Davis (trans. & eds): *Clausewitz on Small War* (Oxford: Oxford University Press, 2015).

Devereux, Robert, 2nd Earl of Essex: *An Apologie of the Earle of Essex* (written 1598; printed London?, 1600).

Devereux, Walter B. (ed.): *Lives and Letters of the Devereux, Earls of Essex, in the Reigns of Elizabeth, James I, and Charles I, 1540–1646* (London: John Murray, 1853).

Digges, Thomas & Dudly Digges: *Four Paradoxes, or Politique Discourses Concerning Militarie Discipline* (London: H. Lownes for Clement Knight, 1604).

Dumas, Matthieu: *Précis des événemens militaires, ou Essai historique sur la guerre présente, avec cartes et plans . . .*, 2 vols. (Paris: Treuttel et Würtz, 1800–1801).

Emmerich, Andreas: *The Partisan in War or the Use of a Corps of Light Troops to an Army* (London: H. Reynell, 1789).

Ewald, Johann: *Abhandlung über den kleinen Krieg* (Cassel: Johann Jacob Cramer, 1785); trans. into English by Robert A Selig and David Curtis Skaggs: *Treatise on Partisan Warfare* (New York: Greenwood Press, 1991).

Ewald, Johann: *Abhandlung von dem Dienst der leichten Truppe* (Flensburg: Korte, 1790 & 1796).

Ewald, Johann: *Belehrungen über den Krieg, besonders über den kleinen Krieg, durch Beispiele großer Helden und kluger und tapferer Männer* (Schleswig: J.G. Röhß, 1798).

Ewald, Johann: *Gedanken eines Hessischen Officiers über das, was man bey Führung eines Detachements im Felde zu thun hat* (Cassel: Johann Jacob Cramer, 1774).

Feuquières, Antoine de Pas, Marquis de: *Mémoires sur la Guerre* (Amsterdam: François Champetier, 1731).

Folard, Jean Charles Chevalier de: *Nouvelles découvertes sur la guerre, dans une dissertation sur Polybe* (Paris: Jean-François Josse & Claude Labottière, 1724).

Frontinus, Sextus Iulius, *Stratagematon* (between A.D. 84–96), trans. & ed. by Charles E. Bennett, *Frontinus: The Stratagems and the Aqueducts of Rome* (London: William Heinemann for Loeb, 1925).

Grenier, Jacques Raymond, vicomte de: *L'Art de Guerre sur Mer, ou Tactique navale, assujettie à de nouveaux principes et à un nouvel ordre de bataille* (Paris: Fermin Didot, 1787).

Grotius, Hugo: *De Jure Belli ac Pacis* (1609), trans. Louise R. Loomis (Roslyn, NY: Walter J. Black, 1949).

Guibert, Comte de: *Défense du Systême de Guerre Moderne, ou Réfutation complete du Systême de M. de M. . . . [Ménil] D. . . . [Durand] Par l'Auteur de l'Essai général de Tactique*, 2 vols. (Neuchâtel: s.e., 1779).

Guibert, Jacques Antoine Hippolyte Comte de: *Essai général de Tactique* (1770), in Guibert: *Stratégiques* (Paris: L'Herne, 1977).

Guibert, Jacques-Antoine-Hippolyte de: *Essai général de tactique* (London: Librairies associés, 1772), in Guibert: *Stratégiques*, ed. by Jean-Paul Charnay and Martine Burgos (Paris: Herne, 1977).

Gundermann, Iselin (ed.): *Das Politische Testament Friedrichs des Grossen* (1768, repr. Vienna: Archiv-Verlag, 2000).

Hahlweg, Werner (ed.): *Carl von Clausewitz: Schriften, Aufsätze, Studien, Briefe*, 2 vols. (Göttingen: Vandenhoek & Ruprecht, 1966 & 1997).

Hakluyt, Richard: *Discourse of Western Planting* (1584), https://ebooks.adelaide.edu.au/h/hakluyt/voyages/v13/planting/complete.html

Hakluyt, Richard (ed.): *The Principal Navigations, Voyages, Traffiques of Discoveries of the English Nation*, Vol. 6 (1589, repr. New York: Augustus M. Kelley, 1969).

Heuser, Beatrice (trans. & ed.): *The Strategy Makers: Thoughts on War and Society from Machiavelli to Clausewitz* (Santa Monica, CA: ABC Clio for Praeger, 2010).

Hoste, Paul, S.J.: *L'art des armées navales, ou Traité des Evolutions navales* (Lyon: Anisson & Posuel, 1697).

Hoste, Paul, S.J.: *Théorie de la Construction des Vaissaux* (Lyon: Anisson & Posuel, 1697).

Instrumentum Pacis Caesareo-Suecicum Osnabrugense, *Instrumenta Pacis Westphalicae: Die Westfälischen Friedensverträge 1648* (Bern: Herbert Lang & Cie., 1949).

Jomini, Antoine Henri: *Traité des grandes Opérations militaires*, 4 vols. (2nd edn, Paris: Magimel, 1811), trans. by Col. S.B. Holabird: *Treatise on Grand Military Operations, or a Critical and Military History of the Wars of Frederick the Great*, 2 vols. (New York: D. Van Nostrad, 1865).

Jomini, Baron de Henri: 'L'art de la Guerre' (The Art of War), *Pallas: Zeitschrift für Staats- und Kriegskunst*, No. 1 (1808), pp. 31–40.

Jomini, Baron de Henri: *Principes fondamentaux de l'art de guerre* (written in 1804, first printed in Glogau, 1807).

Jomini, Baron de Henri: *Tableau analytique des principales combinaisons de la guerre, et de leurs rapports avec la politique des Etats, pour servir d'introduction au Traité des grandes opérations militaires* (Paris: chez Anselm, successeur de Magimel, 1830).

Le G. de W. . .y [sic; presumed to be General Charles Emmanuel de Warnery]: *Remarques sur l'Essai général de Tactique de Guibert* (Warsaw: s.e., 1781).

Le Mière de Corvey, J.F.A.: *Des Partisans et des corps irréguliers* (Paris: Anselin & Pochard et al., 1823), p. xiv f.

Legnano, Giovanni da: *Tractatus de Bello, de Represaliis et de Duello* (1360), ed. by Thomas Erskine Holland, trans. by James Leslie Brierly (Oxford: Oxford University Press for the Carnegie Institute, 1917).

Leicester, Robert Dudley, Earl of: *Lawes and Ordinances* [for the English forces in the Low Countries] (London: Christopher Barker, 1586).

Leo VI, Byzantine emperor: *Taktika*, trans. & ed. by George Dennis: *The Taktika of Leo VI* (Washington: Dumbarton Oaks, 2010), trans. John Checo of Cambridge: *De bellico apparatu liber* (Basle: s.e., 1554).

Linnebach, Karl (ed.): *Karl u. Marie v. Clausewitz: Ein Lebensbild in Briefen und Tagebuchblättern* (Berlin: Martin Warneck, 1917).

Lloyd, General Henry Humphry Evans: *Continuation of the History of the Late War in Germany, between the King of Prussia, and the Empress of Germany, and Her Allies*, Part II (1781), in Patrick J. Speelman (ed.): *War, Society and Enlightenment: The Works of General Lloyd* (Leiden: Brill, 2005).

Londoño, Sancho de: *Discurso sobre la forma de reducir la Disciplina Militar a mejor y antiguo estado* (originally 1594?, Madrid: Ministry of Defence, 1992).

Machiavelli, Niccolò: *The Art of War*, trans. by Ellis Farneworth (originally 1521; Indianapolis: Bobbs-Merrill, 1965, repr. New York: Da Capo, 1990).

Machivelli, Niccolò: Discorsi . . . sopra la prima deca di Tito Livio (Florence: Bernardo di Giunta, 1531).

Marmont, Maréchal, Duc de Raguse: *De l'Esprit des Institutions militaires* (Paris: Librairie militaire J Dumaine, 1845).

Marquis of Pidal & Miguel Salvá (eds): *Colección de Documentos Inéditos para la Historia de España*, Vol. 29 (Madrid: Imprenta de la Viuda de Calero, 1856), Pt I.

Melzi, Francesco Ludovico: *Regole militari sopra il governo e servitio della cavalleria* (Venice: Deuchino, 1626).

Mendoza, Don Bernardino de: *Teórica y práctica de la guerra* (Madrid: Pedro Madrigal, 1595, repr. Madrid: Ministerio de Defensa, 1998), p. 128, trans. by Sir Edwarde Hoby: *Theorique and practise of warre* (Middelburg: Richard Schilders, 1597).

Montecuccoli, Raimondo: *Dalla relazione della congiura del Wallenstein* (1634), trans. into German in Hauptmann Alois Veltzé (ed.): *Ausgewählte Schriften des Raimond Fürsten Montecuccoli*, Vol. 3 (Vienna: Wilhelm Braumüller, 1901), pp. 3–8.

Montecuccoli, Raimondo: *Del arte militare* (MS K. und K. Hof-Bibliothek, Vienna, Cod 10.966; written at Hohenegg, 20 März 1653), trans. into German in Hauptmann Alois Veltzé (ed.): *Ausgewählte Schriften des Raimond Fürsten Montecuccoli*, Vol. 2 (Vienna: Wilhelm Braumüller, 1899), pp. 27–117.

Montecuccoli, Raimondo: *Della Guerra col Turco in Ungheria* (1670), trans. into German in Hauptmann Alois Veltzé (ed.): *Ausgewählte Schriften des Raimond Fürsten Montecuccoli*, Vol. 2 (Vienna: Wilhelm Braumüller, 1899), pp. 195–563.

Montecuccoli, Raimondo: *Discorso della Guerra contro il Turco* (Vienna, 1 March 1664).

Montecuccoli, Raimondo: '[Discorso] Sulle Battaglie' (1639–1642?), ed. & trans. by Thomas M. Barker: *Military Intellectual and Battle: Raimondo Montecuccoli and the Thirty Years' War* (Albany, NY: State University of New York Press, 1975), pp. 73-173.

Montecuccoli, Raimondo: 'L'Ungheria nell'anno 1677', in Hauptmann Alois Veltzé (ed.): *Ausgewählte Schriften des Raimond Fürsten Montecuccoli*, Vol. 3 (Vienna: Wilhelm Braumüller, 1899), pp. 423, 459–472.

Montecuccoli, Raimondo: 'Mal governo della camera aulica' (7 August 1670), trans. into German by Alois Veltzé (ed.): *Ausgewählte Schriften des Raimond Fürsten Montecuccoli*, Vol. 3 (Vienna: Wilhelm Braumüller, 1900), pp. 385–389.

Montecuccoli, Raimondo: *Memorie Militari* (1681), printed in Ugo Foscolo & Giuseppe Grassi (eds): *Memorie militare di Raimondo di Montecuccoli*, 2 vols. (Torino: Tipografia Economica, 1852).

Montesquieu: *De L'Esprit des lois* (Paris: Garnier, 1990).

Nassau, Johann von: *Das Kriegsbuch*, in Werner Hahlweg (ed.): *Die Heeresreform der Oranier* (Wiesbaden: Selbstverlag der Historischen Kommission, 1973), J.W. Wijn: 'Johann der Mittlere von Nassau-Siegen', in Werner Hahlweg (ed.): *Klassiker der Kriegskunst* (Darmstadt: Wehr- und Wissen-Verlag, 1960), pp. 119–133.

Nikephoros Phokas (mid-950s), *Peri Paradromes*, trans. & ed. by George Dennis: *Three Byzantine Military Treatises* (Washington, DC: Dumbarton Oaks, 1985), 146–239.

Noue, Seigneur de: *Discovrs politiqves et militaires du Seigneur de la Noue* (2nd edn, Bâle: François Forest, 1587).

Oliveira, P.ᵉ Fernando: *Arte da guerra do mar novamente escrita* (Coimbra: s.e., 1555, repr. in facsimile Lisbon: Edições 79, 2008).

Oppenheim, M. (ed.): *The Naval Tracts of Sir William Monson*, Vol. 1 (London: The Navy Records Society, 1902).

Pizan, Christine de: *Le chemin de longue étude* (1403/1404), ed. by Andrea Tarnowski (Paris: Le Livre de Poche, 2000).

Pizan, Christine de: *Le Livre de Fais d'Armes et Chevalerie*, first printed as *L'art de cheualerie selon Vegece* (Paris: Anthoine Verard, 1488), trans. into English by William Caxton: *Boke of the fayt of armes and of chyualrye* (Westminster: William Caxton, 1489), new trans. by Sumner Willard, ed. by Charity Cannon Willard: *The Book of Deeds of Arms and of Chivalry* (University Park, PA: Pennsylvania State University Press, 1999).

Pizan, Christine de: *Le Livre des Fais et Bonnes Mœurs du Sage Roi Charles V* (1404), ed. by S. Solente (Paris: Librairie ancienne Honoré Champion, 1936).

Pizan, Christine de: *Le Livre du Corps de Police*, ed. by Angus J. Kennedy (Paris: Honoré Champion, 1998), I.11.

Pizan, Christine de: *Livre de la Paix* (1413), trans. by Karen Green, Constant J. Mews, Janice Pinder & Tania Van Hemelryck: *The Book of Peace by Christine de Pizan* (University Park, PA: Pennsylvania State University Press, c. 2008).

Porcia, Count Giacomo/Jacopo di: *Clarissimi viri Jacobi Pvrliliarvm comitis de re militaris liber* (Venice: Joannis Tacuinus di Tridino, 1530).

Puységur, Brigadier Marquis de (ed.): *Art de la Guerre, par principes et par règles, ouvrage de M. Le Maréchal [Jacques François] de Puységur* (Paris: Charles-Antoine Jombert, 1748), p. 3.

Ralegh, Sir Walter: *Historye of the World* (London: Walter Bvrre, 1614).

Rogers, Clifford J. (ed. & trans.): *Edward III's Wars* (Rochester, NY: Boydell Press, 1999), Document No. 55.

Rohan, Henri Duc de: *Le parfait capitaine, autrement l'abrégé des Guerres de Gaulle* (Paris: A. Courbé, 1638).

Rohan, Henri Duc de: *Le Parfaict Capitaine, Autrement l'abrégé des guerres de Gaule des commentaires de César* (Paris: Iean Hovzé, 1636).

Rothfels, Hans (ed.): *Carl von Clausewitz: Politische Schriften und Briefe* (Munich: Drei Masken Verlag, 1922).

Rousseau, Jean-Jacques: *Jugement sur la Paix perpetuelle* (MS 1756) (Neuchâtel, 1782), para. 1175, http://oll.libertyfund.org/index.php?option=com_staticxt&staticfile=show.php&title=710&search=extend+their+domination&layout=htmla_2011872, accessed on 14 Sept. 2008.

Rühle von Lilienstern, Otto August: *Apologie des Krieges* (1813), reprinted as *Vom Kriege: ein Fragment aus einer Reihe von Vorlesungen über die Theorie der Kriegskunst* (Frankfurt: Wenner, 1814).

Rühle von Lilienstern, Otto August: *Handbuch für den Offizier zur Belehrung im Frieden und zum Gebrauch im Felde*, Vol. 1 (Berlin: G. Reimer, 1817), and Vol. 2 (Berlin: G. Reimer, 1818).

Rühle von Lilienstern, Otto August: 'Review of *On War*', *Allgemeine Militär Zeitung*, Vol. 8 No. 1 (1833), col. 6–25.

'Rühle's Review of *On War*', *Allgemeine Militär Zeitung*, Vol. 8 No. 3 (1833), col. 22–24. and Clausewitz: *On War*, II.2.

Santa Cruz de Marcenado, Don Alvaro de Navia Ossorio y Vigil, Vizconde de Puerto, Marques de: *Reflexiones Militares*, 11 Books in 5 volumes, of which vols. 1–5, i.e. Books 1–10 (Turin: Juan Francisco Mairesse, 1724–1727), vol. 6 i.e. Book 11 (Paris: Simon Langlois, 1730).

Santa Cruz de Marzenado, Marquis de: *Réeflexions militaires et politiques*, trans. from Spanish (Paris: Jacques Guerin, 1735).

Saxe, Maurice de: *Rêveries sur l'Art de la Guerre* (written 1732, published posthumously in The Hague: 1756), trans. by US Army in Brig. Gen. T.R. Phillips (ed.): *Roots of Strategy*, Vol. 5 (Mechanicsburg, PA: Stackpole Books, 1985).

Scharnhorst, Gerhard [later: von]: *Militärisches Taschenbuch zum Gebrauch im Felde* (2nd impression 1793, 3rd impression Hanover: Helwigsche Hofbuchhandlung, 1794).

Schering, Walther Malmsten (ed.): *Kleine Schriften: Geist und Tat – das Vermächtnis des Soldaten und Denkers Carl von Clausewitz in Auswahl aus seinen Werken, Briefen und unveröffentlichen Schriften* (Stuttgart: Alfred Kröner Verlag, 1941).

Schwendi, Lazarus von: *Consilium, Oder: Bedencken An Kaiser Ferdinanden, wie deß Bapsts in Rom Pij V unbillichen anmassen wider Ihrer Kays. Majest. ordentliche Wahl durch die Churfürsten des H. Römischen Reichs ohne des Bapst Consens und Bewilligung geschehen, zu begegnen sey. . . . II. Bedencken An Kaiser Maximilian den Andern, von Regierung deß H. Römischen Reichs . . .* (Frankfurt: Kopf, 1612).

Schwendi, Lazarus von: 'Kriegsraht und Bedencken des Freyherrn Lazarus von Schwendi weiland Römischer Kais. Majstaet tapfern und glückseligen Kriegs-Obersten', in Erasmus Francisci (ed.): *Türckischen Staats und Regiments Beschreibungen; Das ist: Gründliche Nachricht von der Ottomannischen Monarchi Ursprung, Wachsthum, derselben Form zu regieren, Landschafften, Städten, Vestungen, [et]c. Item was vor Potentaten auf dasselbe Reich zu praetendiren: Diesen sind beygefügt etliche der berühmtsten so woln alten als neuen Weissagungen, Muthmassungen und Erklärungen, von gedachten Türckischen Reichs Tyranney und Untergang* (s.l. [Nürnberg?], 1664).

Schwendi, Lazarus von: *Mein Lazarus vonn Schwendis etc. Warhaffter und unwidersprechlicher Bericht, was ich, die niderwerffung und fengknus, weyland Sebastian Vogelsperger belangend, gehandelt und gethon habe* (Speyer: Nolt, Anastasius, 1548; repr. ReInk Books, 2016).

Schwendi, Lazarus von, Freyherr zu Hohen Landsperg et al.: *Kriegsdiscurs, von Bestellung deß ganzen Kriegswesens unnd von den Kriegsämptern* (Frankfurt: Andree Weichels Erben Claudi de Marne & Johan Aubri, 1593).

Selden, John: *Mare Clausum sev de Dominio Maris Libri dvo* (London: William Stanesbeius for Richard Meighen, 1636), published subsequently in English: John Selden: *Of the Dominion, or Ownership of the Sea, Two Books* (London: William Du-Gard, 1652).

Selden, John: *Mare Clausum sev de Dominio Maris Libri dvo* (London: William Stanesbeius for Richard Meighen, 1636), p. 337, published subsequently in English: John Selden: *Of the Dominion, or Ownership of the Sea, Two Books* (London: William Du-Gard, 1652).

Sikora, Michael & Johannes Kunisch (eds): *Gerhard von Scharnhorst, Schüler, Lehrer, Kriegsteilnehmer (Kurhannover bis 1795)* (Cologne: Böhlau, 2002).

Smythe, Sir John: *Certain Discourses Military*, ed. by J.R. Hale (rev. edn, 1590, Ithaca, NY: Cornell University Press, 1964), pp. 3–5.

Strype, John: *Annals of the Reformation*, Vol. 4 (originally 1735, repr. Oxford: Clarendon Press, 1824).

Sutcliffe, Matthew: *An abridgement or suruey of poperie . . .* (London: Melchisedech Bradwood for Cuthbert Burbie, 1606).

Sutcliffe, Matthew: *An ansvvere to a certaine libel supplicatorie . . .* (London: The Deputies of C. Barker, 1592).

Sutcliffe, Matthew: *An ansvvere vnto a certaine calumnious letter*, published by M. Iob Throkmorton . . . (London: The Deputies of C. Barker, 1595).

Sutcliffe, Matthew: *Apologia pro christiano batavo* (London: s.n., 1610); *The Blessings on Mount Gerizzim, and the Curses on Movnt Ebal* (London: Andrew Hebb, 1625?).

Sutcliffe, Matthew: *The Blessings on Mount Gerizzim, and the Curses on Movnt Ebal: Or, The Happie Estate of Protestants Compared with the Miserable Estate of Papists vnder the Popes Tyrannie* (London: Printed for Andrew Hebb, 1625).

Sutcliffe, Matthew: *A Briefe Examination, of a Certaine Peremptorie Menacing and Disleal Petition . . .* (London: W. Cotton, 1606).

Sutcliffe, Matthew: *A Challenge concerning the Romish Church, Her Doctrine and Practises* (London: A. Hatfield, 1602).

Sutcliffe, Matthew: *The Practice, Proceedings and Lawes of Armes* (London: Deputies of C. Barker, 1593).

Sutcliffe, Matthew: *A Treatise on Ecclesiastical Discipline* . . . (London: George Bishop & Ralph Newberie, 1590).

Thukydides: *The hystory writtone by Thucidides the Athenyan of the warre, whiche was betwene the Peloponesians and the Athenyans*, trans. from French by Thomas Nicolls (London: William Tylle, 1550).

Traverse, Baron de: *Extrait de la première partie de l'Art de Guerre de M. le Maréchal de Puysegur* (Paris: chez Charles-Ant. Jombert et Hochereau l'Aîné, 1752).

Tressan, Comte de: 'Guerre', in Diderot & d'Alembert (ed.): *Encyclopédie ou Dictionnaire raisonné des Sciences, des Arts et des Métiers*, Vol. 7 (Paris: Briasson, David, Le Breton & Durand, 1757), p. 986.

Tronson du Coudray, Charles: *L'ordre profond et l'ordre mince considérés par rapport aux effets de l'artillerie* (Metz: Ruault et Esprit, 1776).

'A True Discourse (as is thought) by Colonel Antonie Wingfield emploied in the voiage to Spaine and Portugall, 1589 . . .', in Richard Hakluyt (ed.): *The Principal Navigations, Voyages, Traffiques of Discoveries of the English Nation* Vol. 6 (1589, repr. New York: Augustus M. Kelley, 1969).

Turpin de Crissé: *Essai sur l'Art de la Guerre*, 2 vols. (Paris: Prault & Jombert, 1754).

Twiss, Sir Travers (ed.): *The Black Book of the Admiralty*, Vol. 1 (London: Longman etc. for Monumenta Juridica, 1871).

Valentini, Georg Wilhelm Freiherr von: *Abhandlung über den kleinen Krieg und über den Gebrauch der leichten Truppen mit Rücksicht auf den französischen Krieg* (3rd edn, 1799, Berlin, 1810).

Veltzé, Alois (ed.): *Ausgewählte Schriften des Raimond Fürsten Montecuccoli*, 4 vols (Vienna: Wilhelm Braumüller, 1900).

W[arner]y, Le G[énéral Charles Emmanuel de] de: *Remarques sur l'Essai général de Tactique de Guibert* (Warsaw: s.e., 1781).

Welvvod [Welwood], William: *An Abridgement of all Sea-Lawes; Gathered Forth of All VVritings and Monuments, Which Are to Be Found among Any People or Nation, vpon the Coasts of the Great Ocean and Mediterranean Sea* (London: Humfrey Lownes for Thomas Man, 1613).

William (Guilhelmus) Count of Nassau & Alain Claude de Mestre: *Annibal et Scipion, ou les grands Capitaines, avec les ordres et plans de batailles* (The Hague, 1675).

Secondary literature (unpublished)

Anderson Covington, Samuel: 'The Comité militaire and the Legislative Reform of the French Army, 1789–1791' (PhD dissertation, University of Arkansas, 1976).

Margetts, Michele: 'Stella Britanna: The Early Life (1563–1592) of Lady Penelope Devereux, Lady Rich (d. 1607)' (MS PhD Yale, 1992).

Redding, Benjamin: ''Divided by *La Manche*: Naval Enterprise and Maritime Revolution in England and France, 1545–1642' (MS PhD University of Warwick, 2016).

Secondary literature (books)

Abel, Jonathan: *Guibert: Father of Napoleon's Grande Armée* (Norman, OK: University of Oklahoma Press, 2016).

Ackerl, Isabella: *Von Türken belagert – von Christen entsetzt: das belagerte Wien 1683* (Vienna: Österreichischer Bundesverlag, 1983), pp. 134–138; Johannes Sachslehner: *Wien Anno 1683: Ein europäisches Schicksalsjahr* (Vienna: Pichler Verlag, 2004), p. 308.

Barker, Thomas M.: *The Military Intellectual and Battle: Raimondo Montecuccoli and the Thirty Years' War* (Albany, NY: State University of New York Press, 1975).

Beckett, Ian Frederick William, *Modern Insurgencies and Counter-Insurgencies: Guerrillas and Their Opponents since 1750* (London: Routledge, 2001).

Black, Jeremy: *European Warfare 1494–1660* (London: Routledge, 2002), pp. 32–54.

Black, Jeremy: *A Military Revolution? Military Change and European Society, 1550–1800* (Basingstoke: Macmillan, 1991).

Bluche, François: *Louis XIV* (Paris: Fayard, 1986).

Booth, Max: *War Made New: Technology, Warfare, and the Course of History, 1500 to Today* (New York: Gotham Books, 2006).

Boroughs, Sir John: *The Soveraignty of the British Seas, Proved by Records, History, and the Municipall Lawes of This Kingdome, Written in the Year 1633* (London: Humphrey Moseley, 1651).

Bridge, Sir Cyprian Arthur George: *Art of Naval Warfare* (London: Smith, Elder, 1907).

Burkhardt, Johannes: *Der Dreissigjährige Krieg* (Frankfurt/Main: Suhrkamp, 1992).

Castex, Raoul: *Théories stratégiques*, Vol. 1 (2nd edn, Paris: SEGMC, 1937).

Cénat, Jean-Philippe: *Le roi stratège: Louis XIV et la direction de la guerre, 1661–1715* (Rennes: Presses Universitaires, 2010).

Childs, David: *Pirate Nation: Elizabeth I and Her Royal Sea Rovers* (Barnsley: Seaforth, 2014).

Colomb, Philip Howard: *Naval Warfare: Its Ruling Principles and Practice Historically Treated* (London: W.H. Allen, 1891).

Contamine, Philippe: *La Guerre au Moyen Age* (2nd revised edn, Paris: Presses Universitaires de France, 1986); English trans. of the first edn: *War in the Middle Ages*, trans. Michael Jones (Oxford: Blackwell 1984).

Corbett, Julian S.: *Drake and the Tudor Navy* (London: Longmans, 1898).

Corbett, Julian S.: *For God and Gold* (London: Macmillan, 1887).

Corbett, Julian S.: *Papers Relating to the Navy during the Spanish War 1585–1587* (London: Macmillan, 1898).

Corbett, Julian S.: *Sir Francis Drake* (London: Macmillan, 1890).

Corbett, Sir Julian: *Some Principles of Maritime Strategy* (1911, repr. Annapolis, MD: US Naval Institute Press, 1988).

Corbett, Julian S.: *The Successors of Drake* (London: Longmans, Green, 1900).

Coutau-Bégarie, Hervé (ed.): *Evolution de la Pensée navale*, Vols. 1–7 (Paris: Economica, 1990–1998), pp. 13–35.

Creveld, Martin van: *Technology and War from 2000 BC to the Present* (New York: Free Press, 1991).

Dain, Alphonse: *Naumachia* (Paris: Les Belles Lettres, 1943).

Daudet, Léon: *La guerre totale* (Paris: Nouvelle Librairie, 1918).

Delbrück, Hans: *Geschichte der Kriegskunst im Rahmen der politischen Geschichte* (originally Berlin: Walter de Gruyter, 1901, repr. Hamburg: Nikol, 2003).

Depeyre, Michel: *Tactique et Stratégies navales de la France et du Royaume-Uni de 1690 à 1815* (Paris: Economica, 1998).

Donker, Paul: *Aphorisumen über den Krieg und die Kriegführung as the first version of Clausewitz's masterpiece* (Breda: Publications of the Netherlands Defence Academy, 2016).

Drévillon, Hervé: *L'impot du Sang* (Paris: Eds Tallandier, 2006).

Duby, Georges: *France in the Middle Ages, 987–1460: From Hugh Capet to Joan of Arc*, trans. by Juliet Vale (Oxford: Blackwell, 1993).

Edelmayer, Friedrich: *Philip II: Biographie eines Weltherrschers* (Stuttgart: Kohlhammer, 2009).

Esdaile, Charles J.: *Fighting Napoleon: Guerrillas, Bandits and Adventurers in Spain, 1808–1814* (New Haven: Yale University Press, 2004).

Esdaile, Charles J. (ed.): *Popular Resistance in the French Wars: Patriots, Partisans and Land Pirates* (Basingstoke: Palgrave Macmillan, 2005).

Foerster, Stig & Joerg Nagler (eds): *On the Road to Total War: The American Civil War and the German Wars of Unification, 1861–1871* (Cambridge: Cambridge University Press, 1997).

Forhan, Kate Langdon: *The Political Theory of Christine de Pizan* (Aldershot: Ashgate, 2002).

Franklin, Julian Harold: *Jean Bodin and the Rise of Abolutist Theory* (Cambridge: Cambridge University Press, 1973).

Frauenholz, Eugen von: *Des Lazarus von Schwendi Denkschrift über die politische Lage des Deutschen Reiches von 1574* (München: Beck, 1939).

Frauenholz, Eugen von: *Lazarus von Schwendi: der erste deutsche Verkünder der allgemeinen Wehrpflicht* (Hamburg: Hanseatische Verlagsanstalt, 1939).

Freedman, Lawrence: *Strategy: A History* (Oxford: Oxford University Press, 2013).

Frost, Robert: *After the Deluge: Poland-Lithuania and the Second Northern War, 1655–1660* (Cambridge: Cambrige University Press, 2010).

Frost, Robert: *The Northern Wars: War, State and Society in Northeastern Europe, 1558–1721* (London: Routledge, 2000).

Fryde, Natalie: *The Tyranny and Fall of Edward II, 1321–1326* (Cambridge: Cambridge University Press, 1979), *passim.*

Fryde, Natalie: *Why Magna Carta? Angevin England Revisited* (Münster: LIT Verlag, 2001).

Fulton, Thomas Wemyss: *The Sovereignty of the Sea* (Edinburgh: William Blackwood & Sons, 1911).

García Hernan, Enrique: *Ireland and Spain in the reign of Philip II* (Dublin: Four Courts Press, 2009).

García Hernán, Enrique & Davide Maffi (eds): *Guerra y Sociedad en la Monarquía Hispánica: Política, Estrategia y Cultura en la Europa Moderna (1500–1700)*, Vols. 1 & 2 (Madrid: Ediciones del Laberinto, 2006).

Gat, Azar: *The Origins of Military Thought: From the Enlightenment to Clausewitz* (Oxford: Clarendon Press, 1989).

Goldsworthy, Adrian: *The Punic Wars* (London: Cassell, 2001).

Hainsworth, Roger & Christine Churches: *The Anglo-Dutch Naval Wars 1652–1674* (Stroud: Sutton, 1998).

Hale, John R.: *The Art of War and Renaissance England* (Washington ?: Folger Shakespeare Library, 1961), p. 1.

Hale, John R.: *War and Society in Renaissance Europe, 1450–1620* (1985, this edn Baltimore, MD: Johns Hopkins University Press, 1986).

Hall, Bert S.: *Weapons and Warfare in Renaissance Europe: Gunpowder, Technology and Tactics* (Baltimore, MD: The Johns Hopkins University Press, 1997).

Hammer, Paul E. J.: *The Polarisation of Elizabethan Politics: The Political Career of Robert Devereux, 2nd Earl of Essex, 1585–1597* (Cambridge: Cambridge University Press, 1999).

Heuser, Beatrice: *The Evolution of Strategy: Thinking War from Antiquity to the Present* (Cambridge: Cambridge University Press, 2010).

Hillgarth, J.N.: *The Spanish Kingdoms 1250–1516, vol. II: 1410–1516, Castilian Hegemony* (Oxford: Clarendon Press, 1987).

Jardine, Lisa & William Sherman: 'Pragmatic Readers: Knowledge Transaction and Scholarly Services in Late Elizabethan England', in Anthony Fletcher & Peter Roberts (eds): *Religion, Culture, and Society in Early Modern Britain* (Cambridge: Cambridge University Press, 1994), pp. 102-124.

Joes, Anthony James: *Modern Guerrilla Insurgency* (Westport, CT: Praeger, 1992).

Kelsey, Harry: *Sir Francis Drake: The Queen's Pirate* (New Haven, CT: Yale University Press, 1998, repr. 2000).

Kennedy, Paul M. (ed.): *Grand Strategies in War and Peace* (New Haven: Yale University Press, 1991).

Kennedy, Paul M.: *The Rise and Fall of British Naval Mastery* (1976, Amherst, NY: Humanity Books, 1983²).

Kenny, Robert W.: *Elizabeth's Admiral: The Political Career of Charles Howard Earl of Nottingham 1536–1624* (Baltimore, MD: Johns Hopkins University Press, 1970).

Kenz, David El & Claire Gantet: *Guerres et paix de religion en Europe, XVIe-XVIIe siècles* (2nd edn, Paris: Armand Colin, 2008).

Kia, Mehrdad: *The Ottoman Empire* (Westport, CT: Greenwood Press, 2008), pp. 59–94.

Lacey, Robert: *Robert Earl of Essex: an Elizabethan Icarus* (London: Weidenfeld & Nicolson, 1971).

Lauerma, Matti: *Jacques-Antoine-Hippolyte de Guibert (1743–1790)* (Helsinki: Suomalainen Tiedeakatemia, 1989).

Lauring, Palle: *A History of Denmark*, trans. by David Hohnen (Copenhagen: Høst & Son, 1995³).

Le Bohec, Yann: *La Guerre romaine* (Paris: Tallandier, 2014).

Lecoq, Anne-Marie (ed.): *La Querelle des Anciens et des Modernes, XVIIe – XVIIIe siècles* (Paris: Gallimard, 2001).

Lee, Sidney (ed.): *Dictionary of National Biography*, Vol. 55 (London: Smith, Elder, 1898), pp. 175–177.

Lemnitzer, Jan Martin: *Power, Law and the End of Privateering* (Houndsmills, Basingstoke: Palgrave Macmillan, 2014).

Leng, Rainer: *Ars belli: deutsche Taktische und kriegstechnische Bilderhandschriften und Traktate im 15. und 16. Jahrhundert*, 2 vols. (Wiesbaden: Reichert, 2002).

Liddell Hart, B.H.: *The Decisive Wars of History: A Study in Strategy* (London: G. Bell & Sons, 1929).

Loades, David: *England's Maritime Empire: Seapower, Commerce and Policy, 1490–1690* (Harlow: Longman 2000).

Ludendorff, Erich: *Der Totale Krieg* (Munich: Ludendorff, 1935); trans. by A.S. Rapoport: *The Nation at War* (London: Hutchinson, 1936).

Luttwak, Edward: *The Grand Strategy of the Byzantine Empire* (Cambridge, MA: Belknap Press, 2009).

Luttwak, Edward: *The Grand Strategy of the Roman Empire: From the First Century A.D. to the Third* (1976, repr. London: Weidenfeld & Nicolson, 1999).

Lynn, John (ed.): *Tools of War: Instruments, Ideas, and Institutions of Warfare 1445–1871* (Urbana, IL: University of Illinois Press, 1990).

Lynn, John: *The Wars of Louis XIV, 1667–1714* (Harlow: Pearson Education, 1999).

MacCaffrey, Wallace T.: *Elizabeth I: War and Politics, 1588–1603* (Princeton: Princeton University Press, 1992).

Mahan, Alfred Thayer: *The Influence of Sea Power upon History, 1660–1783* (Boston: Little, Brown, 1890).

Mahan, Alfred Thayer: *Sea Power in Its Relations to the War of 1812*, 2 vols. (Boston: Little, Brown, 1905).

McKay, Derek: *Prince Eugene of Savoy* (London: Thames & Hudson, 1977), p. 28.

Meynert, Hermann: *Geschichte des Kriegswesens und der Heeresverfassung in Europa*, Vol. 1 (Graz: Akademische Druck- u. Verlagsanstalt, 1973).

Mignet, M. (ed.): *Négociations relatives à la succession d'Espagne sous Louis XIV*, Vol. 1 (Paris: Imprimerie Royale, 1835).

Murphy, Rhoads: *Ottoman Warfare, 1500–1700* (New Brunswick, NJ: Rutgers University Press, 1999), p. 144f.

Neff, Stephen: *War and the Law of Nations* (Cambridge: Cambridge University Press, 2005).

Neuhaus, Helmut: 'Montecuccoli, Raimund Fürst von', in: *Neue Deutsche Biographie*, Vol. 18 (Munich: Bayerische Akademie der Wissenschaften: 1997), pp. 44–47.

Nicholson, Helen: *Medieval Warfare* (Basingstoke: Palgrave Macmillan, 2004).

Nicklas, Thomas: *Um Macht und Einheit des Reiches: Konzeption und Wirklichkeit der Politik bei Lazarus von Schwendi (1522–1583)* (Husum: Matthiesen Verlag, 1995).

Olivier, David H.: *German Naval Strategy 1856–1888: Forerunners of Tirpitz* (London: Frank Cass, 2004).

Papirer, Eugène: *Kientzheim en Haute-Alsace: La Ville de Lazare de Schwendi* (Colmar: Editions d'Alsace, 1982).

Paret, Peter: *Clausewitz and the State* (Oxford: Clarendon Press, 1976).

Parker, Geoffrey: *The Army of Flanders and the Spanish Road, 1567–1659: The Logistics of Spanish Victory and Defeat in the Low Countries' Wars* (London: Cambridge University Press, 1972).

Parker, Geoffrey: *The Grand Strategy of Philip II* (New Haven: Yale University Press, 1998).

Parker, Geoffrey: *Imprudent King: A New Life of Philip II* (New Haven: Yale University Press, 2014).

Parker, Geoffrey: *The Military Revolution: Military Innovation and the Rise of the West 1500–1800* (Cambridge: Cambridge University Press, 1988).

Parrott, David: *The Business of War: Military Enterprise and Military Revolution in Early Modern Europe* (Cambridge: Cambridge University Press, 2012).

Parrott, David: *Richelieu's Army: War, Government and Society in France, 1624–1642* (Cambridge: Cambridge University Press, 2001).

Poirier, Lucien: *Les voix de la stratégie* (Paris: Fayard, 1985).

Purton, Peter: *A History of the Late Medieval Siege, 1200–1500* (Woodbridge: Boydell Press, 2010).

Ramatuelle, Audibert: *Cours élémentaire de Tactique navale* (Paris: Baudouin, Year X/1802).

Recio Morales, Óscar (ed.): *Redes y espacios de poder de la comunidad irlandesa en España y la América española, 1600–1825* (Valencia: Albatros Ediciones, 2012).

Redworth, Glyn: *The Prince and the Infanta: The Cultural Politics of the Spanish Match* (Newhaven, CT: Yale University Press, 2003).

Reynolds, Susan: *Fiefs and Vassals: The Medieval Evidence Reinterpreted* (Oxford: Oxford University Press, 1994).

Richardot, Philippe: *Végèce et la Culture militaire au Moyen Âge (Ve-XVe siècles)* (Paris: Economica, 1998).

Rink, Martin: *Vom 'Partheygänger' zum Partisanen: Die Konzeption des kleinen Krieges in Preußen, 1740–1813* (Frankfurt/Main: Peter Lang, 1999).

Roberts, Michael: *The Military Revolution, 1560–1660* (Belfast: Marjory Boyd, 1956); reprinted in Michael Roberts: *Essays in Swedish History* (London: Weidenfeld & Nicolson, 1967), pp. 195–225.

Robot, Luis (ed.): *Historia Militar de España III Edad Moderna Part II Escenario europeo* (Madrid: Ministerio de Defensa, 2013).

Rodger, N.A.M.: *The Command of the Ocean: A Naval History of Britain, 1649–1815* (originally 2004, London: Penguin, 2005).

Rodger, N.A.M.: *The Safeguard of the Sea: A Naval History of Britain, 660–1649* (1997; London: Penguin, 2004).

Rogers, Clifford J.: *War Cruel and Sharp: English Strategy under Edward III, 1327–1360* (Woodbridge: The Boydell Press, 2000).

Rose, Susan: *Medieval Naval Warfare 1000–1500* (London: Routledge, 2002), pp. 123–131.

Saul, Nigel: *A Companion to Medieval England, 1066–1485* (Stroud: Tempus, 2000).

Schmidt, Peer: *Spanische Universalmonarchie oder 'teutsche Libertet'* (Stuttgart: Franz Steiner Verlag, 2001).

Schnerb, Bertrand: *Armagnacs et Bourguignons: la maudite guerre, 1407–1435* (Paris: Perrin, 2009).

Schreiber, Gerhard: *Raimondo Montecuccoli: Feldherr, Schriftsteller und Kavalier* (Graz: Verlag Styria, 2000).

Seché, Alphonse: *Les Guerres d'Enfer* (Paris: Sansot, 1915).

Sobiecki, Sebastian: *The Sea and Medieval English Literature* (Cambridge: D.S. Brewer, 2008).

Strachan, Hew: *On War: A Biography* (New York: Atlantic Press, 2007).

Tallett, Frank: *War and Society in Early-Modern Europe, 1495–1715* (London: Routledge, 1992).

Tallett, Frank & David Trim (eds): *European Warfare, 1350–1750* (Cambridge: Cambridge University Press, 2010).

Talmon, J.L.: *The Origins of Totalitarian Democracy: Political Theory and Practice during the French Revolution and Beyond* (London, 1952).

Tilly, Charles (ed.): *The Formation of National States in Western Europe* (Princeton, NJ: Princeton University Press, 1975).

Toefler, Alvin & Heidi Toefler: *War and Anti-War* (Boston: Little, Brown, 1993).

Twiss, Sir Travers (ed.): *The Black Book of the Admiralty, vol. 55 of the Rerum britannicarum medii aevi scriptores or Chronicles and Memorials of Great Britain and Ireland during the Middle Ages*, Vol. 1 (London: Longman, 1871).

Ungerer, Gustav (ed.): *A Spaniard in Elizabethan England: The Correspondez on Antonio Pérez's Exile*, Vol. 1 (London: Thamesis Books Ltc, 1974).

Usherwood, Stephen & Elizabeth Usherwood: *The Counter-Armada 1596: The Journal of the Mary Rose* (London: Bodley Head, 1983).

Verbruggen, Jan Frans: *The Art of Warfare in Western Europe during the Middle Ages; from the Eighth Century to 1340* (2nd edn, Woodbridge: Boydell Press, 1997).

Verrier, Frédérique: *Les Armes de Minerve: L'Humanisme militaire dans l'Italie du XVIe Siècle* (Paris: Presses universitaires de Paris-Sorbonne, 1997), p. 40f.

Weigley, Russell F.: *The American Way of War: A History of United States Military Strategy and Policy* (New York: Macmillan, 1976).

Wernham, Richard Bruce: *The Return of the Armadas: The Last Years of the Elizabethan War against Spain, 1595–1603* (Oxford: Clarendon Press, 1994).

Wheatcroft, Andrew: *The Enemy at the Gate: Habsburgs, Ottomans and the Battle for Europe* (London: Pimlico, 2009), p. 13f.

Wilkinson, Henry Spencer: *Command of the Sea and Brain of the Navy* (Westminster, London: Archibald Constable, 1894).

Williamson, James A.: *Sir John Hawkins, the Time and the Man* (Oxford: Clarendon Press, 1927).

Secondary literature (articles)

Adams, Simon: 'Tactics or Politics? The "Military Revolution" and the Habsburg Hegemony, 1525–1648', in John A. Lynn (ed.): *Tools of War: Instruments, Ideas, and Institutions of Warfare 1445–1871* (Urbana, IL: University of Illinois Press, 1990), pp. 28–42.

Ágoston, Gabor: 'La frontière militaire ottomane en Hongrie', in Marie-Françoise Vajda-Saudraix & Olivier Chaline (eds): *L'Hongrie ottomane, XVIe-XVIIe siècles*, Special Issue of *Histoire, Economie & Société*, Vol. 34 (Sept. 2015), pp. 36–54.

Armitage, David: 'The Elizabethan Idea of Empire', *Transactions of the Royal Historical Society*, 6th series, Vol. 14 (2004), pp. 269–277.

Barnes, Jonathan: 'The Just War', in Norman Kretzmann, Anthony Kenny & Jan Pinborg (eds): *The Cambridge History of Later Medieval Philosophy* (Cambridge: Cambridge University Press, 1982), pp. 775–777.

Barron, Caroline: 'The Tyranny of Richard II', *Bulletin of the Institute of Historical Research*, Vol. 41 No. 103 (1968), pp. 1–18.

Belissa, Marc & Patrice Leclerq: 'The Revolutionary Period, 1789–1802', in Anja Hartmann & Beatrice Heuser (eds): *War, Peace and World Orders from Antiquity until the 20th Century* (London: Routledge, 2001), pp. 203-213.

Black, Jeremy: 'A Military Revolution? A 1660–1792 Perspective', in Clifford Rogers (ed.): *The Military Revolution Debate* (Boulder, CO: Westview Press, 1995), pp. 95–114.

Brinton, Crane, Gordon A. Craig & Felix Gilbert: 'Jomini', in Edward Mead Earle (ed.): *Makers of Modern Strategy From Machiavelli to Hitler* (Princeton, NJ: Princeton University Press, 1943), pp. 77-90.

Brunelli, Giampiero: 'Montecuccoli, Raimondo', *Dizionario Biografico degli Italiani*, Vol. 76 (Rome: Istituto della Enciclopedia Italiana, 2012), pp. 22-30.

Brunt, P.A.: 'The Aims of Alexander', *Greece & Rome*, Vol. 12 (1965), pp. 205–215.

Brunt, P.A.: 'Spartan Policy and Strategy in the Archidamian War', *Phoenix*, Vol. 19 No. 4 (Winter 1965), pp. 255–280.

Carroll, Berenice A.: 'Christine de Pizan and the Origins of Peace Theory', in Hilda L. Smith (ed.): *Women Writers and the Early British Political Tradition* (Cambridge: Cambridge University Press, 1998), pp. 22–39.

Carroll, Berenice A.: 'On the Causes of War and the Quest for Peace: Christine de Pizan and Early Peace Theory', in Eric Hicks (ed.): *Au Champs des Escritures: IIIe Colloque international sur Christine de Pizan* (Paris: Honoré Champion, 2000), pp. 337–348.

Cazaux, Loïc: 'Pour un droit de la guerre? La discipline militaire et les rapports entre combattants et non-combattants dans le *Livre des Faits d'Armes et de Chevalerie* de Christine de Pizan', in Dominique Demartini, Claire Le Ninan, Anne Paupert & Michelle Szkilnik (eds): *Une femme et la guerre à la fin du Moyen Âge: Le livre des faits d'armes et de chevalerie de Christine de Pizan* (Paris: Honoré Champion, 2016), pp. 89–102.

Charnay, Jean-Paul: 'Portraits de Guibert', in Centre d'études et de recherché sur les strategies et les conflicts (ed.): *Guibert ou le Soldat Philosophe* (Paris: CERSC, 1981), pp. 10-50.

Coutau-Bégarie, Hervé: 'L'émergence d'une Pensée navale en Europe au XVIe Siècle et au Début du XVIIe Siècle', in Hervé Coutau-Bégarie (ed.): *Evolution de la Pensée navale* Vol. 4 (Paris: Economica, 1994), pp. 13–35.

Cranfield, Nicholas W.S.: 'Sutcliffe, Matthew (1549/50–1629)', in H.C.G. Matthew & Brian Harrison (eds): *Oxford Dictionary of National Biography 53* (Oxford: Oxford University Press, 2004), pp. 351–353.

Cruz, Anne: 'Vindicating the *Vulnerata*: Cádiz and the Circulation of Religious Imagery as Weapons of War', in Anne Cruz (ed.): *Material and Symbolic Circulation between Spain and England, 1554–1604* (Aldershot: Ashgate, 2008), pp. 43-60.

Dohrn-van Rossum, Gerhard: 'Novitates-Inventores: Die "Erfindung der Erfinder" im Spätmittelalter', in Hans-Joachim Schmidt (ed.): *Tradition, Innovation, Invention: Fortschrittsverweigerung und Fortschrittsbewusstsein im Mittelalter* (Berlin: Walter de Gruyter, 2005), pp. 27–49.

Drévillon, Hervé: 'Vauban stratège', in Jean Baechler & Jean-Vincent Holeindre (eds): *Penseurs de la Stratégie* (Paris: Hermann, 2014), pp. 99–110.

Esdaile, Charles: 'De-Constructing the French Wars: Napoleon as Anti-Strategist', *Journal of Strategic Studies*, Vol. 31 No. 4 (2008), pp. 512–552.

Fonck, Bertrand & George Satterfield: 'The Essence of War: French Armies and Small War in the Low Countries (1672–97)', *Small Wars and Insurgencies*, Vol. 25 No. 4 (Aug. 2014), pp. 767–783.

Fryde, Natalie: 'Innocent III, England and the Modernization of European International Politics', *Innocenzo III, Urbs et Orbis*, Vol. 2 (1998), pp. 971–984.

Garcia Fitz, Francisco: '¿Hube estrategia en la edad media? A propósito de las relaciones castellano-musulmanas durante la segunda mitad del siglo XIII', *Revista da Faculdade de Lettras*, 2nd series, Vol. 15 No. 2 (1998), pp. 837–854.

García Hernán, Enrique: 'Planes militares de Felipe II para conquistar Irlanda, 1569–1578', in Enrique García Hernán, Miguel Ángel de Bunes, Óscar Recio Morales & Bernardo J. García García (eds): *Irlanda y la Monarquía hispánica: Kinsale 1601–2001: Guerra, Política, Exilio y Religión* (Madrid: Universidad de Alcalá, CSIS, 2002), pp. 185–204.

García Hernan, Enrique: 'Tratadística militar', in Luis Robot (volume ed.): *Historia Militar de España* III *Edad Moderna* Part II *Escenario europeo* (Madrid: Ministerio de Defensa, 2013), pp. 401–419.

Gat, Azar: 'Montecuccoli: The Impact of Proto-Science on Military Theory', in Azar Gat: *The Origins of Military Thought from the Enlightenment to Clausewitz* (Oxford: Oxford University Press, 1991), pp. 13–24.

Gillingham, John: 'War and Chivalry in the *History of William the Marshal*', reprinted in Matthew Strickland (ed.): *Anglo-Saxon Warfare: Studies in Late Anglo-Saxon and Anglo-Norman Military Organisation and Warfare* (Woodbridge: Boydell Press, 1992), pp. 251–263.

Glete, Jan: 'Naval Power and Control of the Sea in the Baltic', in John Hattendorf & Richard Unger (eds): *War at Sea in the Middle Ages and the Renaissance* (Woodbrige, Suffolk: Boydell Press, 2003), pp. 217–232.

Glete, Jan: 'Warfare, Entrepreneurship, and the Fiscal-Military State', in Frank Tallett & David Trim (eds): *European Warfare, 1350–1750* (Cambridge: Cambridge University Press, 2010), pp. 300–321.

Greyerz, Kaspar von: 'Lazarus von Schwendi and late Humanism in Basle', in Kaspar von Greyerz (ed.): *Von Menschen die glauben, schreiben, und wissen* (Göttingen: Verderhoeck & Ruprecht, 2013), pp. 53–67.

Groves, Bryan N.: 'The Multiple Faces of Effective Grand Strategy', *Journal of Strategic Security*, Vol. 3 No. 2 (2010), pp. 1–12.

Grummit, David & Jean-François Lassalmonie: 'Royal Public Finance, 1290–1523', in Christopher Fletcher, Jean-Philippe Genet & John Watts (eds): *Government and Political Life in England and France, c. 1300-c. 1500* (Cambridge: Cambridge University Press, 2015), pp. 116–149.

Guilmartin, John F. Jr: 'The Origins and First Tests of the Military Revolution Abroad', in Clifford Rogers (ed.): *The Military Revolution Debate* (Boulder, CO: Westview Press, 1995), pp. 299–333.

Hale, John R.: 'The Early Development of the Bastion: An Italian Chronology, c. 1450–c. 1534', in J.R. Hale, J.R.L.Highfield & B. Smalley (eds): *Europe in the Late Middle Ages* (London: Faber & Faber, 1965), pp. 466–494.

Hall, Bert & Kelly DeVries: 'Essay Review: The Military Revolution Revisited', *Technology and Culture*, Vol. 31 No. 3 (July 1990), pp. 500–507.

Hammer, Paul: 'The Earl of Essex, Fulke Greville, and the Employment of Scholars', *Studies in Philology*, Vol. 91 No. 2 (Spring 1994), pp. 167–180.

Hammer, Paul: 'Essex and Europe: Evidence from Confidential Instructions by the Earl of Essex, 1595–6', *English Historical Review*, Vol. 111 No. 441 (Apr. 1996), pp. 357–381.

Hammer, Paul: 'Myth-Making: Politics, Propaganda and the Capture of Cadiz in 1596', *The Historical Journal*, Vol. 40 No. 3 (1997), pp. 621–642.

Hammer, Paul: 'New Light on the Cadiz Expedition of 1596', *Historical Research*, Vol. 70 No. 172 (June 1997), pp. 182–202.

Hammer, Paul: 'The Uses of Scholarship: The Secretariat of Robert Devereux, Second Earl of Essex, c. 1585–1601', *English Historical Review*, Vol. 109 No. 430 (Feb. 1994), pp. 26–51.

Hardesty Doig, Kathleen: 'War in the Reform Programme of the Encyclopedie', *War and Society*, Vol. 6, No. 1 (May 1988), pp. 1–9.

Hayes-McCoy, G.A.: 'Strategy and Tactics in Irish Warfare, 1593–1601', *Irish Historical Studies*, Vol. 2 No. 7 (Mar. 1941), pp. 255–279.

Hegyi, Klára: 'Les origines ethniques et la confession des soldats de l'armée turque servant dans les châteaux forts en territoire hongrois', in Marie-Françoise Vajda-Saudraix & Olivier Chaline (eds): *L'Hongrie ottomane, XVIe-XVIIe siècles*, Special Issue of *Histoire, Economie & Société*, Vol. 34 (Sept. 2015), pp. 54–64.

Henry, L.W.: 'The Earl of Essex as Strategist and Military Organizer (1596–7)', *English Historical Review* Vol. 64 No. 268 (July 1953), pp. 363–393.

Hernando Sánchez, Carlos José: 'Non sufficit orbis? Las estrategias de la Monarquía de España', in Luis Robot (volume ed.): *Historia Militar de España* III *Edad Moderna* Part II *Escenario europeo* (Madrid: Ministerio de Defensa, 2013), pp. 29-78.

Heuser, Beatrice: 'Exploring the Jungle of Terminology', *The Origins of Small Wars: From Special Operations to Ideological Insurgencies*, special issue, *Small Wars and Insurgencies*, Vol. 25 No. 4 (Aug. 2014), pp. 741–753.

Heuser, Beatrice: 'Small Wars in the Age of Clausewitz: Watershed between Partisan War and People's War', *Journal of Strategic Studies*, Vol. 33 No. 1 (Feb. 2010), pp. 137–160.

Heuser, Beatrice & Patrick Porter: 'Guerres asymmétriques: l'orientalisme militaire contre la Voie de la guerre en Occident', in Albert Galvany & Romain Graziani (ed.): *La Guerre en perspective: Histoire et culture militaire en Chine* (Paris: Presses universitaires de Vincennes, 2014), pp. 207–218.

Honig, Jan Willem: 'Reappraising Late Medieval Strategy: The Example of the 1415 Agincourt', *War in History*, Vol. 19 No. 2 (2012), pp. 123–151.

nalcik, Halil: 'The Heyday and Decline of the Ottoman Empire', in P.M. Holt, Ann Lambton & Bernard Lewis (eds): *The Cambridge History of Islam*, Vol. 1A (Cambridge: Cambridge University Press, 1970, repr. 1985), pp. 324-353.

Jiménez Moreno, Augustín: 'Las Órdenes Militares y la defensa de la Monarquía hispánica. Un proyecto de organización naval atlántica: el memorial de Ramón Ezquerra (1596)', in Enrique García Hernán & Davide Maffi (eds): *Guerra y Sociedad en la Monarquía Hispánica: Política, Estrategia y Cultura en la Europa Moderna (1500–1700), vol. II: Ejército, economía, sociedad y cultura* (Madrid: Laberinto, 2006), pp. 700–705.

Kagan, Kimberly: 'Redefining Roman Grand Strategy', *The Journal of Military History*, Vol. 70 No. 2 (2006), pp. 333–362.

Kent, H.S.K.: 'The Historical Origins of the Three-Mile Limit', *The American Journal of International Law* Vol. 48 No. 4 (Oct. 1954), pp. 537–553.

Kessel, Eberhard: 'Zur Genesis der modernern Kriegslehre: die Entstehungsgeschichte von Clausewitz' Buch "Vom Kriege"', *Wehrwissenschaftliche Rundschau*, Vol. 3 No. 9 (1953), p. 408.

Kluckhohn, August von: 'Schwendi, Lazarus Freiherr v.', *Allgemeine Deutsche Biographie*, Vol. 33 (1891), pp. 382–401, and Thomas Nicklas: 'Schwendi, Lazarus Freiherr von', *Neue Deutsche Biographie*, Vol. 24 (2010), pp. 65–66.

Laget, Frédérique: 'Guerre sur Mer et Usage stratégique de la Mer, Manche, XIVe-XVe siècle', *Revue du Nord*, Vol. 95 No. 402 (Oct.–Dec. 2013), pp. 947–966.

Lambert, Andrew: 'Sea Power', in George Kassimeris & John Buckley (eds): *The Ashgate Research Companion to Modern Warfare* (Farnham: Ashgate, 2010), pp. 73–88.

Le Saux, Françoise: 'War and Knighthood in Christine de Pizan's *Livre des faits d'armes et de chevallerie*', in Corrine Saunders, Françoise Le Saux & Neil Thomas (eds): *Writing War: Medieval Literary Responses to Warfare* (Woodbridge: D.S. Brewer, 2004), pp. 93–105.

Luis Corral, Fernando: 'Alfonso VIII of Castile's Judicial Process at the Court of Henry II of England: An Effective and Valid Arbitration?', *Nottingham Medieval Studies*, Vol. 50 (2006), pp. 22–42.

Luraghi, Raimondo: 'Montecuccoli's Plans for a General War against the Turks', in Johann Christoph Allmayer-Beck (ed.): *Beiträge zum Internationalen Congress für Militärgeschichte* (Vienna: gedr. durch Österreichische Kommission für Militärgeschichte, 6.–10. Juni 1983), pp. 71–78.

Lynn, John: 'The Trace Italienne and the Growth of Armies: The French Case', *Journal of Military History*, Vol. 55 No. 3 (July 1999), p. 297.

Maffi, Davide: 'El reducto desdeñado. el ejército de Flandes y la monarquía de Carlos II (1665–1700)', in Enrique García Hernán & Davide Maffi (eds): *War and Society in the Spanish Monarchy: Politics, Strategy and Culture in Early Modern Europe, 1500–1700*, Vol. 2 (Valencia: Albaros, 2016), pp. 277–300.

Malone, Edward A.: 'Wingfield, Anthony (*b. c.* 1552, *d.* in or after 1611)', in: *Oxford Dictionary of National Biography* (Oxford: Oxford University Press, 2004) [www.oxforddnb.com. idpproxy.reading.ac.uk/view/article/29734, accessed 17 Nov. 2014].

Mews, Constant J.: 'The Literary Sources of *Le Livre de la Paix*', in Karen Green, Constant J. Mews, Janice Pinder & Tania van Hemelryck (trans. & eds): *The Book of Peace by Christine de Pizan* (University Park, PA: Pennsylvania University Press, 2008), pp. 33–40.

Moneera Laennec, Christine: 'Unladylike Polemics: Christine de Pizan's Strategic Attack and Defense', *Tulsa Studies in Women's Literature*, Vol. 12 No. 1 (Spring 1993), pp. 47–59.

Neill, Donald A.: 'Ancestral Voices: The Influence of the Ancients on the Military Thought of the Seventeenth and Eighteenth Centuries', *Journal of Military History*, Vol. 62 (July 1998), pp. 487–520.

Nolan, John S.: 'The Militarization of the Elizabethan State', *Journal of Military History*, Vol. 58 No. 3 (July 1994), pp. 391–420.

Otte, Thomas: 'Educating Bellona: Carl von Clausewitz and Military Education', in G.C. Kennedy & K. Neilson (eds): *Military Education: Past, Present and Future* (New York: Praeger, 2001), pp. 13–33.

Pagès, Jean: 'Un traité de tactique navale du XVIe Siècle: le Libre III *Della Milizia Marittima* de Cristoforo da Canal', in Hervé Coutau-Bégarie (ed.): *Evolution de la Pensée navale*, Vol. 4 (Paris: Economica, 1994), pp. 37–64.

Parker, Geoffrey: 'Early Modern Europe', in Michael Howard, George J. Andreopoulos & Mark R. Shulman (eds): *The Laws of War: Constraints on Warfare in the Western World* (New Haven: Yale University Press, 1994), pp. 40–58.

Parker, Geoffrey: 'The "Military Revolution", 1560–1660: A Myth?', *The Journal of Modern History*, Vol. 48 (June 1976), pp. 195–214.

Parker, Geoffrey: 'Mutiny and Discontent in the Spanish Army of Flanders, 1572–1607', *Past & Present*, Vol. 58 No. 1 (Feb. 1973), pp. 38–52.

Parrott, David: 'Strategy and Tactics in the Thirty Years' War: The "Military Revolution"', in Clifford Rogers (ed.): *The Military Revolution Debate* (Boulder, CO: Westview Press, 1995), pp. 227–251.

Pepper, Simon: 'Castles and Cannon in the Naples Campaign of 1494–95', in David Abulafia (ed.): *The French Descent into Renaissance Italy, 1494–95: Antecedents and Effects* (Aldershot: Variorum, 1995), pp. 263–294.

Piersdorf, Kurt von: 'Brandt', in Kurt von Piersdorf (ed.): *Soldatisches Führertum*, Vol. 6 (Hamburg: Hanseatische Verlagsanstalt, 1938), p. 575.

Rauscher, Peter: 'Kaisertum und hegemoniales Königtum: Die kaiserliche Reaktion auf die niederländische Politik Philipps II. von Spanien', in Friedrich Edelmayer (ed.):

Hispania-Austria II: La época de Felipe II (1556–1598) (Vienna: Verlag für Geschichte und Politik, 1999), pp. 57–88.

Reinhardt, Volker: 'Goldenes Zeitalter, Zyklus, Aufbruch ins Unbekannte: Geschichtskonzeptionen der italienischen Renaissance', in Hans-Joachim Schmidt (ed.): *Tradition, Innovation, Invention: Fortschrittsverweigerung und Fortschrittsbewusstsein im Mittelalter* (Berlin: Walter de Gruyter, 2005), pp. 51–67.

Richardot, Philippe: 'La datation du *De Re Militari* de Végèce', *Latomus*, Vol. 57 No. 1 (Jan.–Mar. 1998), pp. 136–147.

Richardot, Philippe: 'Y a-t-il une pensée navale dans l'Occident médiéval?', in Hervé Coutau-Bégarie (ed.): *Evolution de la Pensée navale*, Vol. 7 (Paris: Economica, 1999), pp. 13–23.

Rink, Martin: 'The German Wars of Liberation 1807–15: The Restrained Insurgency', in: *The Origins of Small Wars: From Special Operations to Ideological Insurgencies*, special issue, *Small Wars and Insurgencies*, Vol. 25 No. 4 (Aug. 2014), pp. 848–842.

Roberts, Michael: 'The Military Revolution, 1560–1660', in Clifford Rogers (ed.): *The Military Revolution Debate* (Boulder, CO: Westview Press, 1995), pp. 13-35.

Roberts, R. Julian: 'Dee, John (1527–1609)', in *Oxford Dictionary of National Biography* (Oxford: Oxford University Press, 2004; online edn, May 2006) [www.oxforddnb.com.idpproxy.reading.ac.uk/view/article/7418, accessed 7 Dec. 2014].

Rodger, N.A.M.: 'The Law and Language of Private Naval Warfare', *The Mariner's Mirror*, Vol. 100 No. 1 (Feb. 2014), pp. 5–16.

Rodger, N.A.M.: 'Queen Elizabeth and the Myth of Sea-Power in English History', *Transactions of the Royal Historical Society*, 6th series, Vol. 14 (2004), pp. 153–174.

Rogers, Clifford: 'The Anglo-French Peace Negotiations of 1354–1360 Reconsidered', in J.S. Bothwell (ed.): *The Age of Edward III* (York: York Medieval Press, 2001), pp. 193–212.

Rogers, Clifford: 'The Military Revolutions of the Hundred Years' War', in Clifford Rogers (ed.): *The Military Revolution Debate* (Boulder, CO: Westview Press, 1995), pp. 55-93.

Rogers, Clifford: 'The Vegetian "Science of Warfare" in the Middle Ages', *Journal of Medieval Military History*, Vol. 1 (2002), pp. 1–19.

Rothenberg, Gunther: 'Maurice of Nassau, Gustavus Adolphus, Raimondo Montecuccoli, and the 'Military Revolution' of the Seventeenth Century', in Peter Paret, Gordon A. Craig & Felix Gilbert (eds): *Makers of Modern Strategy: From Machiavelli to the Nuclear Age* (Princeton, NJ: Princeton University Press, 1986), pp. 56–63.

Rowlands, Guy: 'Louis XIV, Vittorio Amedeo II and French Military Failure in Italy, 1689–96', *The English Historical Review*, Vol. 115 No. 462 (June 2000), pp. 534–569.

Rupp, Daniel A.: 'Vom Gegner lernen? Zur Taktik französischer Heere in den Schlachten von Kortrijk, Arques und am Pevelenberg', *Militärgeschichtliche Zeitschrift*, Vol. 65 No. 1 (2006), pp. 89–112.

Sander, Erich: 'Der Verfall der römischen Belagerungskunst', *Historische Zeitschrift*, Vol. 149 (1934), pp. 457–476.

Scheipers, Sibylle: '"The Most Beautiful of Wars": Carl von Clausewitz and Small Wars', *European Journal of International Security*, Vol. 2 No. 1 (Feb. 2017), pp. 47-63.

Schzl. [sic]: 'Montecuccoli, Raimund Fürst von', in: *Allgemeine Deutsche Biographie*, Vol. 22 (Leipzig : Duncker & Humblot, 1885), pp. 183–189.

Sutherland, N.M.: 'The Origins of the Thirty Years' War and the Structure of European Politics', *The English Historical Review*, Vol. 107, No. 424 (July 1992), pp. 587–625.

Szkilnik, Michelle: 'Le Jouvencel oule Roman des Faits d'Armes et de la Chevalerie', in Dominique Demartini, Claire Le Ninan, Anne Paupert & Michelle Szkilnik (eds): *Une femme et la guerre à la fin du Moyen Âge: Le livre des faits d'armes et de chevalerie de Christine de Pizan* (Paris: Honoré Champion, 2016), pp. 165–178.

Taylor, Andrew: '"Dame Christine" et la Chevalerie savante en Angleterre', in Dominique Demartini, Claire Le Ninan, Anne Paupert & Michelle Szkilnik (eds): *Une femme et la guerre à la fin du Moyen Âge: Le livre des faits d'armes et de chevalerie de Christine de Pizan* (Paris: Honoré Champion, 2016), pp. 179–190.

Teague, Frances: 'Christine de Pizan's *Book of War*', in Glenda McLeod (ed.): *The Reception of Christine de Pizan from the fifteenth through the Nineteenth Centuries* (Lewiston: Edwin Mellen Press, 1991), p. 25f.

Thorau, Peter: 'Panzerreiter im Pfeilhagel?', *Militärgeschichtliche Zeitschrift*, Vol. 65 No. 1 (2006), pp. 63–78.

Tipton, Alzada: '"Lively Patterns . . . for Affayres of State": Sir John Hayward's *The Life and Reigne of King Henrie IIII* and the Earl of Essex', *Sixteenth Century Journal*, Vol. 33 No. 3 (Autumn 2002), pp. 769–794.

Traina, Giusto: 'La guerre mondiale des Romains', *L'Histoire*, No. 405 (Nov. 2014), pp. 76–81.

Webb, Henry: 'Dr. Matthew Sutcliffe', *Philological Quarterly*, Vol. 23 (1944), p. 86f.

Willard, Charity Cannon: 'Christine de Pizan on the Art of Warfare', in M. Desmond (ed.): *Christine de Pizan an the Categories of Difference* (Minneapolis: University of Minnesota Press, 1998), pp. 3–15.

Williams, Philip: 'The Strategy of Galley Warfare in the Mediterranean (1560–1630)', in Enrique García Hernán & Davide Maffi (eds): *Guerra y Sociedad en la Monarquía Hispánica: Política, Estrategia y Cultura en la Europa Moderna (1500–1700), vol. I: Política, estrategia, organization y guerre en el mar* (Madrid: Ediciones del Laberinto, 2006), pp. 891–920.

Wilson, Peter: 'Habsburg Imperial Strategy during the Thirty Years War', in Enrique García Hernán & Davide Maffi (eds): *Guerra y Sociedad en la Monarquía Hispánica: Política, Estrategia y Cultura en la Europa Moderna (1500–1700)* (Madrid: Ediciones del Laberinto, 2006), Vol. 1, pp. 245–267.

Younger, Neil: 'The Practice and Politics of Troop Raising', *English Historical Review*, Vol. 127 No. 526 (2012) pp. 566–591.

Ziegler, Theobald: 'Sturm, Johann', in: *Allgemeine Deutsche Biographie*, Vol. 37 (Leipzig: Duncker & Humblot, 1894), pp. 21–38.

INDEX OF PERSONAL NAMES

Abel, Jonathan 182
Abrey, Friar Pedro de 108
Adams, Simon 55
Agrippa, Menenius 38
Alava y Viamont, Diego de 60
Alba, Duke of 28, 60, 98, 143
Alberti, Leon Battista 51
Alexander VI, Pope 12, 126
Alexander VII, Pope 152
Alfonso VIII, King of Castile 38
Alfred, King of Wessex 129
Angevins 118, 121, 191
Anne of Austria, consort of Philip II of
    Spain 121
Antonio, Dom, Pretender to the Portuguese
    Throne 19, 76, 82
Apostles, the 56
Aristotle 33
Armenians 140
Arne, Thomas 122, 129
Artois, Robert d' 10
Aryans 181
Athenians 181
August, Prince of Prussia 186
Austrian(s) 151f; Habsburgs 13, 17, 22, 26,
    71, 136, 143, 151f, 166

Bacon, Anthony 93, 123
Bacon, Sir Francis 93f, 123, 126
Barker, Christopher 98
Barret, Robert 55
Basta, Giorgio 151
Bath, William Bourchier, Earl of 94

Bavarian(s) 140
Bayard, Chevalier de 146
Berenhorst, Georg Heinrich von 58, 196f
Bigi, Anna 150
Black, Jeremy 54
Böcklin von Böcklinsau, Anna, wife of
    Lazarus von Schwendi 144
Böcklin von Böcklinsau, Wilhelm 144
Boethius 33
Boguslawski, Anton Andreas von 187
Bonaparte, Jerome King of Westphalia 188
Boroughs, John 120, 127
Bouvet, Honoré 33, 35, 40, 43
Brandt, Heinrich von 190f
Bridge, Sir Cyprian 130
Briene, Loménie de 176
Brienne, Count 176
Brodie, Bernard 43
Bueil, Jean V de 34, 44, 69
Bülow, Dietrich Heinrich Freiherr (Baron)
    von 193–6
Burgundy, Duchess of 121
Bynkershoek, Cornelius van 129

Caesar, Julius 60–2, 122
Callois, Roger 168
Callwell, Charles 131
Canal, Cristoforo Da 69f
Carlos II, King of Spain 25
Carnot, Lazare 168, 176, 187
Castel, Etienne de 32
Castel, Jean 34
Castex, Raoul 69f

Caxton, William 44, 57
Cecil, Sir Robert 83, 107, 112
Cecil, William Lord Burghley 72f, 107
Celts 181
Cénat, Jean-Philippe 26
Chamlay, Jules-Louis Bolé de 22, 24, 26
Charlemagne, Emperor 4, 13, 17, 23
Charles, Count of Valois, son of Philip III of
 France 6
Charles, Duke of Lorraine 161
Charles I (Stuart), King of England and
 Scotland 62, 112, 126, 128
Charles II (Stuart), King of England and
 Scotland 25, 129
Charles IV, Holy Roman Emperor 122
Charles V, Holy Roman Emperor 4, 6, 14,
 140–3
Charles V (Valois), King of France 6, 11,
 32–7, 42
Charles VI (Valois), King of France 6, 32–6
Charles VII (Valois), King of France 6, 11, 174
Charles VIII (Valois), King of France 51, 58f
Charles IX (Valois), King of France 18
Charles the Bold, Duke of Burgundy 50
Chartres, Bernard of 48
Chastelet Jr, Paul Hay du 23, 67n
Chastenet, Jacques François de 61, 186
Chaves, Alonso de 69
Christina, Queen of Sweden 128, 152
Cicero 33, 43, 100, 154, 163n, 165n
Clausewitz, Carl von 1, 41, 62, 96, 171, 176,
 Chapter 9
Colbert, Jean Baptiste 22, 24
Colin, Jean 167
Columb, Philip Howard Vice Admiral 85, 130
Columbus, Christopher 12
Condé, Prince of 13, 72
Contamine, Philippe 8
Corbett, Sir Julian 70, 75, 82, 85–7, 131f
Cortés, Martin 69
Corvey, Jean-Frédéric Auguste Le Mière
 de 191
Coudray, Charles Tronson du 62
Crecentio Bartolommeo (Barotolmeo
 Crescenzio) 69
Creveld, Martin van 54
Crissé, Count Lancelot Turpin de 186, 199

Danton, Georges 168
Daudet, Léon 180
Decker, Colonel Carl von 199
Dee, Dr John 124–6, 128
D'Este, Cardinal Alexander 151
D'Este, Cesare, Duke of Módena 150f

Devereux, Robert 72, 92
Diderot, Count de Tressan 60
Dietrichstein, Margarete von 152
Digges, Thomas 59f
Doig, Kathleen Hardesty 167
Douhet, Giulio 107
Drake, Sir Francis 14, 19, 75–85, 95, 104,
 107f, 126
Dudley, Robet Earl of Leicester 92–4, 98
Dudley, Sir Henry 121
Due Repulse, HMS 103
Dumas, General Matthieu 186, 203n
Dyer, Sir Edward 124

Edgar, Anglo-Saxon King 118
Edward (the Confessor), King of England 9
Edward I, King of England 5, 122
Edward II, King of England 3, 119, 122
Edward III, King of England 3–12, 24–8, 34,
 37, 102, 118f
Egmont, Count 143
Elizabeth I, Queen of England 12–20,
 Chapter 4, Chapter 5, 122–6
Emmerich, Andreas 188
Eric III, King of Norway 120
Eric VII, King of Denmark 120
Eric XIII, King of Sweden 120
Essex, Earl of 72f, 76, 78f, 83f, Chapter 5,
 123–6, 132, 134
Estrades, Count d' 22, 24f
Eugene, Prince of Savoy 26, 161
Euler, Leonard 194
Ewald, Johann von 188

Fabius, Quintus Fabius Maximus Verrucosus
 (Cunctator) 145, 154
Farnese, Alexander Duke of Parma 80
Ferdinand, King of Aragon 51, 70
Ferdinand I, Holy Roman Emperor 4, 14,
 143, 160
Feuquières, Marquis de 62, 186
Fichte, Johann Gottlieb 195, 197f
Fitz, Francisco García 11
Fitzgeralds, of Desmond 75
Foerster, Stig 180f
Folard, Jean de 170, 174
Forhan, Kate 34, 38, 42
Fourquevaux, Raymond de Beccarie de
 Pavie Baron de 67n 145f
Francis, Duke of Guise 70
Frederick II (the Great), King of Prussia 60,
 62, 168–70, 174, 177, 180, 189, 197, 203n
Frederick William I, King of Prussia 28
Frederick William III, King of Prussia 189, 197

Frobisher, Sir Martin 76
Frontinus 33
Frost, Robert 54
Fulbecke, William 191
Fuller, J.F.C 194
Fulton, William 120–2, 129f

Gat, Azar 136
Ghengis Khan 2
Gilbert, Sir Humphrey 71
Giles of Rome 33
Gillingham, John 8
Giraldi, Lilio Gregorio 69
Gneisenau, August Neidhardt Count 187,
    189–90, 193
Godefroi, Count d'Estrades 22
Great Michael, RSN 52
Gregory XIII, Pope 19, 72
Grenier, Jacques Raymond Viscount de
    69f, 85
Grotius, Hugo 117, 122, 126f, 130, 154
Grynaeus, Simon 141
Guibert, Jacques Antoine Hippolyte Comte
    de 43, 60, 62, Chapter 8, 187, 190, 196f
Gustavus II Adolphus, King of Sweden 52,
    58, 174f
Guyenne, Louis de 33, 36

Habsburgs 5–26, 50, 62, 70–3, 112, 121,
    126, 136–60, 176, 199
Hale, John 52–4
Hall, Bert 57
Hakluyt, Richard 82
Hammer, Paul 93, 103, 110, 193
Hanoverians 126–30
Hawkins, Sir John 76, 78, 80, 95, 104
Hector, Prince of Troy 37
Hegel, Georg Wilhelm Friedrich 198
Henri, Duc de Rohan 60, 151
Henri II (Valois) King of France 120
Henri III (Valois), King of France 120
Henri IV (Bourbon), King of France, King
    of Navarre 13f, 16f, 20, 72f, 76, 78, 95,
    99, 102, 107
Henry, King of Navarre *see* Henri IV King
    of France
Henry I, King of England 122
Henry II, King of England 5, 38
Henry IV (Bolingbroke), King of England
    4, 6, 121
Henry V, King of England 6, 11, 118, 120
Henry VI, King of England 6, 33, 44, 121
Henry VII (Tudor), King of England 44,
    70, 99

Henry VIII (Tudor), King of England 12,
    71, 73, 99, 102
Herberg-Rothe, Andreas 198
Hernán, Enrique García 71
Herodotus 61, 165n
Holofernes (Biblical) 35
Homer 61
Honig, Jan Willem 8
Howard, Charles Lord of Effingham 78,
    103, 107, 109–11
Howard, Lord Thomas 76, 78
Howard, Lord William 121
Howard, Michael 43
Huguenot(s) 72, 181
Hussites 52
Huyrluyt, Commodore Jacob 129
Hydra 40

Isabella, Queen of Castile 51
Isabella Clara Eugenia, Infanta of Spain 13, 20
Isabeau of Bavaria, consort of Charles VI of
    France 33

Jagellonian(s) 143
James I, King of Scotland a.k.a James VI,
    King of England and Ireland 20, 22, 85,
    112, 122, 126f
James VII, King of England and Ireland 129
Jesus (Biblical) 39, 56
Joan of Arc 6, 39, 66n
John, Don of Austria 17, 19
John, King of England 5, 9, 121
John (the Fearless), Duke of Burgundy 35f
John I (the Magnificent), Duke of Berry 33
John II (the Good), King of France 6, 39
John of Salisbury 38, 42
Jomini, Antoine Baron de 62, 192–5, 206n
Juan, Don of Austria, illegitimate son of
    Emperor Charles V 71
Judith (Biblical) 35

Kagan, Kimberly 2
Kant, Immanuel 169, 186, 198
Kiesewetter, Johann Gottfried 186
Klein, Jean 177
Knights of Malta 17, 149

Lacey, Robert 100, 106
Lancastrians 4, 6, 9
Lazare de Baïf, Antoine de Conflans 69
Legnano, Giovanni da 191
Lemkin, Raphael 181
Leng, Rainer 51
Leo VI (the Wise), Byzantine Emperor 58, 69

Leopold I, Holy Roman Emperor 153, 156
Lessing, Ephraim Gotthold 198
Lilienstern, August Rühle von 185, 191–5, 198f
Lindenau, Karl Friedrich von 198
Lipsius, Justus 58, 151, 155
Lloyd, Henry Humphrey Evans 62, 170
Londoño, Sancho de 60, 98
Losau, Constantin von 199
Louis, Duke of Orleans 35
Louis (Lajos) II, King of Hungary 148
Louis IX, King of France (Saint) 38
Louis XIII, King of France 61
Louis XIV, King of France 3–5, 11, 17,
    22–8, 60–2, 79n 129, 152, 174, 177
Louis of Guyenne, Dauphin of France 33
Louvois, Marquis of 22
Ludendorrff, Erich von 180–2
Luraghi, Raimondo 161
Lynn, John 54

Machiavelli, Niccolò 40–3, 56–8, 100, 141,
    144, 174f, 186, 195, 197–9
Mahan, Alfred Thayer 85–7, 131f
Manuel I, King of Portugal 19
Margaret, of Parma 142
Margaret I, Queen of Denmark 120
Margaret of Anjou, consort of Henry VI of
    England 44
Marmont, Auguste de 62
Mary (Biblical) 56, 109
Mary I Tudor, Queen of England 14f, 70f, 120f
Mary II, Queen of England and Scotland 129
Mary Stuart, Queen of Scots 13, 19f, 70,
    72, 123
Maurice, Emperor Byzantine Empire 58
Maximillian II, Holy Roman Emperor 14,
    143f, 149
Mazarin, Cardinal Jules Raymond 22f
Medici, Viginia de' 150
Mehmet II Fatih (the Conqueror), Sultan
    59, 141
Mehmet IV Avcı (the Hunter), Sultan 152
Mehmet Köprülü Paşa 152
Melians 181
Melzi, Francesco Ludovico 151
Mendelssohn, Moses 198
Mendoza, Don Bernardino de 21, 67n,
    69–71, 123, 126
Minerva, Goddess 33
Moltke (the elder), Helmuth von 195
Montecuccoli, Anna Aloisia 152
Montecuccoli, Carlotta Polizena 152
Montecuccoli, Ernestina 152
Montecuccoli, Ernesto 151

Montecuccoli, Leopold Philip 152
Montecuccoli, Massimiliano 151
Montecuccoli, Raimondo 23, 61f,
    Chapter 7, 193
Montesquieu, Charles-Louis de Secondat,
    Baron de La Brède et de 169, 171, 173,
    181, 187
Mountgomerie, John 73
Müller, Johannes 198

Naegler, Joerg 180f
Napoleon I, Emperor of France 1, 17, 27,
    62, 98, 146, 167f, 173, 176, 180, 182, 187,
    189–96; Warfare 168; Wars 17, 182
Nassau, Family of 57f, 175
Nassau, Maurice of 52, 174
Nassau-Siegen, Count John of 57f
Neill, Donald 49, 63
Nemours, Gaston de Foix Duke of 146
Newton, Sir Isaac 194
Nolan, John 99
Normans 191
Norris, Sir John 76
Noue, Seigneur de la 151

Olivares, Count-Duke 12
Oliveira, Fernando 69f
Oresme Nicolas d' 33
Othéa, Goddess 37
Ottomans 13, 17f, 27, 51f, 71, Chapter 7;
    Empire 17, 19, 22, Chapter 7; Navy 15, 17
Ouranos, Nikephoros 69
Ovid 33

Pantera, Pantero 69
Paret, Peter 192, 197f
Parker, Geoffrey 15f, 22, 51–4, 58, 63
Parrot, David 54f
Pérez, Antonio 73
Perrault, Charles 60
Pestalozzi, Heinrich 197
Philip II, King of France 9
Philip II, King of Spain 3f, 11–23, 28, 33,
    Chapter 4, 102, 107–9, 111, 121, 123f, 142f
Philip III, King of France 34
Philip III, King of Spain 22f
Philip IV, King of Spain 14, 21, 23f
Philip VI, King of France 6
Philomenes 61
Phoenicians 126
Phull, General Karl Ludwig 198
Pius V, Pope 17, 71
Pizan, Christine de 3–6, 11, Chapter 2, 57,
    69, 195

Pizzano, Tomaso de 32
Plantagenets 6, 9, 11, 23, 34, 49, 66, 118, 128
Plato 33, 40, 46n, 124, 141
Plutarch 61, 97
Poirier, Lucien 168, 175
Polybius 61, 63, 165n
Pufendorf, Samuel 191
Puységur, Marquis de 61f, 186

Quadra, Alvaro de 18, 21

Rákóczi, Francis I 151
Rákóczi, George I 151
Rákóczi Family 151, 153, 160
Ralegh, Sir Walter 75–85, 107–10, 126f
Ramatuelle, Audibert 85
Raynal, Abbé (pseudonym for Guibert) 178
Reynolds, Susan 172
Richard I (the Lionheart), King of England
    51, 118, 133n
Richard II, King of England 4, 6, 121
Richard III, King of England 4
Richelieu, Cardinal 23f
Richmond, Herbert 132
Robert Curthose, Duke of Normandy 4
Roberts, Michael 52f, 63
Robespierre, Maximilien 168
Rodger, N.A.M. 13, 122, 130
Rogers, Clifford 8f, 11, 50, 54
Rousseau, Jean-Jacques 170
Rubens, Peter Paul 14, 30n

Saint-Germain, Count 176
Saint-Just, Louis Antoine de 176
Sancho VI, King of Navarre 38
Santa Cruz de Marcenado, Marquis of 62,
    146, 157, 186, 195, 199
Saracens 42
Sassoferrato, Bartolus da 122
Saux, Françoise Le 33, 43
Saxe, Maurice de 62, 170, 193
Saxons 140; Anglo 5, 9, 118; Translyvanian 160
Scharnhorst, General Gerhard von 186, 188,
    191–4
Scheipers, Sibylle 198
Schill, Ferdinand von 189
Schlegel, August 197
Schlegel, Friedrich 197
Schlieffen, Count 63
Schwendi, Lazarus von 1f, 14, 28, Chapter 7
Schwendi, Rutland von Hohenlandsberg 141
Scipio Africanus 58
Scots 5, 10, 13, 19, 49f, 70–2, 99, 128
Scrope, Stephen 44

Sebastian, Dom, Portuguese Pretender 76
Sebastian I, King of Portugal 126
Séché, Alphonse 180
Ségur, Marshal de 176
Seignelay, Marquis of 22
Selden, John 118, 122, 128
Seneca 33, 40, 141
Shaftesbury, third Earl of 198
Sidonia, Duke of Medina 108, 120
Sigismund, King of Bohemia 52
Smith, Adam 199
Smith, John 112
Smythe, Sir John 59–60, 63
Sobiecki, Sebastian 122
Staël, Germaine de 187, 197
Stuarts 11, 100, 112, 126–30
Sturm, Johann 141
Suárez, Francisco 191
Suetonius 171
Süleyman I, (the Magnificent) Sultan 160
Sulzer, Johann George 198
Sun Tsu 145, 193
Süssmilch, Captain von 188
Sutcliffe, John 92
Sutcliffe, Mathew 79, 83f, 86, Chapter 5,
    112, 123f, 126, 161
Swiss 50, 53, 57, 72, 175, 197
Szapolyai, János 160

Tacitus 62, 171
Talbot, John 44
Tallet, Frank 54, 65
Teutonic Knights 148f
Thomson, James 129
Thucydides 11, 61f, 117, 122–4, 141, 165n, 186
Till, Geoffrey 132
Toledo, Don García de 69, 123
Traverse, Baron de 61
Tudors 11, 19f, 71, 100, 125
Turenne, Viscount 61, 153
Turner, Sir James 50
Tyrone, Earl of 21, 78

Ubaldis, Baldus de 127

Vadés, Jaime 14
Valentini, Georg Wilhelm von 188
Valerius Maximus 33
Valois 10, 13, 18, 34f
Vauban, Sébastien Le Prestre de 22, 24, 26,
    63, 65n, 169
Vegetius 33, 42f, 56–8, 61–3, 69, 145, 154,
    165n, 186
Verbruggen, Jan Frans 57

Vere, Sir Francis 108
Vergil (Virgil) 141
Vogelsberger, Sebastian 142
Voltaire 167, 169

Wallenstein, Prince of Friedland 158
Warney, General de 178
Washington, George 167
Wellington, Duke of 189
Welwod, William 127
Wencken, Apollonia 141
Wilkinson, Henry Spenser 130
William I (the Conqueror), King of
    England 3, 9
William II (Rufus), King of England 4
William III, King of England and Scotland,
    Prince of Orange 14, 24f, 72, 143f
William Louis, Count of Nassau 58

Wingfield, Antony Sir 81f, 86, 89n, 123
Witt, Johan de 24f
Worcester, William 44
Wright, Robert 93

Xenophon 61f 165n

Young, Anthony 129

Zanthier, Friedrich Wilhelm von 199
Zapolya, John 143
Zerotin, Charles of 144
Zimmern, Eleonore von, wife of Lazarus
    von Schwendi 144
Zimmern, Froben Christoph von 144
Zizka, Jan 52
Zuñinga, Don Baltasar de 12
Zrínyi, Miklós 151

INDEX OF PLACE NAMES AND STATES

Académie Française 60
Afghanistan 100
Africa 17, 21, 49, 51, 104
Agincourt, Battle of (1415) 6, 34, 49
Algarve 105
Alps 26, 111, 136, 152
Alsace 23, 143f, 179; Alsations 191
Altenburg 153
America(s) 12, 22, 64, 74, 78, 104, 106, 109;
     North 26f, 111, 125f, 128, 131, 188f
Andalucía 105
Antilles 27
Apennines 150
Arabia 50f, 66n, 138
Aragon 21, 70, 73
Artois 23
Asia 12, 21
Atlantic, Ocean 15, 26, 28, 72f, 77f, 85, 98,
     103f, 109, 124, 128
Atlantis 124
Auerstedt, Battle of (1806) 196
Augsburg 137, 142; Diet of (1555) 142;
     Edict of (1555) 14; League of 24
Austria 71, 121, 136, 152, 164n, 188
Azores 19, 74, 76f, 79, 104, 109, 111

Balkans 22, 140
Baltic, the 121, 128; Sea 128, 189; Wars 54
Bannockburn, Battle of (1314) 50
Basque, country 26
Bastille, Storming of the (1789) 176
Bavaria 33, 188
Belgrade 161

Berlin 187, 198
Berne 44
Biskay, Bay of 105
Bohemia 124, 151
Bologna 32, 37; University of 122
Bonn 153
Brandeis 151
Breisach 142
Breisgau 142, 144
Breitenfeld, Battle of (1631) 151
Brescia 146
Brétigny, Treaty of (1360) 6, 8
Brill (Brielle) 16, 74, 98
Britain 25–7, 85, 87, 117, 124, 129f, 169,
     188; British Empire 125, 128; British
     Isles 16, 98, 111, 122, 127, 129; (British)
     Royal Navy 125; British Strategies 76
Britain, Great 11, 22–7, 49, 84, 100, 111,
     117f, 122, 127–30
Brittany 7, 20, 26, 73–6, 124
Buda 143, 152
Budapest 161
Burg 185
Burgundy 7, 12, 111
Byzantine Empire 5, 58, 69, 140, 147

Cádiz 19, 74f, 78, 83f, Chapter 5, 127
Calais 7, 20, 71, 73f, 78, 98, 107, 111, 120,
     133n
Cambridge University, Trinity College 81,
     92–4, 117, 123f
Canada 52, 129f
Canaries 74, 79, 83

Cape Roca 83
Cape Verde 75
Caribbean 27, 75, 78
Carpathian, mountains 152
Carthage 126, 181
Caschau 143
Caspian, Sea 138
Castelnuovo 59
Castile 12, 18, 21, 38, 70, 73
Castillon, Battle of (1453) 6
Castro, Duchy of 151
Catalonia 23, 26
Cevennes 23
Channel, English 7–11, 16, 18, 20, 34, 44, 73–80, 107, 118, 122, 128
Chelsea College 112
China 49f, 51
Collège des Quatre Nations 23
Constantinople (Konstantinyya) 51, 59, 138, 140, 149, 152, 161
Cornwall 21, 78, 95
Corsica 176
Coruña, La (the Groyne) 74f, 84, 103, 111
Courtrai 50, 66n
Crécy, Battle of (1346) 39, 49
Crimea 138

Damme, Battle of (1213) 9
Danube, river 49, 152, 160
Dark Ages 181
Denmark 81, 120, 124, 128, 139
Devonshire 94, 103
Dover, Straits of (Narrow Sea) 122
Drava, river 160
Dublin 19, 71
Dutch *see* Netherlands
Dutch Insurgency/Uprising 13–27, 71–6, 143
Dutch West India Company 25

Ecole Militaire 167
Edirne (Adrianople) 138
England 3–28, 33–42, 44, 50, 58–63, Chapter 4, Chapter 5, 118–29, 139, 180, 190
Erdöd, Battle of (1568) 143
Exeter 94

Faro 109
Ferrara 150
Ferrol 78, 84, 103, 111
Flanders 7, 10, 18, 26, 49, 51, 76, 81, 94, 102, 118, 179
Florence 39, 58
Flushing (Vlissingen) 16, 74, 98

France 3–28, 32–42, 51–63, 65n, 70–81, 87, 94f, 98–102, 107, 119–22, 129f, 139, 141f, 152, 161, 169–81, 186f, 193; Estates-General 177; French Convention 176; French Revolution 1, 3, 17, 55f, 69, 87, 167f, 173, 175–8, 182, 187–91; Instut de 23
Friesland 124

Gaillard, Château 51
Galicia (region of Spain) 105
Gascony 7, 179
Genoa 17, 77, 111
Germany 52, 147, 151f
Gibraltar 26, 98, 105, 111
Golden Spurs, Battle of (1302) 50
Granada 18, 51, 59
Grandson, Battle of (1476) 50
Gravelines, Battle of (1558) 143
Graz 152
Great Britain *see* Britain
Greece 49, 61f
Guadalquivir, river 75

Hainault 23
Halifax, Yorkshire 92
Hofburg, Imperial Palace 143
Hohenlandsberg 143
Holland 24, 83, 124
Holy Roman Empire 3–28, 57, 128, 136–44, 161; Imperial Diet 23, 142, 149; War Council 149, 152f, 156, 160
Hudson Bay 27
Hungary 12, 138–60

Iberia 5, 13, 20, 72, 74, 76, 78f, 81, 103f, 106–11
Iceland 129
India 52
Iraq 100
Ireland 19, 21f, 31n, 71–9, 84, 98, 100, 102f, 109, 122, 124f, 128f; Irish Channel 75; Irish Navy 75; Irish Resistance 21, 79, 111
Italy 3, 19, 24, 26, 32f, 39, 59, 69f, 87, 94, 102, 107, 120, 127, 136, 146, 149, 151f, 186, 198; City States 8, 17

Jamestown 111
Jena, Battle of (1806) 196
Jericho 52
Judaea 49

Kientzheim 144
King James' College 112
Kinsale, Battle of (1601) 21, 79

Kirchhofen 144
Königsberg 169
Konstantinyya *see* Constantinople
Konzer Bridge 153
Kövar, Battle of (1568) 143
Kutná Hora 52

Leiden, Leyden 127, 172
Lepanto, Battle of (1571) 17, 71, 123, 149
Lisbon 73–88, 94, 100–11
Lithuania 139f
London 7, 21, 25, 39, 72, 77, 94, 111, 123, 172
Lorraine 27, 161, 191
Louvre 23
Low Countries *see* Netherlands
Lützen, Battle of (1632) 151

Magdeburg 142, 181, 185
Main, river 153
Malta 149
Marseillais 69, 105
Mediterranean 7, 9, 12, 14–15, 17f, 26, 49, 52, 120, 123, 126, 138, 149, 179
Melnik 151
Melos 181
Memmingen 141
Metz, Siege of (1552) 142
Milan 14, 16, 26, 34, 111
Minden, Battle of (1759) 169
Mittelbiberach 141
Módena 151
Mohács, Battle of (1526) 148
Monte San Giovanni 59
Montreuil-sur-Mer 119
Moravia 144, 151f
Morgarten, Battle of (1315) 50
Morocco 109, 139
Moscow 149
Moushole 21
Muncas, Battle of (1568) 143
Münster Treaty of (1648) 23
Murten, Battle of (1476) 50

Nagykanizsa 148
Nancy, Battle of (1477) 50
Naples 58f
Netherlands 4, 9, 14–26, 26, 50, 52, 57, 59f, 66n, 70f, 74, 76, 78, 80f, 87, 92, 94, 98, 102–11, 117, 119–21, 129, 142f, 151, 153, 189
Neuchâtel 177
New England 112
Newfoundland 27
Newlyn 21

New World 12, 14, 99
Nördlingen, Battle of (1635) 151
Normandy 7, 20, 51, 74, 76, 118, 124
North Sea 124, 128f
Norway 124, 128f
Nova Scotia 27, 129

Osnabrück Treaty of (1648) 23
Oxford University 93

Panama 78, 95, 107
Paris 7, 32, 37, 167, 169, 176; Declaration on Maritime Law (1856) 86
Penzance 21
Persia 137
Picardy 124
Pizzano 32, 44n
Plymouth 74, 94, 108, 121
Poland 4, 22, 139, 149, 151, 190
Portsmouth 73
Portugal 12, 14f, 19, 69, 73f, 76, 81, 94, 104f, 126, 188
Prague 124, 136, 143f, 162n
Prussia 17, 28, 60, 149, 168f, 176f, 186; General War School (Allgemeine Kriegsakademie) 186–8, 190–2, 194f
Pyrenees 18, 73, 111; Peace of (1659) 23

Raab (Györ) 148, 152; Liberation of 161; River 152, 160; Siege of 138
Ratisbon 142
Rhine, river 49, 144, 153
Roanoke, colony 111
Rome 11, 17, 33, 61–2, 77, 126, 171f; Roman Empire 3, 11, 24, 49, 57, 122, 136, 189; Roman Empire, East (*see* Byzantine Empire); Roman Empire, West 5, 24
Rossbach, Battle of (1757) 169
Roussillon 23
Rumania 140
Russia 22, 120

St. Andrews, University of 127
St. Gotthardt, Battle of (1664) 152
St. James, Court of (London) 21, 70f
St. Martin, Battle of (1568) 143
St. Quentin, Battle of (1557) 70, 143
St. Vincent (South Cape) 83
San Lucar 83
Saragossa, Treaty of (1496) 12
Savoy 17, 24–7
Schmalkaldic League 142
Scotland 6, 8, 11, 24f, 62, 76, 85, 124–8, 139
Seine, river 23

Seville 75, 81, 104
Siam, King of 27
Sicily 14, 21, 123
Silesia 151
Sluys, Battle of (1340) 118
Sorbonne University (Paris) 41
Southsea Castle 73
Spain 3–28, 51, 59, Chapter 4, 92–104,
    106–12, 120f, 123–6, 139, 142f, 149, 153,
    186, 188f, 190f
Stettin (Szczecin) 151, 157
Stralsund 189
Strasbourg 141f
Styria 152
Sublime Porte (Constantinople) 138, 149
Swabia 141
Sweden 13, 22, 52, 58, 120, 128, 139, 152, 174
Switzerland 49, 177, 187, 197
Szatmár, Battle of (1568) 143
Szerencs 143

Tagus, river 104
Tatar 153
Tauber, river 153
Taunton, Somerset 94
Tirol 188f

Tokaj 143
Tordesillas, Treaty of (1494) 12, 77
Toulon 26
Transylvania 138, 140, 143, 149, 153, 160
Troyes, Treaty of (1430) 6

Ukraine 138
United Provinces 22, 129
Utrecht: Peace of (1813) 27; Treaty of
    (1713) 129

Vasvár, Peace of 152
Vendée 189, 191
Venetia 32, 29, 42, 70
Venice 4, 17, 32, 39, 98
Virginia 112, 126; Company 111

Wales 6, 129
Washington, D.C. 149
Weimar 151
West Indies 21, 72, 74, 76, 79f, 83, 104
Westminster, Peace Treaty of (1674) 129
Westphalia, Treaties of (1648) 128, 137
Worcester 118

Zaragoza (Saragossa) 73

INDEX OF WARS AND STRATEGIC CONCEPTS

absolute war 176
aggression 19, 145, 187
alliances (alliance warfare) 1, 5, 8, 10, 24–8, 70, 72, 76, 101f, 107, 156
American War of Independence (1775–1783) 188f
Anglo-Dutch Wars 25, 129
Anglo-Spanish War (1585–1604) 17, 20, 22, Chapter 4, 106
annihilation, strategy of 176, 182
appeasement 147, 160f
Armada (Spanish navy) 10, 20f, 31, 75, 78, 99, 104, 109, 125; *Gran Armada* (1588) 20
Armagnacs-Bourguignon Civil War (1407–1435) 4
attack and capture 95

Barbicans Strategy 8
blockade 9, 74, 76, 79–81, 86
bricks-and-mortar defence 73
bridge of gold (offering the enemy a ~ to retreat) 97

Cabinet War 187, 199
Cabocherie Uprisings (1413) 34
camino español 16, 111
Camisard Uprising (1702–1715) 23
cavalry interregnum 49
centre of gravity 192
chance (luck, fortune) 40, 56, 96, 145, 148, 154
chasse gardée 126
chequebook diplomacy 2, 141
chevauchee 8f, 26, 28

citizen-soldier 167, 172, 175, 178, 187, 197
civil war 3–6, 13, 17, 23, 33–6, 137, 157, 188, 205n
Cold War 13, 19, 149
command of the sea 85–7, 106f, Chapter 6; rule the ocean/waves 84, 106
commerce raiding 74, 84, 86, 106, 110, 127
counterinsurgency 16, 138, 143, 157–60, 189
crusades 42, 48f, 53n, 140; Albigensian (1209–1229) 181

deception 41
decisive battle 102–3, 131, 168–70, 175f
defence in depth 26f, 52, 56
democracy 38, 172, 182
deterrence 19, 177
Dutch War of Independence a.k.a. Eighty Years' War or Dutch Rebellion (1568–1648) 13, 17–22, 73, 102

economic warfare 86
Eighty-Years War *see* Dutch War of Independence
'English School' of International Relations 41
Enterprise of England (Strategy of Philip II of Spain) 19, 21
equester 34, 57
esprit de corps 178
expansionism 27, 137, 140, 152, 161

Fabian strategists 20
First World War (1914–1918) 63, 90, 180
fleet in being 82, 86

force concentration 5, 27f, 85, 99, 192f
fortune *see* chance
Freikorps 189
French Wars of Religion (1562–1598) 18, 143

gazi (soldier-farmers along the borders of
   the Ottoman Empire) 138
genocide 180–2
Grenzer (Christian soldier-farmers
   defending the Holy Roman Empire) 138
guerre de course see commerce raiding
guerra di corsar see commerce raiding
guerrilla warfare 21, 188, 190f

Haufen see pike formations
hearts and minds campaign 97, 146
Hundred Years' War (1337–1453) 4, 6, 8f,
   11, 26, 34, 39, 50, 59, 118, 175

indirect approach 18, 21, 72f, 86, 107, 131,
   153, 155
insurgency 13, 28, 35, 43, 153–4, 156–60,
   188–290
interior lines 193
internal rebellion 35, 158
inter-service rivalry 91, 110
interstate war 23, 38, 137
intimidation 27

Jacquerie uprisings (1353) 34
just war (*ius ad bellum*) 25, 35–43, 96–8,
   123, 144f, 169

Knights Hospitaller 98

Landwehr see militia
law of nations 126, 129, 181
laws of war (*ius in bello*) 24, 36, 144f, 169
League of Nations 38
letters of marque 75, 127
levée en masse 168–82, 187–91
limited battles 175
limited war(s) 170, 176, 179
lines of communication 16–18, 20, 22. 73f,
   98, 104, 109, 118, 130

magnum concilium 5
maritime joint operations 75, 82
massacre(s) 28, 98, 109; St Bartholomew
   (1572) 181
mediatory council 38f, 43f
mercenaries 39, 59, 74, 100f, 142, 170, 172, 174
military revolution Chapter 3; intelligence
   revolution 49; nuclear revolution 49; PGM
   revolution 49

military service 164n, 175
militia 53, 60, 99f, 106f, 146, 148, 172, 175,
   177–9, 189f, 202
mobilization 86; total mobilization 180–2

nationalism 168
Nine Years' War (1594–1603) *see* Tyrone's
   Rebellion
Nine Years' War (1688–1697) 24f
nova militia 48

Organisation for Security and Cooperation
   in Europe 38

partisans, partisan warfare 186f, 189, 191;
   see also guerrilla warfare
peaceful coexistence 136–61
Peloponnesian War (431–404 B.C.E) 11,
   61, 117
Peninsular War (1807–1814) 190f
people's war 190, 198
phalanx 50, 62, 174
pike formations 50, 57, 63
pogrom 181
pre-emptive war 83, 96, 107, 114, 123
pressed men 100
preventive war 27, 95f, 107, 169
Privy Council 103, 105f, 110
proto-nationalism 39, 141
Providence 41, 123
Prudence 40f, 120

Reconquista 15, 19; *see also* roll-back strategy
roll-back strategy 136–61

sanctuarisation 27
schiltron see pike formations
scorched earth tactics 26, 28, 71, 98, 161
Second World War (1939–1945) 13, 43,
   131, 138
Seven Years' War (1756–1763) 62, 168, 170, 176
siege warfare 8, 42, 50–68, 97, 170
small war 151, 187–93; *see also* guerrilla
   warfare; partisan warfare
Spanish Succession, War of the (1701–1714)
   4, 17
stratégiste 43
surprise attack 19f, 81, 108
système de guerre 197

Thirty Years' War (1618–1648) 17, 22–4, 52,
   54f, 62, 128, 137f, 151f, 154, 175, 181
Three Graces tax for defence against the
   Turks 19
total war Chapter 8

trace italienne 51
treasure fleet 74, 80
trinity, Clausewitz's concept of the 194
Trojan War 60
Türkensteuer Tax for defence against the
   Turks 144
tyrannicide 35
Tyrone's Rebellion (1594–1603) 21

United Nations 38

virtù 41, 141

wagon fort, defensive barrier 147
War of Devolution (1667–1668) 24f
war of liberation 189
Wars of Religion (1524–1648) 18, 137
wars of self-defence 35, 39, 145, 169
Wars of the Roses (1455–1485) 4, 36
Wars of the Three Kingdoms (1639–1651)
   21f, 78